PARTIAL
PAYMENTS

PARTIAL PAYMENTS

ESSAYS ON WRITERS AND THEIR LIVES

JOSEPH EPSTEIN

W. W. NORTON & COMPANY
NEW YORK
LONDON

First published as a Norton paperback 1991

Printed in the United States of America.

The essays in this volume originally appeared in the following publications: *The New Criterion, Commentary, The Times Literary Supplement,* and *Encounter*. They are reprinted here with the kind permission of the editors.

The text of this book is composed in ITC Galliard, with display type set in Michelangelo and Old Style Garamond. Composition and manufacturing by The Maple-Vail Book Manufacturing Group.

Library of Congress Cataloging-in-Publication Data

Epstein, Joseph, 1937–
    Partial payments : essays on writers and their lives
    Joseph Epstein. —1st ed.
       p.   cm.
    1. Books and reading. 2. Literature, Modern—20th century—History and criticism. 3. Books—Reviews. I. Title.
    Z1003.E67 1989
    081—dc19   88–6059

ISBN 0-393-30716-6

W. W. Norton & Company, Inc.
500 Fifth Avenue, New York, N.Y. 10110
W. W. Norton & Company Ltd
10 Coptic Street, London WC1A 1PU

  2 3 4 5 6 7 8 9 0

FOR HILTON KRAMER,
A YOUNGEST SON, WHO FOR MORE
THAN TWENTY-FIVE YEARS HAS
BEEN MY IDEAL OLDER BROTHER

Acknowledgments

I wish to acknowledge the help of Neal Kozodoy of *Commentary,* Erich Eichman of *The New Criterion,* and Carol Houck Smith of W. W. Norton in the making of this book. I am grateful to these three editors for encouragement, sound advice, and much laughter.

Contents

Introduction

IN AN EARLIER BOOK of literary essays, *Plausible Prejudices,* I remarked upon my unwillingness to see myself as a literary critic. But to continue to insist upon this point, now that I am about to publish a second volume of such essays, may, I realize, be pushing it. For nearly a quarter of a century, after all, I have been producing what the world, or at least that minuscule portion of it interested in such stuff, roughly agrees to call literary criticism. And yet I continue to think of myself as someone who is essentially a reader— a man who takes a deep pleasure in good books, who views reading as a fine mode of acquiring experience, and who still brings the highest expectations to what he reads. By the highest expectations I mean that I am perhaps a naive person who has never ceased to believe that books can change his life, and decisively so.

One of the principal differences between most readers and me is that I am paid to write about a great deal that I read. Often editors ask me to do so, using a new or reissued book or a biography or critical study of an author as the occasion; sometimes I ask editors if they would be interested in my doing so, seeing in the occasion of the newly published book a chance to read—and often reread—an author about whom I have inchoate thoughts that I should like the chance to formulate more carefully, first for myself and then for anyone who chooses to read what I write. Nothing so concentrates the mind as having to write. In my own case, I frequently do not know what I really think about a writer, a general subject, an event, a person, until I set out my thoughts on the page. "Never put anything in writing," young men of a former age used to be warned, lest they supply evidence against themselves in a future suit for breach of promise. I find I have to put nearly everything in writing, especially my somewhat complicated feelings, arguments, and general assessments of writers who, when read at all closely, are never less than complicated themselves.

My *modus operandi*—or M.O., as they say down at the station house—is to read everything authors have written and much that has been written about them in the effort to discover what they have attempted to achieve in their novels or essays or poems. I try to trace lines of development, find preoccupations, locate (where they exist) obsessions, analyze literary strengths and weaknesses, and, before closing up the joint for the day, say as plainly as I can what I think it all comes to. Where possible I like to set out my understanding of why a certain writer writes as he or she does—in a particular style and form and with a set point of view—and not in another way. Interest in a writer's work leads, for me, into interest in his life. I was pleased to discover that V. S. Naipaul feels much the same way. "To take an interest in a writer's work is, for me, to take an interest in his life," Naipaul has written, "one interest follows automatically on the other." When I write about authors, I am keen to know not only what they have done and how they have done it, but, near as I can discover, what kind of man or woman is behind the work.

In my earlier book of literary criticism, *Plausible Prejudices,* this biographical interest, though present in many of the essays about writers no longer living, was generally less strong. This was partly because the earlier book, when it dealt with contemporary writers, tended to go on the attack; and the attack seemed more honorably made on literary than on biographical or personal grounds. The tone and general approach are considerably different in *Partial Payments,* whose essays are chiefly about writers who are not alive. On this matter of literary likes and dislikes, Harold Nicolson once wrote: "A given individual's attitude toward life and literature is moulded far more by the things he dislikes than by the things he likes, by his rejections rather than by his acceptances." Interesting if true, but I am not at all certain that it is true. Better in any case to have both likes and dislikes on record.

At some point in the composition of nearly all the essays in this book, I found myself asking, with a slight Yiddish lilt, "So what's the story?" By this question I meant, What has been the personal drama of the writers who wrote the books that are the ostensible reason for my writing about them in the first place? I say "ostensible" because I often found myself quite as interested in this drama as in their books. The books would send me back to consider the life; knowing about the life, in turn, helped me to understand a good deal more about the books. Why did homosexuality seem to me at the center of E. M. Forster's books but not at the center of Somerset Maugham's? How does one account for the depression that suffuses so much of E. B. White's work? What was it that kept S. J. Perelman, a fairly unpleasant man, from being a better writer than he was, while Evelyn Waugh, a scarcely more pleasant man, was an altogether superior writer? Only biography can help answer these, to me, absolutely fascinating questions.

I ask such questions not as a Freudian or a Marxist or a structuralist or a member of any other school or clique of criticism. I have, that is to say, no set program; I set out in search of no previously assumed answers. I read a writer who has impressed or puzzled or delighted me, and, like one of the innocent townsfolk at the end of each segment of the old *Lone Ranger* radio show, I ask: "Who was that masked writer?" Unlike those townsfolk, I ride off in pursuit, less to unmask the writer than to seek an explanation for his particular power, or to discover what led him to fail, or (sometimes) to thank him by way of a tribute in prose for the instruction and pleasure his work has provided.

The book now in your hands may in some quarters be considered old-fashioned. It uses literary criticism as an occasion—"excuse" may be the better word—for literary portraiture. Its tradition is a long and thoroughly international one. Its practitioners have included Sainte-Beuve in France, V. S. Pritchett (among many others) in England, Edmund Wilson in the United States. Its assumption is that there is a general, not necessarily academic, public interested in good writing—or, to be in one stroke more precise and more vain, a general public interested in good writing about good writing. To those of us who love and attempt to turn out this kind of writing, it does not in the least seem old-fashioned, but always newly minted and the most sensible way to go about expressing our devotion to literature.

In the contemporary university, however, this manner of writing about literature is felt to be a bit out-of-it. Peter Brooks, a professor of French at Yale, has remarked on the "ever widening rift between academic literary studies and journalistic literary criticism." This rift, Professor Brooks believes, really lies "between a literary criticism that has a good conscience about the traditional goals and methods of its work, and another kind of reflection on literature that is full of doubts about its status and purpose, yet continues to feel that talking, lecturing, writing about literature and its language touches—as no other 'discipline' quite does—on certain key issues in culture and on the very definition of the human."

At the risk of seeming immensely shallow, the author of the essays in this book must own that he does not struggle greatly over "the very definition of the human." He does not find himself dawdling over the meaning of meaning, either; nor does he think that all writing is at base political. All these matters, which the contemporary literary academic mind has found so diverting (in every sense of the word), I find, to put it gently, not very interesting. I think it true, too, that serious writers have been less interested in them than in the wide variety of human behavior and the moral dramas that continue to be at the center of the human struggle to make sense of life. I know my own sense of life has been adjusted, altered, at times radically changed by the writers I have read, beginning when I was a boy with the sports novels of John R. Tunis, and doubtless it will continue to change with the novelist or poet, essayist or philosopher, that I shall be reading three or four months from now. I am indebted to these writers.

Anyone who takes reading seriously has accrued a similar debt. To quote the epigram by G. C. Lichtenberg that stands near the front of this book, "To read means to borrow; to create out of one's reading is paying off one's debts." Repayments to writers who have been important in one's own development can never be made in full. I do hope, though, that the essays in this book constitute at least partial payments, in the sense Lichtenberg intended. My grandfather, a man with scholarly interests who failed in several businesses, used to say: "You want a job where you will never run out of work—be a debt collector." If he were alive today, I might reply: "Grandpa, you could accomplish the same thing, from the debtor's side, by reading all your life. You will acquire more debts than you can ever hope to pay off."

To read means to borrow; to
create out of one's reading
is paying off one's debts.

—G. C. Lichtenberg

PARTIAL PAYMENTS

Matthew Arnold
and the Resistance

IN NOVEMBER 1883, when Matthew Arnold was lecturing in America, Henry James wrote from England to his boyhood friend Thomas Sergeant Perry: "I am very sorry you didn't like poor old Mat. I like him—I love him rather—as I do my old portfolio, my old shoe horn: with an affection that is proof against anything he may say or do today, and proof against taking him too seriously." Not take Matthew Arnold seriously! Now there is a very strange notion indeed—so strange that Max Beerbohm once drew a caricature of Matthew Arnold being addressed by his niece in a caption that read: "Why, Uncle Matthew, oh why, will you not be always wholly serious?" The joke here is that Matthew Arnold, the great high priest of culture in Victorian England, seems hardly ever to have been anything else.

In his letter to Perry, James noted that he had only recently completed an article on Matthew Arnold for the *English Illustrated Magazine* "in which I have expressed nothing but tenderness and in a manner absolutely fulsome." The article appeared in the issue of January 1884, and is worth consulting for the light it casts upon James's odd verdict in his letter to Perry. Henry James was of course a literary critic of great subtlety and penetration, but what is perhaps less commonly known about him is what his dear friend Edith Wharton called his "merry malice." One had to attend most diligently to catch the note of merry malice in James, for he could toss about what he himself called "gracious twaddle" with the best of them. But the one subject on which James allowed no twaddle was art. About it he was always in earnest—about it he could not lie.

James begins his article by listing Matthew Arnold's special qualities. He is the most English of Englishmen and yet, despite this, the most conscious of national idiosyncrasy, for he has developed a style with "a kind of European accent" and "certain ways of looking at things." Arnold is "representative of the critical spirit." He resembles Sainte-Beuve—a high compliment, this, for James—and has an even more ample horizon than the Frenchman, though James wishes Arnold had more closely emulated Sainte-Beuve in writing more on contemporaries and on more strictly literary subjects. Although he recognizes that religion has a reality for Arnold, and has even given his writing a certain power, he regrets that he spends so much time writing about religion, writing which James scores as "a certain amount of misdirected effort." Arnold is for James in some ways a cross between Sainte-Beuve and Renan: "And if he has gone less into the details of literature than the one, he has gone more than the other into the application of religion to questions of life."

Now for a touch or two of Jamesian merry malice. "The felicity of his illustrations is extreme," writes James, meaning that he wished Arnold did not quote so much, or seem to find in his quotations "a little more than is visible to the average reader." As for Matthew Arnold the poet, James writes: "But this limited, just a little precarious, character of his inspiration adds to his value for people who like the quality of rareness in their pleasures, like sometimes to perceive just a little the effort of the poet, like to hear him take breath." I take that last phrase—"to hear him take breath"—to mean that Arnold's poetry rather creaks. James concludes by saying that Arnold is the poet "for the man of culture," that his verse "has a kind of minor magic," and "that it rests the mind, and I think I may add nourishes it." Has a body of poetry ever been buried under higher drifts of faint praise? It would be cruel, if it were not, in Arnold's case, also accurate.

Rolling up his sleeves without quite taking off his jacket, James next sets out to place Matthew Arnold. He calls him a "general critic," a job that Arnold "may really be said to have invented." He did not quite invent culture, James says, with the lightest touch of merry malice, but "he made it more definite than it had been before—he vivified and lighted it up." He spoke, moreover, with the impartiality of culture, said things that immensely needed saying and that no one had said before him, in consequence of which "all criticism is better, lighter, more sympathetic and informed." He was also, no small thing, "one of the two or three best English prose-writers of one's day." After a bit more in the way of cavil—perhaps Arnold's tact has sometimes been found wanting, the idiosyncrasies of his prose pushed too far—James concludes that Matthew Arnold was, "more than any one else, the happily proportioned, the truly distinguished man of letters."

Although James insists, in his article, on Matthew Arnold's seriousness, as one follows James through his totting up of Arnold's weaknesses and strengths, it becomes clear that he, James, does not take Arnold altogether seriously. He has placed Arnold, taken his measure—and yet somehow, even though everything he writes about Arnold is true, it does not seem to be the *whole* truth. But then critical justice for Matthew Arnold, as F. R. Leavis noted in a *Scrutiny* essay of 1939, is not easily achieved. "He seems at present to the appraising reader," Leavis wrote, "a peculiarly elusive quantity." At present and, one needs to add, in the past.

Leslie Stephen, the Victorian man of letters, presents a balance sheet on Matthew Arnold that tilts much more on the debit side than Henry James's. Stephen begins his essay by saying that he does not like the notion of ranking poets, but, so saying, he goes on to say that Arnold is not of the same stature as the two major poets of the high Victorian era, Browning and Tennyson. As a critic, though, Arnold is viewed by Stephen as "primarily a poet," which is to say that he, Arnold, was notable neither for "logical analysis" nor for "convincing proof." Arnold perhaps delighted too much "in discovering catchwords, and repeating them sometimes to weariness." This applies to such phrases as "sweetness and light"—a phrase that originated with Swift and supplies the heavy motif in Arnold's *Culture and Anarchy*. As for Arnold's definition of poetry as "criticism of life," Stephen owns to confusion about what Arnold could possibly have meant. Arnold's belief in culture, true enough, was part of his heritage and thus of his nature; the effect of his work, granted, was civilizing; reading him, Stephen allows, is always useful as "a shock, unpleasant at times, but excellent in its effects as an intellectual tonic." As in Henry James's essay, so in Leslie Stephen's, there is much back and forth, weak and strong, good and bad. One comes away from Stephen thinking that it is better that Matthew Arnold wrote than not—but not very much better.

Reading T. S. Eliot's essay "Arnold and Pater," one is likely to think perhaps it would have been better had Matthew Arnold never written at all. Eliot harbors for Arnold a respectful distaste. He calls him "rather a propagandist for criticism than a critic," and he has a lower view of Arnold's intellectual gifts than do either James or Stephen: "Arnold had little gift for consistency or for definition. Nor had he the power of connected reasoning at any length: his flights are either short flights or circular flights. Nothing in his prose works, therefore, will stand very close analysis, and we may very well feel that the positive content of many words is very small." Worse: "He was a champion of 'ideas' most of whose ideas we no longer take seriously." (There is that word "seriously" again.) But Eliot's real complaint against Arnold is that he "set up Culture to take the place of Religion," without giving a very clear notion of what exactly culture is. "And Culture is a term," Eliot writes, "which each man not only may interpret as he pleases, but must indeed interpret as he can." The best that Eliot can seem to say for Arnold is that, coming alongside Carlyle and Ruskin, he "taught English expository and critical prose a restraint and urbanity it needed." On the other hand, "he produced a kind of illusion of precision and clarity; that is, he maintained these qualities as ideals of style." Thus the Lord giveth and the Lord taketh away.

Jerked free of their contexts the phrases for which Matthew Arnold is best known do not today seem much above the level of slogans. Poetry is "criticism of life"; culture is "the study of perfection"; criticism is "a disinterested endeavor to learn and propagate the best that is known and thought in the world." And let us not forget—as Arnold, in *Culture and Anarchy,* scarcely for a moment allows us to forget—"sweetness and light." But Henry James was right to remind his readers that even though the freshness of these Arnoldian formulations was beginning to fade—and James wrote this, recall, more than a century ago—it was through Arnold, as James noted, "and through him only that we have grown familiar with certain ideas and terms which now form part of the common stock of allusion." Still, they seem little more than clichés now, roughly at the same level of sophistication and usefulness as "knowledge is power" or "time is money"; they seem, that is to say, yawn-inducing pieties which, though they may be true, are not very interesting.

But when the worst has been said about Matthew Arnold—and I have here tried to say it, and summarized others saying it—the fact stands that Arnold remains in the great tradition of literary criticism; that much of his work is still alive and to the point; and that, because of the peculiar turn that contemporary literary culture has taken, Matthew Arnold has become perhaps more important than ever before. Nor is it correct to leave the impression that Arnold has been without admirers within fairly recent times. Lionel Trilling wrote a book-length study of Arnold (originally his doctoral dissertation, a work more than a decade in the making), and his own, more mature work as a critic everywhere shows the influence of Arnold. F. R. Leavis, though one tends not to think of so intellectually combative a critic as an Arnoldian, was nevertheless an admirer of Matthew Arnold, and thought him one of only four commanding figures in the history of English literary criticism, the other three being Johnson, Coleridge, and T. S. Eliot.

Yet Trilling is dead, Leavis is dead, and any serious revival of Matthew Arnold's reputation appears highly improbable. Certainly, refreshed interest in Arnold seems unlikely. The not entirely shocking findings of Arnold's most recent biographer, Park Honan, support the statement made by the master of Balliol College, Benjamin Jowett—he whose name was made tidily to rhyme with the line, "There's no knowledge, but I know it"—who of Arnold said: "He was the most sensible man of genius whom I have ever known and the most free from personality." And it is true that of the great Victorian prose writers—Ruskin, Carlyle, J. S. Mill, Dickens—Matthew Arnold was the most sane. Modern taste has been trained to prefer geniuses who appear as wounded personalities, maniacally obsessed, psychologically crippled, and here Arnold disappoints entirely.

Reading Park Honan's *Matthew Arnold* one is if anything impressed by the opportunities that Arnold had to turn neurotic, or even a little mad, and how he failed—that is to say, came through—them all. Matthew Arnold wore iron braces on his legs when a small child to correct a deformity; he grew up in the shadow of a strong father, who of course was Thomas Arnold, the great Victorian controversialist and headmaster of Rugby (later one of Lytton Strachey's four subjects of attack in *Eminent Victorians*); he competed among many children for his parents' affection; he roundly disappointed his family by not getting a first at Oxford, he the son of Thomas Arnold; his poetic inspiration dried up on him in mid-career; he lost three of his own children in the span of a few years. . . . The list of setbacks, natural difficulties, and disasters in Arnold's life could be extended, and Honan extends it whenever he can. He is keen to render a psychological portrait of Matthew Arnold, and lines of the following kind, so à la mode and yet so unpersuasive, pop up wherever possible, as in this exegesis of a poem: "The 'pit of fire' suggests a deep vein of guilt in Arnold's elder-brotherism or his rivalry with siblings, in his tendency to love and hate those who came between himself and his mother."

But that Matthew's heart belonged to Mamma—or, as Honan elsewhere maintains, to one of his sisters—seems quite beside the point. Psychological portraiture, in Arnold's case, renders little of value. Matthew Arnold's personality seems to have been remarkably of a piece, wall-to-wall, and the figure in his carpet, if one must be found, lies in the triumph of character over psychology. Psychology wants to know what a man's problems are; character has to do with how he surmounts them. Matthew Arnold surmounted all the problems life put in his way, he played on through, he made a life that was a work of art, not a case study. "In all his work," Honan writes, "Arnold in effect explained himself to his parents." That may or may not be so—Honan does not convince me that it is—but the chief thing is that others read Arnold, that he, Matthew Arnold, as Honan writes, "is the Victorian who matters most."

When Honan takes down his shingle and returns to the stacks, his accomplishments are rather more impressive. He has discovered, for example, the identity of the woman, hitherto unknown, who is the "Marguerite" in some of Arnold's lyric poems: a young German-born woman named Mary Claude whom he had met while on holiday in the Swiss Alps. (Such a discovery, in scholarly circles, ought to be good for tenure at, say, Rutgers or below.) Of more interest to the nonacademic reader is the account that runs through the pages of Honan's biography of Matthew Arnold's workaday life as a traveling school inspector. Arnold worked thirty-five years as one of Her

Majesty's inspectors of schools. The job was no sinecure; it was closer to the reverse: a job offering a very great deal of work for very little pay. Arnold was of that generation of English men of letters who had to earn their living by work other than letters. Work Arnold did, without stint or complaint, for the better part of his adult life as a school inspector. "The actual achievement in producible criticism," wrote F. R. Leavis of Arnold's body of writing, "may not seem a very impressive one." Yet when one considers that—apart from a term as professor of poetry at Oxford—Arnold wrote under the lash of a full-time job, it seems quite impressive.

The job of school inspector put Matthew Arnold and his family to many hardships, and yet it could be argued that, as a critic, it was the making of him. His work gave him a view across England's classes, for it involved reporting on the sad, often squalid schooling arrangements then set up for the children of the working class and paupers in such cities as Liverpool and Birmingham. He witnessed the misery visited upon the underclasses at first hand, and it increased his sympathy while fortifying his belief in the necessity of raising up the beaten down. Yet Arnold never idealized the poor; seeing them, working with them, he knew how far they had to go to reach the purlieus of decent living, let alone culture as he understood it. He knew that more was involved in raising them up than certain obvious welfare measures that were likely to create, as he once put it, "not only more poor men's bread but more poor men."

Arnold also reported on the schools and universities of France, Germany, Italy, and, later, Switzerland. His reports gave him a certain national celebrity, for the schools of these other countries compared, in Arnold's view, far too favorably with England's, and the comparison caused, predictably, a stir. But the travel that was required to write these reports also widened Arnold's perspective as a writer. Of English critics, he has always seemed the least parochial, and this, too, is owing in part to his work as a school inspector. Continental and classical influences had earlier been a part of Arnold's reading: Herder, Goethe, Spinoza, Epictetus above all. But Arnold's travels as a school inspector put him in close touch with French and German culture, and he wrote a good deal about the writers of both countries, thus contributing to the critic's job, as Edmund Wilson once put it, of cross-fertilization of culture.

In his book Honan takes a swipe at Lionel Trilling's biography, *Matthew Arnold* (1939), for its "remorseless politicizing of Arnold's thought." So it seems to go with biography, figures of the past get Marxed in one generation, Freuded the next. Not that Lionel Trilling's biography of Arnold is Marxist, but Trilling, for all that his book is filled with learning and intelligence, would like Matthew Arnold to be a figure more congenial to the 1930s, the years during which the book was composed. Yet it must be said that, inconveniently enough, Matthew Arnold does not make for a biographical subject of overpowering interest. His was a life, like most lives, without a ripping, a rivening crisis. Even his literary life knew no sharp divisions. "Without consciously renouncing poetry," Honan writes, "Arnold wrote less and less verse after 1853." Later Honan notes: "With 'My Countrymen' in 1856 he dropped literary criticism for ten years, and with the new and at times desperate worry over the violence in the United Kingdom, he turned to social comment." This is a little too calm, too commonplace for modern taste in biography, which tends to prefer subjects who provide sexual extravaganzas, dangerous addictions, abrupt political shifts. Arnold's life provides nothing of the sort.

Quite the reverse. The very shape of Arnold's career seems to resist the biographer's art. As a young man, Arnold's chief mental effort was given over to poetry, work that is now, apart from "Dover Beach" and a few other anthology pieces, largely of academic interest. (In both Trilling's and Honan's books, the lengthy explanations of Arnold's poems make for rather dreary longueurs.) The preponderance of Arnold's later work is given over to writing on religious subjects, about which Henry James, accurately, observed: "There is something dry and dusty in the atmosphere of such discussions, which accords ill with the fresh tone of the man of letters, the artist." All of which is a roundabout way of saying that Arnold's life has for us a middle vastly more interesting than either its beginning or its end. It is, almost exclusively, Matthew Arnold the critic who is of interest today.

What the biographical view does display, though, is that Matthew Arnold was a good man, and a good man, in literature as in the old popular song, is hard to find. He was, as John Morley put it,

> incapable of sacrificing the smallest interest of anybody else to his own; he had not a spark of envy or jealousy; he stood well aloof from all the hustlings and jostlings by which selfish men push on; he bore life's disappointments, and he was disappointed in some reasonable hopes and anticipations, with good nature and fortitude; he cast no burden upon others, and never shrank from bearing his own share of the daily load to the last ounce of it; he took the deepest, sincerest, and most active interest in the well-being of his country and countrymen.

Whenever it was appropriate to do so, Arnold, in his own criticism, attempted to discover the quality of a man or woman through his or her writing. "The personality of an author had a peculiar importance for him," Arnold wrote of Sainte-Beuve, and the remark applies nicely to himself. "Whatever else we have or have not in Count Tolstoy," Arnold wrote, "we have at least a great soul and a great writer."

Van Wyck Brooks was the last critic to define literature as great men writing. It is not a silly definition, even if less than comprehensive. In nearly all of Matthew Arnold's literary criticism the point of reading is in large part to be in the company of great souls. (Would any critic today think to call a writer a great soul? Are there any great souls among our writers?) Modern criticism, of course, has long taught that one does not inquire too deeply into the life of the writer, for it is his writing, the work itself, that is the main, the great, the supreme thing (except of course for the heavily psychologizing critics for whom the state of the writer's psyche is the only thing). In so teaching, modern criticism forced the first of the fissures between the writer and the work, which would in time be followed by fissures between the work and reality, until we come to the situation of the present day and the opaque lucubrations of structuralists, semioticists, and deconstructionists, in which the work itself is denied any fixed reality whatsoever.

Not only did Matthew Arnold wish to understand the man behind the writing, he wished to change the souls of men through his own writing. He was clear enough about his intentions. As he himself put it, without becoming directly political he nonetheless wished "to work inwardly upon the predominant force in our politics—the great middle class—and cure its spirit." How Arnold went about this is nicely formulated by Lionel Trilling: "To discover and define, then, the dominant tendency of his age, to analyze the good from the bad, foster the good, diminish the bad—this will be Arnold's program of criticism."

As Matthew Arnold entered on this critical program, doubtless somewhere in his mind he must have known that what he wrote in another of his essays on Sainte-Beuve also had application to himself: namely, that "excellent work in a lower kind counts in the long run above work that is short of excellence in a higher; first-rate criticism has a permanent value greater than that of any but first-rate works of poetry and art." After all the disclaimers about Arnold are lodged, the qualifications inserted, that he was a first-rate critic is incontestable. T. S. Eliot once famously remarked that the only way to be a good critic is to be very intelligent—a statement as true as it is unhelpful. Reading Matthew Arnold's criticism, though, one gets a clearer idea of what constitutes intelligence in literary criticism and why certain literary criticism is "compellingly alive," as Leavis once called Arnold's, and most is stillborn.

Some critics can turn criticism into a work of art, others into a work of philosophy, but both kinds are extremely rare. Most academic critics—and almost all critics today are academics— write term papers into old age: "The Problem of Identity in D. H. Lawrence," "Pater as Poltergeist," and so forth. No great literary critic has ever had, in the strict sense of the word, a method; no great critic ever formed or was part of a school. Certain critics through their writing have played a decisive role in their time—Vissarion Belinsky, the nineteenth-century Russian, was such a critic—though their criticism can, after its time, seem quite unreadable (as Belinsky's does to me, at least in English). No, great critics are quite as rare, possibly rarer, than great poets, and Randall Jarrell was surely correct when he wrote: "Unless you are one critic in a hundred thousand, the future will quote you only as an example of the normal error of the past, what everyone was foolish enough to believe then. Critics are discarded like calendars. . . ."

Matthew Arnold is the one in a hundred thousand—a critic whom we do not discard, for his work is still alive, still readable, still significant. How does this happen to be so? Prose style is part of the answer. Arnold had the gift of style, and his prose, when it was flowing well, combined winningly the qualities of stateliness and intimacy: he could be witty and ironic and thunderously earnest by turns. But other critics have written well, even beautifully—Van Wyck Brooks comes to mind— who are not so rereadable as Arnold; while still other critics have often written wretchedly—F. R. Leavis—and can still be reread. Prose style alone is not the way for a critic to escape oblivion.

Nor is right opinion. To be correct in all one's literary opinions is, similarly, no guarantee of enduring as a critic. Arnold was often wrong in his opinions. There were important opinions he never registered; he never, as Honan points out, wrote about any of the major living English writers of his time: Dickens, George Eliot, Browning, Tennyson, Carlyle, Ruskin. Literary sensibility weighs in more heavily than correct opinion in a critic, and literary sensibility Arnold had *in excelsis*. His pages are filled with glittering observations, examples of seeing both the forest and the trees, such as the following fine distinction between the characters of Anna Karenina and Emma Bovary:

> *Madame Bovary* . . . is a work of *petrified feeling;* over it hangs an atmosphere of bitterness, irony, impotence; not a personage in the book to rejoice or console us; the springs of freshness and feeling are not there to create such personages. Emma Bovary follows a course in some respects like that of Anna, but where, in Emma Bovary, is Anna's charm? The treasures of compassion, tenderness, insight, which alone amid such guilt and misery, can enable charm to subsist and to emerge are wanting to Flaubert. He is cruel, with the cruelty of petrified feeling, to his poor heroine; he pursues her without pity or pause, as with malignity; he is harder upon her himself than any reader ever, I think, will be inclined to be.

What superior perspective and large-mindedness were behind observations of this high caliber!

Still, adding up right and wrong literary opinions is not, finally, very useful, and Arnold himself apparently did not think so. On the subject of literary opinion he quoted, approvingly, Sainte-Beuve: "I hold very little to literary opinions; literary opinions occupy very little place in my life and in my thoughts. What does occupy me seriously is life itself and the object of it."

"Life itself" was always at the center of Matthew Arnold's critical writing, and here, combined with his sheerly literary gifts, is to be found the secret of the survival of his criticism unto our day. As a critic, Arnold was able to grasp life in its interrelatedness: literary, moral, and spiritual values were for him twined. As a record of man's yearnings and imaginings, defeats and triumphs, literature was flush with morality, with things of the spirit, and was therefore a human activity of absolute centrality. Trained in reading this record, in understanding it, the literary man took a privileged place, and it was not, in Arnold's view, off on the sidelines. "I have a conviction," Arnold wrote to his sister in 1865, "that there is a real, an almost imminent danger of England losing immeasurably in all ways, declining . . . for want of what I must still call ideas, for want of perceiving how the world is going and must go, and preparing herself accordingly. This conviction haunts me, and at times overwhelms me with depression." As this quotation shows, ideas for Arnold were not things to play with, intellectual toys to last a season. They shaped reality, and on how reality was perceived hung the fate of nations. And who is to say that, in this fundamental belief, Arnold was wrong?

Professor Honan writes that, in his lifetime, Arnold "gained fame because he was audacious, challenging, fresh, witty, on the move in his ideas and topics, in the thick of controversy, and undaunted in probing the weakness of an industrial society. He was not ephemeral or superficial . . . but he was unique in his voice and presence, irony, range, urbanity, and sensitivity, as he brought into his essays a sense of the Western literary heritage." And, one is tempted to add, so on and so forth. One has seen all these qualities lined up fore and aft of Arnold's name, and, true enough, legitimate claim to them can be made for him. For all his shortcomings, there can be no doubt that, when Arnold was writing well, we are, as Leavis put it, reading the work of "an extraordinarily distinguished mind in complete possession of its purpose and pursuing it with easy mastery—that, in fact, we are reading a great critic."

But what made Arnold great, along with his distinctive literary skills, was his assumptions. Chief among these were that nothing was quite so important as literature and that literature was never to be treated as an end in itself. Literature's effect on the general culture, though always subtle and never all that easy to make out, was decisive, even crucial. Arnold put the point neatly in his essay "The Bishop and the Philosopher": "Literary criticism's most important function is to try books as to the influence which they are calculated to have upon the general culture of single nations or of the world at large. Of this culture literary criticism is the appointed guardian, and on this culture all literary work may be conceived as in some way or other operating." Guardians of the culture, literary critics are akin to philosopher-kings, but of the spirit; in the same essay, Arnold notes: "The highly instructed few, and not the scantily instructed many, will ever be the organ to the human race of knowledge and truth." And to whom do these guardians of the culture talk? Arnold answered the question in his essay "Dr. Stanley's Lectures on the Jewish Church": "The few who live this life stand apart, and have an existence separate from that of the mass of mankind; they address an imaginary audience of their mates; the region which they inhabit is the laboratory wherein are fashioned new intellectual ideas which, from time to time, take their place in the world. Are these few justified, in the sight of God, in so living? That is a question which literary criticism must not attempt to answer."

Such notions are today nicely calculated to bring cries of "Elitist!" Arnold, though, is scarcely likely to have been troubled by them; standards, for him, were essential, and without them all else collapsed. In his essay "The Literary Influence of Academies," Arnold deplored that there was in England "no body of opinion . . . strong enough to set up a standard." One of his complaints about the United States was that "the *average man* is too much a religion there; his performance is unduly magnified, his shortcomings are not duly seen and admitted." The problem, as Arnold viewed it in a brief essay on Milton, is that "when the right standard of excellence is lost, it is not likely that much that is excellent will be produced." Arnold would have agreed with Renan, who wrote: "All ages have had their inferior literature; but the great danger of our time is that this inferior literature tends more and more to get the upper place."

It was the job of the literary critic to set the right standard of excellence, and by doing so, as Arnold put it in "The Function of Criticism at the Present Time," "to make an intellectual situation of which the creative power can profitably avail itself." And more: "It [criticism] tends to establish an order of ideas, if not absolutely true, yet true by comparison with that which it displaces; to make the best ideas prevail. Presently these new ideas reach society, the touch of truth is the touch of life, and there is a stir and growth everywhere; out of this stir and growth come the creative epochs of literature." And, though Arnold does not say so, the greater enrichment of all.

Because Matthew Arnold understood the relationship between literature and society, because he knew the significant function of the critic as a broker in that relationship, because he practiced that function consummately, his criticism continues to live. Because Arnold knew that literature is never an end in itself, he is serious in precisely the way that T. S. Eliot—who, as we have seen, did not think much of Arnold—accused Paul Valéry in his criticism of failing to be serious: in showing the relation of literature to experience. And because, finally, all that Matthew Arnold believed important about literature is generally flouted by practitioners of academic literary criticism today, Arnold is, or at any rate ought to be, a figure, the leading one, in what I have come to think of as the Resistance.

What the Resistance is resisting is the major trends in the study of literature in the United States at the present time. A shorthand way of grasping what is going on in literary studies today is to understand that nearly everything which Matthew Arnold most ardently believed about the importance of literature has been rejected. Culture, Arnold felt, was skeptical of systems and system-makers, and of course it is precisely such systems that are on the rise in our day: structuralism, semiology, deconstructionism (even though the last is a kind of anti-system system). Their adherents are critics who treat literature as an end in itself, as Arnold never did, and who manage to make literature seem much more complicated while at the same time a good deal less interesting than one would have thought possible. These critics are of course all academics. Arnold saw the beginnings of the professionalization of literature, but he was perhaps fortunate not to see its nearly complete professorialization, which is what, in criticism, we have today. Arnold had a not very favorable view of teaching, calling it, in his essay on Maurice de Guérin, "that common but most perfidious refuge of men of letters. . . ." That the study—and increasingly the creation—of literature was one day to be almost wholly in the province of universities, as it is now, would have seemed to Arnold depressing in the extreme.

One of the reasons behind the professorialization of literature has been vastly increased university enrollments. Even though Arnold might have thought these increased enrollments represented a victory for culture—conceiving as he did "of no perfection as being real which is not a *general* perfection, embracing all our fellow-men"—it seems greatly unlikely that Arnold would have been other than saddened at the negligible effect of the spread of higher education on standards. Arnold thought to bring culture, "by means of reading, observing, thinking." Much depended, it hardly needs saying, upon what one read, observed, thought about. Under the current dispensation of teaching popular culture in universities, the new notion seems to be to bring the children of the middle classes *down* through courses in science fiction, movies, detective stories, and the like.

Considering popular culture, Thomas Edwards, writing in *Raritan,* a journal of professorial criticism, asks if some of its "advanced" developments may not be "as interesting as many recent developments in high arts," and then proceeds to note that we are living "at a time when high art, and its serious criticism, seem to be moving even farther from the idea of a common high-cultural center." Edwards thinks that the interest in popular culture puts "intellectual seriousness to the kind of test *it* deserves." He may think so but he apparently does not have the heart (or the courage) to say that "the common high-cultural center"—an ideal taken over from Matthew Arnold—is finished. Leslie Fiedler, though, has no difficulty saying it: ". . . the hierarchical view of literature at its heart is a vestige of a defunct, class-structured society, no longer viable in the world of mass communications and advanced technology, whether capitalist or socialist." Under the banner of such advanced thought, Arnold's old definition of criticism as "a distinterested endeavor to learn and propagate the best that is known and thought in the world" is out. A semiological study of Woody Woodpecker is the wave of the future.

"When the right standard of excellence is lost," Arnold wrote, "it is not likely that much that is excellent will be produced." Standards in literary matters have been shaky for a long while now. True, there is still, in universities, a consensus that holds Shakespeare to be above Arthur Miller, Pushkin above Pynchon, but there is no similar consensus of what ought and what ought not to be taught. This might seem a healthy thing, if it did not proceed largely from shot confidence and an absence of the kind of intellectual authority that is prepared to argue that some subjects, books, authors, are more important than others and that, this being so, the former ought to be taught and the latter excluded, at least from university study. As things stand, inclusion is increasingly by professorial whim and convenience and, above all, politics. Novelists who write, as it sometimes seems, chiefly for exegesis have made it into the literature curriculum; so have subjects that have only a strong student demand to recommend them.

As in the university, so outside it, standards have not so much slipped as disappeared. Criticism has increasingly become an arm of cultural publicity. The house specialty here seems to be the five-year genius—the cultural figure who holds the publicity foreground for half a decade or so, then is shunted off stage to make way for the next such figure. Criticism could have prevented such febrility, but can anyone name three book reviewers whom, on the most fundamental level, he can trust? By fundamental level, I mean that if these reviewers tell you that a work is serious you can count on its being so; and can count as well on their opinion not being the result of cowardice, vanity, or politics.

Matthew Arnold had his politics, but it was the politics of culture. He thought anarchy "intolerable," but also thought that the nineteenth-century liberalism ascendant in his day—"the mechanical and material civilization in esteem with us"—was, as he put it, "inadequate." Arnold set culture above politics, writing: "But if despondency and violence are both of them forbidden to the believer in culture, yet neither, on the other hand, is public life and direct political action much permitted to him." Again, Arnold could hardly be other than dismayed at our own contemporary scene, where politics is permitted not only to transcend but to shape culture, so that, to cite only the most obvious example, the idea of a central common culture is chipped away to accommodate the claims of several political groupings—minorities, women, the young—as if culture were spoils to be divided up in a smoke-filled room.

Revulsion does not seem too strong a word to apply to Matthew Arnold's likely reaction to those novelists and poets, philosophers and critics, who spend the better part of their time devising techniques that attempt to demonstrate that reality does not exist; or at least not in so substantive a way that a text can have a generally agreed upon meaning, one idea be more persuasive than another, or that literature can be taken for anything other than a self-referential activity. One can only imagine Arnold rubbing his eyes at the spectacle of bloated self-importance as he reads such sentences from contemporary critics as this from Leo Bersani: "I would now like to propose a model of fantasmatic sexuality supplemental to, and subversive of, the model just derived from Laplanche's reading of Freud"; or this from Harold Bloom: "The promulgation of the catastrophe is indeed already the condition of language, the condition of the ruins of time, and of the defense against time, the deep lie at every reimagined origin"; or this from Richard Poirier: "Thus it is that Foucault and Nietzsche offer, in my view, an occasion for participating in the only momentarily exhilarating and cleansing imagination of self-eradication." One can as readily imagine Matthew Arnold reeling at a Modern Language Association meeting, in his hand a program announcing one goofy paper after another, while in the room the graduate students come and go, talking of Michel Foucault.

If T. S. Eliot disapproved of Matthew Arnold for substituting culture (chiefly literary culture) for religion at a time when religious traditions were wearing thin, today it is the literary tradition that is wearing thin, if not altogether coming apart. F. R. Leavis made essentially this same point, and it is a compelling one. In this situation Arnold remains the man for those who revere the tradition and wish to resist the forces, literary, critical, and political, that have done so much to undermine it. Arnold is the man because, for all that can be said against him, he anticipated the issues of our day, and on every one his own position is admirable—admirable and tenable and usable in our time. Not least, he knew that literature is itself very real, that the perception of literature shapes the way reality itself is perceived, that literature is about life and is part of life. If Matthew Arnold was wrong about any of this, then perhaps it is just as well that the literary tradition die out, while, like astrologers, writers and critics continue to practice an art dead and in disrepute, and the rest of us turn to the crossword puzzle.

Commentary 1982

H. L. Mencken
for Grownups

APART FROM being forgotten altogether, surely the lowest circle in literary hell is for a writer to be chalked up as a period piece. Such a fate is usually— and mercifully—a posthumous one, but H. L. Mencken, the American essayist and publicist, felt something of its sting in his lifetime.

Mencken's birth and death dates are 1880–1956, though, in one of the gods' crueler practical jokes, he suffered a stroke in 1948 that allowed him, one of the most bookish of men, to read only with the greatest difficulty and to write not at all. But H. L. Mencken's apogee came in the period between the end of World War I and the onset of the Depression. "So many young men got their likes and dislikes from Mencken," runs a sentence from Hemingway's *The Sun Also Rises* (1926). And so they did; and so, in an oddly angled way, they would continue to. Along with being considered a writer very much of his period—associated with good but now moribund causes: the struggle against the genteel tradition in literature, against censorship in politics, against puritanical restraints in social life— Mencken has also been considered chiefly a young man's writer. He was, certainly, deemed a writer an intelligent fellow would soon outgrow. Such then is Mencken's current reputation: a writer of the 1920s and a writer for the young. Damned, you might say, and double damned.

Not that this unenviable literary reputation is entirely askew. For a long while reading H. L. Mencken was part of the tradition of growing up for young men with intellectual interests in America, though perhaps now the tradition is beginning to thin out. For myself, he was a writer I adored at eighteen. What I adored about him above all was his iconoclasm, even though the icons he set about busting, by the time I came to read him in the middle 1950s, were long gone: the politicians William Jennings Bryan, Woodrow Wilson, Theodore Roosevelt, Warren Gamaliel Harding, and Calvin Coolidge; Prohibition; fundamentalist religion; all the habits and attitudes and hidebound views that for him marched under the flag of twentieth-century American Puritanism. The pleasure in reading Mencken came in witnessing a man lashing out so handsomely, bashing away with an exuberance I did not even know was allowed in literature till encountering him. Such at any rate was the reaction of a middle-class boy at the University of Chicago, which, as it turns out, was not so very different from the reaction to Mencken, some three decades earlier, of Richard Wright, who in his autobiography, *Black Boy,* tells of sneaking a Mencken volume out of the Memphis library:

> That night in my rented room, while letting the hot water run over my can of pork and beans in the sink, I opened *A Book of Prefaces* and began to read. I was jarred and shocked by the style, the clear, clean, sweeping sentences. Why did he write like that? And how did one write like that? I pictured the man as a raging demon, slashing with his pen, consumed with hate, denouncing everything American, extolling everything European or German, laughing at the weakness of people, mocking God, authority. What was this? I stood up, trying to realize what reality lay behind the meaning of the words. . . . Yes, this man was fighting, fighting with words. He was using words as a weapon, using them as one would use a club. Could words be weapons?

Well, yes, for here they were. Then, maybe, perhaps, I could use them as a weapon? No. It frightened me. I read on and what amazed me was not what he said, but how on earth anybody had the courage to say it.

What is of interest here is the universality of Mencken's appeal to the young, for his attraction for Richard Wright, a Mississippi Negro raised in poverty and terror, and for me, a young man with so many material advantages, was nearly identical. And he had the selfsame effect on thousands of other young Americans.

But as I grew older I pulled away from Mencken. Too many of his opinions clashed with my own. He held low views of human nature. He was anti-government, not keen for democracy, thought capitalism the least evil of all economic arrangements. He held idealism to be little more than a swindle. In the 1930s Mike Gold, then the editor of the *New Masses*, accused Mencken of "killing social idealism in young America." He was opposed to the New Deal and even more opposed to Franklin Delano Roosevelt.* In short, I found H. L. Mencken

---

*Mencken's decline in popularity set in with the Depression. He had very little regard for Marxism and kept himself free from the sectarian politics that exerted so strong a pull on intellectuals and writers in the 1930s.

If not lining up for the great left-wing causes of the 1930s cost Mencken a large part of his earlier following, his late recognition of the true intent of Adolf Hitler cost him the remainder. Mencken had a "German problem." As a journalist of German ancestry, he suffered greatly during World War I, being viewed as insufficiently patriotic. U.S. participation in World War I brought with it a state of frenzied hatred of all things German unmatched in the nation's history. The German language was barred from many public and private schools; German Americans were often ridiculed and sometimes attacked on the streets; sauerkraut was renamed "liberty cabbage." With this history of American anti-German hysteria in mind, Mencken was most hesitant to believe the worst about Hitler, though it cannot really be said that he was neutral on the subject. In a letter of 1936 he wrote: "I don't know a single man of any reputation in America who is in favor of the Nazi scheme. As it stands, Germany has completely lost the sympathy it had during the years following 1920."

politically objectionable. Were he alive and had we met I suspect he would have found me boring and laughable—the very type, as he would characterize it in a famous essay, of "the forward looker."

I came back to reading Mencken because I had been asked by an American magazine to write about Professor Carl Bode's edition of *The New Mencken Letters*. In the course of reading these letters and other of Mencken's writings, along with writings about him, I made a number of small but to me impressive discoveries. One was that, although I thought I had put away the scribblings of H. L. Mencken along with other childish things, I now found I took greater pleasure and sustenance from them than ever before. For me at least, H. L. Mencken is one of those writers who get better as they get older—and such writers, of course, are the best kind.

And I discovered something else. Although Montesquieu says, "I have never had a sorrow that an hour of reading did not dissipate," Montesquieu was not under the burden of staying *au courant* with literary and intellectual life in the last quarter of the twentieth century. He did not have to cast his eyes over the literary criticisms of Fredric Jameson or Jacques Derrida, the fictions of Joseph Heller or John Barth, or the humorless social commentary of Christopher Lasch; otherwise he would not have spoken so readily about reading dissipating sorrows. But some writers, it is true, do lift one out of gloom, and away from the valley of small and large woes; and, for myself, I have found three writers who perform this service for me almost unfailingly: Montaigne, Justice Holmes (in his letters), and Henry Louis Mencken.

Mencken lifts the spirit—how appalled he would be to find himself accused of uplift!—but such undeniably is his effect on me. Does the reason for this lie in his power as a comedian? To be sure, few American writers have been funnier. Who but Mencken could refer to clichés as "the old wheezing of the melodeon"; or to a hot dog as "a cartridge filled with the sweepings of the abattoir"; or to college teachers as "the average drover of undergraduates"? When sex hygienists explain sex by analogy with botany all they achieve is to "make botany seem obscene." As for Freud, he simply translated the age-old fact that most men and women are frauds "into pathological terms, adding a bedroom scene, and so laid the foundations for psychoanalysis." Mencken is one of that too-small company of modern writers who can make one laugh aloud. Mencken's comedy—of phrase, of formulation, of perspective—partly explains his ability to lift the spirits, but only, I think, partly.

Might the explanation be found in his prose, with its boundless energy? Along with Ernest Hemingway, H. L. Mencken devised one of the few original and unmistakable American prose styles of the current century. He had great orchestral power. Karl Kraus once described journalists as men who, given time, wrote worse. Not Mencken: everything he wrote, whether composed on the run or after leisurely cerebration, had his characteristic energy, music, and elegance. How Mencken achieved his effects can, on a technical level, be easily enough understood. What is entailed is rather easily formulated: strong verbs, exotic nouns, outrageous adjectives, a confident cadence, superior humor, and wide learning. Walter Lippmann, in an essay of 1926, said of the effect of reading Mencken: "When you can explain the heightening effect of a spirited horse, of a swift athlete, of a dancer really in control of his own body, when you can explain why watching them you feel more alive yourself, you can explain the quality of his influence."

During the years that he edited the *American Mercury* it was sometimes alleged that entire issues of the monthly magazine read as if written by Mencken himself. There are two possible explanations here: one is that Mencken rewrote many of the things that appeared in the magazine; the other—which seems more likely—is that contributors felt the pull of his influence and succumbed to it. Many a young man in the 1920s scribbled away à la Mencken, composing tirades against the local minister or YMCA, and even today Mencken has his imitators. But, finally, for none of them does the imitation really come off. The reason is that none of them truly has H. L. Mencken's point of view. And it is point of view that cannot be imitated.

Point of view in a writer is always a matter of the keenest interest, and in a writer who is not a novelist or poet or dramatist it is a matter of central interest. The sense in which I intend point of view to be taken is suggested by a line in V. S. Naipaul's novel *Guerrillas,* in which Naipaul remarks about the novel's only female character, a woman who has been a camp follower for many causes, that "she had a great many opinions but these did not add up to a point of view." Everyone has opinions—writers, academics, people who do intellectual work of one kind or another—but not everyone has a point of view.

Part of the tribute that we pay great artists is to ignore many of their opinions. If one took all of Tolstoy's many opinions to heart, one would have to discard his best novels as contradictions of his stated views. If believing the full parcel of Dostoevsky's opinions were the price of admission, no non-Christian could afford to read his novels. Theodore Dreiser, whom Mencken once cited for his "incurable antipathy to the *mot juste,*" had an equivalent antipathy to consistency of opinion, and could go from Communism to Fascism almost as easily as Mencken himself from dessert to cigar. Sometimes an artist will go too far, even for an artist—witness Ezra Pound's speeches for Mussolini—and is brought to book for it (though in Pound's case we have an instance of opinion backed up by action). But artists holding egregious opinions are an old story. The modern tendency is by and large to forgive artists their prejudices, to say, well, if these opinions do not spoil the artist's work, then the devil take his opinions; and the modern tendency is, for the most part, correct.

But for writers who are not poets or novelists or dramatists, who deal more directly with the experience and materials of

life—for, that is, essayists and certain critics—opinions do seem
to weigh in more heavily. For some among these writers their
opinions define them almost completely. Certain political writers are eager, in fact hot, to be identified with their cause, be
it conservatism, radicalism, or liberalism. Other writers are
specialists in holding only up-to-the-moment and certifiably
O.K. opinions; these are men and women who stay in mental
shape by jumping on and off political and cultural band wag-
ons. Yet other writers are so consistently mistaken—or vicious,
or cowardly—in their opinions as to give irrefutable evidence
of bad character. And there are writers who ask to be judged
solely by the purity of their opinions, even though these opinions have nothing to do with the way they actually live: critics
of capitalism driving Saabs, professors of ethics sleeping with
their students. As Mencken said of the Puritan of his day, so
one might say of the large number of intellectuals who fit snugly
into this last category, that with them "moral obligation is
something quite outside personal conduct, and has very little
to do with it."

But the best writers, I maintain, cannot be defined by their
opinions alone, or even chiefly. Take, as an instance, George
Orwell, who called himself a socialist and thought himself a
radical but today is most admired by people quite on the other
side. And he is admired less for his discrete opinions than for
his general point of view, his way of "looking out at the world."
So it has always been: Hazlitt was fervently for Napoleon, but
this is an attitude that scarcely matters to those of us who care
about Hazlitt today. Lamb's views seem of negligible interest;
and Emerson seems to moot the entire question by holding all
opinions, many of them canceling one another out. No, it is
not their opinions but the possession of an interesting point
of view that separates the great essayists from their fellow
workers, making them, in their own fashion, artists in prose.
H. L. Mencken was an artist, perhaps the greatest of the Amer-

ican essayists, and what makes him an artist is his special point
of view.

The problem in the case of Mencken is that most people,
even if they have not read him since adolescence, think they
know what his point of view is. Edmund Wilson, who wrote
about Mencken on several occasions (and always with respect),
in 1921 noted of him: "Mencken is the civilized consciousness
of modern America, its learning, its intelligence and its taste,
realizing the grossness of its manners and mind, and crying out
in horror and chagrin. . . ." Nice though it might at first seem
to have this little boutonniere of praise pinned to one's coat,
Mencken, I suspect, would have declined to wear it. Wilson's
praise makes H. L. Mencken sound like nothing quite so much
as a member of the Bloomsbury group on a Peace Corps mission to help civilize the natives of the United States. Wilson's
mention of Mencken's taste, for example, is quite off target.
Taste was not a thing Mencken prided himself on, or set out
to demonstrate in his writings. In an essay entitled "Education," in fact, he speaks of a high-school teacher—Mencken
never went to college—who "introduced me to Shakespeare,
Congreve, Wycherley, Marlowe and Sheridan, and so filled me
with that taste for coarseness which now offends so many of
my customers, lay and clerical. . . ."

As for Wilson's remark about Mencken "crying out in horror and chagrin," this, as Mencken himself might have said,
was sheerest fustian, buncombe, bosh, tosh, balderdash, blather,
blague, pother, rodomontade . . . and other epithets that he
reserved for those statements that fell into the category of the
obviously not true. Mencken rather enjoyed America, and
probably for precisely the reasons that he gave in his essay "On
Being an American": "Me [he wrote], I like it because it amuses
me to my taste. I never get tired of the show. It is worth every
cent it costs."

Possibly Mencken confused Wilson as Mencken said the cynic

confused people, who thought him an unhappy man; this is "a false deduction," Mencken said, deduced "from the obvious fact that cynics make other men unhappy."

Mencken thought, true enough, that the cynic was in a privileged position in life, and compared him to "a wedding guest who has known the bride for nine years and has had her confidence." Yet define a cynic as one may, any durable definition must allow that at bottom a cynic feels a distaste for life. This requisite distaste Mencken sorely lacked. The late Philip Rahv—a Marxist in politics and a modernist in literature, and hence a man with a real appetite for gloom—once referred to H. L. Mencken as "the ideologue of enjoyment." I am not sure what Rahv intended by this lumpish phrase; I am sure, though, that for Rahv enjoyment was no good thing—certainly nothing that ought to occupy a serious mind. And if under the banner of enjoyment one includes mirth, then, who can say, Mencken may have been its ideologue. "Mirth," Mencken wrote, "is necessary to wisdom, to comfort, above all, to happiness."

Mirth Mencken could be counted upon to supply. But his laughter, like that of all first-class humorists, is at bottom serious. His essay "Professor Veblen" might serve as a model. The energy of Mencken's prose in this essay is Olympic; one can almost visualize its author, before sitting down to the writing of it, slipping off his jacket, rolling up his shirt sleeves, spitting on his palms. He begins by citing Thorstein Veblen as the latest in a chain of "geysers of pish-posh," and would prefer to waste no further time upon his "incomprehensible syllogisms." Nonetheless, out of a sense of duty, he read all Veblen's writings, from which he emerged weakened but with the "good news" that, to have "a fairly good general acquaintance with the gifted metaphysician's ideas," all that any of the rest of us need read is *The Theory of the Leisure Class* (1899) and *The Higher Learning in America* (1918). If pressed for time, Mencken tells us, the former volume alone will suffice.

But even this will be a bit of a struggle, because Veblen's

style interposes itself so obdurately between his ideas and his readers. As anyone who has read him will recall, Veblen was something of a specialist at getting as little thought into as many words as possible. Such thought as he has is, according to Mencken, "simply Socialism and water." If the style be the message, what Veblen's style conveys to Mencken is "a relentless disease, a sort of progressive intellectual diabetes, a leprosy of the horse sense." Mencken then takes off after the most notable notion in *The Theory of the Leisure Class,* "the theory of conspicuous consumption."

> On page 135 of *The Theory of the Leisure Class* he [Veblen] turns his garish and buzzing search-light upon another problem of the domestic hearth, this time a double one. First, why do we have lawns around our country houses? Secondly, why don't we employ cows to keep them clipped . . . ? Why do we renounce cows and hire Jugo-Slavs? Because "to the average popular apprehension a herd of cattle so pointedly suggests thrift and usefulness that their presence . . . would be intolerably cheap." With the highest veneration. Bosh! Plowing through a bad book from end to end, I can find nothing sillier than this. Here, indeed, the whole "theory of conspicuous waste" is exposed for precisely what it is: one per cent platitude and ninety-five per cent nonsense. Has the genial professor, pondering his great problems, ever taken a walk in the country? And has he, in the course of that walk, ever crossed a pasture inhabited by a cow (*Bos taurus*)? And has he, making that crossing, ever passed astern of the cow herself? And has he, thus passing astern, ever stepped carelessly, and—
>
> But this is not a medical work, and so I had better haul up.

This is vintage Mencken, the throttle full out; and the real force propelling it is Mencken's jocose wonder at the simple unreality of a man like Thorstein Veblen. Mencken had an appreciation for the reality of things, a quality rare in men who deal in art or ideas. He always strained to see things plain and as they really were. His animus against the Veblens of the world is that, with their concepts and notions, they flattened out reality—and, in the act of doing so, not only got things wrong but made them less interesting than they are. Veblen's ideas were at bottom nothing more than higher platitudes, and Mencken defined a platitude thus: "on the one hand it is universally admitted and on the other hand it is not true."

If Mencken was the great scourge of the platitudinarians, high and low, he was also something of a poet of common sense. Justice Holmes (in a letter to Harold J. Laski) remarked on Mencken's "sense of reality," adding, "and most of his prejudices I share." Walter Lippmann said that Mencken was "in touch with life." Two of his earliest books were on Nietzsche and on Shaw ("It is his life work to announce the obvious in terms of the scandalous"). Like Nietzsche, Mencken could be wildly extravagant; but unlike Nietzsche he was always sane. Like Shaw, Mencken made a living out of detesting hypocrisy; but unlike Shaw, he was without the pretensions of the pundit. He could be relied upon to seize the central point. Thus, in a brief piece about Ring Lardner, he writes: "He has grasped the primary fact that no conceivable ingenuity can save a story that fails to show a recognizable and interesting character; he knows that a good character sketch is always a good story, no matter what its structure." That is still true, and renders nugatory all the dark lucubrations of our modern theorists of fictions.

Common sense of Mencken's kind is also, surprisingly, long-lived. Although today the media are a great subject of study, and in America there are writers and teachers of journalism who are called "media ecologists," surely the following short passage from Mencken's essay "Journalism in America" is, *mutatis mutandis,* the first thing that anyone who has had any contact with journalism in our day knows or needs to know. Mencken is discussing whether publishers are to blame for the shoddiness of newspapers:

But do they [the publishers] issue orders that their papers shall be printed in blowsy, clumsy English? That they shall stand against every decent thing, and in favor of everything that is meretricious and ignoble? That they shall wallow in trivialities, and manhandle important news? That their view of learning shall be that of a bartender? . . . Or that helpless men, with the mob against them, should be pursued without fairness, decency or sense? I doubt it. I doubt, even, that the Babbitts turned Greeleys are responsible, in the last analysis, for the political rubbish that fills their papers. . . . The average newspaper proprietor, I suspect, gets nine-tenths of his political ideas from his own men. . . . What they tell him is, in the long run, what he believes, with certain inconsiderable corrections by professionals trying to work him. If only because they have confidential access to him day in and day out, they are able to introduce their own notions into his head. He may have their jobs in his hand, but they have his ears and eyes, so to speak, in theirs.

In Mencken's day, as in ours, the platitudes came in from all sides, from journalists, professors, politicians, novelists, intellectuals, clergymen (more then than now, of course), and the bilge bids fair to flood the joint. Mencken's reason for attacking ignorant religion, as he did so often in his day, was that he felt that if someone didn't there would "be no security for sound sense among us, and little for common decency." Similarly, he mocked psychology because he believed that it did not "make the world more comprehensible, and hence more bearable"— which it may not even to this day. "For it is the natural tendency of the ignorant to believe what is not true. In order to counter that tendency it is not sufficient to exhibit the true; it is also necessary to expose and denounce the false." This, then as now, was a full-time job, with plenty of opportunity for overtime.

Did H. L. Mencken know the truth? I do not believe that he ever claimed that he did. He did, however, know a thing or two. He knew what honor was, and valued it. He said that, of all things in the world, he most admired craftsmanship; and he knew it when he saw it. He could spot "phonies" of all sorts, either singly or by the herd. He knew the arts of literature and music well, and language even better. But above all he knew what he did not know—and what he felt could not be known. Included in the unknowable was the following:

> No one knows Who created the visible universe, and it is infinitely improbable that anything properly describable as evidence on the point will ever be discovered. No one knows what motives or intentions, if any, lie behind what we call natural laws. No one knows why man has his present form. No one knows why sin and suffering were sent into this world—that is, why the fashioning of man was so badly botched.

Mencken was of course famously agnostic, but his agnosticism was far from the kind that expressed itself in indifference. True, fundamentalist religions were in their heyday when he was in his; America was still preponderantly a Protestant country, and Protestantism, in its various forms, gave the United States its tone—a tone that H. L. Mencken felt, to put it gently, was highly uncivilized. But more, I think, is entailed than that religion offered Mencken a large and important and regular target at which to shoot his rationalist arrows.

I have recently read the six volumes of *Prejudices* (1919–27), and in reading through them I was especially struck with how often Mencken refers to godly things—and not mockingly but in connection with what he thought to be the tragedy of existence. In his essay "The National Letters," he criticizes American fiction for not often enough taking up the subject of the "man of delicate organization in revolt against the inexplicable tragedy of existence." He refers to the "poignant and significant conflict between a salient individual and the harsh and meaningless fiats of destiny, the unintelligible mandates and vagaries of God. . . ." Of Beethoven, he writes: "He is a great tragic poet, and like all great tragic poets, he is obsessed by a sense of the inscrutable meaninglessness of life." Of Conrad and Dreiser, his two favorites among novelists roughly contemporary with himself, he wrote that they are "forever fascinated by the 'immense indifference of things,' the tragic vanity of the blind groping that we call aspiration, the profound meaninglessness of life—fascinated and left wondering. . . . God and man are eternal antagonists." This is not quite the iconoclastic Mencken.

Underlying Mencken's many views and opinions, then, is a tragic sense of life. His belief that the great questions in life were unanswerable, the great problems unsolvable, issued in a pervasive skepticism. But Mencken's skepticism did not in turn issue in mere negation. "The natural state of reflective man is one of depression," he wrote. Yet he himself seems to have been one of the most ebullient of men. Is there a contradiction?

L'homme moyen sensuel; the averagely sensual man with the brilliantly active mind. A tragic sense of life Mencken indubitably had, a skeptic he undeniably was, yet he also retained a love for all that life had to offer, esteeming the pleasure of food and drink (the world would be a kindlier place, he held, if most people went about "gently stewed"), of music and literature, of work and friendship. His tragical reading of the ultimate meaninglessness of existence made these things seem not less but more important.

Nor did Mencken neglect the pain in the world. He scoffed at the extravagant complaints of writers about their hard and lonely work: "If authors could work in large well-ventilated factories, like cigar-makers or garment workers, with plenty of their mates about and a flow of lively professional gossip to entertain them, their labor would be immensely lighter. . . ." Mencken once set the portion of the "human race that had the ability to think at one-eighth of one percent." (As for the rest, he said: "The only thing to do with them is to make PhD's of them, and set them to writing handbooks on style.") He spoke more than once of the need for a cultural aristocracy—"secure in its position, animated by an intelligent curiosity, skeptical of all facile generalizations, superior to the sentimentality of the mob, and delighting in the battle of ideas for its own sake"— but there was never anything snobbish about this. He valued the workingman rather more than he did intellectuals and professors; he thought printers, for example, clearly superior to journalists as a human type; and in the Caedmon recording he made in 1948, he said sadly that he had heard that printers had descended to playing golf. He thought well of the "saloon culture" of his day. And he was far from unmindful of the endless burdens of the mass of humanity. At the close of his Third Series of *Prejudices,* Mencken placed a little piece entitled "Suite Américaine" that was a list of the sadnesses inherent in the lives of Americans.

> College professors in one-building universities on the prairie, still hoping, at the age of sixty, to get their whimsical essays into the *Atlantic Monthly.* . . . Car conductors on lonely suburban lines, trying desperately to save up $500 and start a Ford garage. . . . Women hidden away in the damp kitchens of unpainted houses along the railroad tracks, frying tough beefsteaks. . . . Ticket-choppers in the subway, breathing sweat in its gaseous form. . . . Women confined for the ninth or tenth time, wondering helplessly what it is all about. . . . The old lady in Wahoo, Neb., who has read the Bible 38 times. . . . The boss who controls the Italian, Czecho-Slovak and Polish votes in Youngstown, O. . . . The youngest murderer in Chicago. . . .

As is well enough known, H. L. Mencken was no great advocate of the theory or practice of democracy; quite the reverse. Yet what I make him out to have believed is not that all people are created equal—a notion contradicted by daily experience— but that people are to be equally valued: an ideal more realistic, more generous, more humane.

The American booboisie, *homo boobiens*—these are perhaps the two of Mencken's phrases that are remembered best. Yet the reason Mencken brought these phrases into play cannot, I think, have been simply contempt for his countrymen. He viewed them, true enough, as endlessly gullible—always prepared to believe (as he more than once put it) that "Jonah swallowed the whale." But in an odd way it was the common man, so regularly bilked by his clergymen, journalists, professors, politicians, in whose defense Mencken wrote. Life might be harsh and meaningless, an endless struggle with its outcome known in advance to be cheerless, but that was only all the more reason not to live out one's days hostage to ideas that denied reality or outraged human nature. *Homo boobiens* was, well, *boobien,* precisely because he fell, time and again, for shoddy mental goods that made his life less good than it might have been, even under the restrictions of the tragic view.

H. L. Mencken once averred that "life, fundamentally, is not worth living." But why, then, did he himself live it so marvelously well? Mencken may be exceptional among modern writers in living his life honorably, discharging his responsibilities with manly promptitude, never less than decent to colleagues, friends, and family, and utterly without sordor. What is more, whenever Mencken registers what might be construed as an objectionable or cruel opinion, one can count on discovering acts of particular kindness that contradict that opinion. He attacks religion, then enters into friendships with nuns and ministers; he relentlessly mocks the pursuit of men by women, then, in middle life, himself marries a woman whose death within a few years is certain. No evidence of envy or unseemly ambition is to be found in the record of his life. Although he did his best to hide it, the "Holy Terror," the "Bad Boy of Baltimore," as the press used to refer to him, appears to have been a quite good man.

Finally, what of H. L. Mencken's "point of view"? There is his tragic sense of life—which is to say, his ability to look into the pit of existence without flinching or whining; his skepticism, which, while it set him to attack those people who claimed to know the unknowable and to have solutions to the unsolvable, nonetheless bred a certain humility in him; and there is his life, which, though he claimed to be an antinomian from the age of eleven, had about it, in its essentials, a rare virtuousness. Add to all this his humor, and his sensible reminder that "one good horselaugh is worth 10,000 syllogisms."

Mencken once noted that "men work simply in order to escape the depressing agony of contemplating life." But he lived his own life (in the phrases of Justice Holmes, another tough-minded and high-spirited American skeptic) by "the divine folly of honor" and with "the senseless passion for knowledge." Mencken knew what made life worth living: the pursuit of ideals that may never—quite possibly can never—be achieved. He once wrote of Joseph Conrad: "One approaches him in various and unhappy moods: depressed, dubious, despairing; one leaves him in the clear yellow sunshine. . . ." After reading H. L. Mencken one basks in that same sunshine and for essentially the same reason: one has just left the company of a superior man and artist.

Encounter 1980

Anton Chekhov: Worse Even than Shakespeare

FOR SOME YEARS now I have been telling an anecdote—always prefacing it by announcing that it is my favorite literary anecdote—large parts of which, I have come to discover, I seem to have invented. I have not made the anecdote up out of whole cloth, but the cotton, the nylon, and the filaments of polyester in it are mine. In this anecdote Tolstoy and Chekhov are walking about Yasnaya Polyana, Tolstoy's country estate. Tolstoy is in his standard rustic rig: loose tunic, baggy trousers held up by a hemp rope and tucked into boots that come up to his knees, a beard that resembles a triple serving of California sprouts, his famous potato nose (which was much like the actor Karl Malden's), and a floppy peasant hat. He is old and slightly crouched yet still sinewy and looking, as someone once described him, like a giant dwarf. Chekhov is in black suit and vest, a black round-brimmed hat pushed back off his forehead, a black goatee and mustache, a black-rimmed monocle affixed to his right eye and held to his lapel by a black string, black shoes, and no tie but a white shirt buttoned at the collar. He is bent and frail and looking, as I don't believe anyone has ever described him, like an elongated and russified Charlie Chaplin. They stroll amid graceful poplars, slender birches, brooding willows. Tolstoy, his arm around the shoulder of his younger companion, speaks in a voice that knows no doubt, though, in my rendering of it, there is a slightly Yiddish lilt to his inflection and syntax.

"Anton Pavlovich," he says, "believe me when I say I admire your stories. No one, dear Anton Pavlovich, admires your stories more than I. More stories, Anton Pavlovich, I implore you to write more stories: wonderful stories, true stories, imperishable stories. But your plays, Anton Pavlovich, really dear boy, of your plays what can one say? Your plays, Anton Pavlovich, are vile stuff—worse even than Shakespeare."

In this anecdote the landscaping and much of the dialogue turn out to be mine. The clothes are Tolstoy's and Chekhov's, and the sentiments are for the most part Tolstoy's, though I have him admiring Chekhov's stories rather more than he actually did. What I have done, I now see, is stitch this anecdote together out of two biographies of Tolstoy I read many years ago. Henri Troyat, in his biography, has Tolstoy put an arm around Chekhov's shoulder not at Yasnaya Polyana but at Gaspra, in the Crimea, and say to him, "Shakespeare's plays are bad enough, but yours are even worse." In his biography, Ernest J. Simmons has Chekhov at the then-ill Tolstoy's bedside, when the older man takes him by the hand, looks into his eyes, and says, " 'Anton Pavlovich, you are a fine man.' Then, smiling, he releases Chekhov's hand and adds, 'But your plays are altogether vile.' "

What I love about this anecdote is, in part, the nature of the insult. "Worse even than Shakespeare," after all, is not everyone's notion of a strong insult; as an insult, it is in the same class as calling a poet not even as good as Homer. (Was it Robert Southey who once told another poet that his, the other poet's, works would be remembered long after Homer's were forgotten—but not *until*?) But for Tolstoy, who detested Shakespeare's plays and never understood what all the fuss over them was about, to call someone's plays worse than Shakespeare's was a serious put-down. Which brings me to my second reason for adoring this anecdote: it is a story about the stupidity of genius, and such stories always comfort those of us who are not geniuses. If geniuses can on occasion be stupid, cannot the rest of us, perhaps, on occasion be geniuses?

Yet this anecdote is not entirely a laughing matter. For the truth seems to be that Tolstoy and Chekhov, though each respected and may even have loved the other, had radically different views about the purpose of literature—radically different and perhaps irreconcilable views. Because of their high reciprocal regard—even though Tolstoy was thirty-two years older than Chekhov and would survive him by six years—these differences were never allowed altogether out into the open. "Chekhov was with us," Tolstoy wrote to one of his sons, "and I like him very much. He is very talented and he must have a good heart, but so far he has given no evidence of possessing a definite point of view." Chekhov was briefly enamored of Tolstoyan ideas, but when he shucked them off he did so emphatically, writing to his publisher and friend Alexei Suvorin: "Prudence and justice tell me there is more love for mankind in electricity and steam than in chastity and abstention from meat. War is an evil and the court system is an evil, but it doesn't follow that I should wear bast shoes and sleep on a stove alongside the hired hand and his wife, and so on and so forth."

When Chekhov published "The Darling," a story about a woman who has no true existence apart from the men and a child she loves, Tolstoy published a rejoinder to the story, calling it charming but making plain—as if Tolstoy knew how to write other than plainly—that, although Chekhov evidently meant to mock his heroine, the effect of reading the story is to remind one how "marvelous and holy" is "her faculty of devoting herself with her whole being to any one she loves." Chekhov was, Tolstoy claimed, unfortunately writing under the influence of "the absurd and evil activity of the fashionable woman movement." When Tolstoy began to publish segments of *What Is Art?*, Chekhov, writing to a friend, remarked that

Tolstoy's "idea is not new; it's been reiterated in various forms by clever old men in every century." Tolstoy's reaction to *The Seagull* was to think it a shoddy imitation of Ibsen. Chekhov's mature opinion of *The Kreutzer Sonata* was that it was "ridiculous and confused"; he also thought Tolstoy's ending for *Resurrection,* relying as it does on a gospel text, bogus in the extreme. The very paragraph before he makes this criticism of *Resurrection,* however, Chekhov indites what is perhaps the most magnificent tribute that one writer has ever offered to another:

> I fear Tolstoy's death. His death would leave a large empty space in my life. First, I have loved no man the way I have loved him. I am not a believer, but of all beliefs I consider his the closest to mine and most suitable for me. Second, when literature has a Tolstoy, it is easy and gratifying to be a writer. Even if you are aware that you have never accomplished anything and are still not accomplishing anything, you don't feel so bad, because Tolstoy accomplishes enough for everyone. His activities provide justification for the hopes and aspirations that are usually placed on literature. Third, Tolstoy stands firm, his authority is enormous, and as long as he is alive bad taste in literature, all vulgarity in its brazen-faced or lachrymose varieties, all bristly or resentful vanity will remain far in the background. His moral authority alone is enough to maintain what we think of as literary trends and schools at a certain minimal level. If not for him, literature would be a flock without a shepherd or an unfathomable jumble.

While Tolstoy said, apropos of Chekhov's stories, that "his mastery is of the highest order," the real burden of his complaint against Chekhov was his feeling that the younger writer was without a clear point of view. Tolstoy was of course a dominant, and by implication a domineering, figure, and his accusation might be read to mean that Chekhov, far from being without a point of view, merely had a point of view too far from Tolstoy's own. Yet there is good reason to doubt that this is quite so. To be sure, a great many other people had no difficulty in finding a clear point of view in Chekhov's writing; or, it is more accurate to say, a great many people found a great many opposed points of view in Chekhov's writing. But in its own way this tends to confirm Tolstoy's feeling that Chekhov's art, however high its technical mastery, was in some sense curiously unfocused.

When critics and fellow writers tended to find a ready point of view in Chekhov's writing, it only made him edgy and sometimes angry. From fairly early in his literary career, readers used Chekhov as something akin to a Rorschach test in which they would discover their own sympathies and antipathies, obsessions and politics. At one time or another Chekhov was thought to be decadent, religiously orthodox, unfeeling, almost sappily tenderhearted, indifferent to the issues of his day, hostage to the issues of his day (note Tolstoy's remark about his writing under the influence of the "woman movement"), and of course both liberal and conservative. The revolutionary Maxim Gorky, for example, wrote to Chekhov that *"Uncle Vanya* is a completely new species of dramatic art, it is a hammer with which you pound in the public's empty heads" and he praised Chekhov for his coldness, which was exactly what others blamed him for. As Simon Karlinsky notes in his excellent edition of the *Letters of Anton Chekhov* (1973), this was "the kind of Chekhov Gorky wanted to exist and the kind he could have loved, rather than the Chekhov who actually lived and whom we know from his stories, plays and letters." That is very well said, but it leaves open the answer to a serious question that has never been altogether satisfactorily dealt with—namely, who was the Chekhov who actually lived and whom we know from his stories, plays, and letters?

The first of the many complications about Anton Chekhov is that he was a good family man who had had a miserable childhood. Chekhov was born in 1860 in Taganrog, a southern port town of roughly sixty thousand inhabitants some six hundred miles from Moscow. He was the third of six children. His father, Paul Chekhov, was a grocer who went bankrupt when Anton was still in adolescence, an event from which he, the father, never quite recovered. (His father's father had been a serf, but, through impressive energy and thrift, had saved 3,500 rubles with which to buy his freedom.) Before he crumbled, Paul Chekhov was a tyrant in his own home, forcing his children to undergo interminable church services, work long hours at his store, and perform well at school; floggings were not irregular occasions. Yet such treatment did not crush the young Chekhov, as their painful childhoods did such writers as Dickens, Kafka, and Hemingway. "He had less pride and greater simplicity than a person born in the West," writes Irene Nemirovsky, one of Chekhov's biographers. "He was unhappy, but he did not brood over the subtler causes of his unhappiness, nor add to it the poison of wounded vanity."

The harsh narrow-mindedness Chekhov faced at home was complemented by the brutality and squalor endemic to the streets of a nineteenth-century provincial Russian town. In a story entitled "My Life," which is not otherwise about Chekhov's own life at all, Chekhov, through the story's narrator, recalled life in a town similar to Taganrog:

> I remembered the tortured dogs, driven mad, the live sparrows plucked naked by boys and flung into the water, and a long, long series of obscure lingering miseries which I had looked on continually from early childhood in that town; and I could not understand what these sixty thousand people lived for, what they read the gospel for, why they prayed, why they read books and magazines. What good had they gained from all that had been said and written hitherto if they were still possessed by the same spiritual darkness and hatred of liberty, as they were a hundred and three hundred years ago?

One of the advantages a writer has over someone who doesn't write is that the writer can at least find use for his early unhappiness in his later writing. Not that Chekhov appears to have suffered more sorely than his brothers and sisters. But unlike them he seems to have been equipped from the outset with an exceptionally good mental gyroscope, which throughout his life helped him to maintain equilibrium. True, the rough conditions of his childhood endowed him with a *sang-froid* that at moments can chill one's own blood, for he had no illusions about natural affection and could say of his own father that he was "a man of average caliber unable to rise above his situation." But his youth made it impossible for him ever to become interested in conventional religion, and he could never understand intellectuals who were religious. His upbringing also gave him a permanent hatred of brutishness and filth. When he was sixteen, after it became clear that his father would not recover his fortunes in Taganrog, the Chekhov family departed for Moscow, leaving Anton pretty much to fend for himself while finishing his secondary education, which, in a less than ideal way, developed self-reliance in him. It was a hard, even wretched life—stripping away illusions, inducing the illusion of skepticism, revealing brutality, demanding independence—but excellent training for becoming Anton Chekhov.

None of the biographies of Chekhov speak with any certainty of how it came about that he decided to become a physician. He was not an outstanding student, not particularly able at acquiring foreign languages; he finished eleventh in a class of twenty-three at Taganrog in a curriculum built around language study. Medical school was a five-year course; then, as now, it was a grind; then, unlike now, there was no pot of gold waiting at its end. What is impressive to contemplate is that Chekhov not only managed to get through his medical studies but did so while managing the beginning of a career as a writer—a very active writer, too—and becoming the head of his family, which meant having the financial responsibility for from anywhere between four and eight people.

No more is known about what lay behind Chekhov's decision to become a writer. The only aptitude he had shown in this line was an adolescent knack for mimicry. Certainly as a young man Chekhov never thought of writing idealistically— as the pursuit of truth and beauty and all that—nor, at least in his early years, did he think of it as a serious vocation. Once he had rejoined his family in Moscow, he wrote to bring in the rubles—though, given the comic periodicals in which his first writings appeared, to bring in the kopecks would be more precise, for Chekhov's early comic sketches earned him roughly a nickel a line. Chekhov became adept at knocking this stuff out; he had no choice but to become adept. His two older brothers' activities in the fields of drinking and whoring had certified them as unreliable; his two younger brothers and his sister were still of school age and hence too young to work. The father earned a menial wage for doing menial work. In three years in Moscow the family moved eleven times. Without brother Anton's earnings from his scribbling, the Chekhov family might well have slipped into beggary, or worse.

The world, it sometimes seems, is divided between those people who leave a mess and those who agree to clean it up. Chekhov, though not particularly happy about it, was clearly among those who clean up. He had become head of his family by default, and its head he remained, for his parents lived the remainder of their lives with him, and his sister Mariya (Masha) lived under his roof even after he was dead, whence she served as the custodian of his works and reputation long after the Bolsheviks had captured Russia. Would Chekhov have written differently if he had not had to serve his literary apprenticeship under the financial pressure of having to support a family? Perhaps. But then again he might not have written at all. As it was, in 1885, his first year out of medical school, Chekhov, in the most un-Yaddo-like conditions imaginable, working on a dining-room table, with family and boarders strolling by as if along the Grande Jatte, published something like 129 stories, sketches, and articles. But then, as Simon Karlinsky says, there is "no word in Russian to convey the concept of privacy."

It is sometimes difficult to get a clear fix on Chekhov's distribution of energy between medicine and literature. Apropos of pursuing two careers, he wrote, "I don't see what's so impossible about chasing two hares at once," and added, "Medicine is my lawful wedded wife and literature my mistress. When one gets on my nerves, I spend the night with the other." Yet things appear to have been more often the other way round; that is, literature appears to have been Chekhov's wife and medicine his mistress. At any rate, apart from a period he spent as a student assistant in a *zemstvo* hospital, and his work during the Russian cholera epidemic of 1892–93, medicine rarely dominated his life. During his 1890 trip to Sakhalin Island, the Russian version of Devil's Island in Siberia, Chekhov combined his careers of physician and writer, first scientifically surveying conditions on the island and then writing a dissertation-like book on them. Otherwise, he saw patients whenever they approached him, as peasants near his later abodes in the Melikhovo region and in Yalta had no hesitation in doing; he rarely charged a fee and he never had anything like a regular medical practice. The chief source of his income was literature; and literature was his regular practice.

Chekhov allowed that his work as a physician had greatly influenced him as a writer. As he put it in a biographical note he wrote for a medical-school class reunion, medicine "significantly broadened the scope of my observations and enriched me with knowledge whose value for me as a writer only a doctor can appreciate." Medicine was, he went on in effect to say, a reality instructor, and it is true that Chekhov's scientific training gave an empirical bent to his writing. People come to physicians in extreme situations, and Chekhov, as a physician, had a greater than ordinary dose of humanity stripped of its dignity. He did not come to literature loaded down with ideas he wished to prove; he found the passionate pronouncements of other writers about the grandeur of mankind not only pompous but slightly laughable—and these things, too, are doubt-less owed to his medical training and practice. His experience as a physician also lent Chekhov a coolness of perspective that could sometimes seem a bit ghastly, as when he spoke of chol-era "making hors d'oeuvres of our local rustics," but that same perspective could turn hot when he was viewing what he took to be the inanity of the political idealists of his time: "All their inactive sanctity and purity are based on hazy and naive sym-pathies and antipathies to individuals and labels, not to facts. It's easy to be pure when you can hate the Devil you don't know and love the God you wouldn't have brains enough to doubt." So much for political purity, and even less for opin-ionation. "There are a great many opinions in the world," Chekhov wrote, "and a good half of them are held by people who have never been in trouble."

Chekhov did not automatically come by such strong opin-ions—opinions, even, about opinions. He was talented, he was almost movie-star handsome, yet his own view of himself as a young man was far from a confident one. "What aristocratic writers take from nature gratis, the less privileged must pay for with their youth," he wrote to a friend, adding that a writer as lowborn as he had to squeeze "the slave out of himself drop by drop" before "he finds that the blood coursing through his veins is no longer the blood of a slave, but that of a real human being." Part of the fascination of the story of Anton Chekhov's life is to be found in watching him become "a real human being," free and courageous and not a man to be trifled with.

Certainly Chekhov's youthful low opinion of himself extended to his early writing. He was perfectly content to think himself a *pisaka*—the Russian equivalent for "scribbler," with an extra dollop of contempt thrown in. He signed much of his early published work with various pseudonyms (Antosha Che-khonte being the one he used for his first published book), and referred to it as "literary excrement." The turning point in the revision of Chekhov's opinions about his own talent came not from within but from without—from, specifically, a letter of praise in 1886, when he was twenty-six years old, from Dmitry Grigorovich, a writer of the generation of Turgenev and Dostoevsky. In this letter Grigorovich wrote that Chekhov was the most talented writer of his generation and predicted great things for him if he would learn to husband his talent by working more slowly, carefully, and conscientiously. The effect on Chekhov of Grigorovich's letter was to make him, for the first time, take his own writing seriously.

Before long other people began to take Chekhov's writing seriously. One important figure among those who did was Alexei Suvorin, a literary man-of-all-work and publisher of the right-wing newspaper *New Times*. Suvorin sought Chekhov out as a contributor and, beginning in 1886, published a flood of his stories that were of a higher caliber than any Chekhov had hitherto published. Simon Karlinsky claims that Suvorin was the decisive influence in launching Chekhov on his career as a serious writer, and the claim is entirely persuasive. The reason the claim needs to be asserted at all is that Suvorin's role in Chekhov's career, and the friendship between the two men, have been vastly diminished in the Soviet account of Chekhov's life. It will not do, in Soviet hagiography, for Anton Chekhov to have had a friend such as Alexei Suvorin, who was for most of his career pro-government and hence anathema to Russian liberals; not exactly an honorable conservative's ideal either, Suvorin was a baiter of Poles and Finns and an anti-Semite, which put his newspaper smack on the wrong side during the Dreyfus Affair. Chekhov, who was convinced of Captain Dreyfus's innocence, dispensed with tact in telling Suvorin how repulsive he thought his paper's position on the Dreyfus Affair was. That the two men could remain friends—and true friends, for many of Chekhov's best and most intimate letters were written to Suvorin—despite such strong disagreement was a testament to the strength of their feeling for each other.

But it also complicates the problem for those who wish to position Chekhov according to his views. Was he a man of the Left or of the Right? Did he tend toward optimism or pessimism in his writing? Was he the writer in whom Simon Karlinsky finds "unfailing humanity and compassion," or the writer in whom Lev Shestov finds a "pitiless talent" and whose advice to humanity, as Shestov says, was to bang its head against the wall and then sleep the sleep of the brute. It is not so much a question of discovering a message in Chekhov. But it is a question of the kind that Henry James, writing about Turgenev, put when he noted: "The great question as to a poet or novelist is, how does he feel about life? What in the last analysis is his philosophy? This is the most interesting thing their works offer us. Details are interesting in proportion as they contribute to make it clear."

Chekhov, there is reason to believe, would not have agreed. In a letter to Suvorin, who complained of his inconclusiveness about a problem raised in one of his stories, Chekhov replied that solving problems was not the artist's job. Nor was "the artist meant to be a judge of his characters and what they say; his only job is to be an impartial witness. . . . Drawing conclusions is up to the jury, that is, the readers." In this same letter there follows an astonishing statement for a writer to make: "It's about time that everyone who writes—especially genuine literary artists—admitted that in this world you can't figure anything out." Chekhov was twenty-eight years old when he wrote that. (He only lived, recall, to forty-four.) Did he really believe it? There is no reason to think that he didn't believe it absolutely.

What is the price for believing that in this world you can't figure anything out? For Chekhov the man, it may not have come to much. Certainly, it did not constrain him from good works. It did not put him off wishing to see conditions alleviated for the prisoners on Sakhalin Island; it did not stop him from building four schools for peasants during his lifetime; it did not restrain him from being passionately on the side of Zola in the Dreyfus Affair; it did not even prevent him from marrying, late in his life, even though no writer, with the exception of Strindberg, has held out in his writing less hope for marriage than Anton Chekhov, for the guttering and final extinguishing of the flame of love is one of the great Chekhovian subjects. No, if one were to judge Chekhov by his actions alone, he would seem a man who believed in education, justice, the family, and who held enlightened and not merely *bienpensant* views on most of the questions of his day. He would emerge from such a judgment as a strong liberal of the best type, not of the pusillanimous kind fearful of being caught on the wrong side such as Turgenev appears to have been, but a man of serious conviction who does what he can to relieve suffering and eliminate injustice, and who believes in the possibility of limited but nonetheless real progress.

Chekhov was not an angel, though he is sometimes made out to be all soul, with a heart of gold. Ronald Hingley wrote *A New Life of Anton Chekhov* (1976), in my view the best biography of Chekhov, in partial reaction to the clichés about Chekhov's tenderness and sensitivity; and while he turns up evidence of Chekhov's evasiveness, his coldness, his occasional unreliability and social hypocrisy, he concludes that the result of assembling Chekhov's defects "has been to provide a character reference more impressive than can come from those who degrade him with their mindless adulation." Believing that in this world you can't figure out anything did not make Chekhov a less decent man. The belief that one is living in a puzzling and indifferent universe might even increase one's sympathy and one's hatred of unnecessary brutality, and in Chekhov's case it actually appears to have done so.

But for a writer whose name is in contention to appear among that small and sacred circle of literary artists of the greatest power, Chekhov's honest disbelief brings with it certain limitations—limitations that make him, as Philip Rahv once put it, "an artist of unmistakable originality, though not of the very first order." Compassionate Chekhov clearly is, and lyrical, and often comic, too, but in the main he is a very dark writer, and admiration for him should not disguise that unarguable fact. Helplessness, hopelessness, misunderstanding, and defeat are chief among his themes. If love crops up in a Chekhov story, it is virtually certain to be mowed down by selfishness or insensitivity or staleness. Serious communication between two people is an impossibility; and in Chekhov's plays, although the conversation goes by the technical name of dialogue, more than half the time his characters are soliloquizing while other people who are not listening are in the same room. In Chekhov's writing, boredom hangs in the atmosphere, palpably there, a spiritual smog created by human inertia; in the story entitled "Uprooted," even a windmill is bored. Music is frequently playing, but usually off in another room; ". . . and then came emptiness, and the sense of the futility of life" is a characteristic Chekhovian line. "Why we live, why we suffer . . . Oh, if only we knew, if only we knew!" moans Olga at the close of *Three Sisters*.

Dark Chekhov undoubtedly is, but darkness, too, has its shades, and Chekhov worked in them all. Twilight was perhaps his favorite among them, for in Chekhov night has not yet—not quite—fallen, but it is coming. One of Chekhov's many artistic innovations was that he was perhaps the first serious writer to take as one of his themes the malaise of modernity—the sense that something in life is awry, something is wrong, something is missing. "We're not happy," says the character Vershinin in *Three Sisters,* "and we can't be happy: we only want happiness." It is this element in Chekhov that makes him seem so modern. At the end of each of Chekhov's major plays—*Ivanov, The Seagull, Uncle Vanya, Three Sisters, The Cherry Orchard*—one can almost sense Samuel Beckett waiting in the wing.

Not that Chekhov is merely Samuel Beckett with Russian cabbage soup, herring, and cucumbers added as props. He is much more than that; he is broader and deeper. His work is a triumph of tone, he was a master of moods. Verisimilitude came naturally to him. Whatever Chekhov writes, one feels, is true: there is no single Chekhov story in which even for a moment one thinks to say that this character doesn't feel right, this situation seems false, life isn't like that. He was a powerful social observer. Another literary line radiates out from Chekhov to Proust, who was born only eleven years after Chekhov. Proust remarked that "every social class has its pathology," but Chekhov, in stories and plays that dealt with every social class from the peasantry to the nobility, had long before already demonstrated the accuracy of Proust's remark.

Yet Chekhov's writing fails to yield up its essence through conventional literary analysis. It won't do with Chekhov to paraphrase a few of his stories, point out the symbolic significance of this or that, fill in the social background, offer a compact interpretation, and knock off for lunch at the faculty club. René Wellek, in the introduction to a useful collection of criticism about Chekhov, remarks, rightly, on the absence in his book of any extended criticism of Chekhov's stories because "selecting a few [of these stories] would falsify Chekhov's achievement." Chekhov's stories are not about good and evil; they have no heroes. With only rare exceptions is there anything resembling intrinsic drama building to a climax—more often, in fact, they descend to an anticlimax. Chekhov himself once told Ivan Bunin that the way to tell a story is to make it as brief as possible and then to lop off the beginning and the ending. (Writing stories without a beginning or an ending is a procedure since picked up by many contemporary writers in the *New Yorker* and elsewhere; the difficulty—it is, unfortunately, an insurmountable one—is that a writer of Chekhov's quality is needed to supply the remaining middle.) Nor will it quite do to say that these stories represent "a slice of life," a grossly inept metaphor, since life, as you may have noticed, is no pie.

There are no plots in Chekhov, and while there are characters in plenty, few of them are memorable in the way that characters in Dickens and Tolstoy and Proust are memorable. "Indeed," writes Virginia Woolf, "it is the soul that is the chief character in Russian fiction," and, double indeed, it is true that the question of souls—lost souls, really—does hover over almost all of Chekhov's pages. But the best account of what goes on in a Chekhov story is Conrad Aiken's. Writing in 1921, reviewing one of the thirteen volumes of Chekhov stories translated into English by Constance Garnett, Aiken notes that "Chekhov is more concerned with the effect of 'actuality' than with the 'story' "—more concerned, that is, with effects than causes. Aiken continues:

> His sensibilities were rich and of an immense range, had thrust their roots, one dares to think, almost as widely and deeply into life as Shakespeare's: his understanding was unsurpassed, and if he falls short of the greatest of artists it is not for a lack of that faculty. No artist has known, by introspection, more "states of mind," no artist has known better, by observation, what shapes they assume in talk or behavior.

What Conrad Aiken calls "states of mind" can as easily be called "condition of soul." This comes through even in translation. It is not easy to obtain a clear verdict on the quality of Chekhov's style in Russian from those for whom the Russian language is not, as it is for me, a locked gate. D. S. Mirsky, an aristocrat who was no great admirer of Chekhov, the grandson of a serf, and who wrote in reaction to the English idolization of Chekhov during World War I, refers to Chekhov's Russian as "another shortcoming," claiming that his language was colorless and without individuality. "He had no feeling for words," Mirksy writes. "Of all Russian writers, he has the least to fear from the treachery of translators." Simon Karlinsky, on a very different hand, compares Chekhov's late prose to "the slow movement of Mozart's Piano Concerto in A major, K.488." Vladimir Nabokov, not exactly a man oblivious to style, says of Chekhov that

> his literary style goes to parties clad in its everyday suit. Thus Chekhov is a good example to give when one tries to explain that a writer may be a perfect artist without being exceptionally vivid in his verbal technique or exceptionally preoccupied with the way his sentences curve. . . . Chekhov managed to convey an impression of artistic beauty far surpassing that of many writers who thought they knew what rich beautiful prose was. He did it by keeping all his words in the same dim light and of the same exact tint of gray, a tint between the color of an old fence and that of a low cloud. The variety of his moods, the flicker of his charming wit, the deeply artistic economy of characterization, the vivid detail, and the fade-out of human life—all the peculiar Chekhovian features—are enhanced by being suffused and surrounded by a faintly iridescent verbal haziness.

One is inclined to believe Karlinsky and Nabokov about Chekhov's Russian style, yet grant Mirsky his point about Chekhov having little to fear about betrayal by translators. Ronald Hingley's Oxford-edition translation of Chekhov seems to me an improvement on Constance Garnett's, but Garnett's reads decently, as does Avrahm Yarmolinsky's and Robert Payne's; I, you might say, have never read a Chekhov translation I didn't like. This is owing, along with the efforts of his translators, to Chekhov's talent, which always shines through: his penetrating analysis of character, his economical and often lyrical descriptions of landscape, his darting truths about human nature and national character ("The Russian loves recalling life, but he does not love living"), his accurate eye and nose for the look and feel and smell of exhausted provincial Russian towns, his really quite magical ability to insinuate a larger significance into even the most minor of incidents. All these qualities, which come across unmistakably in every translation of his work, Chekhov had in amplitude.

What Chekhov didn't have was a strong sense of form. This may seem a minor weakness, especially set beside his impressive strengths, but the absence of a sense of form may, in Chekhov's case, have been more than a mere technical problem. Why, for example, did Chekhov never write a novel? To ask the question is not akin to asking why a sprinter doesn't run a marathon, for Chekhov, early in his career, worked two years on a novel (to be entitled *Stories from the Lives of My Friends*) that he never completed. True, Chekhov once said: "It's much better as a rule to write short works than long ones: fewer pretensions and more success. . . ." Yet he once wrote to Dmitry Grigorovich, and the italics are his: "*I do not yet know how to write long pieces.*" When he came to write at greater length—and such stories as "The Steppe," "In the Ravine," "Three Years," and "My Life" qualify, at least in length, as novellas—he feared that these longer stories sagged in the middle, which they often do. And Ronald Hingley notes that as Chekhov begins to mature as an artist, "we find the more elaborate the plot of a given story is, the less effective it tends to be as a work of art." Chekhov himself was too much the highly self-conscious artist not to recognize his own aesthetic deficiencies.

At twenty-eight Chekhov wrote to Grigorovich: "I still lack a political, religious and philosophical world view—I change it every month—and so I'll have to limit myself to descriptions of how my heroes love, marry, give birth, die, and how they speak." That same year he wrote to Alexei Suvorin: "The artist must pass judgment only on what he understands; his range is as limited as that of any other specialist—that's what I keep repeating and insisting upon. Anyone who says the artist's field is all answers and no questions has never done any writing or had any dealings with imagery." Despite the efforts of various people to pull him ideologically this way and that, Chekhov hewed to the view that it was not the writer's job to answer questions but to formulate them correctly. Of a now-forgotten writer capable of writing such sentences as "The greatest wonder of all is man himself, and we shall never tire of studying him," Chekhov said: "That's no view of life; that's a lollipop."

Not only did Chekhov eschew easy answers but he asked the hardest questions. In a story of 1898 entitled "A Doctor's Visit," a young doctor visits the daughter of a family who owns a large factory. The members of this wealthy family are unhappy; the fifteen hundred or so factory workers are living a barbarous life in unhealthy conditions; only the family's governess, "a stupid middle-aged lady in pince-nez" who eats sterlet and drinks Madeira during the doctor's visit, seems to be deriving any pleasure from these arrangements—all that misery so one insensitive woman may enjoy a rich lunch. Think what a crude writer like Maxim Gorky would have done with this material. Here is what Chekhov does as he has the young doctor sit upon some planks and building materials and contemplate the hideous factory building:

> And he thought about the devil, in whom he did not believe, and he looked round at the two windows where the fires were gleaming. It seemed to him that out of those crimson eyes the devil himself was looking at him—that unknown force that had created the mutual relation of the strong and the weak, that coarse blunder which one could never correct. The strong must hinder the weak from living—such was the law of Nature; but only in a newspaper article or in a school book was that intelligible and easily accepted. In the hotchpotch which was everyday life, in the tangle of trivialities out of which human relations were woven, it was no longer a law, but a logical absurdity, when the strong and the weak were both equally victims of their mutual relations, unwillingly submitting to some directing force, unknown, standing outside life, apart from man.

There are many moments—and the above passage is one of them—when one is glad that Chekhov had the courage of his lack of convictions.

But Chekhov knew there was a price to be paid for not having clear convictions and a strong sense of the meaning of life. If one hasn't something approaching a coherent world view, a sense of the interconnectedness of things and their ultimate meaning, form becomes a tricky matter. Plots become difficult when one hasn't a firm point to make. One can demonstrate life's complexity, observing in the process what recalcitrant material life offers to the writer and how it defies any generalization one can make about it. Chekhov often worked this vein— that of the artist who labors in the criticism of abstractions, never taking sides. "I'm far from an enthusiast for modernity," Chekhov wrote. "But one must be as objective and fair as possible. Bad as things may now be, uncongenial as the present is, the past was quite simply nauseating." One sees something of Chekhov as the artist criticizing abstractions in his many stories having to do with Russian peasants, for Chekhov's treatment of peasants, in its variousness, is a marvelous antidote to Turgenev's treacly sentimentalizing of them and Tolstoy's fantastical idealizing of them. There is a great deal a writer can do without a coherent world view, and Chekhov came close to doing it all, but he knew, being very savvy about such things, that there is also a great deal one cannot do. Chekhov, in his subtlety, made the case against the writer without strong convictions or a coherent world view, and—though he dragged his generation of Russian writers into the indictment—it was finally a cogent indictment against himself. Writing to Suvorin, Chekhov lamented:

> We truly lack a certain something: if you lift up the skirts of our muse, all you see is a flat area. Keep in mind that the writers we call eternal or simply good, the writers who intoxicate us, have one highly important trait in common: they're moving toward

something definite and beckon you to follow, and you feel with your entire being not only with your mind, that they have a certain goal, like the ghost of Hamlet's father, which had a motive for coming and stirring Hamlet's imagination. . . . The best of them are realistic and describe life as it is, but because each line is saturated with the consciousness of its goal, you feel life as it should be in addition to life as it is, and you are captivated by it. But what about us? Us! We describe life as it is and stop dead right there.

And yet one does not think of Chekhov as a writer who can be clapped into the irons of generalizations about his genera- tion, so greatly, as a figure in world literature, does he tower above any other Russian writer of his generation. Besides, among writers generationalism—the regular identification of oneself as part of a literary generation—is the last refuge of a pipsqueak, and Chekhov rarely went in for it. On the contrary, he did not even feel the need for solidarity among writers of his generation. "We can't all think or feel in the same way," he wrote to Ivan Leontyev. "We have different goals or no goals at all. . . . To help a colleague, to respect his person and his work, to refrain from gossiping about him and envying him, lying to him and acting hypocritically toward him, all this requires that one be not so much a young writer as simply a human being." No, it is difficult to believe that Chekhov's shortcomings can be explained by the plight of his generation.

In seeking an understanding of why Chekhov is so good a writer and yet just misses being among the small circle of great writers—that circle wherein reside such figures as Dante and Cervantes, Dickens and Tolstoy—one runs up against the sin- gle important mystery in Chekhov's life: the mystery of how he, a physician always confident in his diagnoses, failed to diagnose his own tuberculosis, probably for fully a decade after he had had it. On March 22, 1897, while dining at the Her- mitage restaurant in Moscow with Suvorin, Chekhov opened his mouth and blood gushed out, causing him to faint at the table. By then, according to Simon Karlinsky, Chekhov "had had tuberculosis for at least ten years without realizing it. All the expected symptoms were there: racking cough, night sweat, palpitations, spitting blood. He still refused to see another doctor about any of these symptoms, and when the possibility of tuberculosis was mentioned by others, he'd reply that if he had it, he would have been dead years ago." Ronald Hingley, who dates the onset of Chekhov's symptoms of tuberculosis to the same time as Karlinsky, remarks that Chekhov's "sickness, with its intimations of ultimate mortality, declared itself on the threshold of a major change in his evolution [as an artist]." Hingley does not push this interesting point further.

I shall. We cannot, of course, know why Chekhov chose, against all the abundant evidence, to ignore or let slide to the back of his mind his knowledge of his apparent tuberculosis. But what does seem tempting to speculate upon is the possibility of Chekhov's knowing that he had an almost certainly fatal disease and the effect of this upon his writing. I believe that Anton Chekhov knew he had tuberculosis, and knew it as early as the late 1880s, when his writing changed radically, becoming darker, more serious, denser, in every way better. I base this belief not alone on the fact that Chekhov, as a highly capable physician, could scarcely have missed knowing it— stranger things have happened—but on the evidence of his writing.

Chekhov, I believe, wrote with knowledge of his own impending death in his bones. It is what gave him his gloom, but his profundity too. Chekhov's stories and plays are filled with people who recognize only too late that life is finite and that they, in their ignorance, have let it pass them by. "Why," asks the chief character in the story "Rothschild's Fiddle," after a misspent life, "do people always do what isn't needful?" Dr. Johnson said that the knowledge that one is to be hanged in a fortnight wonderfully concentrates the mind; the knowledge that one is carrying a fatal disease probably does something similar for the prose. The lyrical descriptions of Chekhov's landscapes, surely, read as if written by a man who knows he may not see them for much longer, and hence is all the more appreciative of them. Mayn't it also be that Chekhov's loftiness—his being above class affiliation, above politics ("Great writers and artists should take part in politics," he wrote during the days of the Dreyfus Affair, "only as a defense against politics"), above taking positions generally—was owing to his foreknowledge of his shortened life? After all, if one knows one's end is near, all such things must seem pretty small potatoes. As a character in Chekhov's story "Gooseberries" puts it: "There ought to be behind the door of every happy, contented man someone standing with a hammer continually reminding him with a tap that there are unhappy people; that however happy he may be, life will show him her laws sooner or later, trouble will come for him—disease, poverty, losses, and no one will see or hear, just as now he neither sees nor hears others."

If I am correct about Chekhov's knowing of his own early death, and if that knowledge gave his work a new depth and a special perspective, such knowledge did not permit him to accept any more readily secondhand answers to life's final mysteries. His own rather arbitrary illness could only have heightened his sense of these mysteries. No ready solutions were at hand. Religion, though he respected it in others, was impossible for him. Science, too, was a cul-de-sac; as the principal character in his story "On the Road" remarks, "The trouble is that every science has a beginning but not an end. . . ." In one of the darkest of Chekhov's tales, "A Dreary Story," a famous professor of medicine, who senses his own death is near, realizes that he hasn't a theory of life, or "what my philosophic colleagues call a general idea." When the young woman who is his most brilliant student beseeches him at a time of crisis in her life for a reason to go on living, the professor, in one of the saddest lines in literature, has to say, "I don't know."

"I don't know" is what Chekhov, in his profound honesty, says to us, his readers. When one recognizes how ardently Chekhov sought to know, how the efforts of his prodigious art were all bent toward the effort of knowing, one has to admire all the more the iron integrity behind such honesty, even if it made him, in the view of a Tolstoy, who felt that he did know, "worse even than Shakespeare." For the truth is that one has to strain very hard to think of a writer who has come after Anton Chekhov of whom one can confidently say, "better even than Chekhov."

The New Criterion 1986

The Outrageous
Mr. Wu

I
N HIS INEVITABLY charming essay "Quia Imperfectum," Max Beerbohm proposed a museum composed of incomplete masterpieces, which would
include among other items Penelope's web, the original drawings for the tower of Babel, the manuscripts of *Edwin Drood*
and "Kubla Kahn," the fragments from Racine's *Iphigénie,* and
the blank spaces and bare pedestals for the paintings and statues that Michelangelo planned but never completed for the
baptistery of San Lorenzo. I wonder if I might suggest yet
another item for inclusion, that of the quite scrappy notes for
an essay that George Orwell had hoped to write about Evelyn
Waugh before death, the ultimate deadline, arrived to rescind
all others in Orwell's active journalistic career. Like the other
items in Beerbohm's museum dedicated to enshrinement of
the incomplete, a full-blown George Orwell essay on Evelyn
Waugh does seem deliciously promising. One imagines that
essay to have been a lengthy piece of work, on the model of
Orwell's essays on Dickens or Kipling, pellucid, shimmering
with good sense, and slicing to the core of Waugh's art as no
other writer has thus far been able to do. "Sorry," as certain
rather sadistic practitioners of the science of librarianship have
been known exuberantly to exclaim, "but that work is not
available."

A very great deal has been written about the art of Evelyn Waugh: *Evelyn Waugh: The Critical Heritage* runs to more than five hundred pages; Christopher Sykes's friendly but not uncritical biography of Waugh has long been in print; and a weighty volume of Waugh's letters, an even weightier one of his diaries, and now *The Essays, Articles and Reviews of Evelyn Waugh* have all appeared. One nonetheless feels that, even though all the pieces are now on the board, no one has quite succeeded in assembling the puzzle presented by this extraordinary writer and his enchanting art. Strip away what one takes to be his mask and one discovers another under it and then yet another under that one. So much seems to interpose itself between his literary career and our understanding of it, not least the preposterous persona he sedulously erected for himself. Yet this much can be said at the outset: A man afflicted by boredom his life long, he unfailingly avoided passing boredom on to his readers. If there is a serious writer in this century who has given more pleasure to his readers than Evelyn Waugh, I cannot think of his name.

One doesn't think of modern literature as strenuously devoted to purveying pleasure. Complexity, yes; seriousness, often; a certain jokiness, occasionally. But pleasure of the kind available in the art of Evelyn Waugh is very rare. I do not mean to imply that aesthetic pleasure of the highest order isn't abundantly available in such modern writers as Joyce and Proust, T. S. Eliot and Wallace Stevens; obviously, it is. But in the work of Evelyn Waugh high aesthetic pleasure—he was a consummate artist, the masculine elegance of whose prose is unrivaled in our time—is combined with pleasure such as only a comic genius can provide. Evelyn Waugh's comedy has had many followers—such British group efforts as "Beyond the Fringe," "That Was the Week That Was," and, on a cruder level, "Monty Python's Flying Circus" are quite unthinkable without the precedent of Waugh—but no successful imitators. There are two reasons why there has never been a convincing parody of

Evelyn Waugh: first, no one else is quite that funny, and second, no one else can write quite that well.

Evelyn Waugh's friend John Sutro coined the word "Wavian"—on the model of "Shavian" for George Bernard Shaw—to apply to the distinctive comedy of Evelyn Waugh. It is comedy that cannot be explained but only displayed. Samples available without request: On our first encountering Waugh's bounder-hero Basil Seal, nearly a third of the way into the novel *Black Mischief,* he is coming awake the morning after a great binge on the sofa of what is to him a totally strange flat. Waugh notes:

> There was a gramophone playing. A lady in a dressing jacket sat in an armchair by the gas fire, eating sardines from the tin with a shoe horn. . . .

Stop the cameras here. That lady eating sardines from the tin with a shoehorn is a pure Wavian touch. So, too, is the following sentence from the first and only installment of Waugh's autobiography, *A Little Learning,* which appears in the chapter in which the author recounts his days at Lancing, his public school: "Apart from general malevolence and particular cruelty, we were not vicious." Finally, from the thesaurus of Wavian anecdotes: Christopher Sykes, in his biography, reports visiting Waugh in the hospital, where he found him grumbling in great pain in the aftermath of an operation for piles. Attempting to solace his friend, Sykes remarked that he assumed the operation, painful though it might seem now, was in any case necessary.

"No," Waugh replied," the operation was not necessary, but might conceivably have become so later on."

"Not necessary?" said Sykes. "They why did you have it done?"

"Perfectionism," answered Waugh.

Sacha Guitry said that a successful joke requires three people: the person who tells it, the person who appreciates it, and the person who doesn't get it. In its whimsy, in its obliquity, sometimes in its cruelty, Evelyn Waugh's comedy is not for everyone. But those who do appreciate it, appreciate it hugely— can scarcely, in fact, get enough of it. Waugh was a man with a ferocious appetite for the ridiculous, and, with his observant eye, he never went hungry for long. In his writing, if not always in his life, he possessed the gift of viewing everything as if from a great distance, *sub specie aeternitatis*—under the aspect, that is, of eternity, from which aspect nearly everything humankind does is of course ridiculous, absurd, comical.

But the comedy of Evelyn Waugh would not have been possible if not dressed out in his carefully measured prose. That prose is the straight face from behind which the smashing punch lines are delivered. There is nothing flashy or idiosyncratic about Waugh's prose style. It has a precision and a delicacy of syntax that elides into an elegance of its own—the elegance of absolute correctness. He commanded a concision that, combined with his towering contempt for cliché, permitted him to write with dead-on directness. He had an interesting though not flamboyant vocabulary, which he was able to assemble in charming juxtapositions (writing of the "desperate levity" of his youth) and unexpected locutions (college bills at this time of desperate levity "engorged his allowance") that gave it a continual freshness. Like his friend Ronald Knox, he was said to have known the exact meaning and derivation of every word he used; perhaps it was this that lent his language its weight and authority. As a writer he thought of himself as a craftsman, and he enjoyed bringing to book those who practiced shoddily the craft he revered. Of a sloppily written book by Harold Laski, Waugh notes that Laski is "so set on preaching the dignity of labour that he shirks his own work." Of another slapdash prose writer, Stephen Spender, Waugh writes: "To see him fumbling with our rich and delicate language is to experience all the horror of seeing a Sèvres vase in the hands of a chimpanzee."

In *A Little Learning,* Waugh wrote that he remembered no Greek and read no Latin for pleasure, yet claimed a great debt to his youthful classical studies for such skill as he had as a prose writer: "Only by them can a boy fully understand that a sentence is a logical construction and that words have basic inalienable meanings, departure from which is either conscious metaphor or inexcusable vulgarity." But more than a grounding in classical studies is required to make an Evelyn Waugh; there were also his fastidiousness and his devilish (I use this word with some forethought) powers of comic formulation. Who but Evelyn Waugh could have devised, as a euphemism for Harold Acton's homosexuality, the phrasing, he "did not fret for female society"? Who but he, in one of his travel books, *Remote People,* could describe two young Germans encountered in Aden as speaking "English, one rather better than the other, but both very fluently, loudly, and unintelligibly." "Proper words in proper places," as Swift famously said, "make the true definition of a style." Waugh knew the proper words and he knew their proper places; he also knew that style, which he thought derived from the conflation of lucidity, elegance, and individuality, was the great preservative of literary art—that which allowed it to live beyond its time.

But then neither Evelyn Waugh's comic genius nor the high quality of his prose has ever been in serious dispute. What is disputed is the use he made of his gifts. There is, to begin with, very little agreement about which are Waugh's best books, why his literary career took the shape it did, or what in summation his nearly forty years of literary effort come to. Edmund Wilson, for example, a great admirer of Waugh's early novels, bailed out on him with the publication of *Brideshead Revisited.* Claiming that this novel "has been a bitter blow to this critic," Wilson, himself always a bit of the village atheist, could neither understand nor endure the Catholicism at the center of the novel. George Orwell, who reviewed, briefly, Waugh's slender novel *Scott-King's Modern Europe*, though properly appreciative of Waugh's skill, was troubled by his politics, and ended his review by suggesting that the author "occasionally turn aside to read a sixpenny pamphlet on Marxism." Christopher Sykes thought *Unconditional Surrender*, the third volume of Waugh's World War II trilogy, *Sword of Honour*, his great masterpiece, while the full trilogy for Kingsley Amis finally neither coheres nor convinces. Martin Green was keenest on Waugh's early novels (excepting *A Handful of Dust* and *The Loved One*), while V. S. Pritchett, an admirer of Waugh's early novels, nonetheless felt that his later novels, particularly *Sword of Honour*, marked an "advance toward a compassionate study of human nature." Clearly, Evelyn Waugh's is not a case in which one can accuse the critics of being in collusion.

Such a critical dissensus has its own interesting implications. It implies, for one thing, that Evelyn Waugh's literary reputation, even now, is far from settled; it implies, for another, that Waugh's work is of a kind that critics feel they can pick and choose from—accepting the Waugh they approve and setting aside the Waugh they disapprove. Perhaps we all do that with authors whom we wish to admire in spite of their holding to ideas that we find uncongenial. (Supposing literature to be a luncheonette, my order is for Dostoevsky, hold the anti-Semitism and Russian Orthodox Christianity.) But with Evelyn Waugh this isn't so easy. It tends to be standard practice to admire the early Waugh while deploring the later, attributing his falling off to his conversion to Catholicism and his deepened reactionaryism. In this reading one admires Waugh's prose style and comic high jinks and leaves the ideas that propel them aside. "It is the business of literature," Desmond MacCarthy once said, "to turn facts into ideas." But Waugh's critics usually either ignore his ideas or set out to attack them for the stirring reason that they disagree with their own. Others choose not to confront those ideas.

The first fact to recognize—a fact wrapped in an idea—is that Evelyn Waugh was a true reactionary. "A reactionary," according to a sprightly definition by Kenneth Minogue, "is someone with a clear and comprehensive vision of an ideal world we have lost." Reactionaryism obviously has a political component, but its politics, in an artist, need not be primary. In her book *Evelyn Waugh, Portrait of a Country Neighbor,* Frances Donaldson remarks that "Evelyn suffered permanently and terribly from nostalgia," and recalls him once telling her, apropos of his not voting in general elections, "The Conservative Party has never put back the clock a single second." He adored the architecture of every century but his own. An essay he wrote in 1955 entitled "The Death of Painting" begins: " 'From today painting is dead,' cried Paul Delaroche in 1839, when first shown a daguerreotype. He spoke too soon." He also wrote: "I think it is time we made up our minds that poetry is one of the arts which has died in the last eighty years." Nothing seemed more absurd to Waugh than whoring after modernity. "There is an unhappy man in Paris called M. Cocteau whose whole life is occupied in trying to be modern," he wrote in 1930, when he was himself only twenty-seven.

Scratch a reactionary and you will find a right-winger—as Christopher Sykes says, Waugh had an "instinctual aversion to all social progress"—but scratch him a little harder and you will find a romantic. It is well to recall that Evelyn Waugh's first published book was a study of Rossetti. The archetypical Waugh hero, from Paul Pennyfeather of *Decline and Fall* through Tony Last of *A Handful of Dust* to the eponymous hero of *The Ordeal of Gilbert Pinfold* is a romantic—and a romantic who, not to put too fine a point on it, gets it in the neck. Not much of a century for romanticism, the twentieth, or so Evelyn Waugh, in his novels, kept pointing out.

This knowledge did not make Waugh any less a romantic; it did, however, make him an extremely interesting one. A romantic is drawn to the heroic, which Waugh was. But he, Waugh, was even more powerfully drawn to the ridiculous. One does not regularly think of the romantic and the ridiculous commingling in the work of a single writer. In Waugh it did. His sense of the ridiculous was nearly all-pervading; to it he owed much of the delight and penetration of his art. Even critics who despised all that he seemed to stand for allowed that he was a greatly gifted man. This did not stop critics from attacking him personally. In 1947, in a letter to Nancy Mitford, Waugh wrote that most of the reviews of his novel *Scott-King's Modern Europe* "instead of being about the book, have been about me, saying I am ill-tempered and self-infatuated. . . . Would you say I was a very ill-tempered and self-infatuated man? It hurts."

Having recently read through Christopher Sykes's biography and Waugh's own *Letters* and *Diaries,* I should say that he was not at all self-infatuated but very ill-tempered indeed. He obviously knew this to be the case. Gilbert Pinfold asks, "Why does everyone except me find it so easy to be nice?"; and the narrator of the brilliant but unfinished novel entitled *Work Suspended* remarks, "I am afraid you greatly overrate my good nature," a thing not many people who knew him were ever likely to do to Evelyn Waugh. He suffered fools not at all, yet boredom frequently—and excruciatingly. Boredom to Waugh was, like a disease, palpable in its effects. In *Work Suspended* he has his narrator say of another character that he was "still smarting with the ruthless boredom of my last two or three meetings with him." *Ruthless boredom*—that is a juxtaposition only an acute sufferer could contrive. Off in Yugoslavia during World War II, Waugh could—and did—scold his second wife for the dullness of her letters:

Darling Laura, sweet whiskers, do try to write me better letters. Your last, dated 19 December received today, so eagerly expected, was a bitter disappointment. Do realize that a letter need not be a bald chronicle of events; I know you lead a dull life now, my heart bleeds for it, though I believe you could make it more interesting if you had the will. But that is no reason to make your letters as dull as your life. I simply am not interested in Bridget's children. Do grasp that. A letter should be a form of conversation; write as though you were talking to me.

To the ardent boredom that always loomed on his horizon Waugh joined a bullying streak, an oddly detached strain of motiveless cruelty that remained with him all his life. Cecil Beaton, who attended the same preparatory school as Waugh, recalled the boyish Evelyn Waugh as "a tiny but fierce" ring-leader of bullies. (Waugh, in his own autobiography, recalling Beaton, remarked coolly of his and his friends' treatment of Beaton: "Our persecution went no further than sticking pins into him and we were solidly beaten for doing so.") Beaton also noted that when he ran into him later in life, Waugh had a knack for making even compliments sound suspicious. Beaton retells an anecdote heard from Lady Diana Cooper about Waugh one day giving quite precise instructions to a stranger who asked the whereabouts of a railway station. When Lady Diana afterwards remarked, "How clever of you to know where the station is," Waugh replied, "I don't. I always give people the wrong directions." Once, when he had behaved with particular rudeness to a young French intellectual at a dinner party in Paris at the home of Nancy Mitford, Miss Mitford, angry at his social brutality, asked him how he could behave so meanly and yet consider himself a believing and practicing Catholic. "You have no idea," Waugh returned, "how much nastier I would be if I was not a Catholic. Without supernatural aid I would hardly be a human being." Was he joking?

The more one learns about the life of Evelyn Waugh, the

less one is inclined to think it a joke at all. In his biography, Christopher Sykes reports Waugh's strong aversion to Dylan Thomas, who used to appear from time to time at evenings at Cyril Connolly's house. Waugh asked Connolly, in fact, never to invite him when he knew that Dylan Thomas was to be there. The reason, as Sykes explains, is that in Thomas—who dressed in checked suits resembling Waugh's, whose language was like Waugh's made up of parody and fantasy, who like Waugh again was small and portly, and who like Waugh still again was often drunk (though Waugh was not, like Thomas, a boisterous drunk)—in Thomas, Evelyn Waugh saw a caricature of himself. "He's exactly what I would have been," Waugh told Sykes, "if I had not become a Catholic."

There can be no greater impropriety than questioning the quality of another person's religious faith. As Evelyn Waugh himself wrote, "every soul in his traffic with God has his own secrets." But in Waugh's case it happens that we do know the motives behind his conversion, in 1930 (at the age of twenty-seven), to Roman Catholicism, for the good reason that Waugh has described them in an essay entitled "Converted to Rome." In this essay he makes plain that he converted to Catholicism not because *"The Jesuits have got hold of him,"* or *"He is captivated by the ritual,"* or *"He wants to have his mind made up for him,"* but because he saw the present phase of European history as one in which "the essential issue" was "between Christianity and Chaos." In this issue he came down on the side of Christianity, and he chose Roman Catholicism because he thought Christianity more universal, better disciplined, and existing "in its most complete and vital form in the Roman Catholic Church." Waugh closed this essay by noting what was for him a crucial distinction in the churchgoing attitudes of Protestants and Catholics: "The Protestant attitude seems often to be, 'I am good; therefore I go to church,' while the Catholic's is, 'I am very far from good; therefore I go to church.' "

Waugh's essay says less about how clearly he perceived God than about how vividly he felt the encroachments of chaos. What had his keen sense of chaos, what had his conversion to Catholicism, to do with his first wife's deserting him for another man in 1929 cannot be known with assurance, but certainly this event can only have contributed to both in no small way. Like so many of the characters in his novels, in his brief first marriage Evelyn Waugh had been a victim. How devastating this must have been to the young man of twenty-six who until now had strode through life without knowing serious set-backs: comfortably upper-middle-class, adored by his parents, befriended by all whom he wished to befriend, gifted as both an artist and a writer, already celebrated as a dazzling comic novelist—only to end up as a dupe and a cuckold through the agency of a woman who now claimed to have married him without ever having loved him. He was shattered and humiliated. (Of Basil Seal, the character who in some respects functions as Waugh's alter-id, Waugh, in *Put Out More Flags,* writes: "He rejoiced, always, in the spectacle of women at a disadvantage.") After the breakup of his first marriage, some of Waugh's friends, according to Christopher Sykes, saw in him "a new hardness and bitterness and an utter disillusion which showed itself in cruelty."

The breakup of his marriage may also have confirmed Evelyn Waugh in his sense of his own unworthiness. Far from being self-infatuated, he was apparently always self-reproachful—friends with a penchant for psychologizing thought him self-hating—always the first to spot flaws in himself. Later in life, now long a Catholic, he chalked this up to a heightened sense of sin; hell, it was said, was his favorite Church dogma. Certainly he tended to feature his own vices. Waugh's diaries are filled with chronicles of his drinking and drugging (he took a drug called chloral for the insomnia that he suffered all his adult life). Reading his diaries one wonders when, between boozing bouts ("Monday 1 August 1955 . . . Uneatable dinner but plenty of champagne"), he was able to get any writing done. In fact, he turned out a great deal of work, scarcely ever missing a journalistic deadline, and needed his literary earnings to keep his large family afloat. But he preferred to emphasize, even if only to himself, how wicked he was. Recall, please, the line about the Catholic's attitude to churchgoing: "I am very far from good; therefore I go to church."

Evelyn Waugh was not the first connoisseur of chaos to sight his earliest specimens of chaos in the laboratory of his own heart. To have found chaos first by looking inward does not mean that chaos does not truly exist outwardly as well. One of the many hallucinations Gilbert Pinfold suffers is overhearing a voice say: "He doesn't really *believe* in his religion, you know. He just pretends to because he thinks it aristocratic. It goes with being Lord of the Manor." Cool and impersonal though Waugh makes his conversion to Catholicism sound, there is no reason to doubt its authenticity nor to doubt his religion's use to him as a barrier to the chaos he found both in his soul and in the world around him. It is also well to remember that with the exception of his youthful book on Rossetti and *Decline and Fall* (1928), all of Evelyn Waugh's books were written while he was a Catholic. Waugh did not like being pigeon-holed as a Catholic writer; and it is not true to say of him, as he once said of J. F. Powers, that his whole art "is everywhere infused and directed by his Faith." Still, it can be said that a fierce sense of chaos looms over all that Evelyn Waugh wrote after his conversion. Not that he made the least pretense to being able to subdue the chaos that haunted him all his days; through his art, though, he was able to wrest a great deal of laughter from it.

As a Catholic, Evelyn Waugh was very legalistic, even pedantic, knowledgeable about minor points of doctrine, and observant of all scraps of ritual. His Catholicism fit snugly into the formality of character he had created in his life. He early set himself up as a back number. He was very keen for old-world courtesy—for, that is, receiving it. (Giving it was something else.) He lived amid heavy Victorian furniture; he became something of a specialist in Victorian painting. He played the lord of the manor, all right, but, it must be added, he usually played it for laughs. He was the curmudgeonly little squire in the thick checkered suit who affixed before his house in the Gloucestershire Cotswolds a notice reading "No Admittance on Business." He refused to use the telephone. He called the day on which the *New Statesman* arrived "Black Friday"; he regularly read that journal as an act of self-provocation. When his hearing began to fail, he took to toting around an ear trumpet; he is usually described as "brandishing" this ear trumpet, which is not imprecise, for he used it as a social weapon to make other people uncomfortable. Once, at a dinner in his honor, when Malcolm Muggeridge rose to deliver a tribute to him, Waugh, seated at a dais, deliberately set his ear trumpet away from him, to make clear to all in the room that nothing Muggeridge was about to say could possibly be worth hearing. He only gave this ear trumpet up when, at a dinner party given by his friend Ann Fleming, after using his trumpet to cause the maximum awkwardness all round, his hostess, having had all she could bear of his shenanigans, soundly thwacked the trumpet with a spoon while it was in his ear, causing, as Waugh later allowed, a sensation akin to that of having had a pistol fired in one's ear.

What lay behind this extraordinary act? Whimsy, for one thing, quite wild whimsy. But it was also very carefully calculated. Evelyn Waugh set out deliberately to outrage. Like his own Mr. Pinfold, he created "a front of pomposity mitigated by indiscretion." Spiritually and intellectually he was at odds with his age—and dressed and acted the part. (Interesting that George Orwell, the other writer of Waugh's generation who is greatly valued, also dressed and acted a part—that of a member of the working class.) Reviewing a book of contemporary etiquette, Waugh wrote: "The need now is for order."

Reviewing a recently issued volume of the *Dictionary of National Biography,* he wrote: "This is not the age of reformation but of defence, when every man of good will should devote all his powers to preserving the few good things left to us from our grandfathers."

The pose of being perpetually outraged and the ploy of consistently outraging was for Evelyn Waugh a clever and useful gambit. Stripped down to his fundamental views, and devoid of his high gifts, Waugh might have seemed quite as drab and grumpy a figure as any other crotchety conservative gremlin. Outrageous though Waugh could be, he outraged with charm. He was never stupid, for, as Donat Gallagher, the editor of *The Essays, Articles and Reviews of Evelyn Waugh* rightly says, his "flourishing extravagances always cling to a solid core of talent and intelligence."

In time people expected the outrageous from Evelyn Waugh, and he usually could be counted upon to deliver. As a young man, he played the radical to conservative friends and the conservative to radicals. Once he sensed which way the wind was blowing, he headed straight into it. Apart from his second wife and a few very close friends, no one knew quite how to take him. In his *Diaries,* Chips Channon, recounting a lunch in London in 1934, notes:

> Also Evelyn Waugh, alias Mr. Wu. I never know . . . is he good trying to be wicked? Or just wicked trying to be nice? He looks like a ventriloquist's doll, with his shiny nose; I feel his ideals are measured by publishers' royalties. He told me today that he thought that anyone could write a novel given six weeks, pen, paper and no telephone or wife.

Serving as a liaison officer in Yugoslavia in World War II, Waugh spread the rumor that Tito was a woman, a lesbian in fact, which supposedly got back to Tito. (Waugh was not precisely an ideal liaison officer, or officer of any kind; at one point he had to be removed from his command because it was feared that, in combat, his own men might shoot him.) He began a review of Randolph Churchill's book about a libel suit by writing: "No one who knows Mr. Randolph Churchill and wishes to express distaste for him should ever be at a loss for words which would be both opprobrious and apt." In the same review he made the point that the journalists found guilty of libel are not sufficiently punished, for their wealthy newspapers pick up the costs when they are found guilty, so he concluded: "The time, I think, is ripe for the restoration of the pillory."

I believe I have established that Evelyn Waugh could be, as they used to note in folders in the personnel departments, "a difficult personality." Was he a snob into the bargain? Snobbery was of course part of his subject as a novelist. He was endlessly interested and amused by the intricacies of the English class system, which was beginning to come apart as he approached maturity. For him the joke was that no one seemed too lowly to look down upon someone else. In *A Handful of Dust,* Tony Last has gone off to a hotel in the countryside with a prostitute to establish his infidelity so that his wife can divorce him. At the hotel, as visitors come swinging through the doors of the dining room, " 'Yids,' explained Milly [the prostitute] superfluously. 'Still it's nice to get a change from the club once in a while.' " (The cruel art in that line of dialogue falls on the word "superfluously.") As for his own social tastes, "Evelyn," Frances Donaldson notes, "liked the smarter of the intellectuals, the more intellectual of the smart—and no one else."

About the age of the common man, Waugh, a most uncommon man, had his qualms, and that is putting it very gently. When someone accused him of not caring for the Man in the Street, he replied that there was no Man in the Street—only men and streets. Upon publication of *Brideshead Revisited* he came in for heavy criticism not only for his often idealized treatment of that novel's aristocratic characters but for his rough portrayal of the young lower-middle-class character he called

Lieutenant Hooper. Hooper is a man without the least shred of romanticism or interest in heroism, who accepts his induction into the army "like the measles," who is bereft of the least scintilla of culture, who has "an overmastering regard for efficiency" without the least aptitude for it, and who for Evelyn Waugh represents the gray crushing wave of the future. *Brideshead Revisited* was written while Waugh was on leave from the British army in 1944. With the victory of the first Labour government in the general election after the war, for Waugh the Age of Hooper had arrived in earnest.

In a review of Edgar Johnson's biography of Charles Dickens, Waugh wrote: "Faults which would be excusable in other men become odious in the light of Dickens's writing." Something like the reverse applies to the life of Evelyn Waugh. Given the coolness of his art and the ferocity of his public mask, one is always surprised to discover him not acting perfectly monstrously. Of Gilbert Pinfold, he wrote: "He was not what is generally meant by the appellation a 'philanthropic' man; he totally lacked what was now called a 'social conscience.' But apart from his love of family and friends he had a certain basic kindliness to those who refrained from active annoyance." Waugh was a faithful husband; at home he played the Victorian paterfamilias, and none of his six children has ever written about him except in a kindly manner. To his small circle of close friends—Nancy Mitford, Diana Cooper, Ann Fleming, Christopher Sykes—he was a devoted if sometimes difficult (and socially dangerous) companion. Along with being modest about his own accomplishments, Waugh never displayed the least jealousy toward writers who were his contemporaries, and with the two among them who might have been considered his greatest rivals, Graham Greene and Anthony Powell, he never wrote nor spoke in other than an appreciative way. He came to the aid of a number of friends whom he found in illness or sore financial condition. And of course when he chose he could be utterly charming.

Studying the arc described by Evelyn Waugh's literary career, one discovers nearly at its middle an uncompleted novel entitled *Work Suspended*. Waugh began the book in 1939 and published it, in its incomplete form, in 1942. It is a brilliant piece of unfinished business, one fully worthy of a place in Max Beerbohm's museum. Waugh makes only two references to it in his *Diaries:* one noting, "I have rewritten the first chapter of the novel about six times and at last got it into tolerable shape"; the other, four years later, noting that Desmond MacCarthy was full of praise for it. What went wrong? Why, after only a hundred pages, did Waugh decide to throw in his pen?

One cannot know with any real precision, but in *Work Suspended* Waugh does offer a few clues. The novel's protagonist, who is a writer, comes into an inheritance that relieves him of the need to work for a few years, which causes him to remark that "it was a matter of pure athletics to go on doing something merely because one did it well." Does it seem pushing things to read into this sentiment Evelyn Waugh's own artistic boredom at continuing in the line of madcap comedy at which he was by now a past master? The protagonist-narrator also remarks, about his father, who is the most splendidly comic of the many comic fathers in Waugh's work—he has strong views on the Jews' being responsible for the vogue of French impressionist painting—"I had not then learned to appreciate the massive defences of what people call the 'border-line of sanity.'" I find this a haunting line, and one that puts one not only in mind of Waugh's own later bout of insanity (recounted in *The Ordeal of Gilbert Pinfold*) but of what seems to me the most penetrating single sentence in all the criticism I have read of Waugh's work; it is a sentence written by V. S. Pritchett that reads: "His early books spring from the liberating notion that human beings are mad; the war trilogy [*Sword of Honour*], a work of maturity, draws on the meatier notion that the horrible thing about human beings is that they are sane."

World War II doubtless played a strong role in turning Evelyn Waugh away from his old sure-fire mode of comic creation. "The Great Bore War" he called it. His was the generation that came to maturity between the wars. Virginia Woolf may have said that "human nature changed in 1910," but the Bright Young People who comprised Waugh's social set could still find spacious margins of leisure and luxury in which to gambol: lunches at the Savoy, bouts of gigglous champagne drunkenness, a ready supply of servants to clean up the mess. But World War II put paid to that kind of life, and no one knew it better than Waugh. Long though he might for the old life, a man as unillusioned as he could scarcely convince himself it was any longer attainable. *Brideshead Revisited,* the first novel he completed after his failure with *Work Suspended,* is easily Evelyn Waugh's most nostalgia-laden book, and sings a threnody to a lavish style of life now quite dead.

After the war the comedy in Waugh's work is still there but much subdued. Waugh's killing off Major Apthorpe in *Men at Arms,* the first of the novels in *Sword of Honour,* is strong evidence of this. Apthorpe, it will be recalled, is the extraordinary character who never traveled without his preposterous kit, which included a portable thunder-box, or water closet, made by the firm of Connolly Chemical Closets. (Whimsical even in his depressions, Waugh loved to drag Cyril Connolly's name into his novels: the ridiculous British military figure in *Black Mischief* is General Connolly; Connolly is the name given to the monstrous children in *Put Out More Flags;* and a cruel portrait of Cyril Connolly himself under the name of Everard Spruce, the editor of a wartime journal entitled *Survival,* appears in the last novel of the trilogy, *Unconditional Surrender.*) Perhaps Waugh killed off Apthorpe for fear that his marvelous comic blandness would take over his trilogy; at any rate, in the second volume of *Sword of Honour* he is replaced by Major Hound, a greatly less delightful figure who, as Waugh has another character note of him, "seems strangely lacking in the Death-Wish." *Sword of Honour* is not barren of comedy—"Guy, how are you?" asks a character of Guy Crouchback, the trilogy's rather drab hero. "Forty," he replies—but the comedy now has a certain edge that it didn't have in the past. Wavian comedy was always cool, and sometimes cruel, yet invariably it had a lovely gaiety about it; now it begins to take on a less attractive asperity. *Sword of Honour* is more ambitious, more mature, than the earlier Waugh novels. No one can accuse this work of not being in pursuit of the largest questions: what is honor, how to achieve personal salvation, is there a will to war propelled by an international death wish, are among the questions raised by the trilogy. Yet Evelyn Waugh in quest of the answers, even though his own earnestness is completely convincing, is now aesthetically less than satisfying.

Is it possible that Evelyn Waugh's was a naturally destructive talent? This sounds a degradation, a put-down, but it is not intended to be. The fact—I see it as a fact—is that Waugh was at his triumphant best on the attack. Think of the subjects that, in his early novels, he had taken on, and how absolutely on target he was in dealing with them—as those of us who have lived beyond his day have reason to know. In *Decline and Fall* he took on the joke of English education; in *Vile Bodies,* the emptiness of gossip-column high life; in *Scoop,* the inanity and insanity of modern journalism ("Look at it this way. News is what a chap who doesn't care much about anything wants to read. And it's only news until he's read it. After that it's dead"); in *Black Mischief,* what is now called the third world (read today, that novel reads like V. S. Naipaul played for laughs); in *A Handful of Dust,* the toll exacted from family and tradition by attempting to live the smart life; in *Scott-King's Modern Europe,* the swindle of modern Communism in Europe. (Forgive me if I neglect *The Loved One,* my least favorite of Waugh's novels, because its target, the nuttiness of California funerary rites, seems to me all too easy to knock off.) Evelyn Waugh did not really know how to write an unreadable novel; but these early novels of his, judged by their craftsmanship, their comic radiance, their intellectual brilliance, are quite without peer.

Writing about his friend Ronald Knox, Waugh noted: "The more learned and philosophic the man, the less likely he is to be 'contemporary,' for he will know that most 'new' ideas are restatements of very old ones and that the latest events are in all essentials repetitions of what has happened before." This remark is not without its applications to Evelyn Waugh himself, who was both attracted to the contemporary and repelled by it. As an artist, he was very much a modernist: a master of irony, of decisive reticences, of abrupt juxtapositions of material that today seem cinematic yet derive from Ronald Firbank, whom Waugh acknowledged as one of his chief artistic influences. As a man, Waugh came more and more to hate modernity. But then, so many modernist artists have come out against modernity. T. S. Eliot wrote: "I will show you fear in a handful of dust"; I believe Evelyn Waugh—who used part of that line for the title of one of his novels—truly saw the fear Eliot spoke about.

The hallucinating Gilbert Pinfold believes he overhears yet another disturbing conversation, in which one party asks another: "Were his books ever any good?" "Never *good*. His earliest ones weren't quite as bad as his latest. He's written out." Not only is this a hallucination; it's poor criticism into the bargain. But it was not half bad as prophecy. After *The Ordeal of Gilbert Pinfold* (1957), Waugh produced only one more novel, *Unconditional Surrender* (1961). Still under the lash of having to earn a living for his large family, he continued to produce a goodly amount of very high quality literary journalism. His last years seem to have been terribly unhappy ones. Plagued by insomnia, bothered as always by boredom, he attempted to fight off the first by stronger drugs, the second by retreating into an alcoholic haze. In a photograph of Evelyn Waugh taken in 1963—three years before his death by heart attack—among the members of an old group of friends from

Oxford days known as the Railway Club, poor Waugh looks like a figure one might meet along the boulevards of hell: porcine, plastered, pathetically done in by life. In his last years he apparently felt his life was over, and wished it soon would be; an aphorism he composed around this time runs: "All fates are 'worse than death.'"

Apropos of Chesterton, a writer for whom he had qualified admiration, Waugh wrote:

> Humility is not a virtue propitious to the artist. It is often pride, emulation, avarice, malice—all the odious qualities—which drive a man to complete, elaborate, refine, destroy, renew, his work until he has made something that gratifies his pride and envy and greed. And in doing so he enriches the world more than the generous and good, though he may lose his own soul in the process. That is the paradox of artistic achievement.

It is a profound paradox, and one that is poignantly illustrated if in no way resolved in the life and career of Evelyn Waugh. All we know is that out of this gifted man's pain and terror has come a great deal of joy and laughter for his readers. It isn't much to know, but a lot for which to be grateful.

The New Criterion 1985

The Comparable Max

MAX BEERBOHM once claimed that there were fifteen hundred readers in England and another thousand in America who knew what he was about. Small enough numbers, one would have thought, but he claimed them with a faint air of boastfulness. When S. N. Behrman first visited Max Beerbohm at his home in Rapallo in the early 1950s, Beerbohm showed him a statement from the firm of Alfred A. Knopf, which had recently reissued a book of his essays. On the right-hand side of the statement was an unbroken column of zeros. *"There's* a publisher's statement!" he announced ("carolled" is the word Behrman uses). As a frequent sojourner in used-book shops, I can testify that Behrman's own book, *A Portrait of Max,* handsomely printed and lavishly illustrated though it is, and charmingly written into the bargain, is an almost inevitable inmate upon the dusty shelves in these shops. Beerbohm would doubtless have been cheered by this, too—evidence that both the life and the work were quite unsalable.

In the closing paragraph of a 1947 essay in celebration of Max Beerbohm's seventy-fifth birthday, Louis Kronenberger remarked: "How big Max's audience will be a generation, or a century, hence is something else again." A generation has now passed, and I think I know how big his audience is: fourteen hundred in England and eleven hundred in America. As for the size of his audience in 2047, my guess is that he will have thirteen hundred readers in England and twelve hundred in America—cultural progress in this colony is slow but steady. Yet all of these readers, I have no doubt, will be devoted. The taste for the writing of Max Beerbohm is a minority taste but a strong one.

If there were a job description for a Max Beerbohm reader, it would, I fear, be severely delimiting. To begin with, the Max Beerbohm reader must be a fairly bookish person, someone who knows a certain amount of literary history and has an appetite for the literary life, for Max Beerbohm, though not an omnivorous reader, was himself literary from his pate down to his spats. The Max Beerbohm reader must have an affection for language and be pleased at witnessing it on exhibit with an always playful but ultimately serious precision, for Beerbohm was, to use one of his own words, a "precisian." Along with having an affection for language, he must enjoy seeing it artfully deployed—he must, that is, adore style, for Beerbohm was one of those writers for whom, without style, there is no message or indeed much of anything else. The Beerbohm reader must take pleasure in irony, for irony, the art of saying one thing and meaning another, was at the center of much that Beerbohm wrote. Delicate, whimsical, sly, his was irony of a kind quick readers are likely to miss. (Test sentence: "To give an accurate account of that period," he wrote in an essay entitled "1880," "would need a far less brilliant pen than mine.") Finally, the Max Beerbohm reader must share the comic view, which means that he can see the prospect for laughter in all but the most dire of human commerce, and especially not fail to see it in himself, for to take oneself altogether seriously, Beerbohm once averred, is to court insanity.

How might one best describe Max Beerbohm to someone who knows nothing about him? Well, for a start, one might imagine D. H. Lawrence. Picture the shagginess of Lawrence, his thick beard, his rough-cut clothes, his disdain for all the social and physical niceties. Recall his passionateness—his passion, so to say, for passion itself—his darkness, his gloom. Think back to his appeal to the primary instincts, his personal messianism, his refusal to deal with anything smaller than capital "D" Destiny. Do not neglect his humorlessness, his distaste for all that otherwise passes for being civilized, his blood theories and manifold roiling hatreds. Have you, then, D. H. Lawrence firmly in mind? Splendid. Now reverse all Lawrence's qualities and you will have a fair beginning notion of Max Beerbohm, who, after allowing that Lawrence was a man "of unquestionable genius," felt it necessary to add: "He never realized, don't you know—he never suspected that to be stark, staring mad is somewhat of a handicap to a writer."

To think of Max Beerbohm as D. H. Lawrence in reverse is a start but a start merely. He really was *sui generis*. George Bernard Shaw was on to something when, on May 2, 1898, in his last column as drama critic for the English *Saturday Review,* before turning the column over to Beerbohm, he wrote: "The younger generation is knocking at the door, and as I open it there steps sprightly in the incomparable Max." Beerbohm had to live with this epithet all his days, and once, writing to his first biographer, John Bohun Lynch, he mildly protested against it:

> Years ago, G.B.S., in a light-hearted moment, called me "the incomparable." Note that I am *not* incomparable. Compare me. Compare me as essayist (for instance) with other essayists. Point out how much less human I am than Lamb, how much less intellectual than Hazlitt, and what an ignoramus beside Belloc; and how Chesterton's high spirits and abundance shame me. . . . Apply the comparative method to me also as a caricaturist.

In this same letter Beerbohm, who was chary of having a biography written about him, especially while he still lived, added:

My gifts are small, I've used them very well and discreetly, never
straining them; and the result is that I've made a charming little
reputation. But that reputation is a frail plant. Don't over-attend
to it, gardener Lynch! Don't drench and deluge it! The contents
of a quite *small* watering-can will be quite enough.

A point to be made about both these passages is that each is
quite accurate. As an essayist, Beerbohm is less human than
Lamb, less intellectual than Hazlitt, and so forth. He never did
strain his gifts; he did use them well and discreetly; he had in
his lifetime, as he has now, precisely a charming little reputation. Frail plant though his reputation may be, the same cannot be said of his talent; it was a delicate flower, no doubt, yet
a hardy one. But let us turn now to examine it at its seedling
stage.

Max Beerbohm's father, a man born in Memel, in Baltic
Germany, of Dutch and German and Lithuanian extraction,
had settled in London at the age of twenty-three and had married an Englishwoman with whom he had three sons and a
daughter. He made a modest success as a grain merchant. When
his first wife died, he married her sister, with whom he had
three more children, two daughters and a final child, a son,
Max. His father was sixty-one when Max was born, his mother
in her forties. The Beerbohms' was by all accounts a happy
household and a comfortable one—so comfortable for Max
that he never left it until his marriage, in his late thirties, to the
American actress Florence Kahn. As one would expect from a
man with a subtle sense of humor, Max Beerbohm had a strong
antipathy to the clichés of conventional psychology, and, given
the fact that he adored his parents and his brothers and sisters,
he wondered if he would one day be thought victim of an
Oedipus complex. After mentioning this to S. N. Behrman, he
paused, then said: "They were a tense and peculiar family, the
Oedipuses, weren't they?"

Max was in awe of his two half brothers Herbert and Julius.

Herbert was an actor and theatrical manager, and was known professionally as Herbert Beerbohm Tree. He was large, red-haired, and robust, with a madcap sense of humor. (Once, when a man walked past him groaning under a grandfather clock he was carting on his back, Herbert announced, "My good fellow, why not carry a watch?") Julius was an unflappable dandy, a gambler with a taste for disastrous financial schemes, whom Max remembered once polishing a translation from Heine while downstairs in his house mover's men were taking away his furniture. Of his brothers Beerbohm wrote: "Herbert was (then and always) a hero to me. But, let me add, Julius was a god."

His half brothers were adult and long out of the house when Max Beerbohm was a boy. The household he grew up in was consequently a feminine one. In it the young Max, a precocious and precise child, was the cynosure. In his biography, *Max,* David Cecil makes the interesting point that Max was not a mother's boy but what "can be described as a sister's boy." Not a bad thing to be, a sister's boy, for it gives one a certain ease in dealing with females; a receptivity to the gentler aspects of culture, over which women have traditionally presided; and a corresponding distance from the brutishness of a steady fare of youthful male companionship. In Max Beerbohm's instance, the sister in question was Dora, who was five years older than he and a child with a talent for drawing and decorative art and a sweet selflessness that later led her to become a postulant of the Anglican Order of Sisters of Mercy. It was in large part from Dora, and within the walls of his family home, that Max Beerbohm learned the rudiments of the art of pleasing—an art that, as he grew older, he would eventually buff to a high sheen of perfection.

So adept was Max Beerbohm at this art of pleasing that he is perhaps the only writer of the past hundred years to go through the English school system without being spiritually scathed. Accounts of his school days present no tales of his being bullied, as was E. M. Forster at the Tonbridge School,

or of him as the victim of a totalitarian monstrosity in miniature, as Orwell makes out the school he calls St. Cyprians to
be. As a schoolboy, Beerbohm loved Latin and was clever at
drawing and had no interest in games. Charterhouse, the public school to which he was sent at age thirteen, was not much
to his taste, but he survived it by reading Thackeray, drawing
charming caricatures of the masters, and when necessary with-
drawing into himself. At Charterhouse he learned, as he later
put it, "the knack of understanding my fellow-creatures, of living in amity with them and not being rubbed the wrong way
by their faults, and not rubbing them the wrong way with
mine." There was never a trace of the rebel in him; even as a
young boy he was too detached for rebellion or even for serious participation in school activities. He was an onlooker, more
comfortable on the sidelines, someone who finds the spectacle
of life rather more interesting than life itself. He was, in two
words, "an artist."

Along with his other gifts, Max Beerbohm had the gift of
an equanimous temperament. He was one of those lucky people to whom life never seemed to present itself as a struggle.
He appears never to have felt the need to dominate; envy was
an emotion unknown to him. It was said that he never had an
adolescence but instead went directly from childhood to young
manhood. When he arrived, at nineteen, at Merton College,
Oxford, he seems to have been fully formed. He was self-con-
tained, self-controlled, self-sufficient. His career at the university was of the kind Evelyn Waugh wished he had had: effortless,
elegant, quietly dazzling.

Shortly after arriving at Oxford, at Ryman's to purchase some
engravings for his room, the young Beerbohm saw Walter
Pater—"a small rock-faced man, whose top-hat and gloves of
bright dog-skin struck one of the many discords in that little
city of learning or laughter"—and judged him to be coarse.
While an undergraduate he published caricatures in some of
London's smartest journals. He placed an essay, a *succès de scan-*

dale entitled "In Defense of Cosmetics," in the first issue of that smartest of all smart literary magazines, the *Yellow Book*. Oscar Wilde announced that he had a prose style "like a silver dagger." A self-declared dandy, Beerbohm was famous for his clothes, his wit, his *sang-froid*. When the artist Will Rothenstein, who was to become his lifelong friend, arrived at Oxford to execute portraits of the leading figures at the university, Beerbohm was among the subjects he chose. Beerbohm did not complete his last year at Oxford, for the life of literature and art beckoned too seductively for him to remain a student. He needed a degree about as much as the pope needs a bowling trophy.

Whom the gods would destroy, they first grant early success. Max Beerbohm, however, was able to elude the gods. He did so through precise knowledge of his own limitations and a sense of humor about himself. At twenty-four he published his first book, a slender volume of seven essays—with a bibliography appended that included a letter to the editor of the school paper at Charterhouse and a schoolboy Latin exercise—which he entitled *The Works of Max Beerbohm*. (His next two volumes of essays he entitled *More* and *Yet Again*.) In the essays of this first little book his entire artistic program is adumbrated. In "Dandies and Dandies" he sets out the aesthetic that was to govern his own creation. Ostensibly writing about Beau Brummell, he notes: "All delicate spirits, to whatever art they turn, even if they turn to no art, assume an oblique attitude toward life." Of Brummell specifically, but of himself more generally, he writes: "Like the single-minded artist that he was, he turned full and square towards his art and looked life straight in the face out of the corners of his eyes," which is as exact a formulation of the method of the ironist as one is likely to find. From the figure of the dandy, too, may be extrapolated Beerbohm's own yearning, in his art, for perfection in detail in all things. Like Brummell yet again (and Beerbohm with him), the dandy is "ever most economical, most scrupulous of means."

There remains only to add that the dandy, like the artist, strives to please chiefly himself. What we have here is the full prescription for Max Beerbohm's art, both as a prose writer and as a caricaturist.

In an essay entitled "Diminuendo," written when Beerbohm was all of twenty-three, he predicts his own early retirement from the hugger-mugger of London for the life of contemplation. (Was this prediction meant to be ironic? "I wish," he once wrote, "I could cure myself of the habit of speaking ironically; I should so like to express myself in a quite straightforward manner.") "What uproar!" he announces in this essay. "Surely I could have no part in modern life." Here he avers that the life of action has no charm for him. It is instead only "the things one has not done, the faces or places one has not seen, or seen but darkly, that have charm." He imagines his retirement spent in some backwater English village, where he will borrow his neighbor's copy of *The Times*. He declares himself already a back number: "I belong to the Beardsley period," which was of course riding its crest at the very moment he indited the sentence. He claims he will stop writing; he is ready to stand aside without regret. The essay closes on the following absolutely accurate predictive sentences: "For to be outmoded is to be a classic, if one has written well. I have acceded to the hierarchy of good scribes and rather like my niche."

Although he lived six decades beyond the 1890s, although all of his best work was done much later than the nineties, Max Beerbohm became—and seemed to wish to become—indissolubly linked to that decade. "I am," he once remarked, "what is known as 'an interesting link to the past.'" But then he himself forged that link and rather insisted upon it. The nineties was the period of his artistic formation, the period of Oscar Wilde and Aubrey Beardsley, Henry James and Walter Sickert, a time when Meredith was still walking the earth and Thomas Hardy and Whistler and Shaw. It was the era of the aesthete—

and an aesthete Max Beerbohm ever was. In later life he returned to draw figures from the nineties over and over; his literary tastes were rooted in the decade as well, causing him to over-rate some writers for their stylishness (Lytton Strachey, in my opinion, for one) and to be antipathetic to all art not grounded in the beautiful. One of his many complaints against Shaw was the latter's blindness to beauty. Of Shaw's panning *The Importance of Being Earnest,* Beerbohm once remarked: "Perhaps while the play was going on he was improving his theory of rent."

If Max Beerbohm was an aesthete, he was an aesthete with a serious difference. The difference was that, unlike almost every other aesthete, from Flaubert to Pater to Pound, he never permitted his aestheticism to override his common sense. S. N. Behrman well says that "the animating spirit of all Max's criticism—as, indeed, of all his writing—is a cultivated common sense." The emphasis needs to be placed on the adjective "cultivated," for his common sense was informed by a true artistic sensibility. He once said of Trollope that he "reminds us that sanity need not be philistine." Of Beerbohm it can be said that he reminds us that one's adoration of art need not extend to lunacy.

It was during the nineties—his own twenties—that Max Beerbohm began to build his reputation. His was the reputation of a charmer, a literary and artistic lapidarian. He worked small and took pride in doing so. "How many charming talents have been spoiled," he wrote, "by the instilled desire to do 'important' work! Some people are born to lift heavy weights. Some are born to juggle with golden balls." Max Beerbohm was, obviously, among the jugglers.

The golden balls he kept in the air were those of the essayist, comic draughtsman, and elegant young man about town. His friends were Aubrey Beardsley, Will Rothenstein, and Reggie Turner. Turner, whom Beerbohm knew from undergraduate days at Merton College, was the wealthy illegitimate son of Lord Burnham, the press lord; he was a homosexual, a failed novelist, and was said by Somerset Maugham to be the most amusing man he had ever known. Of his own novels Turner once said: "Other people's first editions are rare. With me it's the second editions that are rare; in fact they don't exist." Max Beerbohm simultaneously kept up a vigorous social round in the highest reaches of English society; as a charming and socially presentable young man, he frequently dined among the Balfours and Asquiths and Churchills, where he would on occasion meet Henry James, whom he described as looking "like a Russian Grand Duke of the better type." James was nearly thirty years older than he, but paid him the compliment of treating him as an equal. Lord David Cecil tells the story of James and Beerbohm standing together at one such dinner party when a woman came up to declare that they looked very distinguished. "We *are* distinguished," Henry James replied. "But you need not look so terribly so," she responded. "We are shameless, shameless!" said Henry James.

Living at home, earning a few pounds for an essay here, a caricature there, Max Beerbohm never held a serious job until 1898, when he was asked to become drama critic of the *Saturday Review*. He jumped at the opportunity—backwards. He had the gravest doubts about it, but agreed to take it chiefly because, his father having died, he thought the additional money would be useful at home. But he began on a note of disclaimer: his first column is entitled "Why I Ought Not to Have Become a Dramatic Critic." He is not, as he notes in that column, stagestruck. He is happy among pictures, has an unenlightened but real love for music, cares about literature most of all and can talk about it intelligently. Having grown up as the brother of Herbert Beerbohm Tree, he explains, he has never been able to associate the theater with glamour but instead only with "the conclusion to a dinner or the prelude to a supper." He has little interest in branching off, as his predecessor G.B.S. did, into "discussions of ethical, theological or political questions," about which he claims to be "singularly ill-informed."

Worse, his is a satiric temperament, which makes him amusing when laughing at anyone, but deadly dull when praising. He is sure that having to write this column is "quite likely to spoil and exhaust such talent as I might otherwise be exercising in literary art." His one advantage is that, having written these columns, at least he will not be compelled to read them. Talk about blowing one's own trumpet. Has anyone ever organized for himself a more extraordinary fanfarade?

His disclaimers were not made in false modesty; they were, once again, quite accurate. Although Max Beerbohm stayed on as drama critic for the *Saturday Review* for fully twelve years, he is not among that very small group of very special drama critics, a group that includes Hazlitt, Shaw, James Agate, and, in our own day, the young Kenneth Tynan. He was not sufficiently febrile; the missionary spirit did not exist in him; he was temperamentally too cool. He asked that a play be entertaining, convincingly coherent, and intelligent—and in the theater, then as now, that was way too much to ask. As might be expected, he was good at deflation: amusing about the hypocrisy of English audiences, imprisoned in linguistic ignorance, watching Signora Duse play *Hedda Gabler* in Italian; riotously funny about the mad unreality of Sarah Bernhardt's memoirs; penetrating on Shaw "using art merely as a means of making people listen to him." None of his reviews is inept; most have felicitous touches, charming asides, digressions from which one wishes he would never return to the business at hand. But for the vast most part his drama criticisms grow boring when he begins to discuss the play under review—which is another way of saying that Max Beerbohm was an essayist and not a critic.

Which, in turn, is another way of saying that Max Beerbohm was above all else an artist. In a tribute to the music-hall comedian Dan Leno, he wrote: "In every art personality is the paramount thing, and without it artistry goes for little." He went on to say that especially was this so in the art of acting, but I would assert that it is no less so in the art of the essay. Think of a significant essayist and you think of the personality he conveys: the gentle Charles Lamb, the passionate William Hazlitt, the gloomy George Orwell. Max Beerbohm's artistic personality is not so readily captured in a lone epithet. It is complex and elusive, yet distinct for all that. It is the personality of the slightly world-weary spectator, sitting along the sideline, a cigarette in hand, a man far from indifferent to worldly things but not quite caught up in them either; a man of considerable sophistication who has yet retained a certain oddly childish mischievousness; charming but not hotly intimate; ready to admit his own flaws but too exquisitely tactful to point out yours; yet for all his charm, his admitted naiveté, his penchant for fun, decidedly not someone over whose eyes you can ever for a moment hope to pull the wool (make that, in Beerbohm's case, cashmere).

Max Beerbohm was too much the conscious artist not to be aware of the impression his own work conveyed, or of the difficulties that personality in art could make. Cyril Connolly, for example, regarded Max Beerbohm as "a psychological case, a supreme egotist masquerading as a detached observer." Beerbohm once put his case in a letter to his wife:

> I am not thinking that "I am I" and must be interesting to everyone else. I am nothing more than I—a detached and puzzled spectator—detached, yet knowing more about myself than any other subject, and offering myself humbly for the inspection of others. I think there is a difference between this and egotism.

Was this personality a fake, a fraud, a made thing? Beerbohm was of the generation of Wilde and Yeats, a generation that believed in masks. He wrote a longish fairy tale, *The Happy Hypocrite,* about the subject of masks. In it a Regency rake named Lord George Hell sets out to seduce the pure Miss Jenny Mere. In aid of this conquest he wears a mask—an actual mask—that lends him a look of goodness and virtue. So long does he wear the mask, so long does he try to live up to it, that at the book's close, when he is inevitably unmasked, his real face has changed, and "line for line, feature for feature," his own true face becomes the saintly face of the mask he had been wearing. The tale's final paragraph reads:

> So he took her in his arms, as though she had been a little child, and kissed her with his own lips. She put her arms around his neck, and he was happier than he had ever been. They were alone in the garden now. Nor lay the mask any longer upon the lawn, for the sun had melted it.

The moral is not in the least murky: the mask, worn long enough, becomes the man. I suppose it can be said that Max Beerbohm created his own mask. Unlike so many others, he set to work on it young and perfected it early. Most of us would like to create a mask of our own, which would represent us at our own highest self-valuation. The modern injunction to "be oneself" implies one's having a suitable self to be. Many of us, not finding that self suitable, try masks but cannot quite bring them off: the eyebrows won't stay straight, the mustache keeps lapsing into the mouth, the nose permits no breath. It is a botch, which Beerbohm's never was. In him the mask became the man, and the man and mask became, as he signed his caricatures and as devoted readers tend to think of him, Max. It is as Max that I should like to refer to him for the remainder of this essay.

The year 1910 was the turning point in Max's life. It was the year he quit his job as drama critic for the *Saturday Review,* which he had long found onerous in the extreme. As a prose writer he was a perfectionist—writing was always much more difficult for him than drawing—and his weekly deadlines did not permit of the polish perfection requires. He wrote his weekly *Saturday Review* piece on Thursday; even decades later he would wake on a Thursday morning with a clutch at his heart in momentary fear about having to set aside the day to write his criticism. If the pressure of these deadlines was hell, dispensing with them altogether was nearly heaven. That same year, at thirty-eight, he married the actress Florence Kahn, and made his plan to move, permanently, to Rapallo.

A man's marriage is perhaps the appropriate place to put to rest the question of whether or not he was a homosexual. The question only arises because Malcolm Muggeridge raised it some years ago in an essay entitled "The Legend of Max." Not that Muggeridge questioned it; in his essay he asserted it: "Beerbohm, it seems to me to emerge, was in panic flight through most of his life from two things—his Jewishness and his homosexuality." It emerges *for* Muggeridge, though no evidence for either assertion emerges *from* Muggeridge. Even from the old Mugger himself, this is pretty wild stuff.

As for the claim that Max was Jewish, Muggeridge contends he once heard this from a man who once heard it from Herbert Beerbohm Tree. Yet odd, does it not seem, that Max, a man supposedly ashamed of being Jewish, would take to wife a woman, Florence Kahn, who was herself Jewish? The claim for Max's homosexuality is made on even shakier grounds; it is based wholly on association—specifically, on Max's connection with the Wilde-Beardsley circle in the nineties. That Max while an undergraduate had an infatuation with a music-hall performer named Cissy Loftus is not allowed to stand in the way. Nor is the fact that he was later engaged to an actress in his brother's theatrical company, and after that had a love affair with yet another actress. Odd, too, that a man in panic flight from his homosexuality would choose to flee with a wife in tow. Does Malcolm Muggeridge, now that he is an earnest Christian, still believe what he wrote about Max? If he does, I hope Saint Peter will one day ask him to supply more serious evidence for his assertions—will make such evidence, in fact, an unwaivable requirement for his entrance to heaven.

In the event, Max's departure from London for Rapallo proved a most cunning move. "When a man is tired of London, he is tired of life," Samuel Johnson wrote, "for there is in London all that life can afford." But Max was not a man to be put off by a Dr. Johnson quotation; nor, as we shall see, a man to be overly impressed even by Dr. Johnson. Besides, a Londoner born, he really had had all that London could afford in the way of fame, sociability, urbane pleasures. Italy was then so much less expensive than London and would allow him to work at his art at the leisurely pace it required. The Beerbohms acquired a small house in the town of Rapallo, long a haunt of English Italophiles; the house overlooked the Gulf of Genoa and was called the Villino Chiaro. In this small house, working in a small study on the terrace, Max produced some of his best work: the fantasy novel *Zuleika Dobson,* the stories of *Seven Men,* the essays in *And Even Now* and other books, and drawings too numerous to catalogue.

What is of especial interest is how little Max seemed to need the outside world. Living frugally, alone with his wife and a single servant, each day he would suit up, pop a straw boater upon his exceedingly round head, and repair to his terrace overlooking the Gulf of Genoa. From the terraces of nearby villas he was occasionally sighted, alone, laughing, doubtless at some superior joke, or twist of language, or human oddity that occurred to him in his endless ruminations upon the past. He never bothered to learn Italian; he rarely went into the town of Rapallo; he had no interest in touring Italy. In time he became an object of intellectual tourism himself, receiving guests who had just come from visiting Bernard Berenson at I Tatti and would afterward call upon Somerset Maugham at Villa Mauresque. He returned to London from time to time to help mount exhibitions of his drawings (he took a serious interest in all the details having to do with his own work), and he and his wife returned to live in England during the two world wars. But for the rest, from 1910 to 1956, he lived for all intents and purposes imprisoned in Villino Chiaro and utterly free in his own imagination.

Standing on that terrace for the better part of forty years, the sun above, the blue Gulf of Genoa before him, of what did he think? Of the past, doubtless, but the past, one imagines, in very small pieces: the chin of Kipling, the back of Shaw's neck, the beard of Rossetti. From there perhaps he strode to his study on the terrace and redrew these figures from his own past that he had drawn so many times before. "I can draw caricatures at any moment," he once wrote to his wife, "and how I rejoice in them. *They* are what I was put into the world to do." A great many others have rejoiced in them as well, except perhaps those who were their subjects. Edmund Gosse, in a letter to Logan Pearsall Smith, noted that Max had done a caricature of him and, as with most of Max's subjects, he was not likely to appreciate it. "We don't like it, and you won't like it, but must pretend, as we all do, that you like it. You can console yourself, at any rate, with the thought that it will give enormous pleasure to your friends."

Charming Max's caricatures are, but harmless fun they aren't. He claimed he was a Jekyll as a writer but as a caricaturist a true Hyde, and once referred to himself as "a ruthless monstrifier of men." His own elegant definition of a caricature cannot be improved upon: "The most perfect caricature is that which, on a small surface, with the simplest means, most accurately exaggerates, to the highest point, the peculiarities of a human being, at his most characteristic moment, in the most beautiful manner." Yet a Max caricature is never a delineation of physical peculiarities merely, but instead uses these peculiarities to penetrate his subject's personality. The personality caught will be found to be comic in its pretensions, or vulgarity, or stupidity, or obtuseness. He loved, too, to play with comic incongruity. My own favorite of his caricatures in this line comes from the book *Rossetti and His Circle* and is entitled "Mr. Morley of Blackburn, on An Afternoon in The Spring of '69, Introduces

Mr. John Stuart Mill." In this drawing a willowy and bloodless John Stuart Mill, hat in one hand, a little leather bag containing galley proofs in the other, looks off into the distance as a small, sharp-nosed John Morley is speaking to a highly dubious looking Rossetti, who fingers his goatee; in the background hangs a Rossetti portrait of an extremely sensual Pre-Raphaelite woman. The lengthy and perfect caption reads:

> "It has recently," he says, "occurred to Mr. Mill that in his life-long endeavor to catch and keep the ear of the nation he has been hampered by a certain deficiency in—well, in warmth, in colour, in rich charm. I have told him that this deficiency (I do not regard it as a defect) might possibly be remedied by *you*. Mr. Mill has in the press, at this moment, a new work, entitled 'The Subjection of Women.' From my slight acquaintance with you, and from all that I have seen and heard of your work, I gather that women greatly interest you, and I have no doubt that you are incensed at their subjection. Mr. Mill has brought his proof-sheets with him. He will read them to you. I believe, and he takes my word for it, that a series of illustrative paintings by you would," etc. etc.

Max's caricatures were always prettily done. Although he drew them easily, even rapturously, he nonetheless took great pains in perfecting them. What makes them extraordinary is that in his drawings he joined caricature and cartoon. Not only are his drawings salient but so are the situations in which he places his subjects. As John Felstiner has remarked: "Beerbohm's innovation, one that only he was capable of making, was to bring the dynamics of parody into caricature." This invests his caricatures with not only the broad truth of satire but the more delicate truth of irony. It also frees them from the charge to which caricature is most liable, that of crudity, and lends them a weight in insight to which no other caricaturist can lay claim. "It is this immediate clarity of insight, free from all malice or prejudice, which makes Max superior to most caricaturists, even to Daumier," W. H. Auden wrote. "Even his most devastating portraits never strike one as unjust; one never feels that for personal or ideological reasons he had decided to uglify his victim before he looked at him."

Although Max never ceased to draw, later in life his caricatures seemed to lose their merry malice. "I seem to have lost my gift for dispraise," he told S. N. Behrman. "Pity crept in." But not everywhere. Max never lost his distaste for pretension, and for no one did he feel this distaste more sharply than for those men whom the world regarded as geniuses. Something there was about extravagantly large talent that set Max off, that made him wish to find its weakness, to diminish it, to bring it down to size. Perhaps it was the narcissism of genius; perhaps its confidence in its own primacy; perhaps its disregard for everything smaller than itself. Whatever it was, no genius ever quite passed muster with Max.

E. M. Forster once remarked that Goethe was the only genius who wasn't stupid. Max would probably have assented, if Forster would agree to remove Goethe from his generalization. In his essay "Quia Imperfectum" Max ponders why an obscure painter named Wilhelm Tischbein never completed a portrait of Goethe that he worked sedulously to persuade Goethe to sit for. Later in the essay, he conjectures that Tischbein was infatuated with an English woman in Naples, which caused him to break off a number of meetings with Goethe, thus permanently delaying completion of the portrait. Earlier, though, he suggests that Goethe may have "irked" Tischbein. But it is obvious that it is Max whom Goethe irks. It is Goethe's perfection that gets to him, all-embracing Goethe, who, as Max writes, "was never injudicious, never lazy, always in his best form—and always in love with some lady or another just so much as was good for the development of his soul and his art, but never by more than that by a tittle." Or, as he puts it earlier, "a man whose career was glorious without intermission, decade after decade, does sorely try our patience." He certainly tries Max's patience, and throughout this essay Max subtly but relentlessly chips away at the marmoreal German genius.

It is the self-importance of geniuses, their absolute confidence in their own value, that Max cannot abide. It is the chinks in their personality that he prefers to emphasize and, in so emphasizing, to magnify. In his essay "Hosts and Guests," he mentions what a miserable guest Dante was in exile, forever complaining about the conditions he met with in the houses in which he stayed; and Max adds that Dante would probably have been a worse host "had it ever occurred to him to entertain any one or anything except a deep regard for Beatrice." His animus extends even to that most congenial of geniuses, Samuel Johnson. In a brief essay entitled " 'A Clergyman,' " Max recounts a brief but definitive put-down of an obscure fellow whom Boswell, in his *Life of Johnson,* refers to only as "a clergyman." The scene for this little devastation is set just before dinner at Thrale Hall. Boswell, interrogatory as ever, is questioning Johnson about the great sermonizers of the day, when the following exchange ensues:

> A CLERGYMAN, whose name I do not recollect: Were not Dodd's sermons addressed to the passions? JOHNSON: They were nothing, Sir, be they addressed to what they may.

Slam! That is it. The clergyman has popped up and been shot down by the cannon of Johnson's confidence. He is never heard from again; his name isn't even recollected; he is target practice for genius. Max writes: "My heart goes out to the poor dear clergyman exclusively." Max then goes on to recount how, as he imagines it, the clergyman never recovers from this blow, the paw of a lion flicking a mouse, and how, as a result of it, he dies young, never having known a pleasing moment for the remainder of his days. "I like to think," Max ends the essay, "that he died forgiving Dr. Johnson."

Max himself was a good deal less forgiving of the geniuses

of his own day. There was something in strength that made him search out its weakness. He was appalled by the bullyboy in Kipling and detested the violence in his writing. He recognized that Ibsen was a genius but could never forgive him his humorlessness. Of William Morris he wrote: "Of course he was a wonderful all-round man but the act of walking round him has always tired me." He ridiculed the wildness and wooliness of the Russian writers, who were then being translated into English by the Garnetts, in his comic piece "Kolniyatsch," a name deriving from the English lunatic asylum Colney Hatch. Antipathy was the strongest emotion he felt toward Yeats: "Geniuses are generally asinine," he noted, "but his particular asinineness bores me and antagonizes me. . . ." As for Bertrand Russell, of him Max remarked: "It is Bertrand Russell's saving grace that he isn't a woman. As a woman he would have been intolerable." Apropos of T. E. Lawrence's wretched translation of *The Odyssey,* he said: "I would rather *not* have been that translator than have driven the Turks out of Arabia." It was the absence of subtlety he deplored in Shaw—"the best brain in England but no beauty except that of an engine"—and his unwavering self-confidence that caused him to be a bad influence "even on himself." When his secretary told Max that he would have liked meeting Sir Isaac Newton, he replied, "I would have taught him the Law of Levity."

The one genius of his time for whom Max retained reverence was Henry James. Not that this reverence was unmixed with comedy. He saw the humor both in and about Henry James. He drew at least six caricatures of James. In one, James is doubled over, as if in great pain, and the caption reads: "Mr. Henry James in the act of parturiating a sentence." In another, James, his all-seeing eyes bulging beneath his domed forehead, is kneeling by a hotel-room door, outside of which are a pair of male and a pair of female shoes, his ear to the keyhole. The caricature carries no caption, but if it did it would clearly read: "Mr. Henry James learns about sex." (Max waited to publish this caricature until after James's death.) And of course his parody of James, "The Mote in the Middle Distance," is unsurpassed—so good that even James delighted in it.

But the comedy that James occasioned in Max did not lessen his regard for the writer he once described in a poem as "indefatigable alchemist." David Cecil writes, persuasively, that "Henry James was the high priest of Max's chosen and professed faith." Both writers were moral aesthetes, and, as Cecil nicely puts it, "Max's spiritual history may be described as a journey from the crude aestheticism preached by Oscar Wilde to the finer aestheticism—moral as well as literary—manifested in Henry James." Max Beerbohm's favorite line from James reads: "Be generous and delicate and pursue the prize." In New English translation this means: Keep your sympathy, keep your subtlety, and keep the ambition always to write as well as possible. Although Max remained critical of James on small points—he once compared James's penchant for revising his early work in the style of his later phase to "patching pale gray silk with snippets of very dark thick brown velvet"—it was to James, at the close of Max's life, that he returned again and again for replenishment of the ideal of the beauty and moral vision of art.

Does the august phrase "moral vision" seem too high-flown to apply to Max Beerbohm himself? It was Henry James who, in a tribute to Turgenev, said that the great question about any writer is, "How does he feel about life? What in the last analysis is his philosophy?" The word "philosophy" and the name "Max Beerbohm" seem to want to fly apart. In his essay "Laughter," Max allowed that he might have a certain mellow wisdom, but went on to say: "I suffer from a strong suspicion that things in general cannot be accounted for through any formula or set of formulae, and that any one philosophy, howsoever new, is no better than another. That is in itself a sort of philosophy, and I suspect it accordingly; but it has for me the merit of being the only one I can make head or tail of." I believe that in this anti-philosophy a philosophy can nonetheless be found; it is the philosophy held in common by nearly all the great essayists.

To be an essayist is to divest oneself of the belief in a general set or system of ideas. All the great essayists, from Montaigne through Hazlitt to Beerbohm to Mencken to Orwell, are not so much anti-philosophical as a-philosophical. (Orwell, true, claimed to be a socialist, but he is never less convincing than when making that claim.) None is notably religious. The very form of the essay—discursive, tentative, enmeshed in the particular—seems to imply that to life's great questions, there probably are no answers, only hints, shadows, fleeting moments of elucidation. Mencken once put it straight out, announcing that no one knows who created the universe, or what intentions lie behind natural laws, or why sin and suffering were sent into the world, and maintained that anyone who claimed to know the answers to these questions was a con man. The essayist is by nature a skeptic: in Montaigne's case, a truly philosophical skeptic; in Hazlitt's and Orwell's cases, passionate skeptics; in Mencken's and Beerbohm's cases, laughing skeptics.

Max Beerbohm's skepticism grew not only out of the forms in which he worked but out of the methods he applied to those forms. He was a past master at parody; his book *A Christmas Garland* is prized by all who adore parody. Yet isn't parody, despite the parodist's insistence that *on se moque ce qu'on aime,* a criticism of (and skepticism about) excess in style, joined, it is true, to a love of idiosyncrasy? He had the lightest, loveliest ironic touch, yet isn't irony also the perfect medium for the skeptic—irony whose underlying assumption is that nothing is as it seems and hence that nothing may be taken at face value? The reason for Max Beerbohm's antipathy to genius is, I believe, genius's own antipathy to moderation and irony. Genius confidently knows what it knows; the skeptic knows that what genius is so confident it knows probably is wrong or not worth knowing. The fox nips at the hedgehog.

Yet it would be a mistake to leave the impression that Max Beerbohm is chiefly a nipper. While he is a writer who stressed limitation, his range as an essayist is surprisingly wide and he often strikes surprisingly deep. His best single book of essays, which was also his final book of essays, is *And Even Now*. It displays his talent in its full flower. Some of these essays are built around a comic conceit ("How Shall I Word It?" "Kolniyatsch," "Hosts and Guests"), some are reminiscential ("A Relic," "No. 2 The Pines," "William and Mary"), and some are made sheerly out of reflection ignited by a minor incident or curious phenomenon.

In the latter class is a little essay entitled "Something Defeasible." It is about Max watching a small boy taking great pains to build a cottage out of sand at the seashore. Max exchanges a few sentences with the laconic young artist, then returns to his newspaper, about which he remarks (the year is 1919): "During the War one felt it a duty to know the worst before breakfast; now that the English polity is threatened merely from within one is apt to dally. . . ." (Quite a "merely"; Max won't permit speed reading.) He comments on the changes within England; these have mostly to do with the slow destruction of English life as he knew it and loved it as a boy and young man. Meanwhile the sea is rolling in on the boy's sand cottage. Is the boy sad at the destruction of what he had worked so painstakingly to build? Quite the reverse:

> His face had flushed bright, and now, as the garden walls crumbled, and the paths and lawns were mingled by the waters' influence and confluence, and the walls of the cottage itself began to totter, and the gables sank, all, all was swallowed, his leaps were so high in air that they recalled to my memory those of a strange religious sect which once visited London; and the glare of his eyes was less indicative of a dreamer than of a triumphant fiend.

This is the first startling turn in the essay. The next comes in the sentence that follows it, which reads: "I myself was conscious of a certain wild enthusiasm within me." Yet it is "the boy's own enthusiasm that made me feel, as never before, how deep-rooted in the human heart the love of destruction, of mere destruction, is." Thinking back upon the destruction of England, he adds, "but I waived the question coming from that hypothesis, and other questions that would have followed; for I wished to be happy while I might."

So dark a note is far from the characteristic note in the artist whom Louis Kronenberger once called "The Perfect Trifler." Knowing that that note, too, played in Max Beerbohm's head makes the many lovely trifles he contrived all the more delightful, even dear, and their perfection all the more impressive. Max looked into the dark and, without underestimating its density by one jot, laughed, and his laughter has brought laughter to those of us who have discovered his splendor as an artist so that we, too, can be happy while we may.

The New Criterion 1985

Mr. Larkin and
Miss Pym

Has Anglophilia, like virginity past the age of twenty, become a dead letter? Impossible to answer such a question with anything approaching precision, but my suspicion is that if Anglophilia is not yet dead, it is well on its way to dying. In America the love of England and of things English was perhaps based in part on snobbery, in part on a sense of cultural inferiority, but by far in greatest part, or so it seems to an Anglophile like myself, on England's immensely impressive cultural tradition. It takes centuries to build powerful traditions, but only decades for these same traditions to shrivel and disappear. There will always be an England; yet, slightly seedy and exhausted land that it now seems, there is a good deal less likelihood of there always being Anglophiles to admire it.

Forty or so years ago, nearly everything English, from the Anglophile's point of view, stood for quality. From shoes to book reviews, if it was English it was well made. There were exceptions. The English tradition in the visual arts was never strong, and English food was infamously poor. But English statesmen surpassed all others, with Winston Churchill easily the greatest political figure to emerge from a democratic nation in this century. At the highest reaches English public schools put a durable blacking on their students through training in classical languages, and this blacking was often polished to a high sheen at Oxford and Cambridge, with the result that England produced a regular supply of young men and women— mostly men, to be sure—who could think clearly and write fluently.

No doubt it was owing to the English educational system that English literary culture was without peer. Nineteenth-century Russian literature may have produced a greater run of star figures, from Pushkin through Chekhov, but the current of English literature ran deeper, producing wave after wave of important novelists and poets, critics and belletrists, editors and journalists. So rich was English literary culture that two of America's subtlest and most penetrating writers, Henry James and T. S. Eliot, not only felt more at home but took up permanent residence there—relocations signaling a profound tribute to a profound literary tradition.

All this seems gone now—ended not with a bang but with the Beatles. Did England's withdrawal from its vast empire foreshadow the waning of its cultural influence, lending credence to the view that cultural power ineluctably follows political power? Was England brought down from within by socialism, whose standard operating procedure is evidently to establish equality not by raising the lowest up but by bringing the best down? Was it owing to some combination of these and other factors too numerous to tot up here? Or is some higher, indecipherable force at work, acting upon countries the way the heavens act upon stars, running them through the cycle from white dwarf through red giant, at which stage they dissipate and disappear? Whatever the case, it is well to remember that when England's star shone, it lit up the firmament.

It seems unlikely that Henry James or T. S. Eliot, were either man alive today, would depart the United States for England. Not that either would have found contemporary America so very congenial, but England, my guess is, would no longer seem a serious alternative. English food has improved and English acting remains supreme. Anglophilia lives and even pays off at PBS, where such English television productions as *Masterpiece Theater* continue to draw large and appreciative audiences. It lives in some quarters of American academic life, where the old snobbery dies hard and an English accent, even a rather poor one, can still weigh heavily in a man's favor. It lingers in journalism, too, though not so strongly as in the heyday of the *New York Review of Books,* whose contributors were once described by a wag as being made up chiefly of mad dogs and Englishmen.

But literarily, Anglophilia, like England itself, has suffered enormous slippage. Today even hard-case Anglophiles are pressed to make a meal out of the meager literary leftovers in the English larder. The days of "Virginia" and "Morgan," "Evelyn" and "Cyril," thin though they may seem in retrospect, are done and gone. English literary journalism, once so special of its kind, has lost its lovely lilt. Whole issues of the *Times Literary Supplement,* a journal whose importance to literary Anglophiles was once comparable to that of the *Racing Form* for horseplayers, are quite unreadable and might just as easily have been written by second-line American academics. The *New Statesman,* in its current condition, is not a paper one would want in the house. The *Spectator,* for all its reputed conservatism, cannot let go of its anti-Americanism and seems sadly parochial. English novelists rarely cause a stir; English poets seem chiefly to write for other English poets, like their American coevals. There are still English writers whom one cares about: Kingsley Amis, who has had the misfortune of never being able to top his first book, *Lucky Jim;* Anthony Powell, whose productivity does not slacken even as he enters his eighties; John Wain and Anita Brookner, and a few others. But the sense of a strong literary culture, of a tradition sturdy enough to ride out lean times, this in England seems to be—to adapt a title from a Philip Larkin poem about the sad passing of an older England—"Going, Going."

One hesitates to say "Gone," though Philip Larkin himself, in the same poem, comes close to saying it is all over for England:

> And that will be England gone,
> The shadows, the meadows, the lanes,
> The guildhalls, the carved choirs.
> There'll be books; it will linger on
> In galleries; but all that remains
> For us will be concrete and tyres.

Something of this same note is struck, if less insistently, in the novels of Barbara Pym. "If we lamented the decay of the great civilizations of the past," a character in her novel *Less Than Angels* remarks, "should we not also regret the dreary levelling down of our own?" That Barbara Pym and Philip Larkin agreed on this general point ought not to be too surprising. They shared a great deal else besides. Although there was a nine-year difference in their ages—she was born in 1913, he in 1922—Barbara Pym and Philip Larkin seemed very much of the same generation. Both were solidly middle class and quite without interest in the social climb. Neither taught or regularly lectured or otherwise attempted to live off the luster of a literary career; both worked at middling cultural jobs— "toad work," in Larkin's phrase—reasonably divorced from literature: Barbara Pym as an assistant editor at the International Institute of African Languages and Cultures, Philip Larkin as the chief librarian at the University of Hull (where he directed a staff of more than a hundred). Although each was an extraordinary person, both prided themselves on living ordinary lives. He was a bachelor, she a spinster. Loneliness was a subject they shared, its pleasures as well as its pain. ("The position of the unmarried woman—unless, of course, she is somebody's mistress—is of no interest whatsoever to the readers of modern fiction," Barbara Pym noted in her diary.) Another of their common subjects was middle age; in American writing, middle age is not yet recognized as a subject—only as something to flee from.

The work of both Barbara Pym and Philip Larkin goes pretty thoroughly against the grain of much mainstream contemporary American writing. For those who know nothing of either writer, perhaps it would be helpful to note that the literary antonym of Philip Larkin is Allen Ginsberg and that of Barbara Pym is Erica Jong. The great recent subjects of American writing—the politics of alienation, sex considered as a branch of gymnastics, the unreality of contemporary life—are of no serious interest to them. If the distance between Barbara Pym and Philip Larkin and most recent American writers is vast, the affinities between the two English writers are many. Philip Larkin could conceivably be a character in a Barbara Pym novel, portions of Barbara Pym's life the subject of a Philip Larkin poem. (While in the hospital after a stroke, Barbara Pym recorded in her diary: "The mixed ward. The pathos of men in pyjamas and dressing gowns. Philip Larkin type subjects.")

Barbara Pym and Philip Larkin, scarcely surprisingly, admired each other's writing. Shy, reserved, they had corresponded for fully fourteen years before meeting for the first time in 1975. ("May I say 'Philip,' if that is what people call you, or should we go through the academic convention of 'Philip Larkin' and 'Barbara Pym'?") But long before their first meeting, Philip Larkin encouraged and aided Barbara Pym. Both aid and encouragement were needed, for in 1963, after publishing six novels with the firm of Jonathan Cape, she was informed by her editor at Cape that the firm was now keener on books with a more contemporary tone. She was perhaps the clearest literary victim we have of the 1960s concentration on the political and the turbulent in literary production; as another editor was to tell her, in rejecting yet another of her novels, hers was "not the kind of novel to which people are turning."

Philip Larkin, who took the rejection of Barbara Pym's novels seriously, wrote a sharp letter to Charles Monteith, an important editor at Faber and Faber, about her situation. The heart of the letter reads:

> I feel it is a great shame if ordinary sane novels about ordinary sane people doing ordinary sane things can't find a publisher these days. This is the tradition of Jane Austen and Trollope, and I refuse to believe that no one wants its successors today. Why should I have to choose between spy rubbish, science fiction rubbish, Negro-homosexual rubbish, or dope-taking nervous-breakdown rubbish? I like to read about people who have done nothing spectacular, who aren't beautiful and lucky, who try to behave well in the limited field of activity they command, but who can see, in the little autumnal moments of vision, that the so called "big" experiences of life are going to miss them; and I like to read about such things presented not with self-pity or despair or romanticism, but with realistic firmness and even humour. That is in fact what the critics call the moral tone of the book. It seems to me the kind of writing a responsible publisher ought to support (that's you Charles!).

Bracing though that letter is to read today, it apparently had no greater effect when it was sent than a touch of bad conscience for its recipient. Barbara Pym spent fourteen years in the literary desert—she went that long without being able to get any new work published, while her old publisher, Jonathan Cape, was able to find room for the Beatle John Lennon (of whom Barbara Pym remarked that, with his long hair, he looked "like a very plain middle-aged Victorian female novelist," which is precisely what he looked like). Cape, Faber and Faber, Macmillan, Hamish Hamilton, Weidenfeld and Nicolson, Longman's, Cassell, Chatto and Windus, Barrie and Jenkins: the dishonor roll of publishers who rejected Barbara Pym is a lengthy one. In all, twenty-one different publishers turned down her novel *An Unsuitable Attachment,* most telling her it was nicely written but not at present their cup of tea.

Writing without any hope of publishing could not have been other than hell for Barbara Pym. At one point she attempted to alter her writing slightly to meet the market: "I am still going on with something, trying to make it less cosy without actually putting in the kind of thing that would be beyond my range (keep *that* and quote it in my biography, young man from the University of Texas!)." She worked at her job, she lived her life, but she had to think of writing novels as "a nice 'hobby' for one, like knitting." Larkin continued to come up with names of editors who might be sympathetic to her cause, and upon thanking him for the name of yet another such editor she could not resist adding, "If only somebody would have the courage to be unfashionable." Friends suggested that she set aside novels to write a biography. She regretted not having followed an academic career, though she knew it was too late to do anything about it. "By the way," she wrote to Philip Larkin in 1974, after more than ten years of not having any new work in print, "the letter I wrote to *The Author* about not getting published was never published, which seems to be the final accolade of failure."

The second reversal of fortune in Barbara Pym's career came in 1977—three years before she would die of cancer—when the *Times Literary Supplement* published lists chosen by important literary figures of the day, of the most underrated writers of the twentieth century. Barbara Pym was the only living writer to show up twice, having been mentioned by both Philip Larkin and Lord David Cecil. It was the making of her. Macmillan rushed in to publish her unpublished novels; Cape began to republish her earlier novels. E. P. Dutton brought out all her work in the United States. She was published in Sweden. She was taught in universities. She was on the short list for the Booker Prize for fiction (won that year by Paul Scott's *Staying On*). Her novel *The Sweet Dove Died* was on the London *Sunday Times* best-seller list.

She delighted in the attention she was now receiving, yet

even in triumph never lost her cool sense of the comedy of life. Writing to thank Philip Larkin after the Booker Prize dinner, she noted: "Don't bother to answer this—I don't expect or wish it. It's only just a heartfelt expression of thanks from the most overestimated novelist of 1977." The triumph was all too brief. She died on January 11, 1980. At the end, according to Hazel Holt, the editor of *A Very Private Eye,* Barbara Pym's autobiography in diaries and letters, "she was sustained, certainly, by her strong faith and still able, as she had been throughout her life, to draw comfort from small pleasures and ironies, and this is, perhaps, the greatest gift she has bequeathed to all who read her."

The curve of Philip Larkin's career was very different—no abrupt swoops up and down, no dramatic reversals on the graph, but instead a slow yet steady upward line. Since Larkin's death, at sixty-three on December 2, 1985, that line has continued to ascend. Larkin's has been a special place among modern poets. Poetry, an art enjoyed by a small minority, became over the course of Larkin's life the preserve of an even smaller group of what can only be termed, somewhat comically, poetry professionals, made up of people who write or teach poetry. By design, Philip Larkin remained the poet for the nonprofessional.

The critic R. P. Blackmur once remarked that the work of any good modern poet issues in ambiguity; Philip Larkin, I strongly suspect, would not have concurred. T. S. Eliot and Ezra Pound maintained that modern poetry must be difficult; Larkin, again, was not likely to have agreed. Larkin did something really quite extraordinary in the annals of contemporary poetry: he managed to write seriously without being in the least ambiguous and to write beautifully without being at all difficult.

Poetry in our time has become almost wholly a university activity, but Philip Larkin is the poet who best survives the hothouse atmosphere of the classroom. My sense is that people who like Larkin's poetry do not like it merely; in fact, they adore it. Although there is nothing the least cult-inducing about Larkin's poetry, people who adore it tend to think of themselves in the way the narrator of Henry James's story "The Next Time" thought of people with special literary tastes—as a group apart, a club, a band, "partakers of the same repose, who sit together in the shade of the tree, by the plash of the fountain, with the glare of the desert round us and no great vice that I know of but the habit perhaps of estimating people a little too much by what they think of a certain style."

But this Jamesian quotation may make Philip Larkin's poetry seem rather precious, ethereal even. It is quite the reverse; it is, in the root sense of the word, mundane. I should not go so far as to say that the following is characteristically Larkinesque, but in its combination of precision, prosiness, and beauty it is what one has come to expect from a Philip Larkin passage:

> Groping back to bed after a piss
> I part thick curtains, and am startled by
> The rapid clouds, the moon's cleanliness.

Larkin did not always have that combination in control. It was not until his second book of poems, *The Less Deceived* (1955), that, as he himself said, "thoughts, feelings, language cohered and jumped." He had in fact begun as a novelist. "I wanted to 'be a novelist' in a way I never wanted to 'be a poet,' " he once remarked. "Novels seem to me to be richer, broader, deeper, more enjoyable than poems." He wrote and published two novels—*Jill* (1946) and *A Girl in Winter* (1947)—while still in his early twenties, but could never complete a third. Neither of these is an important novel, and if Philip Larkin had not been their author both would have long since met the pulper's blade. But they are of interest in showing how precocious Larkin was and how little, temperamentally, he changed. The gift of precise yet startling phrasing was there from the outset. "The music was slow," runs a line from *Jill,* "with a logical sadness." From the outset, too, he had a penchant for the grim and the gray. Although he never claimed a terrified childhood, as a boy he stammered and was nearsighted, and of his parents, whom he described as "rather awkward people," he observed that they were "not very good at being happy." Lugubrious Larkin ever was, but—and herein lies part of his distinction—wittily lugubrious. Larkin could be dour and funny at the same time because he knew he was by nature dour and that there was nothing to be done but laugh about it. "Deprivation is for me," he once told an interviewer, "what daffodils were for Wordsworth."

Part of the appeal of both Barbara Pym and Philip Larkin is their solid common sense. Not a quality in notably abundant supply among writers of our day, common sense; so rare is it that coming upon it in books, one is inclined to greet it as a radical new trait. Yet it is by the dictates of common sense that most of us attempt to live our lives, in decency and honor. As Barbara Pym at one point remarks about James Baldwin's novel *Another Country,* "One is so really glad never to have had the chance of that kind of life." And one can say the same of the lives lived in the novels of Norman Kurt Updike or Philip Márquez Doctorow, which, with their violence, sex, and politics, come to seem, from the perspective of a certain age, like the Hardy boys with an X-rating. Apart from the X, such books do not seem quite appropriate for grownups.

Barbara Pym and Philip Larkin appear to have been grownups early in life. For the subject of her first novel, *Some Tame Gazelle,* Barbara Pym drew a portrait modeled on her sister and herself at middle age that in many ways turned out to be prophetic: in it she is a spinster, her sister divorced, and they are living together, as they in fact did for the better part of their adult lives. John Wain, in an autobiographical volume entitled *Sprightly Running,* recalls Philip Larkin at Oxford serving as a model for him because of Larkin's seriousness, "his ironic self-effacement, [and] rock-like determination to do whatever it might be necessary to do in order to write well."

Although Larkin found his tone early, he did not find his subject quite so quickly. His first volume of poetry, *The North Ship* (1945), was written under the influence of Yeats and was an obvious mistake, forcing him into false sensitivity ("The walking of girls' vulnerable feet") and Yeatsian music ("If hands could free you, heart, / Where would you fly?") that he simply did not have the pipes to play. The poems in *The North Ship* are brief, but, alas, not brief enough, as Larkin himself knew. In an introduction written for a reissue of the book in 1965, Larkin wrote, "As a coda I have added a poem, written a year or so later, which, though not noticeably better than the rest, shows the Celtic fever abated and the patient sleeping soundly."

Neither Barbara Pym nor Philip Larkin shows any long or intricate lines of development. (It was E. M. Forster who said that, after a certain age, one ceases to be interested in development but only in masterpieces.) Barbara Pym wrote Pymish novels right out of the starting gate, though some of her books, particularly *A Quartet in Autumn,* a novel about the terrors of superannuation, grew darker as she grew older. Once Larkin had shaken off the idea of himself as a novelist—"Novels," he once said, "are about other people and poems are about yourself"—and had fought free of the influence of Yeats, he found his mature and steady and unchanging voice. Thomas Hardy was a crucial figure for him, teaching him, as he put it, "not to be afraid of the obvious." When poems no longer came to him, as happened in the last decade of his life, he stopped writing.

Although both Barbara Pym and Philip Larkin worked on the periphery of academic life—she at her anthropological institute, he at the Hull library—neither was by any serious measure an academic. Characters who are anthropologists figure in several of Barbara Pym's novels, and she sometimes comments on the similarities shared by anthropologists and novelists, but her settings are not university ones. Larkin obviously knew a great deal about university life, but with two exceptions, the poems "Posterity" and "Vers de Societé," the academic life is not his subject, either. Both felt the need of a regular job; neither ever played full time at being "the writer." Larkin remarked with some pride that he "never read my poems in public, never lectured on poetry, never taught anyone how to write it." He once told an interviewer from the *Observer* that it would embarrass him very much to become, in effect, a public poet by giving lectures and readings on a regular basis. "I don't want to go around," he said, very Larkinly, "pretending to be me."

Doctrine seems to have been of little interest to either Barbara Pym or Philip Larkin. Freudianism plays no part in their work, and both wrote as if Marxism never existed. Larkin called himself a right-winger; by this he meant that he identified the Right with the virtues of thrift, hard work, reverence, and the desire to preserve. If Barbara Pym had any politics, I do not know what they might have been. In "Homage to a Government," in his book *High Windows* (1974), Larkin writes, sadly, about England's withdrawal from the world: "It's hard to say who wanted it to happen, / But now it's been decided nobody minds." But politics are far from Larkin's central concern. If any two writers can be said to occupy the zone where art is not invaded by politics, Barbara Pym and Philip Larkin are those writers.

What combination of social conditions, personal temperament, and tension between artistic traditions and ephemeral trends turns writers in one or another direction? It varies in nearly every case. But Barbara Pym, the daughter of a solicitor, who came of age during the Depression, and Philip Larkin, the son of a civil servant, who came of age during World War II, both took the world pretty much as they found it. Perhaps growing up in somewhat straitened circumstances—Larkin noted of his own generation at Oxford: "At an age when self-importance would have been normal, events cut us ruthlessly down to size"—put a hitch in the expectations of both writers. Perhaps both felt themselves less than dazzlingly equipped for happiness in life.

Whatever the case, Barbara Pym and Philip Larkin, without making any great fuss about it, wrote against the grain of their time. For all that the world reverences artists, for the most part they are quite as much the slaves of their time as the rest of us, moving in packs, responding to trends, joining movements, acting in concert. Even an avant-garde remains a garde—a number of people marching together, however far out in front of their contemporaries, but still a number. But Barbara Pym and Philip Larkin, each in her and his respective line, marched quite alone.

"Description," said Wallace Stevens, "is revelation." In her subtle, ironic, dead-on accurate novels, Barbara Pym endlessly describes: clothes, furniture, gardens, houses, food. Although she always has a story to tell, plot somehow is not quite paramount. Not that things fail to happen: people die, rather less frequently they marry, they pay their small courtesies, and those who have not already given it up as a bad job search to give some purpose to their lives through doing things for others. The compass in a Pym novel is kept narrow. Barbara Pym characters go off to their jobs, lunch carefully, sometimes have a boiled egg with their tea, take comfort from hot milky drinks, and put out of mind as best they can that life can be as "empty as the house one was coming back to." As a character in *Some Tame Gazelle* puts it, "Today has been rather trying, it has really—too much happening." Most days are given over to doing dull undramatic things: shopping, cooking, eating, washing-up, then up to bed to read a few pages of a novel by Charlotte M. Yonge or perhaps a poem or two in a sound anthology of seventeenth-century verse. The following day may provide a jumble sale or a conference on copy editing or a tour of a manor house. England has never seemed smaller.

It ought to be excruciatingly dull, but it never is. Barbara

Pym writes novels of the kind that, in her own novel *Jane and Prudence,* one of her characters is said to like: "Well written and tortuous, with a good dash of culture and the inevitable unhappy or indefinite ending, which was so like life." Missing from this formulation, if the correspondence to a Pym novel is to be reasonably complete, is the element of humor. In a Barbara Pym novel strict attention must be paid, lest a quiet cultivated joke pass over one's head. In *An Unsuitable Attachment,* for example, a book in a non-circulating social-science library is discovered to have a red food stain. " 'Of course,' said Mervyn thoughtfully, 'it could just be a genuine tomato sauce from a dish of spaghetti or ravioli. Yet it is difficult to imagine anyone reading Talcott Parsons and manipulating spaghetti at the same time.' " The reference to Talcott Parsons, whose prose could so often be the stylistic equivalent of spaghetti, is exactly right. But then Barbara Pym always gets such things exactly right. In *Some Tame Gazelle,* a single line—a single adverb, actually—sinks a character forever: " 'I shall never understand women,' said Dr. Parnell complacently." In *A Glass of Blessings,* a woman remarks that knitting can be a useful occupation, especially since one can do it while talking. " 'I wonder if women brought their knitting when Oscar Wilde talked,' said Piers. 'I daresay not,' said Sybil calmly, 'but that doesn't mean they wouldn't have liked to.' " As I say, careful attention must be paid.

In her novels Barbara Pym has created a world, by which I mean she has created characteristic scenes and situations and characters that are like no others and yet feel absolutely true. Whether art imitates life, or things work the other way round, remains a serious question, but traveling in England one notices a woman bringing flowers to a church, or two middle-aged women running a tearoom, or a vicar with an abstracted air being led by a wire-haired terrier, and one cannot view them as other than escapees from a Barbara Pym novel.

Within these novels, some characters show up in several

books: a young graduate student in anthropology in *Less Than Angels* is a full-blown professor reading a eulogy to a colleague in *A Few Green Leaves;* a feckless widower in *Jane and Prudence* shows up in the obituary column by a rector in *A Few Green Leaves;* a rather steady-seeming husband in *A Glass of Blessings* turns out to have had a brief affair with Prudence from *Jane and Prudence.* These small connections between novels give Barbara Pym's body of work something of the feeling of an *oeuvre.* Most of her novels run to roughly 250 pages, yet in each of them she manages to make ten or twelve characters come alive, switching points of view, interweaving stories, making the kinds of interconnections that are the hallmark of the true novelist.

Barbara Pym is a very feminine but very far from a conventionally feminist writer. Despite all the interest in writing by women, her novels are unlikely to turn up on an authorized feminist reading list. A novel entitled *Excellent Women* guarantees that; it is about those women who "are not for marrying" but content themselves doing good works for their parish or friends or strangers—women ready to accept a secondary role in life. Such women crop up in almost all of Barbara Pym's novels. "It was sad," thinks the leading character in *No Fond Return of Love,* "how women longed to be needed and useful and how seldom most of them really were." Her title *Some Tame Gazelle* comes from a minor English poet, who wrote: "Some tame gazelle, or some gentle dove: / Something to love, oh, something to love!" A male character in *An Unsuitable Attachment* reflects: "How convenient women were . . . the way they were always 'just going' to make coffee or tea or perhaps had just roasted a joint in the oven or made a cheese soufflé." And if such passages would cook Miss Pym's goose among the feminists, the following line, from *Less Than Angels,* would deep-fry it: "Yes, of course women do think the worst of each other, perhaps because only they can know what they are capable of." And that line is given to a woman we are obviously intended to admire.

At the same time, Barbara Pym partakes of what I think of as the superior feminism. As opposed to the conventional feminism that finds men to be exploitative brutes, out to do women in at every turn, harsh, oppressive, vicious, the superior feminism finds men to be rather amusing creatures who are not quite to be taken seriously. Men in Barbara Pym novels tend to be bumbling, out-of-it clergymen who might almost have strayed over from an Evelyn Waugh novel, self-important anthropologists, vain widowers, charming and handsome younger men who often turn out to be homosexual. They cannot be held quite responsible, really, for they are rather like large children. "Perhaps it was a mistake to have any kind of serious conversation when eating," thinks the heroine of *Some Tame Gazelle,* "or even anywhere in mixed company." Time and again men are rather gently put in their place. "Who could imagine a man who was *never* boring or irritating?" thinks Jane in *Jane and Prudence.* " 'A rare person?' echoed Miss Randall [in *No Fond Return of Love*]. 'A rather good-looking man who has made a mess of his marriage, by all accounts—I shouldn't have thought that was rare at all.' " "One does feel that men need company more than women do." "Men appeared to be so unsubtle. . . ." "Women are prepared to take trouble with sour and difficult things [gooseberries, in this instance], whereas men would hardly think it worthwhile." "Men do seem to require meat with their meal." Read enough Barbara Pym and men and women come to seem as if they are not merely different but of different phyla. And yet, like tame gazelles, men are needed as something to love.

If Barbara Pym's characters seem sometimes to dwell on trivialities—on meals, on churchgoing, on pottering about in the garden—it is not only because life is chiefly made up of trivialities but because they provide comfort in lives that often hide great sorrows, disappointments, lost opportunities. Life can bruise, her novels show, and no one should assume that she has a monopoly on suffering. Everyone must fight loneliness in the best way she can. Not even marriage is a sure protection against loneliness. "Mild, kindly looks and spectacles, thought Jane [in *Jane and Prudence*]; this is what it [marriage] all came to in the end." Or as Catherine, in *A Glass of Blessings*, notes when looking for a book that will take her out of herself after her young man has left her, "The only real book of devotion she had, suitably enough from her headmistress, told her that we are strangers and pilgrims here and must endure the heart's banishment, and she felt that she knew that anyway."

"Miss Pym's novels may look like 'women's books,' " Philip Larkin wrote, "but no man can read them and be quite the same again." That is true. What is also true is that Barbara Pym's novels—comic and sad, bright and dark as each of them all at once manages to be—seem a working out of a passage written many years earlier by Edith Wharton, a novelist, so far as is known, whom she may never have read:

> I have sometimes thought that a woman's nature is like a great house full of rooms: there is the hall, through which everyone passes in going in and out; the drawing room, where one receives formal visits; the sitting room, where the members of the family come and go as they like; but beyond that, far beyond, are other rooms, the handles of whose doors are never turned, no one knows whither they lead; and in the innermost room, the holy of holies, the soul sits alone and waits for a footstep that never comes.

Philip Larkin wrote, briefly, about Barbara Pym, but Barbara Pym, who wrote no criticism nor did any reviewing, never wrote about Philip Larkin. In her last novel, *A Few Green Leaves*, a mother regrets that her daughter "was not better read in English Literature, with all the comfort it could give. A few sad Hardy poems, a little Eliot, a line of Larkin seemed inadequate solace." She, of course, herself read not a line but all of Larkin's poetry and was greatly enamored of it. In her diary she noted: "What is the point of saying (as if for posterity) what Philip is *like*. He is so utterly what he is in his letters and poems." And in a letter to him, written when she had a little more than six months to live, she said: "I had such a nice letter from the USA asking me to 'lecture,' but won't go. It is [from] Carlisle, Pennsylvania, and the man who wrote had got on to my novels because of his interest in *your* work! A nice thought." It is a nice thought, and a smart one, for, literarily and spiritually, the two writers were as brother and sister.

The shape of their two careers, as I have noted, was very different. After the youthful publication of his two novels and the false step of his first volume of poems, Larkin patiently awaited the maturation of his poetic talent, which was in full bloom by his early thirties with the publication of *The Less Deceived* in 1955. Although he was a contemporary and friend of Kingsley Amis—who claims to have got the idea for *Lucky Jim* when visiting Larkin, who was working as a librarian at University College, Leicester—Larkin was not included in the band of Angry Young Men, the journalistic label grafted on to the generation of Amis, John Osborne, John Wain, and John Braine, though Larkin shared that generation's taste for jazz, detective fiction, and deadpan comedy. Living and working in Hull, the parliamentary seat of Andrew Marvell, he was part of no literary community, no poetry clique, no political cause. He did a certain amount of reviewing—"hack work," he invariably called it—and worked away at his poems, which won him a small but devoted and steadily increasing following.

Perhaps the reason Larkin seemed to take a certain pride in never having taught or lectured on poetry or given readings of his own poetry is that, by not doing so, he removed himself from the poetry-university-subsidy nexus. Nor has his poetry been frequently put under the knife of critical dissection, like

T. S. Eliot's "patient etherized upon a table." Unlike that of so many modern poets, from Wallace Stevens to John Ashbery, Philip Larkin's poetry is available for enjoyment without aid of windy explication, reader's manuals, slides, road maps, computer print-outs. He himself strongly felt that the writing and reading of poetry ought to be a pleasure. "To write a poem is a pleasure: sometimes I deliberately let it compete in the open market, so to speak, with other spare-time activities, ostensibly on the grounds that if a poem isn't more entertaining to write than listening to records or going out it won't be entertaining to read." In a brief piece entitled "The Pleasure Principle," he noted that "if a poet loses his pleasure-seeking audience he has lost the only audience worth having, for which the dutiful mob that signs on every September is no substitute." His own critical guide, enunciated when he was a judge for the Booker Prize in England, has nothing of the smell of the seminar room:

> Personally, I found myself asking four questions about every book: Could I read it? If I could read it, did I believe it? If I believed it, did I care about it? And if I cared about it, what was the quality of my caring, and would it last?

About nearly everything Larkin wrote, prose and poetry, there is this same no-nonsense, come-off-it tone. It is the tone of the philistine—but the philistine with a difference: the philistine with the authority behind him of having written some of the great poems of the age. There are after all times when philistinism, if propelled by common sense and not by an animus against art, can be valuable, and ours may be such a time. Who would have thought—recalled, rather—that poetry, its composition and its comprehension, ought to give pleasure? Or in thinking about Sylvia Plath, how useful to be reminded, as Larkin commonsensically reminds us, that "mad poets do not write about madness. . . . Plath did: it was her subject, her *donnée* ('I do it exceptionally well'); together they played an increasingly reckless game of tag." The world could use more such philistines.

There can be no gainsaying how deep this strain ran in Philip Larkin, and until one understands how deep it did, one cannot hope to understand how strongly Larkin's aesthetic views went against the spirit of the age. These views are given their most comprehensive form not in any of Larkin's writings about poetry but instead in the introduction to *All What Jazz,* the collection of pieces on jazz that he wrote for the *Daily Telegraph* between 1961 and 1971. For Larkin, jazz took a turn—a nasty turn— with the ascendancy of the saxophonist Charlie Parker and the musicians who followed in his trail. There was, in Larkin's view, something meant to upset in the tense, febrile music of these men. Theirs was not, Larkin puts it, "the music of happy men," as so much of the jazz of their precursors seemed. "I used to think that anyone hearing a Parker record would guess he was a drug addict, but no one hearing Beiderbecke would think he was an alcoholic, and that this summed up the distinction between the kinds of music." Later, of course, it grew worse; and with musicians like John Coltrane "jazz started to be *ugly on purpose*" (Larkin's emphasis).

Larkin, who grew up loving jazz, found himself unable to enjoy this new work, which critics informed him was revolutionary and spoke for our time and yet was traditional in the best and deepest sense. "I hadn't realized that jazz had gone from Lascaux to Jackson Pollock in fifty years," he writes, tongue firmly in his cheek. "All I am saying is that the term 'modern,' when applied to art, has a more than chronological meaning: it denotes a quality of irresponsibility peculiar to this century, known sometimes as modernism, and once I had classified modern jazz under this heading I knew where I was." As for how modern art has come to this pass, Larkin writes:

My own theory is that it is related to an imbalance between the two tensions from which art springs: these are the tension between the artist and his material, and between the artist and his audience, and that in the last seventy-five years or so the second of these has slackened or even perished. In consequence the artist has become over-concerned with his material (hence an age of technical experiment), and, in isolation, has busied himself with the two principal themes of modernism, mystification and outrage. Piqued at being neglected, he has painted portraits with both eyes on the same side of the nose, or smothered a model with paint and rolled her over a blank canvas. He has designed a dwelling-house to be built underground. He has written poems resembling the kind of pictures typists make with their machines during the coffee break, or a novel in gibberish, or a play in which the characters sit in dustbins. He has made a six-hour film of someone asleep. He has carved human figures with large holes in them. And parallel to this activity ("every idiom has its idiot," as an American novelist has written) there has grown up a kind of critical journalism designed to put it over.

Do understand, Philip Larkin is not merely a pre–Carnaby Street Englishman, left behind by the art of his day. It goes back further and runs deeper. "My dislike of Pound and Picasso, both of whom predate me by a considerable margin, can't be explained in this way," he writes. "The same can be said of Henry Moore and James Joyce (a textbook case of declension from talent to absurdity). No, I dislike such things not because they are new, but because they are irresponsible exploitations of technique in contradiction of human life as we know it. This is my essential criticism of modernism, whether perpetrated by Parker, Pound, or Picasso: it helps us neither to enjoy nor endure."

One might be able to dismiss all this as crankishness and a hatred of the modern if Philip Larkin did not in his own poetry provide such splendid examples of the kind of art that he admired. Obviously the art he aspired to is not cheerful art; nor was he looking for reassuring messages about the dignity of humankind. It is instead an art in which the demands of technique are met—the pleasurable struggle, in poetry, among rhythm and meter and the meaning of words—but in which technique never overwhelms content. It is an art in which the ironic, the comic, the understated, the fearlessly honest, are given full play, while the shocking and the deliberately hideous are excluded. Excitement in such an art derives from precision of language and subtlety of sentiment, not from tension. A poem must not merely be but mean.

The standard line about Philip Larkin is that he is above all the poet of human limitation, and there is some truth to this—within limits. It does not, however, quite comprehend the extent of Larkin's spiritual isolation. His friends—Kingsley Amis, John Wain, Barbara Pym—speak of him with a touching combination of affection and reverence. He was nonetheless a solitary man, one of nature's true bachelors. Barbara Pym, who regretted and finally reconciled herself to not marrying, can be said to have been unlucky in love; Philip Larkin, so far as is known, cannot be said to have advanced to the stage where he could even be called unlucky. The twelve-line poem "Talking in Bed" ends:

> It becomes still more difficult to find
> Words at once true and kind,
> Or not untrue and not unkind.

The poem "Self's the Man" ("Only I'm a better hand / At knowing what I can stand / Without them sending a van— / Or suppose I am") reinforces one's sense of Larkin's radical isolation. And his poem "Mr. Bleaney," about a single man, living alone in a furnished room, spending his summer holidays at Frinton, Christmas with his sister at Stoke, reverberates with the sadness of human solitude. A stammerer as a boy, increasingly deaf in middle age—Larkin's life neatly conspired to set him apart and keep him there. What is impressive is the way that he was able to generalize his own apartness into persuasive poems about the isolation, the loneliness, that is part of the condition of us all. The magic of his art was to have brought a kind of grandeur to life viewed from the bed-sitter under the attic. How he did this is baffling, but, as Kingsley Amis has written of Philip Larkin, "this kind of bafflement is a normal response to an artist of the first rank."

Larkin wrote that "the essence of [the poet's] gifts is to recreate the familiar, and it is from the familiar that he draws his strength." T. S. Eliot, writing about Andrew Marvell, said that the poet possesses the ability to make the familiar strange and the strange familiar. But Larkin did something rather different: he made the familiar important. His poetry is anti-romantic, anti-rhetorical, ending neither in mystification (see the works of John Ashbery) nor in outrage (see those of Allen Ginsberg), but in plain and powerful truth-telling. His poetry exhibits his incapacity for self-delusion. Within the confines of the most careful meter and charming rhymes, writing always in a persuasive mature voice, he was able to formulate home truths of a kind that poetry in our day has too often neglected, as in these lines from "Continuing to Live":

> This loss of interest, hair, and enterprise—
> Ah, if the game were poker, yes,
> You might discard them, draw a full house!
>   But it's chess.

There is no want of bleakness in Larkin's poetry, often covered over by wit, as in "This Be the Verse," with its often-quoted opening line about your mum and dad, but which ends:

> Man hands on misery to man.
>   It deepens like a coastal shelf.
> Get out as early as you can,
>   And don't have any kids yourself.

Yearning is a strong element in Larkin, who once described his childhood as "a forgotten boredom" and who wrote that "the realization that it was not people I dislike but children was for me one of those moments of revelation." He yearns for the youth that is gone, the release from constraint that he is too old to join in—"Sexual intercourse began / In nineteen sixty-three / (Which was rather late for me)"—while being unable to live completely in the present and fearing the death that awaits in the future. To say that intimations of mortality touch everything that Larkin wrote is putting it too lightly. There are the ambulances that "come to rest at any kerb / All streets in time are visited." Religion, "That vast moth-eaten musical brocade / Created to pretend we never die," is no help, nor is rationalism. As the last four lines of "Dockery and Son" have it:

> Life is first boredom, then fear.
> Whether or not we use it, it goes,
> And leaves what something hidden from us chose,
> And age, and then only the end of age.

This all ought to be immensely depressing, and yet, somehow, it is not. On the contrary, it is, somehow, consoling, as are the novels of Barbara Pym. A. N. Wilson, in an obituary article, wrote that "Larkin found the perfect voice for expressing our worst fears." Perhaps the reason is that he expressed these fears so perfectly, writing fearlessly about the universal fear of oblivion. How like a human being to be certain of his extinction, beside which nothing else matters, and yet to create a poem about it, which does matter. "Aubade," which for me is Philip Larkin's single most beautiful poem, a poem in which a man awakes in the middle of the night to contemplate his own approaching death ("Being brave / Lets no one off the grave"), ends on this passage of qualified but real knowledge that life goes on:

> Slowly light strengthens, and the room takes shape.
> It stands plain as a wardrobe, what we know,
> Have always known, know that we can't escape,

Yet can't accept. One side will have to go.
Meanwhile telephones crouch, getting ready to ring
In locked-up offices, and all the uncaring
Intricate rented world begins to rouse.
The sky is white as clay, with no sun.
Work has to be done.
Postmen like doctors go from house to house.

Barbara Pym and Philip Larkin, two at first glimpse small-gauged but finally essential writers, are both quintessentially, untranslatably English. One cannot imagine their novels and poems having been produced in the United States, or Latin America, or Israel, or any other European country. Writing after the end of England's heroic age, laboring in the neutral zone of art where politics do not matter and public events are of negligible interest, they were able to produce work that concentrates wholly on the simple but frequently forgotten condition of being human: on loneliness and yearning and death and on the small but crucial pleasures that make life bearable. Anglophilia may well be dead, but if the nation that gave rise to it can continue to produce writers of the quality of Barbara Pym and Philip Larkin, then long live England.

Commentary 1986

Walter Lippmann:
The Opinion Machine

A jodha could read but thought it more dignified to be read to, and Mr. Biswas was sometimes called to the house to read, for a penny, a newspaper column of which Ajodha was particularly fond. This was a syndicated American column called That Body of Yours *which dealt every day with a different danger to the human body. Ajodha listened with gravity, concern, alarm. It puzzled Mr. Biswas that he should subject himself to this torment, and it amazed him that the writer, Dr. Samuel S. Pitkin, could keep the column going with such regularity. But the doctor never flagged; twenty years later the column was still going.*

—V. S. Naipaul, *A House for Mr. Biswas*

IN THE UNITED STATES at about this time millions of Americans, without the luxury of having a Brahmin boy to read to them, read the syndicated column of Walter Lippmann, which was entitled "Today and Tomorrow," though it might as easily have been called "That Body Politic of Yours." Like Ajodha, they read with gravity, concern, alarm. Like Dr. Pitkin, Lippmann never flagged, finding a new danger to the body politic anywhere from two to four days a week over the course of some thirty-six years. And like Mr. Biswas, one has to wonder why Lippmann's readers subjected themselves to this torment and how he could keep the column going with such regularity.

Among that not always jolly class of mortals known as promising young men, Walter Lippmann was surely one of the most promising of all. Born in 1889, he was a New Yorker by birth, a German Jew by ancestry, a rentier through his family's economic position, and an exceedingly, even toweringly, intelligent fellow by nature. He was an only child, with a potentially domineering mother, whose attempts at domination he early eluded, and a kindly but ineffectual father, his relationship with whom Lippmann later in life described as "never very intimate, but affectionately friendly." Dispassionate, detached, oddly disconnected from political and social moorings—most people were unaware that he was a Jew—Lippmann seemed perfectly equipped to be what in later years his readers took him for: a machine built for dispensing disinterested opinion.

Ronald Steel's *Walter Lippmann and the American Century* is not a heavily psychological biography. With a life so elaborately intertwined with public events as Lippmann's, Steel has his hands full merely laying the carpet, without attempting to find the figure in it. But he does venture the observation that Walter Lippmann may have found his true father in "a succession of strong leaders whom he greatly admired, and in a variety of older men to whom he became attached, men of strong character and personal warmth. . . ." Be that as it may, at the very least the young Walter Lippmann had the knack of making a strong impression on exceptional men. He was also something of what the job advertisements refer to as a "self-starter."

The elderly William James, for example, came to call on Lippmann when the latter, at Harvard, published a rebellious undergraduate article in the *Harvard Illustrated*. Santayana, who was said to have lectured at Harvard while staring out of the window toward the Europe for which he yearned, apparently looked away from the window long enough to take note of Lippmann, whom he offered a job as a graduate assistant in his introductory philosophy course. Lippmann showed up at a seminar which Graham Wallas taught at Harvard in the spring of 1910, and a few years later Wallas's book *The Great Society* was published with a dedication to Walter Lippmann. When Lincoln Steffens, author of *The Shame of the Cities* and then the wielder of the muckiest rake in American journalism, gave an occasional lecture at Harvard, Lippmann arranged to find his way into Steffens's esteem as well, and later became his research assistant.

"Of course Walter Lippmann's mind was of a rather special type," Van Wyck Brooks wrote in his autobiography, "but he was mature at twenty-three or so when most of us were still floundering about in a prolonged adolescence." Another way of saying this is to say that Lippmann had the gift of perpetual middle age: when he was twenty he seemed fifty; and when he was seventy-five, he still seemed fifty. Perhaps the only time Walter Lippmann did not seem fifty was when he was nearly fifty—when he was, to be exact, forty-eight and left his wife for the wife of Hamilton Fish Armstrong, one of his closest friends (though some, I suppose, might argue that no act could be more essentially middle-aged than this).

Not the least advantage of Lippmann's precocity, his rare intellectual equanimity and superior perspective, was that it got him quickly out of the starting gate and onto the course of a career. The only problem—and it was a happy problem— was which of several careers to choose from, for the young Walter Lippmann's possibilities could scarcely have been greater. For a time he thought he might become an art historian. He is easily imagined as an academic—probably a political-philosophy don. A life as a political activist was another prospect; and indeed shortly after leaving Harvard, in a youthful socialist phase, he worked for the then socialist mayor of the city of Schenectady. He was among the founding editors of the *New*

Republic, and could doubtless have left his mark as a magazine editor (it was Lippmann who brought Edmund Wilson to the *New Republic* as literary editor). "He is a born writer," Justice Holmes wrote of Lippmann in a letter to Lewis Einstein; and, judging from early essays Lippmann wrote on H. L. Mencken and Sinclair Lewis, he could have been, had he chosen, a first-class literary critic. But what Walter Lippmann finally became, at the age of forty-two, was a columnist, a man who looks out upon the world and offers his opinions about its condition, at a prescribed length and on prescribed days: a Delphic oracle on a deadline.

Lippmann did not set out to be a columnist, nor did he become such a creature overnight. Before starting his column in 1931, he put in a long apprenticeship as a journalist, author, and general insider. He certainly never made the vulgar error of starting at the bottom. He completed his first book, *A Preface of Politics,* when he was twenty-three. He socialized for a time in bohemia, attending the Greenwich Village salon of Mabel Dodge Luhan, though always, one imagines, with a slight sense of slumming, for Walter Lippmann, whose suits were bespoke and whose hair was professionally shampooed, was very far from being a bohemian. In the presidential election of 1916, when only twenty-seven, he wrote the labor plank in the campaign platform of Theodore Roosevelt, the one American political figure he unstintingly admired. With World War I he became interested in foreign affairs. Having insinuated himself with Woodrow Wilson's man Colonel Edward M. House— who reported to Wilson that Lippmann was "a Jew, but unlike other Jews he is a silent one"—he worked with the United States delegation to the Paris Peace Conference, and was personally responsible for fashioning eight of President Wilson's famous though ill-fated Fourteen Points. "He has a mind like a knife and will be a great power one day," Harold Laski wrote to Justice Holmes.

What Lippmann was becoming was something of an American Harold Laski: the bright young man, the behind-the-scenes wheeler-dealer, the *éminence grise;* but Lippmann was of a higher intellectual caliber than Harold Laski—more thoughtful, less locked into a fixed politics, rather more refined in his interests, tastes, and bearing. Bernard Berenson predicted great things for him; Leonard Woolf thought him a brilliant conversationalist. Thus at I Tatti and among Bloomsbury he was adjudged O.K. As a writer he showed himself not merely precocious but original, and perhaps nowhere more so than in *Public Opinion* (1922), a book published when he was thirty-three, which still has a high standing among serious social scientists.

The same year that *Public Opinion* appeared, Lippmann left the *New Republic* to become an editorialist for the *New York World,* where he would remain for nine years, tapping out opinions on all possible subjects, though chiefly on foreign affairs. Before long he became editor of the *New York World's* editorial page at an excellent salary and with three months' leave each year to travel and to devote to his own writing. The editorial was a form he was comfortable with. "I find the *World* job easy to do," he wrote to Berenson. There was always something of the model editorial about Lippmann's prose, which tended to be judgmental yet cool, slightly high-blown yet even-handed. If he had a reigning tone it was one of dispassion, even in the act of advocacy. As Steel remarks, "Lippmann cared about social justice, but it was not an emotional issue for him."

Mr. Steel would clearly prefer that it had been an emotional issue. He favors, as he puts it, "the voice of Lippmann the romantic, before that voice was muted by caution, eminence, and skepticism. . . ." But Walter Lippmann was decorous by temperament (even deploring, as a socialist at Harvard, bad taste in propaganda). Steel does not, in general, care very much for Lippmann's performance during his years as editor of the *New York World's* editorial page. He disapproves of his not favoring Senator Robert La Follette in the presidential election of 1924, of his dithering over his pronouncements on the

famous Sacco-Vanzetti case, and of his coming increasingly to
distrust the wisdom of the masses. (Steel views Lippmann as—
in one of the fashionable words of contemporary political discourse—an "elitist.") Of Lippmann's turning first one way, then
another, on the Sacco-Vanzetti case, Steel maintains that,
whatever his true views, he also "cared about his influence as a
public person," and that "his fear of being cut off from centers
of power [and] his distaste for too close an association with
radicals often muted his voice." That Sacco and Vanzetti may
have been guilty, that certain radical pronouncements may have
been distasteful, these possibilities are not entertained.

Walter Lippmann and the American Century is a political
biography in the full sense of the term—not only is it about a
political figure but it is also written out of a quite specific political point of view. This is what gives the book its prosecutorial
tone. In foreign policy Steel's point of view is that of a revisionist, which means he believes that the past forty years or so
in American foreign policy have been a period of imperialist
intention, of the thrust—sometimes artfully disguised, sometimes naked—on the part of the United States for world hege-
mony. Steel views the Cold War as more the fault of the United
States than of the Soviet Union; and in his own journalism he
has shown a great impatience with what he construes to be the
screen of moral babble, paranoia, and simple hypocrisy behind
which American policy has operated. The domestic side of the
revisionist point of view is to perceive the United States as a
vaguely racist country, ruled by Big Business, out to squash
radicals, hold back the working class, and by and large make
life hell for all who choose to go against the monstrous wishes
of America's secret rulers. Although Steel never states his position directly, *Walter Lippmann and the American Century* is a
whole-earth catalogue of revisionist presuppositions, assumptions, notions. Much of his biography is scarcely more than a
checklist of Walter Lippmann's opinions. What they are checked
against is Ronald Steel's opinions, and when Lippmann's

opinions and Steel's are not congruent, Lippmann's are found wanting.

Although Steel's political purposes mar his book's standing as a work of biographical art, he does present much interesting detail about the quotidian aspects of Lippmann's life. Lippmann was a beautifully organized intellectual worker. While editorial-page editor of the *New York World,* he also did a monthly article for the magazine *Vanity Fair,* lectured widely, and published a book roughly every two years. This still left him adequate time for political sport, national and international. In the presidential-election campaign of 1928, he was part of the inner strategy group of Al Smith, the Democratic candidate. Earlier, in 1927, he had joined Dwight Morrow, then United States ambassador to Mexico, in a secret diplomatic mission which had entailed working through to a compromise between American oil companies and a Mexican government committed to regaining control of Mexican oil and mineral rights. Nor was he above using his editorials to flatter senators—Senator William E. Borah was a notable example—in order to gain their legislative support for programs which he, Lippmann, favored. In what was to become a fairly common practice, Lippmann took an active hand in events, and then, through his writing, applauded the good sense of something he himself had helped to bring about.

By the time the *New York World* folded in 1931, Walter Lippmann was, at forty-two, a mildly famous man. Certainly he was everywhere known among journalists and intellectuals; and his fame was beginning to spread beyond the world of his professional peers. *A Preface to Morals,* a book he published in 1929, was a best seller. He was offered a chair in government at Harvard; the University of North Carolina at Chapel Hill offered him its presidency. Magazines put out feelers to him. Adolph Ochs, publisher of the *New York Times,* offered him the job of running his paper's Washington bureau. William Randolph Hearst wanted him to write a column for his papers.

But the offer Lippmann finally accepted was from the *New York Herald Tribune;* it was to write a column of opinion four days a week, at a salary of $25,000 a year, with more money to come from syndication—this was at the height of the Depression—long vacations, every expense paid and perquisite seen to, and a guarantee of freedom to write exactly what he pleased.

As for Lippmann's choosing to do a column, there was something quite natural in the choice. Through his other writings he had become too well-known to continue to settle for the anonymity of unsigned editorials or for an editorship itself. As Steel suggests, he had not the temperament for an academic life; so many years of journalism had doubtless quickened his intellectual pulse. If Lippmann was in part a thinker, he was also as much a journalist, who thought best with the clangor of contemporary events in the foreground. Then there was the matter of influence; Lippmann had already had several draughts of that exhilarating brew. Nothing like the Fabian Society existed in the United States. Only with the presidency of Franklin Delano Roosevelt and the advent of his brain trust were professors and "generalist" intellectuals brought into politics. A column, offering a regular platform for disseminating ideas and holding out the possibility of exerting influence, nicely satisfied Lippmann's ambition.

A newspaper column was at that time rather a grander thing than it has since become. Radio never gave the competition to newspapers over the conveyance of news and comment that television now does. For news there was essentially one medium—newspapers—and not yet, in any serious way, media. Nor had the notion yet arisen of an op-ed page—introduced, I believe, by the *New York Times* and since slavishly followed by other American newspapers. The reigning idea of the op-ed page is to represent all shades of opinion. Yet with all shades represented, as they now generally are, the result only seems to be greater darkness. Most American op-ed pages today offer dogs barking from the left and dogs barking from the right, with the consequent cacophony known as "dialogue."

Although other columnists emerged who became great figures in American journalism—Westbrook Pegler, Drew Pear-
son, Marquis Childs, the brothers Alsop, James Reston (who
is still with the *New York Times*)—none has ever exceeded
Lippmann in general esteem. While he was at work it sometimes seemed as if there were four branches of government in
the United States: the executive, the legislative, the judicial,
and Walter Lippmann. In the brief span of six hundred or so
words, a Lippmann column gave off the aura of intellectual
elegance, thoughtfulness, and supreme disinterestedness. Before
deciding what they thought on particular issues, questions, and
problems, hundreds of thousands, perhaps millions of Americans waited to hear what Walter Lippmann had to say. Through
his column Lippmann became a figure, a personage, a power.

But it was his ostensible disinterestedness that gave him his
place well above the ruck of other American journalists. He
wrote, Steel tells us, in a soundproof study, and his loyal readers, had they known, would have thought this entirely fitting.
Their view of Walter Lippmann was that he was immensely
well-informed without in any way being *parti pris*. His views
were invulnerable to outside influence, or so it seemed, and he
came upon them by dint of sheer lucubration. He often spoke
publicly about the need for the columnist to maintain his neu-
trality and not "to think of oneself as engaged in a public career
on the stage of the world."

But in his own career, it turns out, Lippmann followed little
of this Polonian advice, and perhaps the chief merit of Steel's
biography is to make clear how deeply implicated he often was
in the events of his time. For one thing, he was inordinately
interested in his own sphere of influence; for another, he was
almost continuously a behind-the-scenes operator. He was an
adviser to Wendell Willkie in the 1940 presidential election.
During World War II he helped draft the bill for lend-lease.
He apparently saw nothing amiss in writing a speech on for-

eign policy for Senator Arthur Vandenberg and then praising the sagacity of the same speech in his column. He regularly wrote memoranda to American presidents and military leaders offering quite specific advice. Very nearly alone among modern men, Lippmann, as Steel's biography demonstrates, enjoyed the twentieth-century drama as both actor and chorus.

Yet despite all this it remains to be said that as a political writer, Lippmann was very much his own man. He neither traveled with nor sought to lead the pack. His views over the years shifted and changed, sometimes in response to personal crises, but more often in response to the tremor of events. He was often wrong in his judgments—some of them crucial judgments—but never because he worked out of an ideological system. When he was wrong it was usually for the good reason that history is more subtle than the mind of any man can comprehend. He could set too much store by his opinions, but he was always independent. His biographer ought to have said this yet doesn't.

The reason is that Steel is too intent on scoring political points off Lippmann to see him quite whole. Part of the difficulty may be that Steel can only judge a man by his politics. Outside political matters, his biography does not display an excess of general culture. His comments on such men as H. L. Mencken and Bernard Berenson, though brief, are commonplace. His prose is not highly refined; among its flaws is a penchant for such journalistic jargon words as "low-profile" and for the old *Time* magazine habit of describing a career in one word: "journalist Norman Hapgood," "pacifist Oswald Garrison Villard," "lawyer George Rublee." His account of Lippmann's most interesting books—*A Preface to Morals* and *Public Opinion*—is scant. His character of Lippmann's second wife, Helen Byrne Armstrong, is oddly deficient, giving only an inkling of a woman who, the type of the wife as protectress, sounds a true horror. Which is a roundabout way of saying that if one doesn't share Ronald Steel's politics one isn't likely to find much to enjoy in his biography.

In order to review Lippmann's opinions, Steel leads us through nearly all of American history from the period before World War I to the Vietnam War. Summary though this history necessarily is, it is laden with longueurs. The effect is rather like witnessing a man being flogged—but very slowly.

The lash is laid to Lippmann for being wrong, for being reticent, for being insufficiently zealous. Part of Steel's bill of complaint is that Lippmann was detached from the Spanish Civil War; that he waffled and wobbled in his estimation of Franklin Delano Roosevelt; that though "never intimidated by [Senator Joseph R.] McCarthy [he] nonetheless wrote relatively little on the issue"; that he did not come to the defense of the defendants in the Oppenheimer, Hiss, and Rosenberg case; that he was quiescent on the subject of race; that only rarely did he "view foreign policy as a moral issue." Seen through Steel's intellectual bifocals—hindsight on the top portion of the lens, his own political point of view below—Lippmann comes out a miserable fellow: a social climber, a Jew ashamed of the religion of his birth, a contemner of the people's wisdom, a rather bloodless egotist.

But Steel is not alone in his estimation of Walter Lippmann or in his general views. The critical reception accorded the American edition of *Walter Lippmann and the American Century* has been overwhelming in its conclusion that Steel has written a brilliant book and that Lippmann was (as Benjamin DeMott put it) "a confirmed elitist," or (as Alexander Cockburn put it) guilty of "consistent misjudgment," or (as Gary Wills put it) "deeply despicable." Other reviewers—Anthony Lewis in the *New York Review of Books,* Alfred Kazin in the *New Republic*—fell into step in their reviews. Poor Lippmann has now had the whole herd of independent minds trample upon his reputation.

It is almost enough to make one rush to his defense—almost, but not quite. Although Lippmann was surely a more interest-

ing and complicated being than he appears in the pages of
Steel's biography—his own books are a warranty for saying
that—it is noteworthy not only how often he, the great doyen
of American journalism, the pundit of pundits, was wrong in
his depiction and prediction of events, but also how terribly
wrong he was about the two most decisive events of the past
fifty years: the rise to power of the Nazis and its significance,
which he was very slow to understand; and the intentions of
the Soviet Union, which he seems to have been quite blind to,
approving as he did of the Yalta Conference, opposing NATO,
and writing, in 1947: "My strongest impression . . . is that the
Russians have lost the Cold War and they know it."

Toward the end of his career Lippmann came out strongly
against American involvement in the Vietnam War, and this
provides the political scorecard which is Steel's biography with
a happy ending. Until Vietnam, Lippmann, in Steel's reading
of his life, was taken up and over by American power interests—essentially "co-opted," in the popular radical phrase of the
1960s. "Success," Steel writes, "had not so much changed him
as it had brought out his innate conservatism." And: ". . . he
seemed to be going out of his way to show that liberalism and
big business could go hand in hand." But now, with Vietnam,
Lippmann had at last seen the light, and what it lit, in Steel's
view, was the corruption and destructiveness of American foreign policy. "Without Vietnam," Murray Kempton wrote in
his review of this biography, "when [Lippmann] was touched
by fire, we might have had trouble taking notice what he left
behind."

But my guess is that, say, twenty years from now we will
have trouble taking notice of what Lippmann left behind despite
his writings about Vietnam. Twenty years from now, if he is
remembered at all, he will be remembered as a small part of
the history of American journalism, another pundit, wrong
much of the time, part of the contemporary noise of his day.
And there is reason to believe that Lippmann himself knew it.

Time and again in Steel's biography he is shown ready to drop his column to devote himself to the important books he felt it was in him to write—books that would speak to the men of his time yet endure beyond his time.

But the prospect of influence, its magnetic pull, proved too strong; he had grasped its wire and could not release it. While he was alive Lippmann's position was that of the pope of American public opinion, or so it was generally believed. European prime ministers cleared their appointment calendars for his visits; American presidents unfailingly sucked up to him; tyrants felt winning him over was absolutely essential. Whether or not he knew it, Lippmann had made a bargain: he achieved great fame in his lifetime in exchange for the near certainty of obscurity in death.

Fame he had, but influence is another question. In Walter Lippmann's case the pen once again proved less mighty than the sword. Statesmen wanted him on their side, but none so ardently as actually to change his course to get him there. Would the world be any different today if he had not scribbled away at his column for thirty-six years? Probably not. He could neither shape history nor change it. For all his eminence, for all his reputed power during his lifetime, in the end one thinks of Lippmann much in the way that Henry James thought of Hyacinth Robinson and the other characters in *The Princess Casamassima,* toward the close of which James wrote: "The figures on the chessboard were still the passions and jealousies and superstitions of man, and thus position with regard to each other at any given moment could be of interest only to the grim invisible fates who played the game—who sat, through the ages, bow-backed over the table."

And yet, even in spite of those grim invisible fates, one must allow Lippmann a measure of admiration. Apart perhaps only from Raymond Aron, he was the last man to believe that he could direct the tumultuous traffic of contemporary history through the sheer force of his intelligence. There was hubris in the very attempt—how often he was wrong, how little it availed him when he was right, proves that. Yet there was also a certain grandeur in the attempt. Today, when public discourse has become thoroughly politicized, the loss of even the pretense of disinterestedness is a serious one. Wrong though Walter Lippmann often was, vain though he could be of his opinions, he did believe in the importance of unaffiliated intelligence in human affairs. Now that he is gone, and gone unreplaced in American journalism, even that belief is in doubt, and the world in consequence is not a cheerier place.

Times Literary Supplement 1981

Henry James: Assailed by the Perceptions

AFTER PROLONGED ENGAGEMENT with the works of Henry James, one not uncommonly discovers oneself attempting to strike off lovely looping sentences, sentences that seem to unravel without themselves *quite* becoming unraveled, pausing, immitigably, for the oddest adverbial interpositions, pausing again, mitigably, for the most dazzlingly elaborate metaphors, sentences that are dipped, even drenched, in the most delicious irony, yet, for all this oh-so-fragile verbal freight, churn merrily along their way, still full of steam and cadence, to close on some slightly oblique but nonetheless utterly deft perception. I parody, but after reading the four volumes of the *Henry James Letters,* who wouldn't? The Henry James prose style, though surely no disease, is nevertheless highly communicable. In his day anyone long exposed to Henry James seemed to pick up the Jamesian prose vibrations. Among his conscious imitators were the journalist Morton Fullerton and the belletrist Percy Lubbock. Even James's last typist-secretary, Miss Theodora Bosanquet, in her slender volume *Henry James at Work* reeled off a number of very James-like sentences. James himself in the end became implacably Jamesian. Miss Bosanquet reports: "By 1909, when the play [*The Outcry*] was written, the men and women of Henry James could talk only in the manner of their creator."

Love it or loathe it, the late style of Henry James is *sui generis*. It is also the great issue in James's career as an artist. Simply formulated, the issue is this: Is the late style of Henry James, more than a bit of a muchness, altogether too much? Would James have done better to have stayed with the elegant yet still not so insistently parenthetical style of, say, *The Portrait of a Lady?* Not to put too delicate a point on it, Did Henry James cut it too fine? At the outset, this much can be said with confidence: No one ever wrote English prose as Henry James did and no one ever will again. Other writers have made a firm impress with a distinctive style. In this century, Ezra Pound, Wyndham Lewis, Ernest Hemingway, wrote English prose each in his own distinctive way, yet in every case the style was an invention, a work of artifice. But Henry James's style was nothing of the sort. James wrote as he thought and thought as he wrote—between his mind and his pen there appears to have been no slack whatsoever. Buffon's famous formulation, *le style est l'homme même,* for once really does seem to apply; between Henry James the man and Henry James the writer the congruence was complete.

Strong evidence for this assertion is to be found in the way Henry James spoke. It was Buffon (again) who said: "Those who write as they speak, even though they speak well, write badly." But James, in a reversal on Buffon, seems often to have attempted to speak as he wrote. The results could be, to put it softly, immensely inconvenient. "He was a great hesitater, you know, the greatest of hesitaters," recalled Max Beerbohm, who was a great James parodist, you know, the greatest of James parodists. After Edith Wharton introduced James to Finley Peter Dunne, the creator of Mr. Dooley, Dunne commented: "What a pity it takes him so long to say anything. Everything he said was splendid but I felt like telling him all the time: 'Just 'pit it right up into Popper's hand.' " Ford Madox Ford once described hearing James speaking to his, Ford's, housemaid outside the window of his study, "going on and on interminably . . . with the effect of a long murmuring of bees."

But to the people who adored James, his hesitations, his parentheses, his circumgyrations, held their own fascination. Edith Wharton, who adored and admired James, wrote of his conversation:

> To James's intimates, however, these elaborate hesitations, far from being an obstacle, were like a cobweb bridge flung from his mind to theirs, an invisible passage over which one knew that silver-footed ironies, veiled jokes, tiptoe malices, were stealing to explode a huge laugh at one's feet. This moment of suspense, in which there was time to watch the forces of malice and merriment assembling over the mobile landscape of his face, was perhaps the rarest of all in the unique experience of a talk with Henry James.

Such, then, was Henry James the talker, at least late in his life. But as James's talk grew more involuted, trying at times even the patience of admirers such as Edith Wharton, so, in middle age, did his prose style grow more intricate. One explanation sometimes put forth for the increasing complexity of James's style is the advent in his life of the typewriter. In 1896, when James was fifty-three, he developed writer's cramp, in response to which he called upon the services of a typist, to whom he dictated his books, journalism, and all but his most private correspondence. For the rest of his days he continued to avail himself of a typist. "If I could only write as I might talk," James began a sentence to his brother when both were young men and Henry felt the rush of impressions upon him, a rush whose current was too strong for his pen to keep pace with. Now, though, with a typist at the ready, he was able to "talk" his writing.

Talk flows more easily than penmanship, or even than typewritermanship, assuming the author himself at the typewriter. The natural fatigue of fingers and wrist that cause one when

writing or typing to wish to come to the end of a sentence
disappears when one talks one's writing. Talk rolls and flows,
lasting quite as long as breath; and even the need for breath
may be satisfied by a semicolon stop, after which one may roll
on and on. Although James frequently excused himself to his
correspondents for writing in "Remingtonese," he doubtless
greatly enjoyed dictating to a typist, for talking his writing
gave full freedom to his impulse to qualify, his hyper-subtlety,
his need for utmost clarity, and his endless pursuit of nuance.
Yet allowing for all that dictating his books permitted James,
one must go on to allow for James's own abiding love of complexity per se. "I glory in the piling up of complications of
every sort," James once told his niece, adding, "If I could pro-
nounce the name James in any different or more elaborate way
I should be in favor of doing so." Writing by dictation did not
so much change Henry James's style as give full vent to it.

Whence derived this love of complexity in Henry James?
After one allows for his high intelligence, his susceptibility to
impressions, his verbal gifts, one still hasn't accounted for James's
love of complexity. One can only begin to do so by gaining
some elementary sense of that remarkable machine, the mind
of Henry James. It was a mind of rare receptivity. Of James,
Ethel Coburn Mayne wrote: "I have never beheld, for my part,
any creature who struck me as to his degree assailed by the
perceptions." Begin, then, with a mind "assailed by the perceptions" (a very Jamesian-sounding phrase), and now add T. S.
Eliot's notion that Henry James "had a mind so fine no idea
could violate it." Please note that Eliot wrote not "penetrate"
but "violate." James could handle general ideas with considerable facility, and he could do so from a fairly early age, as his
youthful letters show. It happens that general ideas were not
what interested him; richer, more serious truths, for Henry
James, were to be discovered elsewhere. Eliot, who thought
James "the most intelligent man of his generation," had James
very much in mind when he wrote that "instead of thinking

without our feelings [as James did] . . . we corrupt our feelings with ideas." We are talking here about sensibility, that ill-defined and perhaps indefinable quality whose constituent elements are feelings, perceptions, refinement, and taste, for Henry James's was pre-eminently a mind dominated by sensibility, and such a mind, itself fine-grained, tends toward shadings, subtleties, nuances, complexity.

George Santayana, whose mind resided in this same realm of sensibility, recorded another aspect of Henry James in his autobiography. Santayana had met James only once, when James was already an older man. Logan Pearsall Smith and his sister Mary Berenson had arranged the meeting. Of James, Santayana wrote:

> Those were his last years and I never saw him again. Neverthe-less in that one interview he made me feel more at home and better understood than his brother William ever had done in the long years of our acquaintance. Henry was calm, he liked to see things as they are, and be free afterwards to imagine how they might have been. We talked about different countries as places of residence. He was of course subtle and bland, appre-ciative of all points of view, and amused at their limitations.

What a telling formulation—"appreciative of all points of view, and amused at their limitations"—and what it tells is a very great deal about James's simultaneous interest in and detach-ment from life. That Santayana spotted this quality in Henry James is not so surprising. It takes one, as they say, to know one.

What was Henry James's own point of view, and in what ways did this point of view contribute to his penchant for com-plexity? James's nationality—or, more precisely, his lack of nationality—is significant here. It was T. S. Eliot who remarked: "I do not suppose that anyone who is not an American can *properly* appreciate James." Yet it was Eliot who, apropos of

James, noted: "It is the final perfection, the consummation of an American to become, not an Englishman, but a European—something which no born European, no person of any European nationality, can become." This is of course exactly what James did do—turn himself into a European, but of no known country. He penetrated ample segments of three European cultures: English, French, and Italian. He walked about with two full languages in his hand; his command of French appears to have been that of a native speaker. Miss Bosanquet says that James "was never really English or American or even Cosmopolitan." Although he became a British citizen at the close of his life, Henry James was, as an artist of sensibility, supra-national. As such, his point of view was never that of an American or Englishman merely; it was above and beyond that. His was the point of view of the pure artist.

But finally Henry James required a complex, fine-textured style because he had a complex, fine-textured mind. One of the many pleasures of reading through Leon Edel's handsomely produced, intelligently edited, chronologically arranged four volumes of the *Henry James Letters* is in witnessing the mind of James grow more complex and more finely textured. Not that this took very long. Henry James was very smart very young. He had the advantage of having been born into a cultivated family, whose father was freed, by his own father's commercial cunning, from the responsibility of having to earn a living. Henry James, Sr., traveled Europe with his family in tow, and his children took a goodly portion of their early schooling in Paris, Geneva, London, and Bonn. Henry was never a superior student; future artists often aren't. He went at things in his own way, and grew up mentally storing his sensations, accruing his impressions, perpetually sharpening his observational powers. He had another advantage: he knew early that he wanted to be a writer. In this line he was fiercely, unrelentingly ambitious. One can say with fair confidence that every important decision Henry James made in his life—to live in Europe, never to marry, to move out of and then later back into London—was a decision dictated above all by the needs of his art. Complicated though life may have seemed through the eyes of Henry James, in this wise at least it was simple—art, his art, came first.

When Henry James was a small boy one of his tutors could make out no special aptitudes in him, and could commend him only on a pleasing translation into English of some of the fables of La Fontaine. Never much good at games, Henry James was nonetheless from an early age an exceptional verbal athlete. His youthful letters show a boy who could play wonderfully with language, tossing it about, using it ironically, dotting in the occasional French phrase, achieving sweet comic effects. Thus, at age seventeen, toward the close of a letter to his boyhood friend Thomas Sergeant Perry, James writes: "According to my usual habit, having fully satisfied my egotism, I turn to humbler themes. Pray how may *you* be?" He is well on his way, as he might put it, to "taking possession" of the English language. At twenty, once more writing to Thomas Sergeant Perry, James describes listening in church to a hell and damnation preacher and remarks upon how the day of such men is done. "The brimstone fizzles up in the pulpit but fades away into the musk and cologne water in the pews." That is pretty damn good, and James knows it was sufficiently to joke about it, for after this line, in parentheses, he notes: "(Don't it strike you that I am very epigrammatic?)"

I referred to Henry James as an exceptional verbal athlete, by which I mean someone who can really play the language, wringing a wide variety of effects from it, ranging over a vast field of moods, registering the most subtle modulations. The verbal athletes are the great natural writers: they have power over the language, and consciousness of this power, and joy in the consciousness. For them writing is a species of intellectual play; they do not grumble about its difficulties, but turn to it with expectant pleasure. Because they take such pleasure in composition, they are generally highly fertile in their creation. In English the great verbal athletes, in my view, have been Chaucer, Sir Thomas Browne, Shakespeare, Dryden, Pope, Sterne, Dickens, James Joyce, and (a single foreigner) Vladimir Nabokov. The special quality in all of these writers is the joy that one can sense their own writing must have given them. Henry James is of their number.

One of the several delights of the *Henry James Letters* is the opportunity it provides to watch James the verbal artist in performance. Letters are form free, and under but a single constraint—not to be dull. Over four volumes, Henry James's letters rarely are. He more than once describes them as "mere gracious twaddle." True, they are sometimes twaddle; true, they are never less than gracious; but they are never "mere." Attention must be paid to them at all times, for no letter is without its fine touch, however pedestrian the subject. Describing poor weather in Rome to his mother, James writes: "Rain in Rome brings out the dirt as darkness does a photographer's negative. . . ." Or of walking through the Louvre with Emerson, James, not yet thirty years old, remarks: "His perception of art is not, I think, naturally keen; and Concord can't have done much to quicken it." Or this one-sentence description of Mrs. William Morris, favorite subject of Rossetti, whom James first encounters at age twenty-six:

> Imagine a tall lean woman in a long dress of some dead purple stuff, guiltless of hoops (or of anything else, I should say), with a mass of crisp black hair heaped into great wavy projections on each of her temples, a thin pale face, a pair of strange sad, deep, dark Swinburnish eyes, with great thick black oblique brows, joined in the middle and tucking themselves away under her hair, a mouth like the "Oriana" in our illustrated Tennyson, a long neck, without any collar, and in lieu thereof some dozen strings of outlandish beads—in fine Complete.

In Rome for the first time, he reports back that he has seen "the Tiber hurrying along as swift and dirty as history." The mind of the young Henry James swarms with impressions, emotions, and sensations, observations, insights, and fine formulations. Yet to his brother William he writes: "I never manage to write but a very small fraction of what has originally occurred to me." In this same letter, lauding the energy of Michelangelo ("energy—positiveness—courage,—call it what you will"), he notes that this energy alone marks the true man of action in art and disjoins the artist from the critic. Could Henry James have already been thinking of himself when he made this observation? It would scarcely be surprising if he had.

Nothing improves the style like actually having subjects to expand it upon. Reading through the first volume of the *Henry James Letters,* one sometimes feels that the problem presented to Henry James by America was that it didn't sufficiently stimulate the artist in him; the young Henry James in America resembles nothing quite so much as a boy who has mastered the higher calculus forced to attend a school where his classmates are working away at addition and subtraction. "Try to be a young man upon whom nothing is lost" runs a well-known James quotation. If ever there was such a young man, he was Henry James. At the age of twenty-two he wrote a review of *Essays in Criticism* that the book's author, Matthew Arnold, praised. In his middle twenties he could meet and take the correct measure of such men as Mark Pattison ("a desiccated old scholar, torpid even to incivility with too much learning") and John Ruskin (who "has been scared back by the grim face of reality into the world of unreason and illusion, and . . . wanders there without a compass and a guide—or any light save the fitful flashes of his beautiful genius"). When he meets George Eliot—"this great horse-faced blue-stocking"—he knows, at the age of twenty-six, that he has met the real thing: "Altogether, she has a larger circumference than any woman I have ever seen." This notion of the circumference of a human being is one that recurs in James; later, in his early thirties, he will remark that he is able intellectually to see all around Flaubert. Once again, like a superior athlete, James needed always freshly to test himself—not his muscles, of course, but his mind—and America in the 1870s simply did not offer a gymnasium well enough equipped to provide him with the kind of literary workout he required.

We know from Leon Edel's five-volume biography of Henry James about James as a dutiful and loving son and as the best of good brothers; from the same splendid biography we know, in careful detail, the itinerary and chronology of James's life. The *Henry James Letters* add the dimension of allowing a sustained look at James's mind and style as it developed over a lifetime. Although more than 2,300 pages, Professor Edel's four volumes of the *Henry James Letters* are very far from all the letters James wrote. These volumes constitute a selection of James's letters, chosen, as Leon Edel reports, "either because they are documentary, throw light on character or personality, or furnish a picture of family background." Professor Edel adds that he has used "literary content" as his chief criterion in making his selection, with an emphasis on those letters that reveal Henry James the artist and professional writer.

Over a long career as a biographer and editor, Leon Edel has served Henry James extremely well. Certainly he has done an admirable job with the *Henry James Letters*. As editor, he has been self-effacing, writing short and always helpful introductory sections within each of the four volumes. He has chosen the letters so that the redundancy factor from letter to letter is very low. He has permitted none of the barbed wire of modern scholarly apparatus to be erected around the text of the letters. His editorial footnotes are minimal, brief, helpfully explanatory. He has wisely left intact snobbish remarks and anti-Semitic allusions. In almost every other way above his social class, in this latter respect James was, alas, very much a member of his social class—no, none of his best friends was Jewish—though with the passing of years the number of these allusions lessens and lessens and finally disappears.

As for snobbery, in a man of James's abilities the charge is not so easily leveled. A snob is someone who arrogates superiority to himself in order to look down upon others. But what if he is—as James was—truly superior? James's snobbery had nothing to do with social class. The form his snobbery took was to look down upon the thoughtless and unfeeling. While in Rome, still a young man, he wrote that the "sight-seeing barbarians are oppressively numerous"; yet the society of Cambridge, Massachusetts, that of his own social class, he also found wanting, and described its women as "provincial, common and inelegant." But one mustn't understand Henry James too quickly. As soon as one marks him down as a snob, one recalls that in Gilbert Osmond he drew one of the most devastating portraits of a snob in all of literature. One recalls, too, his beautifully imaginative, that is to say his utterly sympathetic, treatment of Hyacinth Robinson and others of the working-class characters in *The Princess Casamassima*. If James was a snob, it was about spiritual decency that he was snobbish, for he looked down upon those who didn't possess it. Desmond MacCarthy once put this same point rather differently when he said that in the fiction of Henry James, only the good are beautiful and there is no shortcut to being good.

But the glory of the *Henry James Letters* is the account its volumes provide of the organization of the life of a major literary artist. I am unaware of the existence in literary annals of anything quite like it. James was a graphomaniac. "I live with my pen in my hand," he wrote, and in his instance this was no mere figure of speech. When he wasn't writing—and he wrote for the better part of his life every morning through lunch (a meal he once referred to as "that matutinal crime") and then often again late at night, seven days a week (in his professional life he abolished the Sabbath)—he was out gathering impressions and experience for still more writing. He knew that "life is effort, unremittingly repeated." He also knew the kind of writer he didn't want to be: "I have a moral horror of seeming to write thin"; and he knew the kind of writer he couldn't be even if he wanted: "a free-going and light-paced enough writer to please the multitude." He viewed himself as a literary artist, but one who had the unshakable temperament of the professional writer. To Charles Eliot Norton, his first editor, then at the *North American Review,* he noted that "experience will cure me of the tendency to waste my substance upon worthless subjects, and teach me to write cheaply about cheap writing." Later, now earning his livelihood as a writer, he complained about "my slow and laborious writing," yet expressed confidence that "with practice I shall learn to write more briskly and naturally."

Had he set his mind to it, Henry James could have been illustrious at two or three different branches of writing. He might easily have made his way—and his name—as a literary critic, and indeed as a young man he wrote to his friend Thomas Sergeant Perry: "Deep in the timorous recesses of my being is a vague desire to do for our dear old English letters and writers *something* of what Sainte-Beuve and the best French critics have done for theirs." Of course, James did write a great deal of literary criticism, much of it by the way and to help earn his livelihood, though as he grew older he wrote—excluding the prefaces to the New York edition of his novels and tales—less and less criticism. What is perhaps not so well known is that Henry James could doubtless have set up as a professional art critic. For an example of how strong he was in this line one has only to read his early letters to his brother William about the great Renaissance masters in Venice, Florence, and Rome. When he later wrote about some of these same painters in the *Nation,* John Ruskin was so moved by it that he told Charles Eliot Norton that he wished James had been appointed Slade Professor of Fine Arts at Cambridge.

"To produce some little exemplary works of art is my narrow and lowly dream," James, not yet thirty, wrote to his friend Grace Norton. There was of course nothing either narrow or lowly about this dream. James hugely admired the amplitude of Balzac's career, after which in some respects he modeled his own, and he tended to think of the literary artist, Napoleonically, as a conquering figure. Before many more years passed he would allow that "my dream is to arrive at the ability to be, in some degree, [England's] moral portrait-painter." As James entered his thirties, these dreams slowly began to come to realization. He took up permanent residence in Europe, first living in Rome, then in Paris, finally settling in London, of which he wrote: "You can live elsewhere *before* you have lived here—but not after."

In Europe he began in earnest his genre-juggling regimen of criticism and journalism while putting his major energies into his fiction. "I find as I grow older," he wrote to William Dean Howells, who throughout his career was so honorably receptive to James's writing, "that the only serious work I can do is in story-spinning." In Paris he came to know Turgenev, whom he admired as an artist but even more as a man: "His whole aspect and temperament [are] of a larger and manlier kind than I have ever yet encountered in a scribbler." His confidence in his own literary abilities grew; so did his critical acumen; and his observations became correspondingly sharper. "Renan is hideous and charming—more hideous even than his photos, and more charming even than his writing." Walter Pater is "far from being as beautiful as his prose." He met Matthew Arnold in Rome, with whom he shared small-talk, and about whom he wrote home: "It remained small-talk and he did nothing to make it *big,* as my youthful dreams would have promised me." The twaddler grew ever more gracious, learning to combine sweet malice with flattery, as when he wrote to his sister-in-law Alice, wife of William, apropos of Josiah Royce: "I shall never, in future, embrace a man's philosophy till I have seen him—and above all till I have seen his wife," adding, "You see that William's own doctrines are by this system very well guaranteed."

"Mysterious and incontrollable (even to one's self) is the growth of one's mind," James wrote not long after his thirtieth birthday. "Little by little, I trust, my abilities will catch up with my ambitions." In point of fact, he would spend the remainder of his life making sure that they, his abilities, did precisely that. But his chief problem would be not his abilities but the ability of his audience to keep up with him. Henry James was neither an avant-garde writer nor a writer out to *épater* his audience in any way. Yet, fairly early in his career, he was presented with the prospect of having to lower his artistic sights in order to hit the large audience that he would have liked but found himself quite unwilling to accommodate. This man so assailed by the perceptions would never in his lifetime find a large audience prepared to be similarly assailed. When Howells suggested that James might give greater pleasure to readers if he would conclude *The American,* which Howells was then serializing in the *Atlantic,* by bringing about a marriage between Christopher Newman and Mme de Cintré, James made clear to Howells that his job was not to provide such ready gratification: "Such readers have a right to their entertainment, but I don't believe it is in me to give them, in a satisfactory way, what they require." Earlier, when he supplied the *New York Tribune* with a regular cultural letter from Paris, James had to be warned against aiming his writing too high. The editor, a decent sort, told James that his letters from Paris were simply too lofty for the readers of a New York newspaper. Once again James gave no serious thought to stooping to conquer. "If my letters have been 'too good,' " he replied, "I am honestly afraid they are the poorest I can do, especially for the money!" All this might come under the rubric of the Integrity Question, except that for Henry James there was no question about it. He believed that it was his job to write as well as he could, while it was his readers' job to keep up with him.

Uncompromising though he was about his art, Henry James nonetheless had his run. The novella *Daisy Miller* brought him a *succès de scandale*. In the late 1870s he seemed perpetually to have a novel being serialized, sometimes simultaneously in English and American magazines. "My fame indeed seems to do very well everywhere," he wrote to Howells, "it is only my fortune that leaves to be desired." Money would never cease to be a problem for him. At this period the bulk of his earnings came from magazine writing. He described his book royalties to Frederick Macmillan, his English publisher, as "the reverse of copious." He had by now moved to London, taking up rooms first on Bolton Street; later he would move to 34 De Vere Gardens, where Robert Browning was his neighbor. To his artistic success was joined a social success: by the 1880s he was dining out among such varied but grand company as Gladstone, Balfour, and Pasteur. Earlier, he ardently wished to become a member of the Reform Club and now succeeded. "*J'y suis, j'y suis*—for ever and a day," he wrote to his father on his admittance. One social season, that of 1878–79, he dined out, by his own reckoning, no fewer than 107 times. Soon enough he would tire of this vigorous social round, struggling as hard to get out of society as some people do to get into it; and at one point, writing to his sister about his yearning for solitude, he noted how he longed for doing "without the need of swallowing inscrutable *entrées* and tugging at the relaxed bell-rope of one's brain for a feeble tinkle of conversation."

With "inscrutable *entrées*" and "the relaxed bell-rope of one's brain" still firmly in mind, perhaps this is the place to insert a point that seems to have escaped generations of Henry James readers but that arises unmistakably in his letters—the point I have in mind is that Henry James was a very funny man. Sometimes his humor will emerge from his phrasings, as when he speaks of his "mountain of 'correspondential' arrears," or describes the room from which he is writing in his bachelor quarters at Rye as "my little old celibatoirean oak parlor," or refers to one Mrs. Greville as part of a family "who form a positive *bouquet* of fools." More often, his comedy derives from his gentle sense of the absurd. After witnessing a ballet in Milan, he writes of "the interminable adventures of a danseuse who went through every possible alternation of human experience on the points of her toes." Sometimes he will stop a sentence to comment on the silliness of words themselves: "I went over to Dover (what a language we have, 'over to Dover'—it would have made Flaubert an even greater maniac than his own did). . . ." Much of Jamesian comedy simply comes from sharp observation: "There are surely bad races and good races, just as there are bad people and good people, and the Irish belong to the category of the impossible" (James himself, of course, came of Irish ancestry.) He can be very funny on the literary manner of the French: "I saw Daudet who is slowly dying and making a book out of it, and Coppée who is slowly living and doing the same." Of Paul Bourget he notes: *"Bourget est tragique—mais est-il sérieux?"* What James called his own "tender chord of perception" turns out to have been threaded with laughter. Here it has to be said that the comic view is at the center of James's vision; and for anyone who cannot comprehend James's comic gifts the works of Henry James figure to remain a hopeless puzzle.

James would have need of his humor along with all his other estimable resources in the years that lay ahead. Although his artistic powers increased, beginning in the 1880s the audience for his work began to dwindle. After *The Portrait of a Lady,* which at least earned critical acclaim, James's next two novels, *The Bostonians* and *The Princess Casamassima,* fell flat, both critically and financially. He now began to find it more and more difficult to write stories to the relatively brief length magazine editors desired. Meanwhile, the commercial success of inferior writers turned him purple with rage. "What you tell me of the success of [Frances Marion] Crawford's last novel sickens and almost paralyzes me," he wrote to Howells. At the same time, doubt about his own prowess began to creep into his letters. "It's always the fault of my things that the head and the trunk are too big and the legs too short." And: "Yes, I reflect too much—or not enough; I don't know which. I ought, that is, to go either much further, or not so far." The demand for his work was reduced to zero—and below zero when a man named Horace Elisha Scudder, Howells's replacement as editor of the *Atlantic*, rejected James's great story "The Pupil." The result was to jolt his confidence severely.

It was now, in 1890, with the hope of achieving "fame and shekels," that Henry James turned to writing for the theater. The story of James's writing for the theater is one of alternating doubts and hopes, oh such towering hopes—hopes that would come rudely crashing down, leaving him spiritually crushed. Leon Edel has provided the definitive account of James's theatrical adventures in the third and fourth volumes of his biography. These adventures culminated with the London production of James's play *Guy Domville*. The audience for the first night of the play—"a brutal mob," as James referred to them in correspondence—"hooted" the play off the stage. At the close of the performance, jeers and catcalls from the gallery were met by applause from James's friends in the audience. When George Alexander, whose company had produced the play and who had himself acted in it, came before the curtain to say that "these discordant notes tonight have hurt me very much" and that if he and his company had failed, they "can only try to deserve your kindness" by doing better in the future, a voice in the gallery shot back: " 'Tain't your fault, guv-'nor, it's a rotten play." One can easily enough imagine James's reaction—and shudder.

What is remarkable about Henry James's experience in writing for the theater is that it marks the first time he was deceived about his own art, or indeed about any art whatsoever. As one reads through James's correspondence, one notices that—despite all the graciousness, despite all the twaddle—the one thing he cannot be merely polite about is art. When sent books by friends or admirers, he duly finds items to praise in them, but at some point in all such letters he shifts gears and turns on the criticism—and the criticism is invariably more persuasive than the praise. The problem, he claims, is that he cannot read a novel without rewriting it as he goes along. "The novel I can *only* read," he writes to Mrs. Humphry Ward, "I can't read at all!" To Howard Sturgis, after subjecting him to a critical workout, he writes: "I am a bad person, really, to expose 'fictitious work' to. . . ."

But it is not only "fictitious work" he is candid about. Some of the funniest letters in the final volume of the *Henry James Letters* are those to the young sculptor Hendrik Andersen, toward whom it is now claimed James had homoerotic feelings. But these feelings, if in fact they existed, did not interfere with James's running critical devastations of Andersen's penchant for creating outsized nude statues. James begins, gently, by hoping that Anderson will soon turn away from such work and toward a *"smaller* masterpiece, the condensed consummate caressed, intensely filled-out thing." But in later letters he refers to Anderson's "great nude army"; and after advising Andersen to try his hand at other subject matter, he writes: "I won't send you any fig-leaves—I need them all myself; besides your ladies' great heaving and straining gentlemen would split them in twain at the end of an hour."

Henry James was fifty-two years old at the time of his theatrical debacle and felt himself completely demoralized. The time had come either to go under or to pick himself up off the floor. In a splendid letter to William Dean Howells, he recounts his condition. The magazine editors no longer want him. "A new generation, that I know not, and mainly prize not, had taken universal possession. The sense of being utterly out of it had weighed me down." He feels he has wasted time, in recent years, because of his theatrical preoccupation, and produced too little. He tells himself: "Produce again—produce; produce better than ever, and all will yet be well." Now, no longer interested in magazine serialization, which has at all events been rendered hopeless by the lack of interest in his work, he decides to turn to the "production of the little *book* pure and simple," the thought of which leaves him serene. And this is precisely what he will do, concentrate his remaining energies on writing the very best books he can. As he will later write to Paul Bourget: "For myself, more than ever, our famous 'Art' is the one refuge and sanatorium." Herewith Henry James enters his major phase.

Henry James's last years are a triumph, but a triumph of a curiously qualified kind. The chief qualification is that he will die, in 1916, not really knowing how triumphant he has been. In a brief span of time, he writes *The Ambassadors, The Wings of the Dove,* and *The Golden Bowl,* the masterpieces of his last years. Yet in 1911, in a letter to Edith Wharton, he refers to *The Golden Bowl* as "the most arduous and thankless task I ever set myself." By "thankless" he means unappreciated. The smallness of his audience, though he pretends otherwise, is forever troubling to him. It wounds him that not even his supremely intelligent brother William thinks well of his late novels, and at one point he ironically promises him that he will someday produce a novel "on the two-and-two-makes-four system," to which his brother's tastes seem to run. He writes as if resigned to being without a large public for his work. He may call the public "a big Booby"; he writes to friends to say that he no longer worries about its indifference to his work or its inability to understand it; still, one feels he should greatly have preferred to have had that big Booby on his side.

"The loneliness of the long-distance artist"—such seems an appropriate caption to the picture presented in the *Henry James Letters* of their author's last years. These are the years of rustification at Lamb House in Rye, Sussex, to which James signed a twenty-one-year lease in 1897. For a man who was a very good friend—"It seems impossible to dislike him," Stephen Crane said. "He is so kind to everybody"—James seems, in his last years, oddly friendless. Part of the reason for this is that he felt himself the last surviving member of the circle around Flaubert, and hence now quite without contemporaries. But in greater part he withdrew more and more within himself. His love of travel grew less, though in 1904 he set out on the trip to the United States that resulted in *The American Scene*. He still made visits and had visitors, but work more than ever consumed him. In these years he became, as he wrote of a character in one of his stories, "a being organized for litera-ture."

Never for a moment did he lose interest in his art. "Nothing, all the same," he wrote to Ford Madox (then) Hueffer, "is ever more interesting to me than the consideration, with those who care and see, or want to, of these bottomless questions of How and Why and Whence and *What*—in connection with the mys-tery of one's craft." Yet he knew that "those who care and see, or want to" are a very small minority. In praising Joseph Con-rad to Edmund Gosse, he could not help adding: "Unhappily, to be very serious and subtle isn't one of the paths to fortune." He received renewed affirmation of this in his own case when the New York edition of his novels and tales, on which he had labored long, flopped financially—"a sort of miniature Ozy-mandias," he called it. He sensed that not even his friends read his work. Miss Bosanquet reports: "He found it safest to assume that nobody read him, and he liked his friends none the worse for their incapacity."

Yet it isn't quite accurate to say that nobody read or under-stood Henry James in his last years. Henry Nash Smith, in a recent work of scholarship, *Democracy and the Novel: Popular Resistance to Classic American Writers,* provides an account of the critical reception of Henry James's mature novels and of their author's reputation that shows a mixed reaction. Scarcely surprisingly, many critics reacted to James's work with irritation of the kind shown by William P. Trent, founding editor of the *Sewanee Review,* who, in a review of *The Awkward Age,* wrote:

> If psychological analysis has to be carried to a point of subtlety considerably beyond any attempted by Shakespeare or Balzac, and if conversations and character analysis are the two poles around which the ellipse of modern fiction is to be drawn—we are willing to commend the novels of today to the careful attention of students of advanced mathematics, and shall content ourselves hereafter with the simple old novelists who were unsophisticated enough to write straight-forward stories.

Others complained that James's novels were too circuitous, too analytic, too laden with psychological suggestion and reticences. Yet a small band of critics—most of them, interestingly, women—did understand what James was getting at; they understood that he had abandoned conventional action in literature in the attempt to get at deeper realities and psychological complexities by tracing events to their secret sources in the heart, there to mine a richer truth about human character than anyone had yet worked. Still, the number of people who understood and appreciated James remained small—and, even though James has long since been picked up for teaching purposes in contemporary universities, it still is small. In the nature of the case, it probably always will be.

"It is art that makes life," Henry James said, and the people who believe this will always adore Henry James as one of the great heroes of art, not only for the art he provided but for the example his own life set. It is all the more gratifying to those of us who think of him thus that, as we now know from his letters, he practiced what he preached—that, in fact, art made life for him. Despite his manifold disappointments, despite the many illnesses of his last years—gout, dark depression, shingles, angina—Henry James never lost his passionate interest in life. Henry Adams, James's contemporary and a man provided with all the advantages life can confer, went sour on life. But not James, who in old age, accounting for his ever freshened interest in life, wrote to Adams: "It's I suppose because I am that queer monster, the artist, an obstinate finality, an inexhaustible sensibility." Henry James is one of those rare writers who does not seem more petty, abject, or repulsive the closer one looks into his life. On the death of his friend Turgenev, James wrote to Edmund Gosse: "Yes, I too like what I read better when I know (and like) the author." The four volumes of the *Henry James Letters* cause one wholeheartedly to concur, with only a slight emendation: the word "like" needs to be changed to "love."

The New Criterion 1984

Is It All Right to Read Somerset Maugham?

*The critic I am waiting for is the one who will explain why, with
all my faults, I have been read for so many years by so many people.*
　　　　　　　　　　　　　　　　　—W. Somerset Maugham

FOUR POWERS govern men: avarice, lust, fear, and
snobbishness." Somerset Maugham didn't write that:
Hilaire Belloc did. But Somerset Maugham, I think
it fair to say, believed it. Avarice, lust, fear, and snobbishness
are Maugham's great subjects; they are everywhere in his work,
as theme, as motive, as background. Small wonder that they
would be, for the same dark quartet—avarice, lust, fear, and
snobbishness—were also the four reigning qualities in Somerset Maugham's own triumphant, lengthy, and finally rather sad
life.

Cyril Connolly once called Somerset Maugham the "last of
the great professional writers." He meant it as an honorific. It
has not always been taken that way. One small step down from
the professional writer is the hack; one large step up is the
artist. A great many more critics have been willing to drop
Maugham a step than have been willing to raise him a step.
Maugham was always highly conscious of this; and one could
string together a quite long necklace composed of the BBs he
shot over his lifetime at highbrow critics, small-public writers,

intellectual-magazine editors, and others who accorded his work less respect than he thought it deserved. "But you must remember the intelligentsia despise me," Maugham in late life told his nephew Robin Maugham. "Take that magazine that's indoors. What's it called? *Encounter?* Well, all the writers on *Encounter* despise me completely. I read it just to find out what's going on and what people are interested in. But I must confess I find it terribly boring." Not the least interesting item in that snippet of conversation is that, whatever his professed views of *Encounter,* Maugham nevertheless subscribed to and read it. He was a man who didn't miss much.

Before considering the quality of Somerset Maugham's writing, the first thing that must be said about him is that he was a very smart man. He was smart about people, absolutely brilliant about their motivations, and nearly a genius at understanding that haziest and most elusive of essential subjects, human nature. He fancied himself a man of few illusions—as don't we all—but in his case he was probably correct to do so. Another word for a man with few illusions is "cynic"; whether it is the correct word is a tangled question. So intent was Maugham on his illusionlessness that he was often called a cynic, a charge he resented. In Oscar Wilde's famous formulation, a cynic is someone "who knows the price of everything and the value of nothing." But Maugham knew both price and value. He also knew that happiness, if it existed, was not for him.

Along with his high intelligence, Maugham had the quality that he himself referred to, in his stories as well as in his autobiographical writings, as character. As Maugham used the term, character has nothing to do with goodness; it is shorn of all moral meaning. Those who have character are not necessarily winning or even particularly likeable. People with character can be quite intelligent, but intelligence alone does not constitute character for Maugham. Instead character is a quality of inner discipline; it comes with having knocked the weakness out of oneself. Having character means that you are someone who cannot be trifled with; you are not negligible; you are a force to be reckoned with; you are serious. Having character may also mean, if you happen to be Somerset Maugham, that no matter how wealthy you are, you sit down at your desk and do your work each morning, and end with a bibliography that includes twenty-eight books of fiction, twelve of nonfiction, and thirty produced plays. "Genius," Maugham wrote to his friend the painter Gerald Kelly, "is a combination of talent and character, but character to a certain extent—I do not know how much, but I believe enormously—can be acquired. . . ." Late in his life he told Desmond MacCarthy that he thought he had more character than brains and more brains than talent.

Somerset Maugham's own character was formed against substantial obstacles: he was orphaned at the age of ten; he had a humiliating stammer; he was a homosexual—this last a fact which he attempted to hide, against which he struggled (going, at one point, so far as to marry and to produce a daughter), and with which he finally came to terms without ever feeling it anything more than a bad card dealt him by life. Much of his early life is recorded in the opening chapters of his novel *Of Human Bondage*. He issued his young hero in that novel, Philip Carey, a clubfoot in place of the stammer life had issued him. But otherwise he recorded fairly accurately the circumstances of his birth in Paris in 1874, where his father, an English lawyer appointed to handle the British embassy's legal affairs, and his mother raised Maugham's three older brothers; and where his mother, who was consumptive, died in childbirth when he was eight, the great and unhealable wound in his, Somerset Maugham's, life. His father died two years later, of cancer of the stomach, and the ten-year-old Maugham was sent to live with his father's only surviving brother, an Anglican clergyman living in the provincial town of Whitstable, and his wife, the childless couple who supplied the models for the arid, unimaginative, and penny-pinching Reverend William and Mrs. Carey in *Of Human Bondage*. Thus first requisite for a writer, an unhappy childhood, was amply met by the young Willie Maugham.

In Ted Morgan's lengthy and very capable biography of Somerset Maugham there occurs a sentence that might be inserted onto the floppy disc of every word-processor-owning biographer of any English writer who went off to school in the late nineteenth or early twentieth century; the sentence reads: "He was small and frail and in poor health, was no good at games, and inhibited by his stammer [this will need to be altered in specific cases], he shrank from his fellow students." Maugham was sent to King's School, in Canterbury. It was not one of the great English public schools; it had no cachet, a point of some interest for the snob Maugham was later to become. The plan was for Maugham, whose youthful intelligence raised him to the top of his class, to win a scholarship to Oxford, and thence to become ordained. Maugham, however, had other plans. From earliest adolescence he had wanted to become a writer.

Maugham was small ("The world," he wrote, "is an entirely different place to a man of five foot seven from what it is to the man of six foot two"), stammering (of his contemporary Arnold Bennett's stammer he noted: "Few knew the distressing sense it gave rise to of a bar to complete contact with other men"), and cheated out of parental love (the only selfless love in the world, he believed, was that of a mother for her child). Although not a Freudian, Maugham would doubtless have agreed with the apothegm of Freud's that has it that the artist forgoes fame, riches, and love for his art, through which he hopes to win fame, riches, and love. The fit, in his own case, was perfect.

From his earliest years Maugham did little that did not bear upon his determination to be a writer. At sixteen, for example, he persuaded his guardian-uncle to permit him to leave King's School to study on his own in Heidelberg, where he would live on the £150 income from his small inheritance. In Heidelberg, he read Schopenhauer and fell under the influence of the plays of Ibsen, a pair that does not exactly qualify as the Abbott and Costello of *fin-de-siècle* European culture. He entered into a homosexual affair. He produced a biography of the composer Meyerbeer, which, when he returned to England, he was unable to get published and subsequently destroyed.

Because he could not own up to his guardian his ambition to be a writer, Maugham, at age eighteen, entered medical school. A lesser-evil choice, medical school at least allowed the young Maugham the freedom of living on his own in London, while granting him a view of the life of the underclasses as seen in the clinics of St. Thomas's teaching hospital in Lambeth Palace Road on the south bank of the Thames. Medicine also provided useful lessons for a would-be writer. In *The Summing Up,* Maugham tells that, when he was unable to discover a certain nerve in the leg of a cadaver in the place his textbook said it would be, he was told by an instructor that the normal is the rarest thing in the world. Maugham in fact never practiced a single day as a physician, yet there is reason to believe he did not regret having gone to medical school. In an essay he later wrote entitled "The Short Story," in which he discussed Chekhov's career as a physician, Maugham noted:

> I have reasons for believing that the training a medical student has to go through is to a writer's benefit. He acquires a knowledge of human nature which is invaluable. He sees it at its best and at its worst. When people are ill, when they are afraid, they discard the mask which they wear in health. The doctor sees them as they really are, selfish, hard, grasping, cowardly; but brave too, generous, kindly and good. He is tolerant of their frailties, awed by their virtues.

Somerset Maugham never worked at any other job but that of writer over the course of his ninety-one years. He never descended to journalism, or worked as a publisher's reader, or took on literary or any other kind of odd jobs. He lived on his £150, not an impressive sum even then. Nor did success come quickly. He published a first novel, *Liza of Lambeth*, at twenty-three, which, though it garnered decent reviews, earned no serious income. He had book-length manuscripts rejected. He wrote plays that were produced but enjoyed only brief runs and others that were not produced at all. At one point he moved to Paris, where he lived, frugally, among English and American expatriate writers and painters, among whom was the businesslike Arnold Bennett, who suggested that Maugham share a mistress with him and a third party. But there was nothing of the bohemian about Maugham, who was an Edwardian under and atop the skin and who, though he took a serious interest in the avant-garde art of his day, wished to avoid the garret style of life that often produced it. It was only in 1907, at the age of thirty-three, that Maugham was able to strike the success gong with a comedy of manners entitled *Lady Frederick,* which ran for 442 performances in London. The music of that gong was something he had longed to hear, for Maugham was a money writer; as he would later aver, "Money was like a sixth sense without which you could not make the most of the other five." Henceforth all that he wrote turned to gold, piles and piles of gold.

Granted that accounting may be no proper part of literary criticism, the amounts of money Somerset Maugham earned by his pen are too impressive to be ignored. As a successful playwright, Ted Morgan asserts, Maugham "bridged the quarter century between Oscar Wilde and Noël Coward," which is chronologically accurate but leaves Shaw out of reckoning. Nonetheless, during these years Maugham always had a play or two running in London and New York theaters and at one point had four plays running concurrently in London's West End. (He generally took no more than three or four weeks to write a play.) No writer to this day has had more novels, stories, and plays turned into movies. There have thus far been two films made of *Of Human Bondage* and two of *The Razor's Edge*. The story "Rain," with its various stage and film adaptions, is said to have earned him more than $1 million in royalties. He was paid a dollar a word for his stories. *The Razor's Edge* (1944) sold 507,000 copies its first month in print; Doubleday's first printing for *Then and Now* (1946), a historical novel about Machiavelli, was 825,000 copies. Outside his study, he bought impressionist paintings, and at a time when one could still do so cheaply. What is more—or, more precisely, what made more—he was sensible enough to turn over much of this money to an astute San Francisco stockbroker named Bert Alanson, who doubled and redoubled it.

The importance of money to Maugham can scarcely be over-emphasized. He claimed it gave him independence, which it did, and allowed him to live exactly as he pleased, which was grandly. In 1926 he bought the house on Cap Ferrat, on the French Riviera, that King Leopold had originally built for his confessor; overlooking the bay of Villefranche, near Nice and Monte Carlo, it included eight acres of land and under Maugham's ownership had a staff of thirteen servants (and four dachshunds). Money also gave him entrée to smart society, which, if one may say so, tended to be a good deal smarter then than it is nowadays (one might meet there Winston Churchill or Moura Budberg or Max Beerbohm). While widening his social horizons, money broadened his subject matter; it made him worldly in a way that a writer who struggles ceaselessly for a living can never quite hope to be. As the Maughamish character named Ashenden says in the story entitled "Guilia Lazzari," "just as the advantage of culture is that it enables you to talk nonsense with distinction, so the habit of luxury allows you to regard its frills and furbelows with a proper contumely."

Not, one hastens to add, that Maugham ever showed anything faintly resembling contumely toward luxury, or smart society, or money and its many emoluments. There were in fact two quite distinct Somerset Maughams: there was the Maugham who appears as the narrator of so many of the stories and of *Cakes and Ale* and *The Razor's Edge,* sometimes under his own name and sometimes under the name Ashenden; and there was the Maugham who lived outside the novels and stories. The first Maugham is one of the second Maugham's most impressive creations. He is every inch the man of the world, a cool hand, a clear head, an observer of philosophical temper who has seen everything and is shocked by nothing. He is the sympathetic gentleman in the beautifully made suit to whom, at the club over brandy and soda, you confess that you harbor murderous thoughts about your wife or have been the cause of your business partner's death or have been sleeping with your dearest friend's mistress. He is of the world yet slightly above it, detached yet not devoid of feeling, a man who holds out the prospect of understanding unaccompanied by harsh judgment.

Then there was the other, the off-the-page Maugham. He was a man never quite comfortable in his own skin, displeased about being short, frustrated and rendered shy by his stammer, endlessly worried about the world's knowing that he was a homosexual. This was the man who could brilliantly mock snobbery in his books yet could never rise above it in his life, so that his biographer could accurately write: "There were four categories of persons who had easy access to the Mauresque [Villa Mauresque was the name of Maugham's estate on Cap Ferrat]: the titled, the wealthy, the famous, and attractive young men." This Maugham could be bitter—so dangerous in repartee that Elizabeth, queen of England, once expressed nervousness about being seated next to him at dinner—remorseless in getting his own way, and utterly suspicious of other people's motives in their dealings with him. This was a tough, an often mean, an always difficult man who came by his dark views through dark experience.

A grave mistake would be to think this second Somerset

Maugham in any wise a fool—after all, it was he who created the first Somerset Maugham. If he was acute at enunciating truths about other people, he was no less acute at understanding himself. In the second of the brief chapters of *The Summing Up,* for example, he can write: "I have been attached, deeply attached, to a few people; but I have been interested in men in general not for their own sakes, but for the sake of my work." That is a statement of remarkable candor about the ruthlessness of writers in pursuit of material. But you have to keep an eye out for the old fraud in him. At the end of the paragraph from which I have just quoted, a paragraph in which he recounts how ordinary people are more interesting to the writer than celebrated ones, for the former's "idiosyncrasies have had more chance to develop in the limited circle of their activity," he concludes on what I take to be a straight-out lie: "For my part I would much sooner spend a month on a desert island with a veterinary surgeon than with a prime minister." Still, the candor enormously outweighs the fraudulence, and I can think of no other modern writer with the introspection and courage to write a passage such as the following:

> My sympathies are limited. I can only be myself, and partly by nature, partly by the circumstances of my life, it is a partial self. I am not a social person. I cannot get drunk and feel a great love for my fellow-men. Convivial amusement has always somewhat bored me. . . . I do not much like being touched and I have always to make a slight effort over myself not to draw away when someone links his arm in mine. I can never forget myself. . . . Though I have been in love a good many times I have never experienced the bliss of requited love. I know that this is the best thing that life can offer and it is a thing that almost all men, though perhaps only for a short time, have enjoyed. I have most loved people who cared little or nothing for me and when people have loved me I have been embarrassed. . . . I have been jealous of my independence. I am incapable of complete surrender. And so, never having felt some of the fundamental emo-

tions of normal men, it is impossible that my work should have
the intimacy, the broad human touch and the animal serenity
which the greatest writers alone can give.

Although Maugham had married and had a daughter—his
wife, with whom he shared a bitter divorce, was Syrie Well-
come Maugham; she went on to become a rather famous interior decorator—he was in the final if not in the first analysis a
homosexual. "You see," his nephew Robin Maugham reports
him as saying, in *Conversations with Willie,* "I was a quarter
normal and three-quarters queer, but I tried to persuade myself
it was the other way round. That was my greatest mistake."
The central love affair of Maugham's life was with a very handsome and very alcoholic young man named Gerald Haxton,
who served as his general factotum and who, while on the
sauce, specialized in making hideously embarrassing scenes.
Theirs was an affair in the Maughamian mode, one very much
of human bondage, with each man bound to the other without
either one deriving anything like prolonged contentment from
it.

Maugham was resigned to his homosexuality. "One day,"
Robin Maugham reports him saying, "it will be realized that
there are people who are *born* homosexual or bisexual and that
there is nothing whatever they can do about it." But he was
never very pleased about his homosexuality. What he had to
say on the subject of homosexuality was not something you
would care to read aloud on Christopher Street at next year's,
or any other year's, Gay Alliance parade. In a brilliant essay on
El Greco toward the close of *Don Fernando,* his book about
Spanish culture in its golden age, he surmised that El Greco,
an artist he much admired, was himself a homosexual. He went
on to catalogue what he, Maugham, took to be the limitations
of homosexuals in the arts:

> Now it cannot be denied that the homosexual has a narrower
> outlook on the world than the normal man. In certain respects

the natural responses of the species are denied to him. Some at least of the broad and typical human emotions he can never experience. However subtly he sees life he cannot see it whole. If it were not for the perplexing *Sonnets* I should say that the homosexual can never reach the supreme heights of genius.

A paragraph later he continued:

I should say that a distinctive trait of the homosexual is a lack of deep seriousness over certain things that normal men take seriously. This ranges from an inane flippancy to a sardonic humour. He has a wilfulness that attaches importance to things that most men find trivial and on the other hand regards cynically the subjects which the common opinion of mankind has held essential to its spiritual welfare. He has a lively sense of beauty, but is apt to see beauty especially in decoration. He loves luxury and attaches peculiar value to elegance. He is emotional, but fantastic. He is vain, loquacious, witty and theatrical. With his keen insight and quick sensibility he can pierce the depths, but in his innate frivolity he fetches up from them not a priceless jewel but a tinsel ornament. He has small power of invention, but a wonderful gift for delightful embroidery. He has vitality, brilliance, but seldom strength. He stands on the bank, aloof and ironical, and watches the river of life flow on. He is persuaded that opinion is no more than prejudice. . . .

As Maugham surmised that El Greco was a homosexual, so one can only surmise that, in putting together this impressive catalogue, Maugham, not publicly known to his readers as a homosexual, was cunningly commenting on the limitations of his own art. Does it make any sense to consider Maugham essentially a homosexual writer—a figure, if you will, in Gay Lit? I, for one, do not think it does. True, in his fiction he tended to be hard on women, but certainly no harder than that figure from Hetero Lit, Norman Mailer. He did not write convincingly about family life—his one attempt at doing so, inserting the family of Athelny Thorpe at the close of *Of Human Bondage,* reads like a poor parody of Dickens—but then neither did Flaubert. More important, unlike so many other modern homosexual writers, from E. M. Forster to Genet to Gore Vidal, Maugham was altogether apolitical; he never sold his artistic birthright, as in another context Max Beerbohm once said of John Galsworthy, for "a pot of message." No, Somerset Maugham was not a homosexual writer but instead that quite different thing, a writer who happened to be a homosexual.

Maugham thought of himself, interestingly, as a professional humorist, which in his stories he calls himself more than a few times, and in one of his Ashenden stories, "The Traitor," he speaks of "the pleasant comedy of life." He meant this, I believe, in the sense in which one speaks of the human comedy. He put his case in *The Summing Up,* where he wrote: "A sense of humour leads you to take pleasure in the discrepancies of human nature; it leads you to mistrust great professions and look for the unworthy motive that they conceal; the disparity between appearance and reality diverts you and you are apt when you cannot find it to create it." If the humorist sometimes misses truth, beauty, and goodness, he is nonetheless tolerant, for he has no interest in moralizing but is "content to understand; and it is true that to understand is to pity and forgive."

While there was nothing of the aesthete about Maugham, nor any aesthetic difficulty about his work, few modern writers have been clearer about their own aesthetic program and, with the exception of Paul Valéry and Henry James, perhaps none has thought more trenchantly about the aesthetic questions raised by literary creation. Maugham thought, for example, that the artist is not justified in wishing to be judged by his intention; for him the crucial moment in the aesthetic transaction is that of communication—that moment when the work of art addresses the viewer or listener or reader. He thought talent to be made up of a natural aptitude for creation combined with a strong outlook on life shorn of the prejudices of the current day. "Sometimes," he wrote in *Don Fernando,* "there will be found a man who has this facility for writing to an extraordinary degree and to this joins an outlook on life which is not only peculiar to himself, but appeals to all men, and then he will be called a genius." Once, when asked the secrets of his own craft by a Chinese professor, he replied: "I know only two. One is to have common sense and the other is to stick to the point."

Maugham may also have been among the best-read of modern writers. He never traveled any distance without a laundry bag filled with books, and he read, as one would imagine, with penetration. He adored the Russian novelists and admired Stendhal. The French called him the English Maupassant, which pleased him greatly. He thought Kipling and Chekhov, along with Maupassant, the ablest of the world's short-story writers. He had mixed feelings about Henry James, on the one hand thinking him amusingly absurd and finding himself unable to believe in the motivations of the characters in his fiction and on the other hand remarking, in his essay "Some Novelists I Have Known": "The fact remains that those last novels of his, notwithstanding their unreality, make all other novels, except the very best, unreadable." But generally he expressed his own personal preference for the straightforward over the ornate, for among prose writers he preferred Dryden and Hazlitt and Arnold and Cardinal Newman over Dr. Johnson and De Quincey and Carlyle and Pater. Here he joined the majority in preferring those who are most like himself.

One cannot read much in Maugham without recognizing that his own straightforward prose style came into being as a result of conscious artistry. He was a careful student of prose, which he wrote about extremely well in an essay on Edmund Burke as well as in *Don Fernando* and in *The Summing Up.* As a beginning novelist, he wrote under the influence of Pater and Oscar Wilde and other of the late Victorian decorative-prose stylists. He soon enough realized he had no talent in this line and set out to write more plainly, taking Swift as his model. (In later life he claimed he would have done better to have studied Dryden.) His own gifts, he recognized, were not poetical: lyricism was not his cup of tea, nor charming metaphors and cogent similes his sugar and milk. What he did have was clarity, logic, and an appreciation for euphonic language. On the subject of the formation of his own prose style, he wrote: "I knew that I should never write as well as I could wish, but I thought with pains I could arrive at writing as well as my natural defects allowed. On taking thought it seemed to me that I must aim at lucidity, simplicity and euphony."

Maugham's was a strong and a serviceable style. His prose tended to be more elegant when he was writing essays than when he was writing novels and stories. He himself remarked, in his essay on Edmund Burke's prose, that the most settled styles in the history of English prose belong to essayists, divines, and historians, and that too settled—that is, too polished—a style might even redound to the disadvantage of the writer of fiction, who is primarily a teller of stories and whose prose needs to remain supple enough to capture so many shades of mood and to insinuate itself into the thoughts of various and often vastly different characters. "But perhaps it is enough if the novelist contents himself with avoiding the grosser errors of grammar," Maugham wrote, "for no one can have considered this matter without being struck by the significant and surprising fact that the four greatest novelists the world has seen, Tolstoi, Balzac, Dostoyevsky and Dickens, wrote their respective languages very carelessly. . . ." Here one can add the name Dreiser, the prose in whose powerful novels on occasion didn't even achieve the level of carelessness.

Not that Maugham was ever close to being in the Dreiser class. (Dreiser himself, truth to tell, wasn't that often in the Dreiser class.) I have recently read what must amount to some four thousand pages of Maugham's prose and found myself seldom brought up by infelicities. In his earlier work he occasionally lapses into cliché; more than once he refers to the heart of one of his characters, in the heat of passion, going "pit-a-pat," when, for such a phrase, once is at least ten times too often. In *Of Human Bondage,* Sally Thorpe, the Dickensian sugar-puss heroine whom Philip Carey eventually marries, says to Carey, "You're an old silly, that's what you are," which causes one to blush, not for Carey but for Maugham. In the same book Mildred Rogers, the waitress who has enthralled Carey, is described as "weak as a rat," when rats are not generally thought weak at all, but rather sinewy and tenacious. Finally in *The Razor's Edge* Maugham, who believed that a writer of one nation has little chance of understanding the people of another nation, has his male American characters use the words "gosh" and "gee" more often than Oogie Pringle on the old *A Date with Judy* radio show. Still, for roughly four thousand pages, that isn't bad.

As a stylist what Maugham had was lucidity, fluency, and economy. In a sheer storyteller, which is what he was, these are the paramount qualities. Often his stories seem almost to tell themselves; such ostensible artlessness, of course, can only be conferred through the exercise of high art. Maugham wrote every morning from 9:45 to 12:45, and he wrote quickly and revised little. He received no editing from his publishers, Heinemann's in England and Doubleday in the United States, for he wanted none. As an author he was the equivalent of what in sports is known as a franchise player; with his huge sales, he could make a publishing house singlehandedly, and publishers know not to fool with success of the kind such an author brings. In 1935, though, that curious figure Eddie Marsh, who had been a private secretary to Churchill, Asquith, and Joseph Chamberlain, offered to inspect Maugham's manuscripts for lapses in precision and errors in usage, and he did so for fourteen of Maugham's books (until his, Marsh's, death in 1953), for which Maugham felt great gratitude. Maugham learned a good deal from Marsh, as he seemed to learn from everyone and everything, and as he grew older his prose grew more confident and more precise.

As a writer of fiction, Maugham had Balzacian ambitions. He believed an important writer needs to produce an ample body of work, and deserves to be judged by the best from that body. He claimed to have small powers of imagination, which caused him to fall back on industry to make up for it. "I have had one advantage," he wrote, "I have never wanted a subject. I have always had more stories in my head than I ever had time to write." He may not have had large powers of imagination, but his powers of observation were of the first order. He plagiarized from life, frequently putting people he knew or had heard about into his stories and novels. (As a result of his writing many stories acquired in his travels in the Malay States, he was said to be considered very much non grata in the British clubs and outposts there.) "I have painted easel pictures," he wrote, "not frescoes." But when he was done he could fill many a gallery.

Why did Maugham write so much? Because, he might have answered, writing is what a writer is supposed to do, and besides, what else was he, who was rather easily bored, to do with his mornings? While at a certain point he no longer needed the money his pen brought in—a pen designed specifically for him, incidentally, with a thick collar that permitted a surer grasp—most assuredly he liked to see it come cascading in. He had, as the small businessmen used to put it, a high nut, with the expenses of maintaining the princely establishment that was Villa Mauresque, paying (always resentfully) alimony to his wife, and traveling in the grand style; doubtless, too, as someone whose young manhood was perforce lived frugally, he had no wish as a middle-aged and older man to dip into interest. But above all he appears to have written as much as he did because he loved to write, to go about with the characters from a story in his head, to work through the technical details of composition, to attempt to bring it all off as nearly perfect as possible. Whatever his motives, working day after day he produced an immense body of writing, although not all of it was of even quality and some of it was pretty poor stuff.

Enter the critics. "This novel, as unmitigated a specimen of fictional drivel as has appeared under respectable authorship within living memory, might be fitly dismissed as the latest triumph of servant-girl's literature were it not for the phenomenal value that still attaches to Maugham's name among modern authors." That explosive sentence is the opening line from a 1943 review by Morton Dauwen Zabel in the *Nation* of Maugham's novel *Up at the Villa*. In its anger this review does not drop off precipitously from this first line. It goes on to attack Maugham for being "hostile to artistic risk," for "his career in the fashionable drawing-rooms and international cocktail sets of Europe," and for his derogations of Henry James; and the review ends by noting that "if the title of 'greatest living English novelist' is to be thrown around any further, it is time it landed in the right quarter. The greatest living English novelist is E. M. Forster." *Up at the Villa*, true enough, is a very poor novel; Maugham himself told Glenway Wescott that he was ashamed of having written it. But the poorness of the novel doesn't quite explain the vehemence of Zabel's review. Whence the anger in that review? Why the personal attack?

Edmund Wilson was even rougher on Maugham, saying that he was "second-rate" and that "his swelling reputation in America"—the year was 1946—showed "a conspicuous sign of the general decline of our standards." The occasion for Wilson's attack was another poor Maugham performance, *Then and Now*, his novel about Machiavelli. The quality of this book, Wilson pronounced, "is never . . . that either of a literary artist or of a first-rate critic of morals; and it may be worthwhile to say this at a moment when there seems to be a tendency to step up Mr. Maugham's standing to the higher ranks of English fiction, and when Mr. Maugham himself has been using his position of prestige for a nagging disparagement of his betters." Who, one may ask, might these betters be? They turn out to be the great modernist writers—Joyce and James and Yeats and Proust—of whom Maugham had, in Wilson's views, a far from adequate appreciation. For example, in a talk at the Library of Congress, Maugham had said:

> Proust, as we know, was enormously influenced by the now largely discredited philosophy of Henri Bergson and great stretches of his work turn upon it. I suppose we all read with a thrill of excitement Proust's volumes as they came out, but now when we reread them in a calmer mood I think what we find to admire in them is his wonderful humor and the extraordinarily vivid and interesting characters that he created in profusion.

Wilson countered that this is, in effect, philistine—true, one doesn't encounter all that many Proust-reading philistines—and that Proust's use of Bergson is crucial to his novel's being "the greatest philosophical novel ever written." I think Maugham was more correct than Wilson, but what we have here is a serious conflict of intellectual temperaments—that between a writer and a reader, which Maugham was, and a pure critic, which Edmund Wilson was. In his publication of this piece in *Classics and Commercials,* Wilson stepped up the vehemence of his attack on Maugham in a postscript in which he called him "a half-trashy novelist, who writes badly, but is patronized by half-serious readers, who do not care much about writing."

Maugham found admirers among men of letters and writers; among his supporters were Cyril Connolly, Virginia Woolf, Desmond MacCarthy, Evelyn Waugh, and V. S. Pritchett; and Orwell wrote of him: "I believe the modern writer who has influenced me most is Somerset Maugham, whom I admire immensely for his power of telling a story straightforwardly and without frills." But among what he termed "highbrow critics" Maugham's name has never been an approved one. He knew this, and, though he pretended to be above it, one finds running throughout his work a sputtering volley of shots against "intellectuals," "highbrows," "the intelligentsia," and "critics of the intelligentsia." Maugham is partly to blame for incitement to critical riot against his own work.

Why did they detest Maugham so? Were they jealous of his success, the vast audience and riches his writing earned? Perhaps this entered into it, but more important, I suspect, was that his writing was an affront to them. He was apolitical, and he wrote dead against the grain of modernism, with all its difficulty, preferring instead to write as plainly as possible about complex things. Say what one wishes against them, no one can accuse the modernist writers of not keeping critics gainfully employed. In an idle fantasy I sometimes think of these writers—Joyce and Eliot and Yeats and Kafka and the rest— mounted on motorcycles in a parade up the Champs-Élysées, a critic or two sitting in a small sidecar attached to each cycle, beaming with pleasure at being allowed along for the ride. But Maugham kept no sidecar; each of his books, to switch metaphors rather abruptly, might have carried a small message, à la the surgeon general's warning on cigarette packages: "No explanation, explication, or exegesis required. Read on without prolegomenon."

But one doesn't have to attack the modernist writers because one admires Somerset Maugham; nor need one think oneself half-serious for admiring him. Maugham remains intensely, immensely readable. Why? One recalls his revealing the secrets of his craft to the Chinese professor: "One is to have common sense and the other is to stick to the point." The point Maugham stuck to throughout his long career was the investigation of that magnificent, comic, admirable, outrageous, depressing, impressive, grim, gracious, grudging, great, and elusive thing called human nature. Human nature was Maugham's enduring subject, and for fiction there is none greater. If you are interested in it, you have to be interested in the writing of Somerset

Maugham. As for his common sense, it was pervasive; the test is that he was an artist who knew that there are things in life greater than art. "I think," he wrote in *A Writer's Notebook,* "there is in the heroic courage with which man confronts the irrationality of the world a beauty greater than the beauty of art." Because he was able to insinuate such sentiments, subtly, dramatically, into his work—see, for an example, the story entitled "Sanatorium"—Maugham will always be a writer for readers who care for more than writing alone.

And yet it is difficult to convey a precise impression of the quality of Maugham's work through naming two or three of his best books. He was right about himself in thinking that he was a writer of the kind for whom the body of his work is greater than the parts taken individually. Of his novels, I find only one, *Cakes and Ale,* completely successful. It is, I think, his masterpiece, a rich comedy about the literary life, its exactions and its delights and its fraudulence. It contains a dazzling portrait of the type of the literary widow and an even better account of the young literary hustler in the character of Alroy Kear, modeled, as it turns out, on Hugh Walpole—a man, as Maugham later averred, "easy to like, but difficult to respect." The literary widow, the literary hustler, the utterly self-absorbed artist, these are types that do not disappear, and Maugham was the first to mount them, like so many butterflies, on a narrative of seamless velvet.

Of his own books, Maugham said he liked *Cakes and Ale* best but tended to agree with the common opinion that held *Of Human Bondage* to be his most important work. In this latter, largely autobiographical book Maugham worked on a larger canvas than he ever would again; it is the sort of novel where one can introduce, for the first time, a major character as late as page 421. I first read *Of Human Bondage* when I was twenty and now I have reread it approaching fifty, and it still seems to me immensely interesting. I tend to think of it as the best nineteenth-century novel written well into the twentieth century. It was publicly promoted at its publication by Theodore Dreiser in a review in the *New Republic* that made its reputation in America. Good as much of the book is, it nonetheless seems badly flawed toward its close by Maugham's need to resolve the action, to put an end to his young hero's troubles in a way that is not only conclusive but happy, and happy in the rather sappiest Dickensian mode.

I shall not run through all of Maugham's books that I have read or reread, but I do think *The Razor's Edge* is in some ways representative of both Maugham's gifts and his deficiencies. This is the novel, it will be recalled, about the quest of a young American named Larry Darrell for the ultimate truths about the meaning of life. In the character Isabel Maturin, Maugham created an extraordinarily vivid and hence persuasive portrait of a grasping American rich girl who wants *merely* everything. In Elliott Templeton, the wealthy expatriate American snob, Maugham created a character of whom it is not ridiculous to say that, after the Baron de Charlus, he may well be the most interesting snob in modern literature. "I don't in the least mind pigging it at the Ritz," he announces at one point. Elliott Templeton is one of those characters whom you don't wish ever to leave the page, in the way one wants certain charming character actors never to leave the stage. Almost everything about *The Razor's Edge* is brilliant—except, alas, Larry Darrell's quest. This may be because goodness, which young Darrell is tiresomely meant to represent, is usually less interesting than its reverse; it may be because ultimate truths about the meaning of life are never quite convincing; it may be because Somerset Maugham's powers of idealization had long since withered. But *The Razor's Edge* resembles nothing so much as a ring with a large rhinestone at the center and smaller but perfect gems all round it.

One is unlikely to encounter Maugham's books in a university curriculum. In my youth his work, because he was an international best seller, was ubiquitous, and if one was at all bookish one was likely, when young, to have read *The Razor's Edge* and *Of Human Bondage;* or if one thought of oneself as artistic to have found self-justification in *The Moon and Sixpence,* his not very good novel modeled on the life of Paul Gauguin. Today I think the best introduction—or reintroduction—to Maugham is through his short stories. So many of these seem so good that it may be unjust to single out a few. But among the four volumes of stories now available in Penguin editions, "Mr. Harrington's Washing" is a work of comic genius; "The Pool" may be the best story ever written on the subject of going native; "The Hairless Mexican" is spy fiction raised to the highest power; and "Lord Mount Drago" is but one of his many stories that provide a cunning anatomy of snobbery. Maugham's nonfiction also bears looking into. At the top of his form he was a very capable essayist—see the volumes entitled *The Vagrant Mood* and *Points of View*—and *Don Fernando,* the book on Spanish culture, contains many clever and wise things. My sense is that it is best to read Maugham's stories and nonfiction first, and let them lead one back to the novels, where one is likely to discover that Maugham is among the novelists who can be profitably read when one is young but get better as one gets older.

Maugham would probably be best served by a single volume, on the order of the Viking Portable Library, except that in his case, the volume, to suit his ample talent, would have to be of a thickness beyond portability. Such a volume, if I were its editor, would include all of *Cakes and Ale,* the better part of *The Summing Up,* the portrait of Elliott Templeton from *The Razor's Edge,* the essays on El Greco, Burke's prose, and Kant's aesthetics, and nearly everything he wrote on prose style. What would make the volume bulge, proving a severe test of the binder's art, would be the number of short stories that would have to be included. The short story really was Maugham's best form, and he published more than a hundred of them— among serious writers, perhaps only Chekhov wrote more. Some of his stories are thin, especially those that attempt to point an easy moral or have a trick ending, but the vast majority are very sturdily made. Those set in the Malay States, taken together, conduce to give as complete a picture of the British abroad as do Kipling's stories of India. Maugham's stories about the artistic life—"The Alien Corn," "The Creative Impulse" chief among them—are also too good not to be included.

Often Maugham's stories seem akin to reading La Rochefoucauld with illustrations—not drawings, of course, but illustrations from life. Maugham resembles La Rochefoucauld in taking avarice, lust, fear, and snobbishness for his subjects. Yet in Maugham, unlike La Rochefoucauld, these dark views about human nature are often stood on their head by evidence of courage, honesty, and integrity, almost always of an unexpected and complicated kind. Maugham is that odd phenomenon, a moralist who is never surprised by immorality. As he puts it in "The Pool," "I held my breath, for to me there is nothing more awe-inspiring than when a man discovers to you the nakedness of his soul. Then you see that no one is so trivial or debased but that in him is a spark of something to excite compassion."

Although he lived long and in splendor, Maugham's life was far from a happy one. As he grew older he grew more suspicious of the people around him—some of whom, it is necessary to add, were fully worthy of his suspicions—and, true to character, he never lapsed into the jolly old man of letters, full of false wisdom for the world. With age the lower part of his face set into a permanent scowl, his eyes acquired a squint, and various people would later describe him as looking like a lizard, a spotted toad, a Gila monster in a robe. The last six or so years of his ninety-one-year life were spent tuning in and out of senility; when turned into senility he was capable of making the kind of devastating remark in company that could make the bubbles disappear from the champagne. S. N. Behrman, who in his memoir *People in a Diary* remarked that he had never "met anyone who had greater will-power, greater self-control than W. S. Maugham," recalls Maugham, toward the end, his stammer still not under control, saying to him: "If you think I'm g-g-ga-ga, you should see W-W-Winston." Like most people who live well beyond the normal span, his was neither a dignified nor an edifying end, when it arrived at long last in a French hospital on December 15, 1965.

Yet for all the unhappiness of Somerset Maugham's outward life, there was still the inward life, which in his case meant the life of the writer, and this brought its own satisfactions. In a passage in *Cakes and Ale* he wrote about the single but powerful compensation of that life:

I began to meditate upon the writer's life. It is full of tribulation. First he must endure poverty and the world's indifference; then, having achieved a measure of success, he must submit with a good grace to its hazards. He depends upon a fickle public. He is at the mercy of journalists who want to interview him and photographers who want to take his picture, of editors who harry him for copy and tax gatherers who harry him for income tax, of persons of quality who ask him to lunch and secretaries of institutes who ask him to lecture, of women who want to marry him and women who want to divorce him, of youths who want his autographs, actors who want parts and strangers who want a loan, of gushing ladies who want advice on their matrimonial affairs and earnest young men who want advice on their compositions, of agents, publishers, managers, bores, admirers, critics, and his own conscience. But he has one compensation. Whenever he has anything on his mind, whether it be a harassing reflection, grief at the death of a friend, unrequited love, wounded pride, anger at the treachery of someone to whom he has shown kindness, in short any emotion or any perplexing thought, he has only to put it down in black and white, using it as the theme of a story or the decoration of an essay, to forget all about it. He is the only free man.

There is little one can add to this, except to say that, through reading the work of a superior writer, which Somerset Maugham was, the rest of us become a little freer, too.

The New Criterion 1985

Señor Borges's Portico

O NE OF THE INTERESTING differences between high art and great science is that the former is unique and its emergence unpredictable in a way that is not quite true of the latter. If Newton had not lived, I have seen it argued, Huygens and Leibniz would have gone on to do his principal work; Wallace was closing in on the theory of evolution for which Darwin has since been recognized as a hero of science; and Edison's work could as readily have been done by Swan (on the incandescent lamp) and Hughes (on the microphone), or so it is said. If Albert Einstein had never lived, it is possible that Ernst Mach or Max Planck or another German physicist would have set to work on the problem of relativity; but if Proust had died in his twenties, there would be no *Remembrance of Things Past,* nor, it seems safe to maintain, any other book remotely like it.

And yet there are some artists, no matter how exotic their origins or how esoteric their gifts, of whom it almost seems as if, had they not existed, they would have to have been invented. Jorge Luis Borges, the Argentine writer who was born in 1899 and died in 1986 at the age of eighty-seven, appears to have been such an artist. In a 1967 essay entitled "The Literature of Exhaustion," the American novelist John Barth, setting out a fairly early claim for Borges as a modern master, allowed that "someone once vexedly accused *me* of inventing" Borges. And indeed Borges was fond of speaking of himself as an invention of sorts, as if there were Borges the writer, who contrived his literary work, and Borges the man, who had gradually become lost in the writer and was destined "to perish, definitively."

But the sense of the word "invention" I have in mind is of another, somewhat different, kind—it is the sense in which invention is spoken of as being the mother of necessity. For Jorge Luis Borges came along in time to justify the kind of writing that certain academic authors and teachers of modern literature had long been awaiting, even if, until his arrival, they themselves perhaps did not know it.

In "The Literature of Exhaustion"—the very title leaves one longing for a nap—John Barth asserts not only that Borges is one of the few writers worthy of being placed alongside such "old masters" of twentieth-century fiction as Joyce and Kafka, but that of the thin line of their successors, Borges is easily the most interesting. What puts Borges in the first rank for Barth is "the combination of that intellectually profound vision with great human insight, poetic power, and consummate mastery of his means. . . ." But beyond these qualities, which define all literary artists of great power, Barth admires Borges for the way he appears to have both understood and transcended the chief aesthetic problems of the day—Barth rather bumpily calls these "the felt ultimacies of our time." In Barth's view, "it may well be that the novel's time as a major art form is up," which is to say that the day for traditional narrative, with its reliance on cause and effect, characterization, lineal anecdote, and the rest of it, is over, done, *kaput*. Barth isn't saying, or even suggesting, that the novel is dead, but instead that some of its traditionally richest possibilities may be. If this is true, the question is, where does one—if one is, as John Barth describes himself, "of the temper that chooses to 'rebel along traditional lines' "—where does one go from here? The answer, for Barth, is in the direction of Jorge Luis Borges.

Jorge Luis Borges is the answer as well for a great many other writers, critics, and teachers of literature. If the tradition of modernism in fiction is not considered at a dead end, the three writers who may be said to have carried it on with the greatest bravura have been Vladimir Nabokov, Samuel Beckett, and Jorge Luis Borges. Each in his different way is a mandarin among modern writers; each has about him the feel of an international figure. Of these three, Nabokov, despite his enormous talent, seems too much a special case—an exile and a man writing out of his own obsessions, a rare and beautiful specimen of butterfly forming a species of one; Beckett, despite his comedy of deadpan precision, is finally too dark, even for teachers and critics who do not seem to mind setting up shop right there on the rim of the abyss. But Borges—well, Borges is a different story. Borges has his obsessions, but one can separate them from his work, in a way that it is difficult to do with Nabokov; Borges has his darkness, but it is not the darkness of the inside of a shroud, as Beckett's increasingly has tended to be. Borges has the additional advantage that his work, in its various preoccupations, would seem to make striking connections with that group of writers and critics, most but not all of them university-based, who think of themselves as post-modernist. To quote a postie novelist named Ronald Sukenick on the post-modernist program in literature: "Reality doesn't exist, time doesn't exist, personality doesn't exist. . . . In view of these annihilations, it will be no surprise that literature, also, does not exist—how could it?"

Although Borges would not have put it quite so blatantly, there is evidence in his work for arguing that he, too, believed that reality, time, personality, literature itself, do not quite exist. This in any case is the gravamen of those stories of Borges that are most widely admired among American academics. Ours may one day be looked back upon as a time when academics in the humanities in the United States spent themselves debating the question of whether reality truly exists: whether meaning is without meaning; whether not only beauty but ethics and morality generally are only in the eye of the beholder; and whether truth is not inseparable from political power. As Dr. Johnson refuted Bishop Berkeley's ingenious argument for the nonexistence of matter by kicking a large stone ("I refute it *thus*," said he), so today might one refute the academic contemners of reality by proposing that in an unreal world they give up their tenure ("Whaddaya, kidding me?" say they).

Although adored by a certain kind of literary academic, Borges was not—at least not until late in his life—himself an academic. He was from the outset, however, entirely bookish. A frail boy growing up behind thick spectacles in a culture that placed a high value on physical prowess and courage, the young Borges hid out in his father's library, unsystematically devouring its contents, enraptured by the encyclopedias, dictionaries, and above all the stories, especially the stories of adventure and the fantastic, that he found there. "When he did not want to give in," Borges's mother once remarked, "I took his books away. That was decisive." In "An Autobiographical Essay," Borges has noted: "If I were asked to name the chief event in my life, I should say my father's library." Elsewhere in the same essay, he writes: "I have always come to things after coming to books"; and he once told an interviewer: "I've always been a greater reader than a writer."

The elder Borges's library was dominated by English books, for the sensible reason that his mother was an Englishwoman from Staffordshire. As Borges's father grew up under his own mother's influence, so was Borges greatly influenced by his father, a lawyer by training, a shy and bookish man by temperament. His father's taste in poetry ran to Shelley, Keats, and Swinburne; in philosophy he had a penchant for metaphysics and psychology, and was partial to the works of Berkeley, Hume, Royce, and William James. He was keen, too, on books about the East, and his library held various editions of *The Arabian Nights*. He wrote and privately printed a lengthy novel, and was a man of serious literary aspirations on which he never made good. He was the fifth generation in his family to go blind because of a hereditary disease. Jorge Luis Borges would be the sixth.

The influence on Borges of his mother was less immediate but of longer duration, in part because she herself endured so long—until, to be precise, the age of ninety-nine, dying when Borges was seventy-six. Apart from a marriage made in his late sixties, which lasted only three years, and another marriage made at the end of his life, Borges lived continuously with his mother, who until her death filled the role for him of nurse and nanny and, after his blindness, reader. Borges's mother was of Spanish descent, and her forebears were heroic figures in the military history of Argentina. Borges appeared to live off the traditions provided by his two parents: English for culture, Spanish for dreams of heroism. While linguistic duality was a fact of life at home, he nevertheless learned to read English before he learned to read Spanish. "When later I read *Don Quixote* in the original," Borges once remarked, "it sounded like a bad translation to me."

With its Italians, its English, its Spanish, Argentina was a land of a thousand snobberies. At the turn of the century, among the upper classes, Francophilia was giving way to Anglophilia. The Borges family was of that class of people who were not rich but were cultivated, with distinguished lineage to draw upon. Borges and his sister were educated by an English governess, until Georgie (as he was known among his family) went off to the state school at the age of nine. Within the Borges household, English was used for cultural matters, Spanish for domestic matters, for the latter was the language of servants and the lower orders. Eventually, of course, Georgie would become Jorge Luis, but to the end of his days Borges claimed to have read much more widely in English than in Spanish.

The Canadian novelist Mordecai Richler once remarked that he divided all experience into the time before he decided to become a writer and the time after, adding that the time before was better. The wisdom of the remark resides in its truth about the nature of experience for those who write and those who do not. Once the decision to write has been made, of course, all experience becomes something to write about—life itself becomes copy, events and emotions judged by their penworthiness above all else. Often, experience before the decision to write has been made seems more central, vivid, real. Perhaps this explains why so many writers—Twain, Hemingway, Salinger—are best at writing about their youth, a time in their lives before they had themselves become writers.

The late Emir Rodriguez Monegal, who was a professor of contemporary Latin American literature at Yale, wrote a most useful and highly interesting biography of Borges, in which he attempted from time to time to Freudianize his subject. Borges is big on inserting labyrinths of one kind or another in his tales (one of his books is entitled, precisely, *Labyrinths*), and Monegal, his psychoanalytical engines roaring, suggested that these various labyrinths might be symbolic of Borges's search for the return to the womb. Yet one wonders if a more significant fact for understanding the kind of writer Borges was may not instead be found in how extraordinarily early he determined to be a writer. At the age of six, Borges informed his father that he had made his decision; he once told an interviewer that by the age of eleven he had begun, when reading, "to identify with the author"; and in his "Autobiographical Essay," he writes: "From the time I was a boy, when blindness came to him, it was tacitly understood that I had to fulfill the literary destiny that circumstances had denied my father."

Never for a moment apparently did Borges, or anyone in his family, ever assume that he would be anything other than a writer. As a boy, he hardly seemed fit for anything else. Physically, he was a perfect target for the young hooligans who were his classmates when he went off to public school in Buenos Aires at the age of nine. At the age of ten, he began to talk about philosophy with his father, who was an idealist, which means that he believed that we are living in a dream world, in which we are dreaming God, or God is dreaming us, but in any case in which existence is of the stuff that dreams are made on. In 1914, when Borges was fifteen, the family departed for an extended visit to Geneva, which was to be more extended than they could have imagined, for the outbreak of World War I detained them in Europe until its conclusion. In Geneva he learned French (the language of instruction at the Collège Calvin, where he went to school) and Latin. Later, reading Carlyle's *Sartor Resartus,* he decided to teach himself German. It was in German that he first encountered Schopenhauer, the philosopher he was to value above all others. And so it would always be with the polyglottal Borges: the reading of books led to the learning of new languages which led to the reading of more books which led. . . . Excepting perhaps only Montaigne, who began writing much later in his life, no more bookish writer than Borges may have ever existed.

After the end of World War I, Borges moved on to Spain, there to continue his studies and to pursue a literary career as a poet. In his first published poem, a bilgy paean to the sea published when he was twenty, he tried to imitate in Spanish Walt Whitman, whom he had himself first read in German. In Madrid he fell in with a group of avant-gardists who styled themselves "ultraists." He was then a lover of mankind: "an anarchist and a freethinker and in favor of pacifism." He wrote poems filled with violent metaphors, essays teeming with bitterness and resentment—in the way that only a young man not yet twenty-two can be bitter and resentful. In an essay about the aesthetics of the whorehouses of Spain, he noted that the curves of one of the girls working there were "sculpted like a phrase by Quevedo." Along with his fellow ultraists, the shy Borges set out to shock the bourgeoisie by reading his discordant poems in public. Was it Valéry who said that everything changes but the avant-garde?

When Borges returned to Buenos Aires, in 1921, he was a published writer, but a writer without a true subject. The city had grown—sprawled, really—during the seven years he had been away, and, as he noted, he now rediscovered it. This city, in its legendary aspect, would one day be among Borges's subjects, but for the time being he was locked into the aridities of the Argentine avant-garde. He ran a number of short-lived magazines, one of which was published on billboards around town; he wrote poetry whose chief intention seems to have been to startle its readers; he took up new affectations, such as trying, in his writing, "to be as Argentine as I could," which meant larding his poems with Argentinisms acquired from a special dictionary. He continued, as always, his reading life, reading in bed each night after dinner; and when he won a literary prize, he used the money to buy a secondhand set of the *Encyclopaedia Britannica* (eleventh edition). Thanks to conversations with a friend of his father's named Macedonio Fernandez, another philosophical idealist who "really believed that we are all living in a dream world," he began to read more skeptically. His poems were favorably reviewed in Ortega y Gasset's new journal, *Revista de Occidente,* and he contributed a single piece, an article on the seventeenth-century Spanish satirist Quevedo, to that journal. But apart from the friendships he made, the years between 1921 and 1930 were regarded by Borges in retrospect as pointless. He later summed them up: "I find myself completely out of sympathy with the priggish and rather dogmatic young man I then was."

Borges's career had a most odd shape; the line describing it would run from precocity to lengthy obscurity to worldwide acclaim to the danger of academic ossification. "By the late 1920's," Monegal writes, "it was obvious in Buenos Aires that [Borges] was the most important young poet there and a leader of the avant-garde." This is all very well, but in a worldly view comparable to being the best shot-putter in the Junior League, or the winner of a national cha-cha contest for people past eighty. Borges was himself too cosmopolitan a young man not to know this. (He once jokingly proposed starting an avant-garde review to be called *Papers for the Suppression of Reality*—some joke.) By 1929, according to Monegal, Borges realized that he would never achieve his ambition of being a cosmic poet and a universally admired one. He was still chiefly living off his father, but now he turned more and more to criticism and reviewing for both obscure and popular Argentine periodicals.

Borges gives much credit to the influence during this period of a writer named Alfonso Reyes, who was the Mexican ambassador in Buenos Aires. Reyes got Borges to knock off the fine writing and the attempts to forge a style built on seventeenth-century models in favor of a prose that was precise, concise, and pellucid. Although at twenty-seven Borges had already had the first of the eight eye operations he would undergo before near blindness set in for good in his middle fifties, he continued to store up vast amounts of desultory reading in subjects erudite and arcane. (Borges always had scholarly tastes without any accompanying illusion that he was himself a scholar.) At this point, in his early thirties, Jorge Luis Borges was still a writer who had not found his form, a talent waiting to burst into fruition.

Curiously, Borges was never a great reader of novels, preferring instead the economy and form of the short story. "As a writer, however, I thought for years that the short story was beyond my powers," Borges writes in "An Autobiographical Essay," and "it was only after a long and roundabout series of timid experiments in narration that I sat down to write real stories." At first he did stories based on incidents from the lives of legendary Buenos Aires toughs, for Borges had cultivated the acquaintance of hoodlums from the city's north side who looked back upon the days when a male virgin was someone who had not yet killed his first man. He then progressed to inventing stories or sketches around the lives of men who had in fact existed, such as Billy the Kid or the Jewish gunman Monk Eastman.

Around 1935 he began to publish tales written in the form of pseudo-essays on books or writers that had never existed; these became not only Borges's trademark but the chief cause behind his eventual fame. For it is precisely this kind of thing that excites a writer and teacher like John Barth, who has noted that, instead of yet another stale narrative, Borges in these tales "writes a remarkable and original work of literature, the implicit theme of which is the difficulty, perhaps the unnecessity, of writing original works of literature. His artistic victory, if you like, is that he confronts an intellectual dead end and employs it against itself to accomplish new human work."

In one such story, "An Examination of the Work of Herbert Quain," Borges begins by announcing the death of an author who has been allotted "scarcely half a column of necrological piety" by the *Times Literary Supplement,* and whose first work, *The God of the Labyrinth,* had been obtusely compared, in the *Spectator,* with Agatha Christie, and others of whose books had been compared with Gertrude Stein. Borges then proceeds I won't say to elucidate but to elaborate upon the kind of writer Quain was. He was a writer who took special pleasure in con- cocting ingenious plots the purpose of which seemed to be to undermine the very notion of plot. " 'I lay claim in this novel,' I have heard [Quain] say, 'to the essential features of all games: symmetry, arbitrary rules, tedium.' " There follows some eru- dite chitchat about what Quain was really up to; a few false interpretations of his work are put up and shot down; it is noted that a fallacious interpretation of one of his comedies as a Freudian work determined its success. Quain, who "was in the habit of arguing that readers were an already extinct spe- cies," produced a final book entitled *Statements* containing eight stories each of which set out a good plot deliberately frustrated by the author. From the third of these stories, Borges tells us, he was able to extract his own story, "The Circular Ruins," which actually happens to exist.

Now this may not be everybody's idea of the way to play parcheesi. But be assured that the board, when Borges sets it up, can be very elegantly laid out, the pieces beautifully carved. One must, it is true, have a taste for puzzles and perplexities to enjoy such a story. It would be a grave mistake, however, to take Borges for a mere gamester. He is playing in earnest. Yet his position is a curious one; he is an aesthete who does not quite believe in the efficacy of art. "Music, states of happiness, mythology, faces belabored by time, certain twilights and certain places," he writes, "try to tell us something, or have said something we should not have missed, or are about to say something: this imminence of revelation which does not occur is, perhaps, the aesthetic phenomenon."

To value art above all else and yet to find art nearly valueless—this, surely, is a strange position. How did Borges come to hold it? Whence did it derive? Valéry remarks that "there is no theory that is not a fragment, carefully prepared, of some autobiography." It is not easy, however, to discover the analogue in Borges's life for his theories about art, unless one looks to his reading, the idealism learned at his father's knee, the avant-garde atmosphere in which he came of age, his penchant for metaphysics. But it all seems somehow cerebral, not quite to touch on life, including Borges's own. Utterly skeptical though he may have been about finding meaning in life, this seems in no way to have prevented him from enjoying it thoroughly. We are used by now to our modern writers' having an edge of coldness, if not outright nastiness about them—the meanness is the message—but none of this was true of Borges, about whom Monegal has no trouble rounding up the most endearing testimonials, such as "I believe that he is the best-humored man I ever met" and ". . . as Borges is so intelligent, when talking to him, he gives us the feeling that we are also intelligent." This most modern of writers was himself a most old-fashioned gentleman.

Not that Borges's life was one of seamless serenity. Beginning in 1937, he worked in a minor position at a branch library
in Buenos Aires for nine years, which he later described as
"nine years of solid unhappiness." His job was to help impose
a systematic organization on a collection of books so small as
to require no such system. He did one hour of actual library
work each day, spending the remainder reading and writing.
But, now in his forties, he felt humiliated by so menial and
dismal a job. Further humiliations were to come. During World
War II, Borges was pro-British, not so easy a thing to be in
preponderantly pro-German Argentina. Borges was an enemy
of totalitarianism of every kind, and in his criticism and journalism attacked Hitler's anti-Semitism and his catastrophic effect
on German culture. Borges was of course also a great enemy
of Colonel Juan Domingo Perón, who, when he came to power,
repaid the writer by keeping him under surveillance. In August
1946, Borges was notified that he had been removed from his
job at the Miguel Cané branch of the municipal library and
"promoted" to inspector of poultry and rabbits in the public
markets of Córdoba Street—clearly a macho-style slap from, as
Borges would later phrase it, "a president whose name I do
not want to remember."

Yet Borges, by his own admission, was never a committed
writer—never *engagé*:

> My political convictions are well known; I am a member of the
> Conservative party—this in itself is a form of skepticism—and
> no one has ever branded me a Communist, a nationalist, an anti-
> Semite, a follower of Billy the Kid or of the dictator Rosa. . . .
> I have never kept my opinions hidden, not even in trying times,
> but neither have I ever allowed them to find their way into my
> literary work, except once when I was buoyed up in exultation
> over the Six-Day War.

As Borges here makes plentifully clear, there was his politics
and there was his writing and, insofar as he could control them,

never did the twain meet. And it is true that Borges's stories do appear drained of all political content: questions of good and evil do not arise in his stories and neither can he ever be said to persuade his readers to any conclusions. He wished to entertain and move them, but to move them in a particular direction—toward wonder and wonderment over life's mysteries.

While still working at the library, in 1938, the year his father died, Borges had an accident, an injury to his scalp, after which septicemia set in, causing him to fear for his sanity. As he began to recover, still uncertain of his mental abilities, he attempted a new kind of story, which turned out to be "Pierre Menard, Author of *Don Quixote*." It is one of Borges's best-known stories and a work of a kind that would become characteristic of the Borges who is most revered in the academy: a narrative discourse upon an imaginary text that pretends to be an analysis of it. What in considerable part accounts for the cachet of this particular story in the university of today is that it is a story about reading. Borges rarely wrote anything more than ten or twelve pages in length. He also professed to believe that "the composition of vast books is a laborious and impoverishing extravagance. . . . I have preferred to write notes upon imaginary books."

A symbolist from Nîmes, a friend of Valéry's, a man whose bibliography reveals him to have been devoted to the arcana of literary study at the highest level, Borges's creation Pierre Menard applies himself to "the repetition of a pre-existing book in another language"—the book in this instance being *Don Quixote* by Miguel de Cervantes. Menard, please understand, wishes to repeat Cervantes's masterpiece *literally*. The project is quite mad, of course, but then, as the narrator of the story avers, "there is no intellectual exercise which is not ultimately useless." After many drafts, which he has destroyed, Menard succeeds in reproducing a few chapters of *Don Quixote* exactly. Although both texts are verbally identical, the narrator argues for the superiority of Menard's, its greater subtlety and rich-ness. To him, that a contemporary of Julien Benda and Ber-trand Russell could turn out such a work, writing in the prose style of a seventeenth-century Spaniard while thinking as a twentieth-century Frenchman, so that the very meanings of his words, and the meanings behind the meanings, have changed, and with it all the meaning of the story—this, truly, is a remarkable accomplishment. The narrator ends the story by noting:

> Menard (perhaps without wishing to) has enriched, by means of a new technique, the hesitant and rudimentary art of reading: the technique is one of deliberate anachronism and erroneous attributions. This technique, with its infinite applications, urges us to run through the *Odyssey* as if it were written after the *Aeneid,* and to read *Le jardin du Centaure* by Madame Henri Bachelier as if it were by Madame Henri Bachelier. This technique would fill the dullest books with adventure. Would not the attributing of *The Imitation of Christ* to Louis-Ferdinand Céline or James Joyce be a sufficient renovation of its tenuous spiritual counsels?

One could organize a whole little Franco-American school of university literary criticism around a story such as "Pierre Menard, Author of *Don Quixote,*" which provides maps of mis-reading, mines of misperception, mimes of unreality. It is very much a story for specialists, for connoisseurs ("kind of sewers," as the playful James Joyce of *Finnegans Wake* might have put it). Although Borges began to write such stories before the new academic criticism was really under way, there is a sense in which the stories anticipate the criticism and play into it. As V. S Pritchett, who is an admirer of Borges, has written, "the risk is—and there are some signs of this already—that criticism of Borges will become an accretion that will force us to see his stories as conceits alone."

But there is more going on in Borges than the organization

of conceits alone. There are stories set in the Argentine past, stories about courage, about fate, about mystery; there is also in much of his work a subtle feeling for drama, even if it is not the drama of good and evil, of men swept up by ambition, love, the ambiguities of morality. His stories are all written with a fine eye for detail, for the arresting juxtaposition of word and event, and with that precision and clarity which, combined, make for the highest literary elegance. Borges was a consummate literary artist—of that there can be no question.

The question is, To what uses did he put his artistry? How good, finally, was Borges? Opinions differ—and strongly. V. S. Pritchett, allowing that Borges can be viewed as "a learned pillager of metaphysical arguments," nonetheless maintains that he passes the test for an artist of ideas by his ability to make "an idea walk," which is to say come alive on the page. But V. S. Naipaul, allowing that Borges's puzzles and jokes can be addictive, nonetheless maintains that "they cannot always support the metaphysical interpretations they receive." Octavio Paz holds that "the great achievement of Borges was to say the most with the least," adding that he was able to combine simplicity with strangeness, "the naturalism of the uncommon, the strangeness of the familiar." This is what "gives him a unique place in the literature of the 20th century." But then there is Vladimir Nabokov, speaking perhaps with the acerbity of the rival, who once told a reporter from *Time:* "At first Vera and I were delighted by reading him. We felt we were on a portico, but we have learned that there was no house."

No one can argue that Borges made extravagant claims on his own behalf. After he achieved fame, he gave hundreds of interviews and wrote various prologues and introductions to his own books and to books about him, and in them he mastered the tone of what might be called the modest genius. "The same few plots, I am sorry to say," he wrote in the prologue to his book *Dr. Brodie's Report*, "have pursued me down through the years; I am decidedly monotonous." It is true that

Borges's stories and poems and criticism seem a remarkably unified enterprise. This enterprise can, I think, be accurately described as the investigation of reality with an eye toward its destruction.

Borges is above all impressed with the mystery of life, and fascinated above all with those who set out to solve the mystery. Scholars and philosophers especially excite his aesthetic interest. "Borges," Alastair Reid once noted, "really did regard scholarship as a branch of fantastic literature." Philosophy was scarcely less fantastic to him, and he found few spectacles as risible as that of a man attempting to interpret the complexity of the world with a theory. In story after story, Borges tells of plans to find order in the world; in story after story, none is finally available. Men are swamped by infinity, chased by time, rattled by memory.

As these stories unfold—"Tlön, Uqbar, Orbis Tertius," "The Babylon Library," "The Aleph," "The Secret Miracle"— the planes of reality and unreality intersect and blur. Labyrinths, mirrors, dreams, strange recurrences, play through these works, with the effect that man's place in the world comes to seem a highly shaky proposition and human destiny, to copy a trope from Borges's story "Averroes' Search," "a blind camel in the desert." Yet if man never seems so helpless or absurd as when searching for the secret meaning of life, Borges, while positing the precariousness of human existence, is also able to infuse poetry into the search, and with it emotion of the kind that results when men are shown alone and at the mercy of a universe they do not begin to understand.

But why would Borges, this gentle and altogether pleasant man, be pledged, in the words of a critic most friendly to him named Ana Maria Barrenechea, "to destroy reality and convert Man into a shadow"? "I am quite simply," Borges has said, "a man who uses perplexities for literary purposes." Yet can it be quite so simple? Skeptical of almost all philosophies, Borges was most partial to idealism, which posits that life does not truly exist outside the mind of the person, or divinity, who beholds it. In the idealistic view, life could well be a dream; and it was this possibility that Borges seemed to prefer to entertain. As a mere window-shopper in philosophy, I have always liked George Santayana's refutation of idealism, set out in *Egotism in German Philosophy*, which runs: "You cannot maintain that the natural world is the product of the human mind without changing the meaning of the word mind and of the word human." But why would a man of so generally skeptical a nature as Borges turn to idealism, or for that matter to playing with perplexities?

My own unfounded speculation about this has to do with the fact that for years Borges suffered from insomnia. So, too, I have recently learned, did Vladimir Nabokov and the Rumanian aphorist E. M. Cioran, two other writers much given to pondering the literary uses of perplexities. So, before them, did Nietzsche, who tried to alleviate it with the use of chloral; and, before Nietzsche, so did De Quincey, who attributed to his insomnia his craving for opium. Borges spoke of "the atrocious lucidity of insomnia." There is something about this tiresome disease, to judge by the roster of writers who have suffered from it, that inflames the imagination, sending it off into dark corners and setting it intricate puzzles.

Some inkling of what a well-stocked mind suffers under insomnia is available in a brilliant Borges story entitled "Funes the Memorius." (Completing this story is said to have cured Borges of his own insomnia.) In it an adolescent boy, Ireneo Funes, a peasant lad who has the unusual ability to tell the precise time of the day without aid of a timepiece, is thrown from a horse and suffers what can only be described as the reverse of amnesia—henceforth, he remembers everything. And he remembers with a vividness of detail that is not only astounding but painful:

> When he fell, he became unconscious; when he came to, the present was almost intolerable in its richness and sharpness, as

were his most distant and trivial memories. Somewhat later he
learned that he was paralyzed. The fact scarcely interested him.
He reasoned (he felt) that his immobility was a minimum price
to pay. Now his perception and his memory were infallible.

Borges goes on to report young Funes's extraordinary accomplishments: his ability to master Latin in an evening, his impatience with numbering or indeed with any system employing
generalization, or even system itself, which, given his memory,
he has no need of. "In the teeming world of Funes there were
only details, almost immediate in their presence." To be able
to forget nothing, never to turn one's mind off, is of course to
live in a kind of hell. Funes's hell is also the hell of the insom-
niac, as well as the hell of a certain kind of writer. Ireneo Funes
cannot bear it past the age of nineteen. "Ireneo Funes died in
1889," Borges concludes his story, "of congestion of the lungs,"
but what he really dies of is perceptual overload.

This story happens to be a little classic of modernism, in the
sense in which Clement Greenberg maintained that "the essence
of modernism lies in the use of the characteristic method of a
discipline to criticize itself. . . ." Yet was Borges a modernist
writer? He himself disdained all artistic labels, saying, "I do
not profess any aesthetic. Why add to the natural limits which
habit imposes on us those of some theory or other?" And yet
it is difficult to disdain them when attempting to place Borges.
For when one compares Borges with the modernist masters of
fiction, he falls short.

As with Proust, time and memory are of paramount importance to Borges; but unlike Proust, Borges does not set them
in the context of love and the intricacies of social relations.
Like Joyce, Borges is a master parodist and student of style;
but unlike style in Joyce, style in Borges never quite achieves
that density of effect that turns it into a way of viewing the
world—a vision. There is a weight to Kafka that Borges does
not begin to possess. Kafka's argument is with reality, which
in his bureaucratic dystopias becomes a nightmare, and he is

anguished at his own inability to adjust to reality of this or almost any other kind. Borges, far from arguing with reality, prefers to postulate its nonexistence. When Kafka argues with reality, one feels his very soul is at stake; when Borges plays with reality, one feels it is all in his head.

Borges had for some time been a great figure in the literary life of Argentina, but only in 1961, when he shared with Samuel Beckett the Formentor Prize (a $10,000 award furnished by six avant-garde publishers in Europe and the United States), did his renown burst the borders of his native country. He was sixty-two years old, and the award had, in many ways, come just in time. Roughly six years before, owing to his increasing blindness, Borges had to cease writing his stories ("critical fictions," his sometime collaborator Adolfo Bioy Casares called them) and his elaborate essays. He now returned to writing poetry—metrical verse, in fact, the meter serving as an aid to the memory of a man who could no longer see his own text. He now had to be read to. Irony of ironies, he was appointed director of the National Library in Buenos Aires, causing him to remark that God had granted him "at one time 800,000 books and darkness." An all too Borgesian story, that.

"As a consequence of that prize, my books mushroomed overnight throughout the Western world," Borges noted. The first consequence was the simultaneous publication of Borges's collection of tales, *Ficciones,* in six different countries. The second consequence was the discovery of Borges by academic literary departments, who fell hungrily on the carcass of his corpus in the middle sixties and are still gnawing on the bones. Honor now followed honor. Borges was appointed to the Charles Eliot Norton Chair of Poetry at Harvard; there was a "Borges Conference" at the University of Oklahoma; magazines published special Borges issues. "An Evening with Jorge Luis Borges" became a not infrequent event on American university campuses. Here Borges gave dollar value, for he was impressive on stage; besides, one could hardly watch him without recalling the blindness of Homer and Milton. In 1971 he was awarded the Jerusalem Prize. He gave more interviews than Hedda Hopper got. Monegal writes that "Borges took to fame with an almost childlike glee." One recalls the triumphal visit of Gertrude Stein to America after the publication of *The Autobiography of Alice B. Toklas*. Apparently few things excite an avant-garde writer like a crashing popular success.

In his last years, Borges, with his deep-set eye sockets, came in his photographs to resemble a wise old monkey of the kind one might see perched amid erotic sculpture on the outside wall of a temple in India. To his blindness was added loss of hearing, encasing him in a labyrinth not of his own but of nature's devising. He came to look upon death as a relief. As he wrote about the Argentine poet Leopoldo Lugones, who committed suicide on one of the islands of Tigre, "he may have felt, perhaps for the first time in his life, that he was freeing himself, at last, of the mysterious duty of searching out metaphors, adjectives, and verbs for everything in the world."

Borges's life is a fantastic, better yet a Borgesian, story, made all the richer by the fact that Borges himself enjoyed nothing quite so much as a fantastic story. He once prophetically wrote:

A man sets himself the task of making a plan of the universe. After many years, he fills a whole space with images of provinces, kingdoms, mountains, bays, ships, islands, fish, rooms, instruments, stars, horses, and people. On the threshold of death, he discovers that the patient labyrinth of lines has traced the likeness of his own face.

So it is with Borges, a writer without quite the power to present his readers with a new and higher organization of experience, such as only the very greatest artists can provide, but whose complexity and richness caused his art to rise above nihilism to become one of the most charming ornaments of the literature of our century.

Commentary 1987

One Cheer for
E. M. Forster

It is devilish difficult to criticize society & also create human beings. Unless one has a big mind, one aim or the other fails before the book is finished. I must pray for a big mind, but it is uphill work—!

—E. M. Forster, letter to Edward Garnett

H OW DID E. M. FORSTER manage to elude the Nobel Prize in Literature? He published his last novel, *A Passage to India*, at the age of forty-five in 1924 and died at the age of ninety-two in 1970. He must have been passed over, then, no fewer than thirty or forty times. Not winning the Nobel Prize put him in a select little club, Tolstoy, Henry James, Chekhov, and Proust being among its most distinguished members—rather a more select club, when one thinks about it, than that comprised by the winners. Still, one wonders, did Forster think much about it?

No mention of the Nobel Prize is made in P. N. Furbank's *E. M. Forster, A Life;* nor does the subject arise anywhere in the two-volume edition of the *Selected Letters of E. M. Forster.* True, Forster's work is relatively unmarked by the rather strenuous thinking on the cosmic level that Nobel Prize committees seem traditionally to favor. Yet E. M. Forster has long held a special place in the hearts of English-speaking readers. He is the novelist par excellence of modern liberalism, and during a period when the liberal point of view has been ascendant. If he had won the Nobel Prize, it would scarcely have been a surprise. On the contrary, it is rather surprising in retrospect that he did not.

The complicated truth is that E. M. Forster was probably better off without the Nobel Prize. It would have been unseemly, even slightly unbecoming to him, a man who made something of a specialty of claiming so little for himself in the way of literary aspirations. But aspirations are one thing, reputation another. Forster's reputation has never been other than high. Even today it sails in the literary stratosphere. The most consistent note in the often strident criticism of David Lean's film version of *A Passage to India,* for example, was that Lean betrayed the richness and subtlety of Forster's novel. What was almost universally judged to be a poor film thus redounded to Forster's posthumous standing.

Not that this standing required much in the way of reinforcement. Apart from his attempt to write a homosexual idyll, the posthumously published novel *Maurice,* Forster's work has received no serious attacks, and his reputation has remained oddly inviolate. During his lifetime it appeared that the less he wrote, the higher his reputation rose. Percy Lubbock is supposed to have said to Forster in 1955: "It's too funny your becoming the holy man of letters. You're really a spiteful old thing. Why haven't people found you out, and run you down?" To which Forster is said to have replied: "They're beginning. But they haven't truly begun; or if they have they are certainly taking their time about it." "Holy man of letters" continues, for the most part, to fit the general view of E. M. Forster today.

Forster is a novelist best read young. I first read him in my early twenties and was greatly moved by him. He did not seem a genius, but very perceptive, wise, and sensitive in a way that made one feel slightly brutish and insensitive in one's own views.

There are certain writers whom we value less for their brilliance than for the fact that they seem rather like ourselves, except that they possess virtues we admire but feel lacking in ourselves. George Orwell is such a writer: one does not consider him a genius or a profound thinker; what one admires—even envies—is his ability to cut through cant to grasp the chief points about a book, or an event, or an argument in a manly and no-nonsense way. Forster once made a not dissimilar point in writing about Samuel Butler's *Erewhon* in an essay entitled "A Book That Influenced Me": "I suggest that the only books that influence us are those for which we are ready, and which have gone a little farther down our own particular path than we have yet got ourselves. . . . You are being influenced when you can say, 'I might have written that myself if I hadn't been so busy.'" Forster himself was just such an influence on many a youthful student of literature. One did not quite think one could have written his books, but he had, as he put it, "gone a little farther down our own particular path than we [had] yet got ourselves." I. A. Richards put it rather differently when he noted that Forster's "real audience is youth, caught at that stage when rebellion against uncomfortable conventions is easy because the cost of abandoning them has not been counted."

I have called E. M. Forster the novelist par excellence of modern liberalism, but I am not the first to have done so. Lionel Trilling did it as early as 1943 in a critical study that over the years has immensely aided E. M. Forster's reputation. As Trilling allowed in a preface to the second edition of this book, his study had "benefited by the special energies that attend a polemical purpose." Trilling had been attacking American writing for what he deemed its "dullness and its pious social simplicities," and against this he now posed Forster's "vivacity, complexity, and irony." Like many of the writers Trilling had attacked, Forster was a liberal, but a liberal with a difference—he was a liberal, in Trilling's view, "at war with the liberal imagination." Forster was of the liberal tradition yet at the same time would have nothing to do with its simple solutions, its crudities, its sentimentality, and its earnest belief in rationalism. In other words, without losing his idealism, neither did Forster lose his head; never for a moment did Forster settle for received opinions, and indeed, according to Trilling, he even "refuses to be conclusive." Forster possessed—a crucial element, this, for Lionel Trilling—"moral realism," which Trilling defined as not only "the awareness of morality itself but of the contradictions, paradoxes, and dangers of living the moral life."

Apart from his doctoral dissertation on Matthew Arnold, Lionel Trilling wrote no other work of sustained advocacy like his *E. M. Forster*. His advocacy was not without qualification, yet advocacy it was, pretty much straight-out and full-blown. The book's opening sentence reads: "E. M. Forster is for me the only living novelist who can be read again and again and who, after each reading, gives me what few writers can give us after our first days of novel reading, the sensation of having learned something." In his qualified manner Trilling remarked that "surely the Greek myths made too deep an impress on Forster," yet he went on to compare such a relatively thin Forster novel as *Where Angels Fear to Tread* with Samuel Butler's *The Way of All Flesh* and Henry James's *The Ambassadors*—surely an instance, as the English say, of over-egging the pudding. Even Forster's flaws were judged raisins in the pudding. If Trilling granted that *The Longest Journey* is the least well-formed of Forster's novels, well, "the responsive reader can be conscious not of an inadequate plan or of a defect in structure but rather of the too-much steam that blows up the boiler." *Howards End*, according to Trilling, "is undoubtedly Forster's masterpiece"; it is "a novel about England's fate." At the close, the bugles are brought out, and the final sentence in *E. M. Forster* reads: "He is one of those who raise the shield of Achilles, which is the moral intelligence of art, against the panic and emptiness which make their onset when the will is tired from its own excess."

Although Lionel Trilling's book about Forster was published after Forster's work as a novelist was complete, it appeared, even in its second edition, before the novel *Maurice* was made public and well before the appearance of P. N. Furbank's biography and the edition of the *Selected Letters*. Trilling did not go into Forster's politics in any detail, except to say that, from his university days on, Forster's was to be an appeal from the Left to the Liberal party and to the middle class. In Trilling's book the word "homosexual" is never mentioned. There is nothing either trivial or silly in the book; it contains much elegant and subtle criticism. Yet my guess is that if Lionel Trilling had known then what the rest of us know now about his subject, he would either not have written his *E. M. Forster* or have written a very different book.

The relation between biography and criticism remains one of the unexplored literary subjects of our day. Ideally, the biography of a writer will chronicle the conditions and explain the travail under which his books—the reason for our interest in him to begin with—were written. Ideally, we come away from having read a literary biography with a widened appreciation of a writer and a deepened understanding of his work. Ideally, after the biographer is done, misunderstandings are cleared up, light is cast into corners where hitherto shadows had clung, lucidity emerges triumphant, and we have another fair and sunny day in the Republic of Letters. *Ideally.* In reality, the results of modern literary biography, given its penchant for psychological and sexual revelation, are rather murkier. Often, where before we had an admired writer, once modern literary biography has done its work we are left with a little pile of secrets revealed. Almost invariably the effect of these revelations does not work in the writer's favor; usually he comes away looking smaller and meaner and less than we thought him beforehand. The only writers I can think of who have come through their trials by literary biography more or less intact are Samuel Johnson, Henry James, and Anton Chekhov; Tolstoy, the only universal genius among modern writers, one tends to admire even for his weaknesses, which somehow make this gigantic figure seem more human. But generally degradation is the result, even when the biographer is favorably disposed toward his subject. This is the way it works, and there is no reason to think it will soon change.

P. N. Furbank, E. M. Forster's biographer, is indisputably well-disposed toward his subject. Forster himself was favorably disposed toward a biography that would tell his life in full. While working on his own biography of his teacher and friend Goldsworthy Lowes Dickinson, Forster told another friend, the writer J. R. Ackerley: "I wish I could get one written about me after I die, but I should want everything told, everything, and there's so far so little." Furbank has evidently taken this as his marching order. He is a biographer with no serious interest in Freudian or other doctrinal psychology. He cites no wound, he speaks of no bow; the carpet of his biography has no strong or subtle figure playing through it. It is facts he sets out, one after another, in more than six hundred pages.

Yet one fact emerges over and above all others—the fact of E. M. Forster's homosexuality. It is a towering fact, one so central to his life as to color almost all the rest. Until reading P. N. Furbank's biography and, more recently, his and Mary Lago's finely edited *Selected Letters,* although I had assumed that Forster was a homosexual, I had no sense of how significant his homosexuality was to his life and work. Not that homosexuality is ever negligible or trivial—certainly it cannot have been when, in England, one could have gone to prison for it—but in Forster's case I even thought his homosexuality possibly of literary advantage. It lent him, I felt, a certain detachment; it set him outside the battle of the heterosexes, and perhaps gave him a small but real advantage in chronicling the emotional entanglements between men and women. Or so I felt.

Certainly there is nothing one can construe as overtly homosexual about E. M. Forster's novels. Apart form *Maurice*, there are no homosexual characters in any of the five novels upon which his reputation rests. Nor is there any animus against women; and indeed as often as not his female characters are genuine heroines. One could not hope to argue that some of his characters are, in effect, got up in drag, as is sometimes true of Proust's characters, for this simply is not so. Can it be, though, that while Forster's novels are in no way patently homosexual, the impulse behind them is homosexual? But then what does it mean to say that the impulse behind a body of work is homosexual? Might the answer to that question be found less in the work than in the life?

About that life nearly everything is now known. The English are supposedly famous for their reserve, but English writers, particularly in this century, are becoming quite as famous for their candor. In the circle of Bloomsbury, of which E. M. Forster was a fringe member, so-called "truth-telling" was a matter of principle and an article of faith. Hence Forster's willingness to have everything about his life known. He kept diaries. He wrote a vast number of letters, in most of which he set no brake on his feelings. He was not in the habit of practicing small deceptions. (The larger deception of his homosexuality was forced upon him.) Although he wrote neither autobiographies nor memoirs, he shows up in the autobiographies and memoirs, diaries and journals, of a great many other writers. No dearth of material here, and no lack of willingness on his biographer's part to set it out for public display.

E. M. Forster was descended from those intellectually minded, evangelically inspired, communally living figures known as the Clapham Sect—so called because of their having settled in the village of Clapham. Among the Clapham Sect were such illustrious names as Wilberforce, Macaulay, Stephen, and Whichelo. Forster's connection was through his aunt Marianne Thornton, about whom he later wrote a domestic biography and who claimed herself to be the last survivor of the sect. His father was an architect, his mother briefly a governess before marriage. Fortunate in his forebears, E. M. Forster was unfortunate in having lost his father, to consumption, when he was but a year old. An only child, he was raised by his mother and a host of aunts in a household that was fatherless and brotherless.

Forster's aunt Marianne Thorton used to refer to him as the "Important One." Freud said that a man assured of his mother's love will be a conqueror; he did not say what became of a man who had *all* his mother's love and much of that of his other female relatives into the bargain. E. M. Forster was brought up with the most gentle and generous concern for his well-being, never punished, always catered to, not allowed to go out into the rain, swaddled in scarves and sweaters—in a sound English word, he was mollycoddled. He was always a dutiful and good son who on more than one occasion had to establish his independence from his mother—she lived to be ninety. In later years he addressed his mother in his letters as "Mummy" and signed them "Poppy."

Convinced by his mother that he was fragile, quite spoiled by the elderly ladies among whom he had grown up, a bit of a prig with preternaturally adult interests in music and church architecture, Forster, by the time he went off to Tonbridge School as a day boy, had acquired all the characteristics essential to the perfect victim of schoolboy bullies. Bullied he was; fearful throughout his school days he remained, a slender boy with sloping shoulders and a receding chin who walked with his eyes cast down and who had a physician's letter excusing him from taking part in games. (He would get his own back at such schools in his description of the muscular and insensitive Christianity of the Sawston School in his novel *The Long-*

est Journey.) Years later, in the *Spectator*, he would write: "School was the unhappiest time of my life, and the worst trick it ever played me was to pretend that it was the world in miniature. For it hindered me from discovering how lovely and delightful and kind the world can be, and how much of it is intelligible."

Cambridge was the true beginning of life for Forster. It meant freedom from his home, freedom from schoolboy bullying, freedom to strike out for himself intellectually and spiritually. At Cambridge, where skepticism mingled in the air with oxygen, he shed any lingering shreds of Christianity he might have retained. He was never drawn to the character of Jesus; nor did the high premium Christianity placed on pain and suffering in any way appeal to him. He read classics at King's College; among his tutors were Nathaniel Wedd and the great academic snob Oscar Browning. He came under the influence of Goldsworthy Lowes Dickinson, who combined in his teaching and in his person Hellenism and liberalism. Mousy though he remained—Lytton Strachey gave him the nickname Taupe (i.e., Mole)—his mousiness no longer prevented him from making friends or from having his merit recognized.

In his last year at Cambridge he was elected to the Society of Apostles, the select coterie of intellectuals whose leading figure was then G. E. Moore and whose membership included Bertrand Russell, John Maynard Keynes, and Strachey. Election to the Apostles was a great event in Forster's life, in effect tying him permanently to Cambridge. While he much enjoyed the friendship of the Society of Apostles, he must have enjoyed even more the implied validation of his intellectual quality. "Someone told me, many years ago, that I was amusing, and I have never quite recovered from the effects," he once wrote to his friend Robert Trevelyan. Neither did he ever quite recover from the effects of being elected to the Apostles, which gave him unshakable confidence in his intellectual ability.

E. M. Forster's intellectual ability was not of the ordinary kind. He never felt he had any commanding power of abstract thought. He never felt the passion of the scholar, though in later years he was commissioned by Dickinson to edit the Dent Classics edition of the *Aeneid* and lectured at workingmen's colleges on the Italian Renaissance. His were the powers of serene observation, often oblique but usually telling. He had quiet wit and a lyrical streak and imaginative sympathy. He had a lucid mind and had early acquired a prose style of unobtrusive elegance that permitted him to state profound things with simplicity. In Forster, intellect united with sensibility, and their tethering in tandem produced the artist that, at Cambridge, he knew he would become.

At Cambridge, too, Forster, according to his biographer, realized that he was a homosexual. Before he had arrived there his sexual experience, to put it softly, was limited. His exceedingly prim upbringing had seen to that; as a child his member was referred to by his mother as his "dirty." When he was a young boy there had been an incident with a stranger in a deerstalker's cap. P. N. Furbank, striking the chilling modern biographical note, writes: "It is true, he rediscovered masturbation when he was 15 or 16, and it was henceforth always to play a large part in his life. . . ." Forster himself allowed that it wasn't until he was thirty that he was quite clear about the mechanics of fornication.

To be sure, there was no shortage of homosexual practitioners in and around Cambridge. Lytton Strachey was a very enthusiastic homosexual; Keynes was mildly famous for his adventures in the line that Mencken once termed "non-Euclidian sex"; and Goldsworthy Lowes Dickinson, Forster's mentor, was someone whose notion of a jolly good time was to have young men stand upon him with their boots on, a fact missing from Forster's biography of Dickinson but not from Dickinson's autobiography. Forster did have a rather chaste affair—embraces and kisses—with a handsome fellow Apostle named H. O. Meredith, who had had love affairs with girls and who later married. P. N. Furbank describes the influence of this relationship on Forster in the following terms:

> But if H.O.M. was the initiator, it was Forster for whom the affair counted most. For him, it was immense and epoch-making; it was, he felt, as if all the "greatness" of the world had been opened up to him. He counted this as the second grand "discovery" of his youth—his emancipation from Christianity being the first—and for the moment it seemed to him as though all the rest of his existence would not be too long to work out the consequences.

Still, the time was the turn of the century; the Oscar Wilde scandal was much in the air; and Forster was by temperament a cautious young man. When he left Cambridge he knew he was a homosexual, but it was not clear what he was prepared to do about it.

A poet, an old Russian proverb has it, always cheats his boss. E. M. Forster, who would grow into a poetic novelist, was under no such compulsion, having been spared the need to work by an inheritance of £8,000 left him by Marianne Thornton. He worked at various jobs over the years—a lecturer, a tutor to a German family at Nassenheide, a cataloguer at the National Gallery, secretary to the maharajah of Dewas, a "searcher" for the Red Cross Wounded and Missing Bureau in Egypt in World War I—but these were as much as anything to give him something to do and make him feel a part of the life around him. He traveled with his mother to Italy, which he later described as "the beautiful country where they say 'yes,' and the place 'where things happen.'" Between the time he left Cambridge and the beginning of World War I he wrote five and published four novels: *Where Angels Fear to Tread* (1905), *The Longest Journey* (1907), *A Room with a View* (1908), *Howards End* (1910), and *Maurice* (written in 1914, published in 1971).

Remarkable though this is as sheer literary productivity, it scarcely seems to have been at the center of Forster's life. That he was a commercially successful, critically honored, and quite famous novelist seemed not to have much mattered to him, either. What was at the center of his being, what did matter terribly to him, appears to have been a relentless yearning, and the haunting feeling of missing out on life.

Although E. M. Forster is generally thrown into that literary group known as Bloomsbury, he was in fact never more than peripheral to it (his name is usually tossed in to lend it additional prestige). True, he attended many of its Thursday-evening sessions, but when things got going he usually departed in time to catch a train to Weybridge or West Hackhurst, where he lived a quite suburban existence with his mother among the dowdy and genteel. Leonard Woolf, though he respected Forster's artistry and was fond of him—his wife Virginia depended on Forster's approval of her own work—always thought him "a perfect old woman." At twenty-five, Forster summed up his life in his diary as "now straightening into something rather sad & dull to be sure . . ." and resolved, among other things, on "more exercise: keep the brutes quiet"; not to "shrink from self-analysis, but don't keep at it too long"; to "get a less superficial idea of women"; and not to "be so afraid to go into strange places or company, & be a fool more frequently." Later he would write erotic homosexual stories "not to express myself but to excite myself." Even after the bountiful success of *Howards End,* he noted: "Good luck has been good to me hitherto but the future is doubtful."

If the grand discoveries of Forster's life were the shedding of Christianity and the realization of his homosexuality, the grand event of his life was a love affair with an Egyptian tram conductor in Alexandria named Mohammed el Adl. He had earlier been in love, though nothing physical came of it, with a Muslim Indian named Syed Ross Masood; it is owing to Masood that Forster made his first visit to and established his lifelong connection with India. Apart from a brief fling later with a London bus driver, and another with an Indian servant in Dewas, the final love of his life was with a policeman, who later married, named Bob Buckingham. All Forster's loves cut through class lines—through and downward. Did sex and politics commingle for Forster? Were his interclass, interracial loves expressions of his liberalism conducted by other means?

What is rather sad about Forster's love affair with Mohammed el Adl is how little it took to make him happy. They struck up a conversation on the conductor's tram. Forster began to ride it daily; the conductor soon refused to collect his fare. Forster proposed they meet at night. They went sometimes to Mohammed el Adl's room, sometimes to Forster's flat. The Egyptian was very dark and his presence shocked Forster's landlady, which made meeting there any longer impossible. One night Forster, bursting with sexual excitement, put his rather inept moves on the tram conductor and a scuffle ensued, in which the former hurt his hand and the latter his eye. ("The idealist, I have noticed," wrote Somerset Maugham in his story "The Human Element," "is apt to be imprudent in the affairs of the flesh.") When Forster again raised the prospect of their going to bed together, Mohammed el Adl replied: "Never, never!" Once he asked Forster: "Do you never consider that your wish has led you to know a tram conductor?" Eventually he gave in to Forster's urgent requests. Forster wrote to Florence Barger, his confidante in England, about this affair: "Wish I was writing the latter half of *Maurice*. I now know so much more." And: "My luck has been amazing."

"It isn't happiness," Forster wrote, "it's rather—offensive phrase—that I first feel a grown-up man." The year was 1917; he was thirty-eight years old. His letters about his relationship with Mohammed el Adl are gushing. He was immensely pleased with himself for having set fear aside and taken the courage to plunge into this relationship: "The practical difficulties—there is a big racial and social gulf—are great: but when you are offered affection, honesty, and intelligence with all that you can possibly want of externals thrown in (including a delightful sense of humor), you surely have to take it or die spiritually."

A political element was also involved, and so to Florence Barger, Forster wrote: "It seems to me that to be trusted, and to be trusted across the barriers of income, race and class, is the greatest reward a man can receive, and that even if the agreement is not attained, even if he goes to Cairo and forgets me, I shall not have failed; and that other people are winning similar victories elsewhere: you and I, too, are winning one." It is difficult to disentangle the kinds of emotion he felt—to know where sexual love leaves off and politics begins, where politics leaves off and sexual love begins: "I have never had anything like this in my life—much friendliness and tolerance, but never this—and not till now was I capable of having it, for I hadn't attained the complete contempt for civilization that provides the necessary calm."

When I say "politics," when I say "liberalism," I mean both words in a special sense. E. M. Forster's was essentially the politics of liberation, his the liberalism of personal emancipation. Edward Shils, a connoisseur of the various shadings of modern liberalism, refers to Forster's as "emancipatory liberalism." Where traditional, progressivist liberalism has always been interested in the manipulation of social and economic institutions toward the end of what it construes to be greater social justice, emancipatory liberalism wishes to change existing institutions and attitudes in order to widen the margin of personal freedom, of sentiment and impulse. The two are of course finely enmeshed, and one of the grave problems of contemporary liberalism is that its adherents do not feel themselves permitted to order their politics à la carte: they want a redistribution of income, they also get the campaign to legalize marijuana; they want an enlarged interpretation of civil liberties, they have to take the lesbian wing of feminism.

Yet the importance of this love affair to E. M. Forster can scarcely be overemphasized. In a perhaps mysterious yet undeniable way it seems to have freed him, both as a writer and as a man. He became a good deal less—in a word I have seen used by Edmund White—"closetty." He had always been a utopian for love, and now, however fleetingly, he had actually experienced something of the love he had hitherto been confined to lauding. He had thought himself dried up as a novelist, but in 1924, fully fourteen years after the publication of *Howards End,* he completed *A Passage to India.* Until now it might have been said that his literary reputation had been melting away; *A Passage to India* solidified it—indeed, set it in marble.

As for the nature of Forster's reputation, it was that of a supreme artist who was also a grand humanitarian. He was a man on the side of art and the downtrodden, the great guru and exemplar of personal relations, the leader of the group he himself designated as the "aristocracy of the sensitive, the considerate and the plucky." In the 1930s he became a man to have at political conferences and an indispensable signatory at the bottom of political petitions. He became a figure in the International PEN Club, a professional civil libertarian, a cheerleader from the Left sidelines who could say, as Forster did from the platform of the International Writers Congress in Paris in 1935: "I am not a Communist, though perhaps I might be one if I was a younger and braver man, for in Communism I can see hope." When Philip Toynbee reviewed Forster's collection of political and literary essays, *Two Cheers for Democracy,* he entitled his review "Too Good for This World," a title not meant to be taken the least bit ironically.

After *A Passage to India,* Forster wrote no more novels. He turned more and more to literary journalism. He wrote a nonfiction book on India, *The Hill of Devi;* he gave the lectures that resulted in *Aspects of the Novel;* he wrote the biography of his aunt; he wrote a libretto for Benjamin Britten's opera *Billy*

Budd. His social circle was almost entirely homosexual. Among his closest friends were Christopher Isherwood, J. R. Ackerley, and William Plomer. He became something akin to the homosexuals' Tolstoy, with King's College, Cambridge, where he lived from 1946 on, his Yasnaya Polyana. ("Tennessee Williams got up too late to reach Cambridge," he wrote to Isherwood. "[Gore] Vidal arrived and I wish he hadn't, as I disliked him a lot.") The fame and money that came with *A Passage to India*, he wrote to Florence Barger, "leave me cold," adding, "my daily life has never been so trying, and there is no one to fill it emotionally." Virginia Woolf, who could cast one of the coldest eyes in the business, wrote apropos of him: "The middle age of buggers is not to be contemplated without horror. . . ." At fifty he entered into the final love affair of his life, with the policeman Bob Buckingham.

To his circle of friends Forster had long been, in P. N. Furbank's words, "a symbol and a hero." Now such feelings about him spread well beyond friends. The thesis-hunters pestered him for interpretations of his novels and requests for interviews. He was much in demand as a lecturer. He turned down various honorary degrees, including one from Oxford. He also turned down a knighthood, though in 1953 he did accept a Companion of Honour, noting after receiving it that if the queen had been a boy he would have fallen in love with her. On his eightieth birthday W. H. Auden sent him a telegram that read: "Old famous loved yet not a sacred cow." Yet a sacred cow was precisely what he had become, for idolization had set in in earnest. Even a hard little number like Dorothy Parker praised him lavishly. Perhaps no man in our time has been more honored not only as a writer but, as P. N. Furbank notes, "for personal goodness and sanctity."

In the history of modern literary reputations, E. M. Forster's is in every way an extraordinary case. No writer put forth fewer claims for himself. Modesty seems to have been his stock in trade, extending even to his personal appearance. Gerald

Brenan was only one among many people who commented on his prim, rather old-maidish aspect. William Plomer called him the very reverse of a dandy: "Incurious fellow passengers in a train, seeing him in a cheap cloth cap and a scruffy waterproof, and carrying the sort of little bag that might have been carried in 1890 by the man who came to wind the clocks, might have thought him a dim provincial of settled habits and taken no more notice of him." Or, as V. S. Pritchett once put it, "he looked like a whim."

As dull as Forster looked, just that bright could he be. One did not often pull that cloth cap over his eyes. In the literary realm, certainly, not very much got by him. Edward Gibbon and Jane Austen were among his most favored authors, and, like them, he could be subtle *and* sharp. In contradistinction to the Rupert Brooke legend, for example, as early as 1915 he wrote to a friend of the sonnets on which Brooke's reputation was based: "They were inspired by his romantic thoughts about war, not by his knowledge of it." He had the English gift of tying common sense to aesthetic sense. Thus, on the subject of Proust and jealousy, he wrote: "He and 'life' are not identical here, life being the more amiable of the two, and future historians will find that his epic of curiosity and despair almost sums up you and me, but not quite." He strikes me as dead on target on Virginia Woolf, about whom he noted: "She is a poet who wants to write something as near to a novel as possible." On Virginia Woolf's feminism he was also quite sharp, writing: "She was sensible about the past; about the present she was sometimes unreasonable." But then his soft liberalism takes control: "The best judges of her feminism are neither elderly men nor even elderly women, but young women. If they . . . think that it expresses an existent grievance, they are right."

Yet, as Lionel Trilling wrote, the "total effect" of Forster's criticism "is not really impressive." For one thing, the authority of much of it rests upon his standing as a practicing artist; for another, though he gave criticism its due for having educational and cultural value as well as for exposing fraud and pretentiousness, he was dubious about its ability to help an artist to improve his work, for criticism, he felt, "cannot help him in great matters." He himself appears to have been little influenced by criticism of his own work, for he believed he had taken his own measure quite as accurately as anyone was likely to do. Writing to the critic Peter Burra in 1934 he noted: "I have been looking at my books lately, partly on account of your article. I think *A Passage to India* stands, but the fissures in the others are considerable." "In fact," he wrote to Robert Trevelyan when he was only twenty-six, "my equipment is frightfully limited, but so good in parts that I want to do with it what I can." That is a very astute judgment, and one that leaves a most interesting question in its trail: What did E. M. Forster do with his literary equipment?

Evelyn Waugh once remarked that most writers, even quite good ones, have only one or two stories to tell. The exceptions are the truly major figures: Balzac, Dickens, George Eliot, Tolstoy, James, Conrad. But E. M. Forster, I don't think many would wish to dispute, is not among their number. He was a one-story man. His is the story of the undeveloped heart. He told it four different times, then set it in India and told it again. In this story a character—an English man or woman of the middle class—is placed in a crucial situation, a crucible of the spirit as it turns out, where his or her heart either develops or permanently stultifies. This crucible invariably entails a confrontation with the primitive, or the preliterate, or the *déclassé*. In all Forster's novels culture is pitted against spirit, mind against feeling. It takes no deep reader to recognize that the author, though himself a habitué of the concert hall and of suburban teas upon English lawns, is on the side of spirit and feeling.

A paradigmatic E. M. Forster story is "The Road from Colonus," a tale written when he was in his twenties. In it a group of English travelers are touring by mule in Greece. Mr. Lucas, the oldest member of the group, comes upon an enormous plane tree near a rather squalid Greek house. The center of the tree is hollowed out, and from it water flows, which irrigates and makes fertile the land below. The tree is a shrine from which little votive offerings hang. The sight of the tree stirs Mr. Lucas, who climbs into its hollow, the water flowing about him. In it he feels overpoweringly the urge to live. "To Mr. Lucas, who, in a brief space of time, had discovered not only Greece, but England and all the world and life, there seemed nothing ludicrous in the desire to hang upon the tree another votive offering—a little model of an entire man." He feels himself utterly at peace—"the feeling of the swimmer, who, after long struggle with chopping seas, finds that after all the tide will sweep him to his goal."

At which moment his daughter and the remainder of the party of English travelers arrive. They exclaim over the beauty of the tree, the crude little Greek dwelling, the entire scene. But Mr. Lucas "found them intolerable. Their enthusiasm was superficial, commonplace, and spasmodic." When Mr. Lucas announces that he plans to remain there, to stay as a guest in the house of the Greeks, his daughter and the other members of the party humor him. For himself, he believes that "in that place and with those people [the Greeks who live in the house] a supreme event was awaiting him which would transfigure the face of the world." But of course he cannot be permitted to stay in any such place. In the end he is dragged off, brusquely set upon his mule by their guide. It is not to be.

In the second part of the story Mr. Lucas and his daughter are back in England. He is complaining about the disorderly behavior of their neighbor's children. She has just received a parcel from Athens containing asphodel bulbs, wrapped up in an old Greek newspaper. It happens that the newspaper carries a story about a small tragedy that occurred in the province of Messenia, where a large tree blew down in the night and crushed to death the occupants of a nearby house. It is of course the very tree and the very house from which Mr. Lucas had been forcibly removed. Now, in England, he is not much interested in the story. His daughter remarks upon what a near miss they have had. Had he stayed in the house as he wished, he might well have been killed, too. But Mr. Lucas is scarcely listening. Instead he rambles on about his neighbors and composes a letter of complaint to their landlord. "Such a marvelous deliverance," says his daughter, "does make one believe in Providence." But in fact Mr. Lucas had to all intents and purposes died the moment he had been dragged away; his heart had shriveled from that very moment and from that very moment, too, he had been consigned to live out his days in middle-class English suburban sterility.

To dwell on "The Road from Colonus" a bit longer, one grants Forster his concluding point: yes, it would have been better to have died happy, even that very night, in the rough-hewn Greek house, feeling oneself in touch with the spirit of the world, than to live out one's days a grumbly, grousing old man. That is conceded. What is less easy to concede is the validity of Mr. Lucas's mystical experience in the tree and the wisdom of the Greek family, who, however squalid the conditions of their lives, had never lost the gift of living in nature and hence had retained the secret of the art of life. Clearly, Forster hated middle-class life, the sterility of its culure, the aridity of its relationships, but all he could pose against it was the superiority of those who, through whatever accidents of geography or social class, eluded it.

For an otherwise remarkably subtle novelist, E. M. Forster could be remarkably crude in his division of characters into those who were and those who were not in touch with life. In the middle were those characters whose personal drama—supplying the drama of his novels—revolved around the question of which side they would fall on. Like many another artist and intellectual of his day, Forster suffered the condition known as horror victorianus; in his novels villains and villainesses are, not very far under the skin, uneminent Victorians: people who believe in progress, empire, the virtues of their social class. As he presents them they are not so much cardboard as metallic; they continually give off sharp pings of their author's disapproval.

Nor did Forster have great powers of invention. All his novels are marred by unbelievable touches. Rickie Elliot in *The Longest Journey* falls in love with his wife-to-be when he sees her being passionately kissed by her fiancé; a bookcase topples onto the pathetic culture-hungry Leonard Bast in the crucial scene in *Howards End;* Lucy Honeychurch is kissed by George Emerson in a field of spring flowers in Italy, which is noted by a female novelist who later publishes a novel reproducing the scene, which causes a scandal that in turn forces the action in *A Room with a View;* a carriage crashes, killing a kidnapped infant in *Where Angels Fear to Tread;* characters regularly die on the instant ("Gerald died that afternoon," is an inspissated but not anomalous sentence in a Forster novel). I do not mean that such things don't happen in life, which provides the trickiest plots of all, but in Forster's novels there is a herky-jerky quality to his plots. If one of the things masterful novelists do is to make the unpredictable seem inevitable, in Forster the unpredictable tends to be expected, which is not at all the same thing. Max Beerbohm's reaction to *Howards End,* the first half of which he thought "beautiful and delightful," might be pressed into service as a general judgment on nearly all E. M. Forster's novels:

> I felt as though I had been taken up for an air-joyride by an "ace" aeronaut, and had mounted high and far, seeing far below me a charming conspectus of things as they are, and had immensely enjoyed the sight, until suddenly the machine began to jerk and wobble, and I looked at the ace, and his face had turned pale green, and his jaw had dropped, and I said, "Is anything the matter?" and he gasped "Yes, I'm afraid I—," and at that moment the machine gave a nose-dive, and, a few sickening moments later, I and my trusted pilot were no more.

But the flight up, as Beerbohm acknowledged, could be dazzling. To shift metaphors abruptly, if E. M. Forster had few cards in his hand, he could nonetheless shuffle them brilliantly. He was an astute judge of character and a potent moralist, in the French sense of the word. Of Mr. Wilcox in *Howards End,* for example, he writes: "But true insight began just where his intelligence ended, and one gathered that this was the case with most millionaires." Adela Quested in *A Passage to India* fails to realize "that it is only hypocrites who cannot forgive hypocrisy." Forster's novels are studded with such small gems. Quite as much as for their action—perhaps rather more than for their action—one anticipates Forster's aphoristic commentary upon his characters.

In his book on Forster, Lionel Trilling remarks that "in Forster there is a deep and important irresolution of whether the world is one of good and evil, sheep and goats, or one of good-and-evil, of sheep who are somehow goats and goats who are somehow sheep." Trilling refers here to Forster's propensity in his novels to allow good actions occasionally to derive from characters of whom he otherwise disapproves, and, going the other way round, to impute qualities of which he clearly disapproves to characters he clearly wishes us to admire. In the most notable instance of the latter, in *A Passage to India,* Forster charges Dr. Aziz, whom he otherwise wishes us to find charming, with sexual snobbery:

It enraged him [Aziz] that he had been accused by a woman who had no personal beauty; sexually, he was a snob. This had puzzled and worried Fielding. Sensuality, as long as it is straightfoward, did not repel him, but this derived sensuality— the sort that classifies a mistress among motorcars if she is beautiful, and among eye-flies if she isn't—was alien to his own emotions, and he felt a barrier between himself and Aziz whenever it arose. It was, in a new form, the old, old trouble that eats the heart out of every civilization: snobbery, the desire for possessions, creditable appendages; and it is to escape this rather than the lusts of the flesh that saints retreat into the Himalayas.

Such curious turnings in character can lend Forster's novels verisimilitude, though sometimes, as in Charlotte Bartlett's radical turning to the side of good in *A Room with a View,* they can be quite unconvincing. But Trilling is at least partially correct in averring that E. M. Forster did not resolve the question of good and evil in his novels. I say partially because, with the exception of *A Passage to India,* I do not believe it loomed as a large problem for him. Forster seemed not to be greatly perplexed by questions of good and evil and of the meaning of life. He thought, within his own set limits, he knew life's meaning. As Mr. Emerson, one of Forster's guru characters in *A Room with a View* says, "Passion is sanity"; and it is he who shows Lucy Honeychurch, the heroine of the novel, "the holiness of direct desire."

The only novel of Forster's in which obeisance to the instinctual life is not central is his most famous novel, *A Passage to India.* It is, interestingly enough, the novel Lionel Trilling liked least. *A Passage to India,* he wrote, "is the least surprising of Forster's novels, the least capricious, and, indeed, the least personal," though Trilling concluded that "Forster's book is not about India alone; it is about all of human life." Certainly, as Forster himself felt, *A Passage to India* is the best-made of his novels: the most elegantly written, in some ways the most filled with wise comment—it is the only one of his novels written when he was in his forties—and the most solidly organized. At the center of the novel is that grand old favorite of symbol-hunting English professors, the scene at the Marabar Caves, which Forster, it transpires, allowed that he had fuddled. Of this scene he wrote to William Plomer: "I tried to show that India is an unexplainable muddle by introducing an unexplained muddle—Miss Quested's experience in the cave. When asked what happened there, *I don't know.*" Still, muddle and fuddle, the novel is an impressive piece of work.

So long has *A Passage to India* held the status of a modern classic that writing about it today one feels almost as if called to comment upon *The Rite of Spring* or *Sunday Afternoon on the Grande Jatte*. Rereading it after more than a quarter of a century, one is struck by how interesting a portrait it provides of the Indian character as viewed by Western eyes. One is also struck by its streak of unfairness. At various points in the novel it is difficult to determine which Forster felt more strongly: his love of India or his hatred of England's presence there. He gives the Anglo-Indians very short shrift, so short that there can be no doubt about his having taken sides. "Over the Anglo-Indians I have had to stretch and bust myself blue," he wrote to his friend E. V. Thompson. "I loathe them and should have been more honest to say so. Honesty and fairness are so different. Isn't it a pity?" To an Anglo-Indian civil servant named E. A. Horne, who criticized Forster for his harsh treatment of Anglo-Indians in the novel, Forster confessed: "I don't like Anglo-Indians as a class. I tried to suppress this and be fair to them, but my lack of sympathy came through."

And it came through accompanied by serious political consequences. As Beatrice Webb was to remark to Forster upon reading *A Passage to India,* the novel "entirely expresses our own view of the situation." The situation, of course, was the British Raj in India. Coming at things from the other side, Paul Johnson, in *Modern Times,* a history of the past sixty years, writes: "In 1924 E. M. Forster published *A Passage to India,* a wonderfully insidious assault on the principle of the Raj, nearly turning upside-down the belief in British superiority and maturity which was the prime justification of the Indian empire."

Books are created in history, and through the events of history is our reading of them influenced. Here it must be noted that history has dissipated much of the glory of *A Passage to India,* by revealing that the treatment of the Indians by the British had been nowhere nearly so cruel, indeed murderous, as the treatment of the Indians by one another, beginning with the massacres following upon independence and continuing even today with the bloody dispute between the Indian government and the Sikhs.

E. M. Forster probably never thought himself a very political writer. He tended, in fact, to think himself rather above politics, and his most famous para-political statement is that contained in "What I Believe," an essay of 1939 included in the collection *Two Cheers for Democracy,* in which he wrote: "I hate the idea of causes, and if I had to choose between betraying my country and betraying my friend, I hope I should have the guts to betray my country." On another occasion he wrote: "We who seek the truth are only concerned with politics when they deflect us from it." To be above politics, to be seeking only truth, is ever the claim of the emancipatory liberal. E. M. Forster, it is well to remember, was the author of a novel *(Maurice)* he could not publish and for the better part of his life was enmeshed in homosexual relationships he could not openly declare. The truth he sought was of a particular kind; it presupposed freedom. For him, without freedom, again of a particular kind, there could be no truth. And the particular kinds, both of truth and of freedom, were at their base political.

In a letter written from Egypt to Goldsworthy Lowes Dickinson in 1916, Forster describes what for him was a utopian scene of hundreds of young soldiers at play at the country palace of the ex-khedive that had been turned into a convalescent hospital. "They go about bare chested and bare legged, the blue of their linen shorts and the pale mauve of their shirts accenting the brown splendor of their bodies; and down by the sea many of them spend their days naked and unrebuked. It is so beautiful that I cannot believe it has not been planned, but can't think by whom nor for whom except me." He then describes a naked man attempting to pull a donkey into the water with him, and concludes:

I come away from that place each time thinking, "Why not more of this? Why not? What would it injure? Why not a world like this—its beauty of course impaired by death and old age and poverty and disease, but a world that should not torture itself by organized and artificial horrors?" It's evidently not to be in our day, not while nationality lives, but I can't believe it Utopian, for each human being has in him the germs of such a world.

In a letter written in 1935 to Christopher Isherwood, Forster notes that a writer on sexual behavior named "Dr. Norman Haire has tittered to William [Plomer] that if my novels were analyzed they would reveal a pretty mess. . . . There are things in my earlier stuff which are obvious enough to me now, though less so when I wrote them. . . ." Such an analysis is perhaps better written by one of the Drs. Norman Haire of our day. But this much can be said: the novels upon which E. M. Forster's reputation rests now seem chiefly screens for their author's yearning for freedom for his own trapped instinctual life. He wrote about men and women, often commenting upon them brilliantly, yet other things must all the while have been at the forefront of his mind.

What these other things were is revealed less in the sadly sentimental novel *Maurice* than in a collection of posthumously published stories entitled *The Life to Come*. These are stories about the suppression of homosexuality and about giving way to it, about its costs so long as society disapproves of it and its pleasures nonetheless. One of them, "Dr. Woolacott," was thought by T. E. Lawrence, to whom Forster showed it, the best thing he had ever written. Another, "The Obelisk," has a touch of nastiness one would not have expected from the great proponent of personal relations. In it a husband and wife on holiday meet two sailors also on holiday. To make a short story even shorter, one sailor goes off into the bushes with the wife, while, though we do not know this until the end, the other sailor has gone off into other bushes with the husband. It

is arch and cruel, a stereotypical homosexual mocking of mar-
iage, which is no prettier than heterosexual mocking of homosexuality. "Only connect," Forster famously wrote in an epigraph
to *Howards End.* Indeed.

What *The Life to Come,* the *Selected Letters,* and P. N. Furbank's biography all conduce to make plain is that in E. M.
Forster the emancipatory liberal appears to have hidden a
homosexual utopian. Ironically, the victories of emancipatory
liberalism, issuing in the breakdown of censorship and with it
the freedom to know and publish hitherto private facts of writers' lives, have resulted in our having to reassess E. M. Forster's novels radically. It is no longer possible to think of Forster
as a writer who happened to have been a homosexual; now he
must be considered a writer for whom homosexuality was the
central, the dominant, fact in his life. Given this centrality, this
dominance, it hardly seems w ld to suggest that the chief impulse
behind Forster's novels, with their paeans and pleas for the life
of the instincts, was itself homosexual. Given, again, all that
we now know about his private life, it is difficult to read them
otherwise.

In a curious way the effect of this is to render E. M. Forster's
novels obsolete, and in a way that art of the first magnitude
never becomes. Filled with wisdom though all of his novels are
at their peripheries, ornamented though all of them are by his
lucid and seductive style, at their center each conducts an argument. E. M. Forster was essentially a polemical and didactic
novelist. He argued against the sterility of middle-class English
life; he attempted to teach the beauty of the passionate instinctual life. In the first instance, he wrote out of his personal antipathies; in the second, out of his personal yearnings.

Viewed from the present, it can be said that in large part
Forster won his argument. An English and vastly more sophis-
ticated Sinclair Lewis (a writer whom Forster himself admired),
with a sexual and spiritual twist added, he has, in his quiet way,
been one of the most successful of those who in our time have

written *pour épater les bourgeois*. As for his teaching about the instinctual life—the sanity of passion, the holiness of desire, and the rest of it—here, too, his side, that of emancipatory liberalism, has known no shortage of victories. If, then, his writing today seems so thin, so hollow, and finally so empty, can it be in part because we have now all had an opportunity to view the progress of emancipationism in our lifetimes, the liberation that was the name of Forster's own most ardent desire, and know it to be itself thin, hollow, and finally rather empty?

Commentary 1985

The Awkward Genius
of Theodore Dreiser

H‘M,’ HE HALF GROANED, clearing his throat. ‘Gee!’ ”
I begin by borrowing a line from Theodore
Dreiser, the master himself, before setting out to
consider the first of many issues that Dreiser's extraordinary
career poses—that of the relationship of style to art. It was his
friend and early champion H. L. Mencken who once remarked
that Dreiser had "an incurable antipathy to the *mot juste*," but
that ain't the half of it. Theodore Dreiser also had an alumi-
num ear (one down from tin), an unfailing penchant for the
purple, an oafish wit, and the literary tact and lightness of touch
of a rhinoceros. Who but Dreiser, in *Sister Carrie*, could cap a
brief description of workers returning home on a winter's night
in Chicago by saying that the crowd was "a spectacle of warm-
blooded humanity"? Only Dreiser, in *An American Tragedy*,
had the innate klutziness to write: "The death house of this
particular prison was one of those crass erections and mainte-
nances of human insensibility and stupidity for which no one
was primarily responsible." No one except Dreiser, in *The
"Genius,"* could roll off this squib of dialogue: " 'Ha! Ha! Ha!
Ha!' laughed Suzanne." For the gracious descriptive touch, there
is this from *The Bulwark:* "Most of them were becomingly
gowned in long frocks of every hue." By now readers who
have not read Dreiser and for whom style in literature is deci-

sive are likely to join in the sentiment of Eugene Witla, the autobiographical hero of *The "Genius"*: " 'Nothing doing,' he exclaimed, in the slang of the day." But I would caution them, before giving up on Dreiser, with a line of snappy dialogue from *Jennie Gerhardt:* " 'Aw, you hush up,' was her displeased rejoinder."

But then it is a good deal easier to make fun of Theodore Dreiser's prose style than it is to account for his genius. A genius he was, of that there ought not to be any serious doubt. He may not always have been able to write a careful sentence or a well-shaped paragraph, but this did not stand in the way of his turning out powerful novels. To put my cards on the table early in the game, let me say that Theodore Dreiser, in my opinion, is America's greatest novelist. Herman Melville may have written the greatest single American novel, Henry James plumbed deeper into the subtleties of human motivation, Mark Twain written more lyrically about this country, but Theodore Dreiser, that clod, bumbler, yokel, creep, wrote the novels that tell more in the way of elemental truth about American life and character, and tell it in a consistently persuasive and powerful manner, than those of any other American writer before or since his time.

While scarcely a courageously lonely opinion, neither is this one on which there is anything like a clear consensus. Dissenting opinions on Theodore Dreiser have never been in short supply. Robert Benchley wrote a hilarious parody of Dreiser in which he skewered the tautological stiffness of his prose while underscoring his propensity for stuffing his novels with density of detail: "(NOTE TO PRINTER: *Attached find copy of Thurston's Street Guide. Print names of every street listed therein, beginning with East Division and up to, and including, Dawson.*)" Stuart P. Sherman lambasted Dreiser in a 1915 essay in the *Nation,* "The Barbaric Naturalism of Theodore Dreiser," a title that speaks for itself, though Sherman was later to reverse his opinion when he wrote, in 1925, is praise of *An American*

Tragedy. Dreiser has never been among the favorite authors of those for whom aesthetic considerations dominate all others. Even Mencken, who helped Dreiser through the censorship wars waged over his early novels and who knew Dreiser's literary worth perhaps as well as any man, was appalled by Dreiser's stylistic horrors. "I often wonder," Mencken once wrote, "if Dreiser gets anything properly describable as pleasure out of [his] dogged accumulation of threadbare, undistinguished, uninspiring nouns, adjectives, verbs, adverbs, pronouns, participles and conjunctions." It was Mencken, too, who called Dreiser "a wholesaler of words."

But a stronger dissent, one based only partly on style, was written by Lionel Trilling in "Dreiser and the Liberal Mind," perhaps the most passionately angry essay that Trilling, not a man famously given to displaying anger in his prose, ever allowed himself.* The year of Trilling's essay is 1946, and the date is important, for, along with Dreiser, there were other targets of attack in this essay. One was the liberal (and Communist and fellow-traveling) critics who failed properly to appreciate Henry James while doing their utmost to elevate Theodore Dreiser.

Trilling's resentment over this is real and reasonable. Among liberal critics James was demoted for his delicacy, his gentility, his powerful subtlety of mind, while what were openly spoken of as Dreiser's low origins, his commonness, and his crudity were viewed by these same critics as sources of strength that issued in Dreiser's greater grip on what was taken to be American reality. For these critics, Dreiser's anti-Semitism was set aside and his support of the American Communist Party was genially understood, in the words of his early biographer Rob-

---

*"Dreiser and the Liberal Mind" was first published in the *Nation* on April 20, 1946. It was revised for publication in Trilling's *The Liberal Imagination* (Viking, 1950), where it appears together with a discussion of V. L. Parrington under the title "Reality in America."

ert Elias, as "a means for establishing his cherished goal of greater equality among men." Trilling rightly argues that when Dreiser attempts to be philosophical "he is likely to be not only foolish but vulgar." He demonstrates that Dreiser, far from being a master of colloquial speech and idiom, as his supporters maintained, can be awkwardly, even hideously, bookish. Finally, taking Dreiser's novel *The Bulwark* for his text, Trilling shows the inconsistency of Dreiser in the "comfortable untroubled way in which [he] moved from nihilism to pietism."

What Trilling writes about Dreiser is by and large true; and yet, somehow, it is not nearly the whole truth. Time has eroded some of the cogency of Trilling's essay. Now, more than forty years after Trilling wrote "Dreiser and the Liberal Mind," Henry James, owing to the admirable efforts of Jacques Barzun, Lionel Trilling, and others, has been thoroughly accepted, even enshrined, in the canon of American literature, while Dreiser's own position, though hardly an obscure one, is far from being the commanding position it once was. Critics of our day tend not so much to overlook his faults as to overlook him generally. Marxist critics may still find much in Dreiser's novels on which to festoon their clichés about the class struggle and alienation under capitalism. Dreiser is still often taught in undergraduate survey courses under the dreary rubric of "Realism and Naturalism." But fashionable Dreiser is not. One cannot readily imagine the flashier contemporary critics deconstructing, semiologizing, trope-a-doping, or otherwise making a critical hash of his bulky books. Nor does the opposition between James and Dreiser—the dichotomy of palefaces and *schleppers,* perhaps—any longer seem productive. One does not, after all, have to choose between them. James is caviar, Dreiser a good boiled potato; one cannot live exclusively on caviar, and there is nothing wrong with a good boiled potato.

Dreiser's contemporary position outside fashion and beyond academic dispute is not an altogether bad place for a writer to be. It leaves his novels the property of those readers who understand novels to be instruments for investigating the connection between character and destiny, and novelists to be investigators on a quest for—I blush to introduce such an old-fashioned word—truth. Although so far as I know Dreiser wrote nothing of sustained theoretical interest on the role of the novelist, his own novels, when they do not spin out of control into philosophical or egocentric divagations, are precisely about the connection between character and destiny. It is this connection, of course, that provides the main line, the great tradition, of the novel—the tradition of Stendhal, Balzac, George Eliot, Dickens, Tolstoy, Hardy, Conrad, and Henry James.

After one has said all that there is to be said against Dreiser, there remain his best novels—especially *Sister Carrie, Jennie Gerhardt, An American Tragedy,* and vast stretches of *The Financier* and *The Titan*—to confront. (If there is a central weakness in Lionel Trilling's essay, it is his failure to confront Dreiser at his best.) How to confront them is no easy matter. I have done so, on occasion, as a university teacher, teaching them to freshmen students, but never, I have felt, anywhere near successfully. At the close of two or three ninety-minute sessions, so much remains unsaid, so much remains unexplored. As a teacher, I invariably feel that I have not encompassed these novels, have not arrived at their true center or conveyed a comprehensive understanding of the serious business that is being conducted in them. Sad to admit, but a sign of great literature may be that it cannot be altogether successfully taught. Confronted with masterworks, pedagogy does not stand mute—never mute—but awkwardly inept.

The best students react well to the novels of Dreiser. They sense that there are big things going on in his pages. And even the very best students have the advantage that, at eighteen, they have very little sense of prose style, and hence no snobbery about it. I am not arguing for the superior wisdom of the young, but rather that the shallow sophistication of the not-so-young can present its own obstacles. Saul Bellow, who has long written and spoken admiringly of Dreiser's novels, puts the point best: "I often think the criticism of Dreiser as a stylist at times betrays a resistance to the feelings he causes readers to suffer. If they say he can't write, they need not experience these feelings."

What are these feelings? I should say that any comprehensive list of them would include humiliation and fear of failure, the craving for respectability, every kind of longing, and the desolation that accompanies an unutterable loneliness in the face of a (probably) uncaring universe. In teaching Dreiser I have always wanted to begin—perhaps some day I shall begin—by saying, "What you must understand about Theodore Dreiser is that he was born poor and homely and raised in ignorance and filled with desire. Write that down and remember it. Now get out of here and go home and read the book again."

How did Dreiser manage to convey such strong feelings in his novels? Certainly not through style. He did it, quite despite style, through the creation of character. All his chief characters—Carrie and Jennie, Clyde and Eugene, Hurstwood and Cowperwood—were of course drawn out of the deep well of his own complex personality, his humiliation and fear and yearning, his lust and loneliness and craving for power. I write "of course," but "of course" doesn't reveal the mystery of how he was able to do it. This Hoosier hick, with a year of college under his belt, without the rudiments of grammar, with low-grade journalism his only training, at the age of twenty-nine was able to create the character of George Hurstwood, the most moving portrait in all literature of the middle-aged man on the way down. *Feinschmecker*s of literature may be put off by Dreiser's describing Hurstwood as the manager of a "truly swell saloon," but I contend that if you cannot sympathize with George Hurstwood's defeat in *Sister Carrie* you are not fit to read novels.

To those of us who care greatly for style in literature, the achievement of Theodore Dreiser is at once an affront and a puzzlement. Dostoevsky, I am told by people who read Russian and who report that his novels have been much "cleaned up" in their English translations, is another writer who worked outside style; and Alexander Solzhenitsyn may be a third. Nor have I ever seen Balzac persuasively praised for his stylistic felicity. Dreiser, Dostoevsky, Solzhenitsyn, Balzac, fast writers all, producers in bulk, each with a powerful vision and an almost missionary zeal to convey it, seem not so much above style as to make style seem somewhat beside the point. Style, sedulously cultivated, can issue in literary power, but if the power is there to begin with style becomes a secondary concern at best, what in encyclopedia sales is known as an "add on." How the power got there in the first place is one of those splendid questions without any convincing general answer.

In the particular case of Theodore Dreiser, one searches for an answer, if answer there be, in biography. The biographical literature on Dreiser is far from scant. To begin with, there is Robert Elias's *Theodore Dreiser: Apostle of Nature* (1949), written by a professor of English at the University of Pennsylvania who knew Dreiser while he was alive and who may be said to have invented Theodore Dreiser as an academic subject. In *Dreiser* (1965), the professional biographer W. A. Swanberg wrote a biography perhaps thin on literary criticism but rich in its clear reporting of the details of Dreiser's long and complicated life. F. O. Matthiessen wrote a volume, *Theodore Dreiser* (1951), in the American Men of Letters Series that suffers for taking Dreiser's strange politics all too seriously. (Matthiessen's book ends on the following note of left-wing piety: "His will provided that, after Helen's [his wife's] death, whatever little property might be left should go to a home for Negro orphans.") In *Homage to Theodore Dreiser* (1971), Robert Penn Warren produced a slender volume that is a fit appreciation of Dreiser's literary achievement on the centennial of his birth, but that does not dwell on the comic, often mad complexities of the man who wrote the books. Easily the most impressive work of literary scholarship devoted to Dreiser is Ellen Moers's *Two Dreisers* (1969), which masterfully illuminates Dreiser's attempts to learn about modern psychology from the Austrian-born psychoanalyst A. A. Brill and about chemical physiology from Jacques Loeb, the master of the mechanistic theory of life. In doing so, Professor Moers enhances Dreiser's stature as a serious artist by removing any notion that he was merely an odd and interesting primitive. Meanwhile, a slow but steady stream of Dreiser's diaries, unpublished manuscripts, and uncorrupted editions of his novels has been issuing from the University of Pennsylvania Press under the general—and very capable—editorship of Thomas P. Riggio. The Library of America plans to issue several volumes of Dreiser's work. And now we have the first volume of what promises to be a blockbuster biography, *Theodore Dreiser: At the Gates of the City, 1871–1907,* by Richard Lingeman.

I say a "blockbuster biography" because Mr. Lingeman has taken more than 470 pages, including scholarly apparatus, to get his subject up to 1907. (Dreiser's dates are 1871–1945.) Still ahead lie most of the vast quantity of Dreiser's writings, the elaborate confusion of his politics, and the astonishing profligacy and tangled skein of his amours. (Mencken once remarked, with only slight hyperbole, that Dreiser enjoyed the sex life of a chimpanzee.) Although only another single volume is promised, it is difficult to imagine Mr. Lingeman landing this whalish work at fewer than a thousand pages, which would certainly be Dreiserian in bulk if not necessarily in other ways. When a writer has been written about as exhaustively as Theodore Dreiser has, the question of the need for such a book arises. As Igor Stravinsky was wont to say late in life, when presented with some new work that threatened to deflect his attention, "Who needs this?"

A new biography of a much-written-about artist is worth doing if something has happened that has made previous ways of telling the subject's life seem outmoded. On the basis of Mr. Lingeman's first volume, it is not clear that any of these conditions obtain. To be sure, there is a greater density of detail in Lingeman's biography than in Swanberg's, but then Lingeman takes more than 400 pages to bring Dreiser's life to a point that Swanberg reached in 125 (in a book that runs to 614 pages). Some of this detail is intrinsically interesting—the account of Doubleday's near scuttling of its own edition of *Sister Carrie,* the chronicle of Dreiser's days as a laborer in the vineyards of mass journalism—but Mae West's famous maxim, "You can't get too much of a good thing," does not necessarily apply to the writing of biography.

As a literary critic, Lingeman is not inept, but neither does he add anything new to our understanding of Dreiser's work. Next to a real literary sensibility such as the one Ellen Moers brought to her criticism of Dreiser, Lingeman's seems rather pale. Part of the problem is in the prose. Lingeman writes a serviceable journalist's prose, but it often lapses into journalistic archaisms in which people "opine" or "pen" short stories. Sometimes it drops two notches farther down into Dreiserian bookish cliché, as when "brightly colored flowers bloomed in lush profusion"; or when Dreiser, under the ministrations of a partner in bed, is sent "into paroxysms of groaning delirium"; or, all engines clanging now, "the seeds of [Dreiser's future books] had been planted in the fallow soil of his silent decade, and the storm brought rain and, lo, the earth bore fruit." Hold that tiger.

But the larger question is whether a fresh interpretation of Theodore Dreiser's life emerges in Richard Lingeman's biography. Thus far it does not seem to, unless one counts as fresh the notion of Dreiser as first the victim and then the triumphal excoriator of American capitalism. Lingeman speaks, for example, of the Dreiser family having "come to identify with the poor," which seems an odd way of putting it when in fact they themselves were blasted poor. In his pages, entrepreneurs and industrialists of the turn of the century are for the most part depicted as robber barons, or simple villains. Thus, Cyrus McCormick is introduced as the "inventor and manufacturer of the mechanical reaper, which swept across the wheat fields of the Great Plains like hordes of locusts," which is a strange way of speaking about instruments, quite as unlocust-like as one could get, that, far from devouring the harvest, helped to bring it in. Although this bias does not thus far ruin his book, one senses Mr. Lingeman, who is the executive editor of the *Nation,* at times struggling manfully to turn Dreiser into a throbbing social conscience and incipient revolutionary— something on the order, if you will, of a contributor to the *Nation.*

One awaits with patient amusement the ideological acrobatics that will be required of Lingeman in his second volume when he will have to deal with some of the jollier political facts of Dreiser's life. To write well about Dreiser, after all, takes a certain political balance, for Dreiser's politics were, as Swanberg (himself a liberal) called them, "a psychopathic potpourri of prejudice and zeal." Dreiser was a man who could compare Joseph Stalin to the White Christ of Dostoevsky, who approved the reports of Hitler's appropriation of Catholic property in Germany, who was an anti-Semitic Zionist on the model of those bigots of yesteryear who wished to send American Negroes back to Africa. ("After L.A.," Dreiser not uncharacteristically wrote to a friend, "New York looks cluttered, grimy and Jewish." Even Mike Gold, the Party-line editor of the *New Masses,* expressed embarrassment at Dreiser's anti-Semitism.) To feature Dreiser, the novelist and the man, as simply the champion of the downtrodden will not wash, dry, or iron. Dreiser, the victim of his own immense egocentric confusions, was finally the champion—of Dreiser. His politics, being despicable, are only worth despising.

To give in to the temptation to read Dreiser's later left-wing politics back into his novels is a grievous mistake. Dreiser the unshakable friend of the Soviet Union, the crackpot social theorist, the man with (as Mencken later called him) "an insatiable appetite for the obviously not true," only emerged after his best books were written. As Ellen Moers rightly points out, "it was only at a fairly late stage in his pursuit of understanding (to be precise, after the publication of *An American Tragedy*) that he grudgingly accorded socio-historical forces a significant and separate role in the destinies of man." Before that Dreiser, the novelist and not the crackpot, was concerned, as he himself put it in a pamphlet entitled "Life, Art and America," with "those sterner truths which life itself teaches—the unreliability of human nature; the crass chance which strikes down and destroys our finest dreams; the fact that man in all his relationships is neither good nor evil but both." This much can be said: Dreiser pitied the weak and admired the strong, but how the weak came to be weak and the strong, strong was the question that ceaselessly perturbed the novelist in him. "Why? Why? I persistently asked myself, and I have yet to find the answer in any code of morals or ethics or the dogma of any religion." His greatness as a novelist is in no small part owing to his refusal, until nearly the end, to accept any easy answers.

How the weak came to be weak was a question that Dreiser's own personal fate set him nearly at birth. He was the ninth of ten children in a family that would never recover from a financial reverse that had occurred five years before his birth. He grew up under an immigrant German father, a defeated man who had retreated into extreme religiosity. His mother was a free spirit of the type of the earth mother, superstitious, with a high capacity for abiding chaos. The family moved from one small Indiana town to another, at one low point sharing quarters, in Vincennes, Indiana, in a firehouse that was also the town's brothel. Poverty vied with scandal as the chief source of shame felt by Dreiser, whose sisters went off with married men, whose brothers lapsed into alcoholism or launched themselves on careers of sporty living, whose mother took in other people's laundry. A whole lot more than family therapy, as they say in the head trades, was indicated.

To the shame and confusion of his home life let us now add Dreiser's physical attributes, which all fell on the debit side. Puny when a child, he was awkward and gangly as he grew older. He had buck teeth and a right eye that wandered. Sand-bagged between his mother's superstitiousness and his father's brimstone religion, his own longings and humiliations left him muddling in a personal hell of insecurity, shame, and fear. While Dreiser still lived with his parents, one of his sisters returned home pregnant, and another ran off with a Hurstwood-like figure named L. A. Hopkins. Although he could not have known it at the time, however wretched he must have been, the young Theodore Dreiser was raised in a laboratory that would later supply the materials for his own early novels.

With his expenses paid by a teacher who had befriended him, Dreiser was able to put in a year at Indiana University, where he felt himself an outcast, inept with girls, gawky and unathletic, a mediocre and dreamy student. Afterward he returned to Chicago, where he took up a number of flunky jobs—driving a laundry truck, collecting installment payments for a furniture company—and then, sensing a dead end to all such jobs, landed part-time work as a reporter on a Chicago paper call the *Daily Globe*. In the early 1890s, and for a long while before and after, newspapers were the graduate school and creative-writing program and national endowment for writers. Twain and Howells, Cather and Crane, had put in their time working on newspapers, and so, later, did Ernest Hemingway and Ring Lardner. Good training for a novelist it was, too, for it allowed the young would-be writer to glimpse life, high and low, and to indulge his curiosity about the world in a way that no other job quite allowed.

Dreiser, whose specialty was feature writing, was by no means a bust as a newspaper man. Unattached and free-roaming, he worked on newspapers in Chicago, St. Louis, Toledo, Cleveland, Pittsburgh, and Buffalo. He covered lynchings and train wrecks and wrote drama criticism; he interviewed celebrities from the worlds of sports and culture and industry. The atmosphere around newspapers at that time was wide open, tinged with bohemianism. Reporters kept a bottle of booze in one drawer and a novel or poem cycle in another. Mr. Lingeman reports that the editor of the *Republic,* one of the papers Dreiser worked on in St. Louis, used to exhort his reporters: "Remember Zola and Balzac, my boy, remember Zola and Balzac." Imagine A. M. Rosenthal or Ben Bradlee saying that. It was a different game.

The year 1894 was a crucial one for Dreiser, and for two reasons. For one, it was the year he met a young man named Arthur Henry—Henry was twenty-six, Dreiser twenty-three— who was city editor of the *Toledo Blade.* A would-be novelist himself, Henry encouraged Dreiser to write fiction. It was at Henry and his wife's summer place in Maumee, Ohio, five years later, in 1899, that Dreiser, now himself married, wrote his first short story. And it was Henry who kept after Dreiser to write a novel, which Dreiser began to do in earnest that winter. The novel was *Sister Carrie,* and it was loosely based upon Dreiser's own sister Emma, who had run off to New York with the manager of a successful saloon in Chicago. When Dreiser bogged down, Henry cheered him on; when Dreiser's finished manuscript was deemed too long, Henry did the cutting. (Throughout his career, Dreiser had little interest in the revising or editing of his own work; he turned it out and let others trim it up.) Without Arthur Henry there probably would have been no *Sister Carrie*.

In 1894, too, Dreiser first read the evolutionist Herbert Spencer's *First Principles* and, not to put too fine a point on it, it blew him off the court. "[Spencer] nearly killed me," Dreiser later remarked, "took every shred of belief away from me; showed me that I was a chemical atom in a whirl of unknown forces; the realization clouded my mind." If Spencer was correct in his argument that the transcendental design of the universe could not be known, and Dreiser was persuaded that he was correct, then religion, notions of a higher justice, ideals of moral order—all were so much screaming into the wind. Spencer did not really explain the world to Dreiser; he explained instead why it was unexplainable. Dreiser's explosive encounter with Spencer set him on a course of extensive reading in biology and experimental psychology. It was this reading transmuted into art that, as Ellen Moers has shown, supplied the power that continues to attract generations of readers to the otherwise seemingly uninspiring story about a country girl who runs off with a middle-aged married man who flops in New York.

In *Sister Carrie,* Dreiser created a novel out of a plot in which no major character even approaches being a highly sentient being—technically speaking, no mean feat. Despite his stylistic crudities, he got the details of his characters' lives right, for he was not himself so far removed from their milieu. He understood their inchoate and often trivial thoughts, and could feel what they felt. (This, wrote Mencken, "takes a kind of skill that is surely not common. Good writing is far easier.") But, more important, he understood that his characters were not so much people who acted in the world as people upon whom the world acted—passive nouns, if a neologism may be permitted. Ellen Moers patiently lays out the way weather and light and warm food and the creak of new clothes and the crinkle of ten-dollar bills alter the moods of Dreiser's characters. Not being thoughtful, they are chiefly desirous, and often of things of which they are not themselves entirely aware. Although Dreiser has been called a determinist, he seems to me nothing of the kind, for while his characters are at the whim of fate, it is by no means clear what fate awaits them. He has also been called a social Darwinian, yet, apart from the Cowperwood novels, this label, too, won't stick. Surely there is nothing of the survival of the fittest to *Sister Carrie*. Carrie Meeber, Charlie Drouet, George Hurstwood—no one character is particularly more fit than another, yet Hurstwood goes under, Drouet survives, and Carrie flourishes. Why this is so is far from clear. What is clear— painfully, profoundly clear—is that life is a mystery.

The inscrutability of life is the obsession at the center of Dreiser's art. In *Jennie Gerhardt,* Lester Kane says to Jennie: "I don't know whether you see what I'm driving at, but all of us are more or less pawns. We're moved about like chessmen by circumstances over which we have no control." Later at his, Lester's, funeral, Dreiser notes of Jennie: "She was suffused with a sense of sorrow, loss, beauty, and mystery. Life in all its vagueness and uncertainty seemed typified by this scene." In *The "Genius,"* Eugene Witla calls religion "a bandage that man has invented to protect a soul made bloody by circumstances; an envelope to protect him from the unescapable and unstable illimitable." Earlier in the same novel Eugene begins to apprehend that "life was nothing save dark forces moving aimlessly."

And yet—another mystery?—somehow in Dreiser this dark view does not issue in antinomianism. "Life was desolate, inexplicable, unbelievably accidental—luck or disaster," he told an early biographer. But that for him only made it all the more interesting. If life was a mystery, it was a damned absorbing one. In "Life, Art and America," he wrote: "A man, if he can, should question the things that he sees—not some things, but everything—stand, as it were, in the center of this whirling storm of contradiction which we know as life, and ask of it its sources and its import." Dreiser bent all his novelistic efforts to understanding life as it truly is—"the game as it is played." In his blunderbuss way, within the frame of fiction, he could break through to say some chillingly true things. In *The "Genius,"* for example, he has this description of his autobiographical hero thinking about his wife: " 'If only she would die,' he said to himself, for we have the happy faculty of hating most joyously on this earth the thing we have wronged the most." In *Jennie Gerhardt* he could strike off the following passage about what is required to make a smashing business success:

> The trouble with Lester was that, while blessed with a fine imagination and considerable insight, he lacked the ruthless, narrow-minded insistence on his individual superiority which is a necessary element in almost every great business success. To be a forceful figure in the business world means, as a rule, that you must be an individual of one idea, and that idea the God-given one that life has destined you for a tremendous future in the particular field you have chosen. It means that one thing, a cake of soap, a new can-opener, a safety razor, or speed-accelerator, must seize on your imagination with tremendous force, burn as a raging flame, and make itself the be-all and end-all of your existence. As a rule, a man needs poverty to help him to this enthusiasm, and youth. The thing he has discovered, and with which he is going to busy himself, must be the door to a thousand opportunities and a thousand joys. Happiness must be beyond or the fire will not burn as brightly as it might—the urge will not be great enough to make a great success.

Impressive though Dreiser's knowledge of the world could be, it did not usually extend to himself. Here, for example, is the way he describes Eugene Witla, the character in *The "Genius"* clearly based on Theodore Dreiser (and let us pass on the question of the tact involved in writing an autobiographical novel with that title): "Eugene was perfectly free and easy in his manner. He was never affected at any time, decidedly eager to learn things from anybody and supremely good natured." Reversing all the terms in that passage—in effect, antonymizing it—gives a much truer picture of the real Dreiser. Far from pleasant to begin with, Dreiser was made more angular, embittered, and rebarbative by the dreary reception accorded his first novel, *Sister Carrie*. Doubleday printed the book in small numbers and a hideous format. Reviewers attacked it for being immoral—Carrie Meeber, reviewers felt, was not made to pay for living outside conventional morality. Dreiser's royalties for this major work of American literature came to $68.40. The novel had a cult following of a sort among younger readers, and it would later garner much appreciation among English reviewers in its William Heinemann edition, yet William Dean Howells, earlier so sympathetic to the work of Mark Twain and Henry James, told Dreiser to his face: "I didn't like *Sister Carrie.*"

Dreiser had already begun work on *Jennie Gerhardt,* but the reaction to *Sister Carrie* drove him to nervous breakdown. The plunge in his morale was accompanied by a plunge in his fortunes. He could no longer turn out the quick journalism by which he had supported his wife and himself. His wife temporarily moved back to Missouri to live with her family, and Dreiser, on a drug regimen for what was felt to be "neurasthenia," moved into dreary quarters in Brooklyn, searched without success for work, and began a general slide not unlike that taken in *Sister Carrie* by George Hurstwood. Dreiser was finally rescued by his brother Paul, the successful songwriter (composer of "On the Banks of the Wabash, Far Away" and "My Gal Sal"), who put him in a sanatorium and arranged work for him when he came out. Dreiser's diaries for this period make painful reading, and so does his recasting of this experience in *The "Genius."* His heavily brooding nature must have had a serious workout trying to understand why, in an arbitrary and unreasoning cosmos, he was selected for this torture.

Even after Dreiser had climbed out of this slough of deepest despond, other obstacles awaited him. It was fully seven years until he returned to the writing of *Jennie Gerhardt* and three more until he saw it published. Publishers were nervous about bringing out the works of an "immoral" author—and immorality in that age meant any hint of sensuousness or any characters let off without severe punishment for, say, living with a man outside marriage. When *The "Genius"* was published in

1915, John Sumner, of the New York Society for the Suppression of Vice, banned the novel as obscene and blasphemous, charging it with seventy-five counts of lewdness and fourteen of profanity: mention of a female breast, at that time, counted as lewdness, taking the Lord's name in vain as profanity. With the help of H. L. Mencken, Dreiser, standing firm, fought Sumner; he also fought publishers who beseeched him to write "moral" books; and he fought more generally for the right of authors to describe the world as they saw it. Dreiser paid the price for doing so, in delayed publication, in reduced audience, in diminished royalties. It took courage and stubbornness, and Dreiser had both. His conduct during these difficult years marks an honorable chapter in the history of the battle against inane censorship, however empty that battle may seem today, when the cunnilinguistic rhapsodies of John Updike and the sodomic violence of Norman Mailer go directly to the best-seller tables.

Certainly his fight against the censors did not make Dreiser's nature any the sweeter. It turned him into a professional flouter of convention. At great boring length, Dreiser, so often the death of the party, would attack American prudery. From here it was only a brief jump to his turning to attack American hypocrisy, and with it everything connected to mainstream American life: religion, business, capitalism generally. This side of Dreiser, the iconoclast who wrote revolutionary books that were suppressed by the forces of American benightedness, earned him a following among the denizens of Greenwich Village and other American bohemias. Unfortunately, Dreiser himself took the role altogether seriously, and it helped steer him into many of his later political imbecilities.

Dreiser was in any case a difficult personality, but his struggle through life made him almost impossible. To his naturally moody, brooding, gloomy temperament, Dreiser added the habit of grievance and the outlook of paranoia. He craved friendship and demanded loyalty, but was unable to sustain the former and unwilling to repay the latter. "And I give you one kindly bit of advice," he once wrote to a young admirer named Harold Husey. "Never bother to know me personally. Remain illusioned, if you can."

Good advice, this, but one may be certain that he never gave it to a woman. Not long after he emerged from his time of breakdown, Dreiser slipped free of the wife who had seen him through it, and his days of heavy, even militant, womanizing began in seriousness. At thirty-eight he blew a well-paying editorial job at the Butterick Publishing Company to chase after the seventeen-year-old daughter of a fellow employee; at sixty-two he was hot on the trail of a freshman girl at Bryn Mawr. He used women as other men used cigars—and frequently had more than one a day. He gave the lie to Baudelaire's famous remark, *Plus un homme cultive les arts, moins il bande*. Professor Thomas Riggio writes: "His sexual appetite matched his appetite for writing and was as compulsive." A pre-Reichian, like many of the Greenwich Village characters of his day, Dreiser believed in the close connection between erotic and creative energy—and acted upon his belief. He was not a man you would want to leave alone in a room with your grandmother, and certainly not with your granddaughter.

"The days of social lies for me is dead," Dreiser wrote to a woman named Bettina Morris in yet another of his many epistolary attempts at seduction. But he continued to avail himself of every other kind of lie. Through sharp dealing he kited up the price of his own manuscripts among collectors. He employed several literary and movie agents at the same time. He asked absolute fidelity from women, which he repaid with something akin to absolute infidelity. He hated capitalism and studied the stock market. The greater the support publishers gave him the readier he was to betray them. Here he was able to tie his general deceitfulness to his very particular anti-Semitism, for the Jewish-owned firms of Liveright and Simon and Schuster, both of which had aided him when he much needed them, he accused of being part of a Jewish plot against him. It was at bottom his anti-Semitism that attracted him to Hitler. The day of the Nazi-Soviet pact, however much it may have shocked other American Communists and fellow travelers, was a day on which everything came together for Dreiser: his anti-Semitism, his anti-capitalism, his Anglophobia, his anti-Americanism. "I ceased following Hitler," he wrote to Mencken, "when . . . he attacked Russia—my pet."

Well, enough beating of a dead author. If I have dwelt at some length on Theodore Dreiser's failures of character, it is not merely because his life provides examples of them in such plentitude but because his life raises a larger issue, namely: How could so clearly unpleasant a man, a man in his life so egocentric, be in his art so sympathetic? a man in his life so mean, be in his art so generous? a man in his life so ignorant, be in his art so intelligent? In George Hurstwood, Theodore Dreiser created the most persuasive portrait in literature of a man in social, psychological, physical, and moral decline. In Jennie Gerhardt he created a pure victim of fate who never loses her inherent goodness of character—and few things in literary art are more difficult than making goodness convincing. In Frank Cowperwood he was able, as Mencken put it, "to give plausibility to the motives, feelings and processes of mind of a man whose salient character is that they transcend all ordinary experience." In Clyde Griffiths, of *An American Tragedy,* he created a character whom, despite his trivial ambitions, his weakness, even his guilt, one wants to survive, and one feels as if a part of oneself has been plowed under when he doesn't. How did Dreiser do it—this bore, crank, celery-juice drinker, and member of the select company of morons who believed that Franklin Delano Roosevelt was part Jewish?

In some artists—Flaubert, James—imagination is at the service of intelligence, while in others—Whitman, Tolstoy—intelligence is entirely at the service of imagination. Dreiser was clearly among the others. Outside his novels, he was powerfully ignorant; within them, he could be dazzlingly penetrating. Fate decreed that he come to literature at a time when the Victorian novel was over—*Sister Carrie* was published in 1900—and the new novel was about to come into being. More than any other novelist, he helped usher it in. He wrote with the confidence of the Victorians but without their optimism. As Ellen Moers noted, "he handled words, sometimes brilliantly, sometimes wretchedly, [but] without the sound of pebbles in his mouth." He broke the rules by speculating in fiction about the nature and purpose of the universe and the status of human beings within it, and got away with it. Goodness was not of necessity rewarded in his novels, nor evil punished—goodness and evil were scarcely at issue. This was revolutionary. In *The "Genius,"* a novel filled with every kind of clumsiness and self-deception, Dreiser writes about Eugene Witla, the artist-hero who is so obviously himself: "He thought that his art was a gift, that he had been sent to revolutionize art in America, or carry it one step forward, and that nature was thus constantly sending its apostles or special representatives over whom it kept watch and in whom it was well pleased." But why would nature choose a man such as Theodore Dreiser for the task? Even to consider the question is to recognize the possibility that we may be in the presence of yet another Dreiserian cosmic mystery.

The New Criterion 1986

Read Marguerite Yourcenar!

IN AN ATTEMPT to arouse interest in the novels of Marguerite Yourcenar, a writer I much admire, perhaps I could do worse than to begin by announcing that the critic George Steiner thinks very little of them. Since so many people who do intellectual work keep a cold spot in their hearts for George Steiner, the fact that he has written with a lofty contempt for Mme Yourcenar may help them to set aside a warm spot in their hearts for her. Steiner wrote about Marguerite Yourcenar in the *New Yorker* shortly after she had been installed as a member—the first woman member—of the French Academy. The first part of his article (which is ostensibly a review of her book *Fires*) is given over to a display of George Steiner's superior knowledge of the history, politics, and inner workings of the French Academy. He then tells us that Mme Yourcenar's renown rests on one work, *Memoirs of Hadrian,* a novel Steiner thinks inferior to Walter Pater's *Marius the Epicurean* and Robert Graves's *I, Claudius.* Yet Steiner, with the portentousness his contemners have come to adore, concedes: "Nonetheless, it retains an undoubted distinction and may one day be heard as having struck a crucial note in the postwar mood of the West."

But this is really all Steiner concedes. The remainder of what he has to say is largely orotund put-down. "A sizeable but textually amateurish and fitfully translated anthology of classical Greek verse" produced by Mme Yourcenar is referred to. Steiner notes that she is "steeped in Pindar, already acquainted, one would guess, with the melancholy postclassicism of Cavafy and other modern Greek lyricists. . . ." (No need to guess, since Mme Yourcenar did in fact write a long and admiring essay on Cavafy that appears in an essay collection of hers entitled *Sous bénéfice d'inventaire*.) Mme Yourcenar's novel *The Abyss* is quickly scored off as "not major work," and she herself, this woman who was not a university teacher and is never studied in universities, as rather academic. At the end of this extravagantly arbitrary piece of pretentiousness, a reader is left with the distinct impression that Marguerite Yourcenar was yet another writer one need not be concerned about.

Not that George Steiner's review is likely to have caused a serious decline in Marguerite Yourcenar's reputation in this country. As far as I can make out, her reputation, both in the United States and in England, has always been unclear. Bookish people have heard of her—many more after her election to the French Academy—but not very many, on my casual inquiries, have read her. If they have, they have read *Memoirs of Hadrian* solely. Meanwhile, no important critic, English or American, has written at any length about her. Even Edmund Wilson, who used to pride himself on what he called his contributions to "the cross-fertilization of culture," somehow missed Mme Yourcenar. In English there has been, quite simply, no serious critical discussion of Marguerite Yourcenar's quality. She seems to have been neither over- nor under-rated—nor even rated at all.

I do not know what Mme Yourcenar's precise reputation is in France. Having been a member of the French Academy, after all, is no more a guarantee of distinction there than having been a member of the American Academy of Arts and Letters here; in both institutions people of the highest intellectual and artistic seriousness sit next to fellow members who are hacks and boobs. Besides, the time is now over when Americans could look to the intrinsic superiority of French literary culture, which has long seemed less old and splendid than tired and a bit preposterous.

Here it needs to be pointed out that Marguerite Yourcenar was neither French nor lived in France. She was born into the upper bourgeoisie in Belgium in 1903, and lived in the United States on an island off the coast of Maine for a great many years. She was elected to the French Academy because she wrote in French, and the French Academy decided that, for its purposes, nationality is determined by the language a writer works in. Still, here we come upon the first impediment to Mme Yourcenar's having a clear literary reputation: a Belgian woman living in Maine and writing in French, she was in some respects the literary equivalent of a man without a country. This is made even more complicated by the fact that her novels are, so to say, written across Europe, being, separately, set in the Baltic provinces, in Italy, in the Low Countries, along the Mediterranean. If Mme Yourcenar had a spiritual home, a cultural nationality, it can only be described as European.

The pattern of publication of Marguerite Yourcenar's novels cannot have helped, if the word pattern applies at all to so erratic a sequence of publications as hers has been. *A Coin in Nine Hands,* for example, originally appeared in French in 1934 under the title *Denier du rêve;* then it reappeared, again in French, in a revised edition in 1959; and it was only in 1982, nearly half a century after it was first published, that we had the book in English. So it has been with her other books: *Coup de Grâce,* published in French in 1939, came out in English in 1957; *The Abyss,* published here in 1976, first appeared in French in 1968; *Fires,* a book of prose poems and aphorisms, was published in French in 1936 and in English in 1981; *Nouvelles orientales* was initially published in 1938, then in a revised edition in 1959, and appeared in English in 1985.

Marguerite Yourcenar treated her novels rather as W. H.

Auden did his poems: revising and reworking and even remak-
ing them over the decades. In between work on her novels she
did a number of translations: of Virginia Woolf, of Henry James,
of Cavafy, of Negro spirituals, of ancient Greek poets. She was
clearly a writer who was interested in what she was interested
in—which is to say, not a writer chiefly interested in doing
what was best for her career. Consequences follow from this.
As a result of the long delays between the publication of Mme
Yourcenar's books, and then of the often even lengthier delays
between their appearance in French and in English, her English-
reading audience has been deprived of anything even faintly
resembling a clear sense of her development as a writer and
any feeling whatsoever of the excitement of fresh work from
her. A new Bellow, a new Naipaul, a new Solzhenitsyn, the
works of such novelists create a stir, an air of intellectual antic-
ipation. Yet there are not—or rather seem not to be—any new
Yourcenars.

As if this were not enough, there is the additionally awkward fact that Marguerite Yourcenar's two most substantial
novels—*Memoirs of Hadrian* and *The Abyss*—are, technically, of
the genre contemptuously known as historical novels. When
most people think of historical novels they think of books like
Gone with the Wind, of costume balls done in prose. (*War and
Peace* is, technically, a historical novel, but let that pass.) Between
Marguerite Yourcenar and Margaret Mitchell there is more than
a vast artistic distance; on purely scholarly grounds the work
of the former has been admired by historians of the ancient
and medieval world. Yet another difficulty with historical novels is that people tend to think of them as not speaking to
contemporary issues, questions, problems. Increasingly, the new
Bellows, Naipauls, Solzhenitsyns do speak to these issues,
questions, problems. Marguerite Yourcenar's novels, it must
be said, do not.

"Among a democratic people poetry will not feed on legends or on traditions and memories of old days," wrote

Tocqueville, thereby partially providing yet another reason that Marguerite Yourcenar has not caught on with American readers. "Democratic peoples may amuse themselves momentarily by looking at nature, but it is about themselves that they are really excited." Which is a roundabout way of saying that Marguerite Yourcenar, who was a writer interested in traditions, legends, memories of old days, was also an aristocratic writer. Someone once observed of her that she was the only living novelist whose characters do not go about with one question uppermost in their minds: Why am I not happier? When a character in a Yourcenar novel is preoccupied with that question, he is rather to be pitied.

One of the marks of the aristocratic novelist is that he writes chiefly about superior people, and in such a way that the identifying factor is almost nil. In a Yourcenar novel one does not "relate to" the characters. To be sure, one does get caught up in her stories, but the pleasures she offers are not those provided by narrative alone. They are also the pleasures of style, and Mme Yourcenar's style is aphoristic and philosophical. Hers is a style well suited for freshly formulating old and new experience. It is also imbued with the intellectual quality known as gravity. She is serious about serious things—and that, nowadays, is not everybody's notion of how novelists ought to conduct their business.

If Marguerite Yourcenar can be said to resemble any twentieth-century writer in her general tone, it is André Malraux. Like Malraux, she is especially good at the abstract expression of passion. Like Malraux, too, her heroes are men of action given to reflection, but reflection of a pitiless kind. "Unlike most men of a reflective turn of mind," says the narrator of *Coup de Grâce,* "I am not disposed to self-depreciation."

Coup de Grâce, a brief novel of 1939, is a good place to begin a consideration of Mme Yourcenar's work. The book is set in the aftermath of World War I, in a town in Eastern Europe that is "an outpost of the Teutonic Order." The town is being fought for in what the narrator of the book, who describes himself as opposed to the Bolsheviks "as a matter of caste," also describes as one of those "Russo-Baltic embroilments." But the novel is above and beyond politics. Its true subject is mad love—love of the kind one dies for.

The object of this love is the narrator of *Coup de Grâce*. He is a man cool and disdainful, a soldier of fortune by profession, who says of himself that "of all the men that I know I am least disposed to seek out ideological incitements in order to love or hate my fellow beings; it is only for causes in which I do not believe that I have been willing to risk my life." The young sister of one of his comrades-in-arms falls in love with him. This girl, whose name is Sophie, is being fed books on revolution by a Jewish student in Riga, about whom the narrator, in his chilly way, remarks: "It must be admitted that the Jewish passion for rising above the paternal pawnshop had produced certain excellent psychological results in young Loew. . . ." But at the heart of the tragedy is the fact that the narrator makes of this young girl a sister, who in him would have a lover.

"Why is it," the narrator asks, "that women fall in love with the very men who are destined otherwise, and who accordingly must repulse them, or else deny their own nature?" The narrator has very little use for women—so little that, as he says, he "has chosen to frequent only the worst of them." But he is not above the vanity of being adored. He notes: "But those who are rejected in love retain one advantage: they have played rather cheaply upon our pride. Our own complacency, and our pleasure at being valued, at last, as each of us always hopes to be, work together to this result, and thus one yields to the temptation of playing God to one's adorer."

"Between Sophie and me an intimacy swiftly sprang up like that between victim and executioner," remarks the narrator, in a metaphor that will reverberate in the novel's final pages. The girl offers herself to him. "Erik," she says, "I'd rather tell you straight out that I've somehow come to love you. . . . So, whenever you wish, do you understand? And even if it's not serious. . . ." The narrator acknowledges that "I soon grew to depend upon the very alcohol which she afforded me, though I certainly never intended to abuse it." His vanity will eventually compromise him as surely as his acting on desire would have done.

Meanwhile there are political complications. In the battle being fought in the background of the novel, Sophie has some sympathy for the Reds. "For a nature like hers," says the narrator, "the supreme elegance evidently was to think that the enemy was right. . . ." Politics and love clash. "She seemed to feel obliged strangely enough to despise everything that I stood for, everything, that is, except me myself." Unrequited love lapses surely into degradation for Sophie, who makes a pathetic attempt to beautify herself with cosmetics, gives herself to another man, falls to drinking. Thinking about her even at her most degraded, though, the narrator is aware of what for him is a fatal truth: "But the unhappy truth about this girl was that although she seemed utterly promiscuous one could not think of committing oneself to her for less than a lifetime." This is of course precisely what the narrator refuses to do. "It is none the less true that I have probably lost out on one of the main chances of my life," he says. "But there are also some chances which, in spite of ourselves, our instinct rejects."

Sophie is finally driven away—away, specifically, to the Reds, on whose side she fights. In the hands of real artists the unpredictable comes to seem inevitable. The narrator, leading a patrol, captures a small band of Red soldiers. Sophie is among them. This is the kind of war in which no prisoners are taken, not even young women. Sophie asks no mercy in any case; she has what the narrator calls an "obstinate will to die." She has only a single request—that she be killed by the hand of the narrator. He obliges: "The first shot did no more than tear open the face, so that I shall never know (and it haunts me still) what expression Sophie would have had in death. On the second shot everything was over." In the concluding paragraph of *Coup de Grâce* the narrator at first thinks that Sophie wished him to kill her as a final sign of her love for him, but he later comes to believe that she really had revenge in mind, leaving him with a permanent aftertaste of remorse, which he does confess to feeling at times. The novel's last line—a line perfect in its flatness—reads: "One is always trapped, somehow, in dealings with women."

If I have recounted the plot of *Coup de Grâce* rather lengthily, it has been to make clear where Marguerite Yourcenar's interests as a novelist lie. They most distinctly do not lie in politics. A character in her novel *A Coin in Nine Hands* remarks that at La Scala, when they need to simulate crowd noises, they get performers to sing the highly sonorous word *rubarbara* in rounds from the wings. He then says, as Mme Yourcenar herself might have done, "Well, politics, whether of the Left or the Right, it's *rubarbara* for me, my boy." She was even less, this writer who was the first female member of the French Academy, interested in the condition of women, or indeed in any contemporary condition. Some novelists pull us more deeply into our own time; she pulls us away from it—or rather above it. Marguerite Yourcenar's subject is human destiny. It was the only serious subject for the Greeks, whom she so much admired. It has always been the great subject of the novel, and always will be, even though few writers in our day have been able to find the means to take it on, let alone so directly as Marguerite Yourcenar has done.

"I have encouraged experimentation with the thought and methods of the past, a learned archaism which might recapture lost intentions and lost techniques." So says the emperor Hadrian in Mme Yourcenar's *Memoirs of Hadrian;* so might the novel's author have said in explanation of her own excursions into the past as a form of literary experimentation. Yet who better to discuss questions of human destiny than a Roman emperor, a man for whom the satisfaction of all worldly desires

can be arranged without difficulty? And who better among
roman emperors than Hadrian (76–138 C.E.), successor to
Trajan, precursor to the Antonines, a competent amateur in
mathematics, literature, and painting, a dabbler in magic and
astrology, a lover of Athens and Greece, a man of wide personal culture?

Memoirs of Hadrian purports to be an account of the Roman
emperor's life as he presents it, in his waning days, to the young
Marcus Aurelius. In it Hadrian recounts to Marcus the expe-
riences of his twenty-year reign and the years that preceded it,
of his travels outward from Rome, of his attempts to penetrate
beneath the conventional ideas of his time. In these memoirs
Hadrian attempts to extract, for the young Marcus but also for
himself, such wisdom as his years have taught him. The novel's
outlook is worldly; its tone philosophical; its feeling completely Roman. The book is a triumph of historical ventrilo-
quism; it is impossible to read it and not think that had Hadrian
left memoirs, this is how they would have read. Next to *Memoirs of Hadrian,* Robert Graves's *I, Claudius* reads like an issue
of *Classic Comics.*

Now, to bring off such a book requires not only artistry and
scholarship but intelligence of a very high order. Intelligence
is not much spoken of in connection with novelists—except to
say that this or that writer is a novelist of ideas—but it looms
larger than most people with literary interests are ready to allow.
In fiction it is difficult—perhaps impossible—to create a character more intelligent than oneself, though this doesn't stop
novelists from trying (or prevent them from failing). When in
his novels the late Henry Miller used to divagate on the subject
of Indian philosophy, only the sheerest intellectual rube did
not know that Miller was out of his water. When John Updike
has a character in one of his novels talk about theology, one's
mind generally takes a walk around the block.

This is not Marguerite Yourcenar's problem. If she has a
problem as a novelist, it is that the quality of talk in her novels

is so superior that it overwhelms the element of story, which, in her longer novels, counts for a good deal less than setting and cerebration (although, it must be added, she is extremely good at constructing chronicles of careers). Something similar occurs in the recent novels of Saul Bellow, whose plots have come increasingly to matter less than the quality of his own observations. Not that Marguerite Yourcenar is quite so essayistic in her novels as Bellow has become in his, but it does often seem that, in recent fiction, plot contracts to accommodate the expansion of mind.

Plot does not figure prominently in *Memoirs of Hadrian*. The dying emperor's reflections are everything. These reflections are pitched at exactly the right—the Roman—level of generality. Here, for example, is Hadrian on both the benefits and the limits of government:

> I lent only half an ear to those well-intentioned folk who say that happiness is enervating, liberty too relaxing, and that kindness is a corruption for those upon whom it is practiced. That may be; but in the world as it is, such reasoning amounts to a refusal to nourish a starving man decently, for fear that in a few years he may suffer from overfeeding. When useless servitude has been alleviated as far as possible, and unnecessary misfortune avoided, there will remain as a test of man's fortitude that long series of veritable ills, death, old age, and incurable sickness, love unrequited and friendship rejected or betrayed, the mediocrity of a life less vast than our projects and duller than our dreams; in short, all the woes caused by the divine nature of things.

It is on the divine nature of things, on the fundamental mysteries of love, food, the body, sleep, the soul, death, that Hadrian's thoughts linger in this novel. "Every bliss achieved is a masterpiece," he writes. As for morals, they "are matters of private agreement; decency is of public concern." The great love of his life had been for the young Bithynian Antinuös;

about it he remarks: "But the weight of love, like that of an arm thrown tenderly across a chest, becomes little by little too heavy to bear." Mme Yourcenar offers the spectacle of a dying emperor, scarcely able to enjoy the simplest pleasures, craving death, taking the measure of the world around him as only a man who soon will have no stake in it can, yet even with death staring him full in the face not utterly devoid of qualified hope:

> Life is atrocious, we know. But precisely because I expect little of the human condition, man's periods of felicity, his partial progress, his efforts to begin over again and to continue, all seem to me like so many prodigies which nearly compensate for the monstrous mass of ills and defeats, of indifference and error. Catastrophe and ruin will come; disorder will triumph, but order will too, from time to time. . . . Not all our books will perish, nor our statues, if broken, lie unrepaired; other domes and other pediments will arise from our domes and pediments; some few men will think and work and feel as we have done, and I venture to count upon such continuators, placed irregularly throughout the centuries, and upon this kind of intermittent immortality.

Passage after passage in *Memoirs of Hadrian* has this marmoreal quality; and reading this remarkable book about a second-century Roman emperor by a twentieth-century Belgian woman one recalls yet another sentence Marguerite Yourcenar has lent to the pen of Hadrian: "A man who reads, reflects, or plans belongs to his species rather than to his sex; in his best moments he rises above the human."

If *Memoirs of Hadrian* seems carved in marble, *The Abyss,* a novel set in sixteenth-century Europe, a Europe with one foot in the Renaissance and the other more firmly planted in the Middle Ages, seems the work of brush on canvas. Bosch and Breughel, as Mme Yourcenar has averred, supply the background for portions of this book; and here, to convey some feeling of texture, is a passage that is pure Breughel:

The traveler stopped in the square to buy a loaf of bread. The doors of the burghers' houses were beginning to open. At one of them a pink-cheeked matron in a crisp linen-wimple loosed a poodle to let it run gaily about; it sniffed the grass before stopping suddenly to settle into that contrite pose all dogs assume when relieving themselves, then bounded off again to its play. A troop of children passed, chattering on their way to school, chubby and merry as robins in their bright attire. . . . A cat stole by, returning home with his prey, the limp claws of a bird protruding from his mouth. From the cook shop came the savory odor of pies and roast meat, mingling with the stale smell from the butcher shop nearby; the butcher's wife stood rinsing her bloodstained threshold with great buckets of water. Outside the town was the customary gallows, raised on a grassy knoll, but the body hanging there had been exposed so long to sun, wind, and rain as to have almost acquired the gentle aspect of old abandoned things; a friendly breeze played through its faded rags. A company of cross-bowmen were setting forth to shoot wood thrush, hearty burghers all, who clapped each other on the back as they exchanged jocosities; each of them had a pouch slung over his shoulder that would soon contain those small warm parcels of life which an instant before had been singing in the open sky. Zeno hastened his step.

Zeno, the protagonist of *The Abyss,* is forever hastening his step. Born in 1509 in Flanders, the illegitimate son of an Italian aristocrat and a mother who becomes an Anabaptist, the young Zeno is a lover of freedom, and his love soon takes an intellectual turn. He studies botany and engineering, astrology and alchemy, earning his keep as a physician and living, detached from society, as a philosopher. Zeno is in quest of the truth, while the Inquisition, more patiently but no less relentlessly, is in quest of him.

Zeno is the pure type of the scientist-philosopher: a man who takes nothing on faith and of whom an ecclesiastic who befriends him says that he has "too little faith to be a heretic." Faithless though he is, he is nonetheless filled with wonder at the simplest objects, not least the wall of flesh covering the human machine, which is the subject of Zeno's unending study as a physician: "This cumbersome envelope of flesh which he had to wash, feed, and water, heat at the fireplace or beneath the pelt of some slaughtered beast, and put to sleep at night like a child or like a helpless old man, was hostage to the whole of nature, and even more hostage to his fellow men."

As man is hostage in his body, concludes Zeno, he is scarcely less so in his mind. "All his life long he had been amazed at the way ideas have of agglomerating, divorced from feeling, like crystals in strange, meaningless formations; and of growing like tumors, devouring the flesh that conceives them. . . . He knew now that ideas die, like men; in the course of half a century he had witnessed the decline of several generations of notions, all falling into dust."

Much as he has striven for freedom himself, Zeno knows he is not finally free. "For no one is free so long as he has desires, wants, or fears, or even, perhaps, so long as he lives." The abyss, Zeno is aware, is "both beyond the celestial sphere and within the human skull." Are we in the end, he wonders, any more sentient than the rabbits given to him one day by a peasant woman and which he looses in the fields?

> Rejoicing in their liberty, he watched them escape into the brush, lascivious, voracious creatures, architects of subterranean labyrinths, timid, yet playing with danger, helpless except for the strength and agility of their loins, and indestructible only by reason of their inexhaustible fertility. If they should manage to avoid the snares and clubs, the falcons and martens, they could still continue their playful leaps and bounds for a time; their fur would whiten in winter along with the snow, and in spring they would begin anew to feed on the fresh green grass. So reflecting, their liberator pushed the basket with his foot into the ditch.

A spectacle of rabbits—lascivious, voracious, timid yet playing with danger—is what Mme Yourcenar offers in *A Coin in Nine*

Hands. No Hadrians, no Zenos, no great men or women move through this novel. The coin of the title is a ten-lira silver piece, which passes from hand to hand in Rome in the year XI (1933) of the Fascist dictatorship. As it passes from a deserted husband to a prostitute with cancer to the owner of a small cosmetics shop to a woman selling votary candles and so forth and so on, Marguerite Yourcenar tells the stories of each of their lives. At the center of the novel is an abortive attempt to assassinate Mussolini.

Montaigne supplies the novel's epigraph: "The right way to prize one's life is to abandon it for a dream." And it is true that in this book everyone is a dreamer of one sort or another. Some dream of love, some of revolution, some of a life of quiet dignity, some of the mastery of art, and some—might these be the greatest dreamers?—that they have grasped reality. In an afterword, Mme Yourcenar wrote that one of the reasons this slender novel "seemed worthy to be published again is that, in its day, it was one of the first French novels (maybe the very first) to confront the hollow reality behind the bloated façade of Fascism. . . ." Yet today this seems rather beside the point. The tragedies of the lives of the characters, however, do not.

"Destiny is lighthearted," begins an aphorism in Marguerite Yourcenar's book *Fires,* and in the pages of *A Coin in Nine Hands* one sees destinies worked out with a lighthearted arbitrariness: cancer for this one, an appetite for revenge for that one; good looks here, poverty of soul there; the belief on one man's part that no faith is worth dying for and the corresponding belief on one woman's part that without a faith worth dying for life is not worth living; an artist who has lived for art and in the bargain perhaps missed out on life: "All in all, I didn't live that much. . . . Painting really takes a lot of discipline. You have to get up early. . . . Go to bed early. . . . I don't have any memories."

Intricate moral questions are usually not at the center of Marguerite Yourcenar's work. Human destiny, its meaning and even more its mysteries, are. She had a clearer sense than any-one now writing of the tragedy yet also the hope inherent in human lives. The great experiment, as her alchemist Zeno says, always begins anew. The effect of reading her novels is to be reminded of the difficulty of life and of its heroic possibili-ties—hardly a thing that contemporary literature does best, if at all. Most of us are undone by life. Ours is but to do, then die. Marguerite Yourcenar's novels make us question why. This is what major writers have always done. This is why she is among their number.

Commentary 1982

E. B. White,
Dark & Lite

WHEN E. B. WHITE DIED, at the age of eighty-six, on October 1, 1985, his obituarist in the *New York Times* referred to him as "one of the nation's most precious literary resources," and the newspaper backed up the statement by running a six-column-across obituary of the kind it generally grants only to indisputably major statesmen and artists. The following day *Times* editors weighed in with "The Elements of White," an editorial that quoted E. B. White in favor of careful prose style and world government and against armed slaughter and destruction. The *Nation*, too, ran an editorial on its front page marking White's death; it used the occasion to point out that the human antonym of E. B. White is New York's mayor Edward Koch and ended by quoting the penultimate sentence from *Charlotte's Web*, one of White's three books for children: "It is not often that someone comes along who is a true friend and a good writer." In the public sense, the *Nation* averred, E. B. White was both. An editorial cartoon by Duffy originally printed in the *Des Moines Register* but picked up around the country—the version I saw was in the *Chicago Tribune*—depicted, again from *Charlotte's Web*, the pig Wilbur looking rather sad beneath a spider web, hanging from the doorway of a barn, in the middle of which is written SOME WRITER.

Some, one might add, career. Famously shy though he was said to have been, E. B. White may nonetheless have also been the most honored American writer of our time. He had more medals than a Soviet marshal: among them, the National Medal for Literature, the Presidential Medal of Freedom, and the gold medal for essays and criticism of the American Academy of Arts and Letters. He was awarded a special Pulitzer Prize citation for "the body of his work." He had honorary degrees from Harvard on down. His books sold very well and his children's books exceedingly well—in the millions, in fact. *The Elements of Style,* a rather bare-bones writing manual originally produced by his Cornell professor William Strunk, which White brought up to date and to which he added material, was a selection of the Book-of-the-Month Club. Any high-school or college anthology that does not contain at least one E. B. White essay—usually the one on his Model T Ford, "Farewell, My Lovely," or "The Death of a Pig"—qualifies as something of a rare book.

Then there is the *New Yorker,* in which the vast majority of White's writing initially appeared and on which he was a major—in some ways, a decisive—influence. Although never formally an editor of the *New Yorker,* White, who came to work for the magazine shortly after its founding in 1925, contributed light pieces and poems and (later) "Letters from the East"; he supplied the captions for a great many cartoons and the tag lines for the excerpts of the unconsciously comical prose published elsewhere that the magazine calls "newsbreaks"; and for decades he wrote the "Notes and Comment" section of " Talk of the Town," which is the closest thing the *New Yorker* has had to an official voice.

Oddly enough, the most disappointing obituary about E. B. White was the one that appeared in the *New Yorker.* A splendid fringe benefit of working for any length of time on the editorial side of the *New Yorker* is that one receives one's own specimen of what are easily the most beautiful obituaries written in the United States. But the obituary accorded to E. B. White, though written by three different hands, somehow fell well short of the mark. The first of the three wrote of White as "an early and brave defender of civil liberties, social justice, and the environment" and also acknowledged his doing "as much as any other single writer to set the tone and create the spirit of the *New Yorker*." The third contributor wrote of taking two children, both of them devoted readers of White's children's books, on a visit to White's farm in Maine, and closed by noting that even though White was not personally on the premises, the farm itself, made immortal by his books, was enough to satisfy the children. He also wrote of White's prose style, remarking that "he seemed to take down the fences of manner and propriety and pomposity in writing." According to this contributor, it was said of E. B. White that he wrote as if neither Marx nor Freud had ever lived, yet if presented with this as a criticism, White "would not then set about becoming more political or more at one with his psyche." Earlier, the first contributor had written that E. B. White "ran counter to our century's fashion for literary despair, and did not try to tamper with his inexplicably sunny inclinations."

The phrase "inexplicably sunny inclinations" caught my attention, as football announcers are wont to say when a quarterback is blindsidedly tackled by a 280-pound defensive lineman. I have recently been reading through the works of E. B. White, a writer of whom I hitherto had a most blurry and inexact picture, and the one thing that can be unequivocally said about him is that one has to search very sedulously indeed to find a gloomier writer than E. B. White. The gloom is not merely incidental but pervasive in his writing. He is, moreover, a relentless preacher, as perhaps befits one whose own favorite writer was that consummate American preacher in prose, Henry David Thoreau. Isaac Rosenfeld's review of *Wild Flag*, a 1946 collection of White's "Notes and Comment" editorials from the *New Yorker*, was entitled "Chopping a Teakettle," from the

Yiddish phrase *hacken a tcheinik*. "Not only does he chop away with an unfailing stroke," Rosenfeld wrote, "but he manages to keep a cloud of steam issuing from the spout as he works." The editorials in *Wild Flag* are about world government, but before he lays down his ax, White has worked on several tea-kettles: the environment, bureaucracy, the horrors of modern life. He turns out to be something of a Jeremiah, but with a plain prose style.

This is not the figure, the precious literary resource, most people think of when they think of E. B. White. Most people, I suspect, think of E. B. White as the archetypical *New Yorker* writer of the early days of that magazine; not quite so anarchical in his humor as James Thurber, or so wickedly witty as Wolcott Gibbs, but very clever, always in good taste, and never heavy—a White Lite, to adapt both the concept and the spelling favored by the American low-calorie-beer industry. Later, when White removed himself from New York to live on a farm on Allen Cove, near North Brooklin, Maine, he became a naturalized New Englander, a man who, it was believed, lived close to the earth and whose prose, it was also believed, took on some of the good sense that comes from plain living among plain people. His success with his children's books served to enhance his reputation—and, into the bargain, to authenticate his sensitivity. You cannot, after all, fool children about these things, can you? There was, then, something of a saintly aura about White, and the older he grew, the more honored he became, the saintlier he seemed. "I wouldn't mind being as old as E. B. White," said Kurt Vonnegut, "if I could actually *be* E. B. White."

Elwyn Brooks White was born in 1899, the sixth, the last, and the late-life child of an upper-middle-class family in Mount Vernon, New York. He was brought up in a rambling Victorian house. His father, who had begun to prosper when White was born, was the general manager and vice-president of Horace Waters and Company, a firm that sold musical instruments.

The single blot on White's otherwise pacific childhood was that his father was charged with, though later acquitted of, fraud in connection with a stock transaction—an event he harks back to in *The Trumpet of the Swan*, the last of his children's books.

From his father, who each summer took the family on vacation to Maine, White acquired a love of the natural world and a respect for order and precision. (In the White family, when a child did not know the meaning of a word, he was sent upstairs to consult *Webster's Unabridged Dictionary*.) From his mother, whose own father was a painter, he acquired a respect for art, shyness, and a strong strain of hypochondria that was never to leave him. (Interesting, is it not, that hypochondriacs seem to be so long-lived?) The large house in Mount Vernon had an expansive lawn, a fine garden, servants, animals—all the things, together with parental love, that ought to make for boyhood happiness, but in E. B. White's case did not, or at least not quite.

Scott Elledge, E. B. White's biographer, begins the second chapter of his book by remarking: 'White was born lucky, as he has often said, but he was also born scared. . . ." And it is true that in his portraits of and random comments about his youth, a combination of melancholy and anxiety hangs over everything. He suffered from hay fever; he had a terror of public speaking; he was more than normally bashful around girls; he felt guilty that his dog, not permitted the run of the house, had to be locked in the basement; he feared failure in school. E. B. White had what in nineteenth-century novels used to be called a very delicate nervous organization. Although not friendless, he seemed most at ease when solitary. He was good at writing, that solitary act, and derived much pleasure from being able to formulate on a page what he often could not say in person. Skating and canoeing, two other solitary acts, were his favorite pastimes. But he spent even more time tending to and sometimes just quietly watching animals. In a memoir of his own boyhood entitled "A Boy I Knew," he wrote: "This boy felt for animals a kinship he never felt for people."

E. B. White may have overdone in his writing the true extent of his shyness as a boy and young man, for his career at college tends to belie his own picture of himself as a youth almost perpetually in the habit of retreat. White went to Cornell, where his two older brothers had preceded him. There he was able to slip the milquetoast name of Elwyn, which his friends exchanged for Andy, after Andrew White, then the powerful president of Cornell. The year of his matriculation was 1917; the United States had just entered World War I, but White did not weigh enough to pass the army physical. With some prodding from his sister he joined a fraternity, a good one, Phi Gamma Delta, and was later elected president. His second year in school he was named to the board of editors of the *Cornell Daily Sun,* and the following year was elected editor in chief. He wrote many of the paper's editorials, and for one of them he won the Arthur Brisbane Award. One of his teachers offered to find him a job as an English instructor, but he had already settled on a career in journalism. The early 1920s were still a time when young people who felt the urge to write could find a home on a newspaper. Willa Cather and Theodore Dreiser began on newspapers and so, later, did Ernest Hemingway.

E. B. White, on his first assignment for his first job (with the United Press), took the wrong train, blew the assignment, and quit. White later wrote features for the *Seattle Times,* publicity for the American Legion News Service, and copy for advertising agencies, but he seemed to fit in nowhere. His chief feelings as a young man seemed to be doubt and self-disgust. Like a great many young men and women, then as now, he had a strong desire to write with nothing particular in mind to write about.

In these, his fledgling years, E. B. White was, as always, self-conscious, but very little the conscious artist. Although he was of the generation of E. E. Cummings and Edmund Wilson,

Wallace Stevens and William Faulkner, high art was never the name of his desire. He had no wish to write the intricate poem or the experimental novel, and so far removed from great artistic ambitions was he that (he once claimed) it took him fully fourteen months to read *Anna Karenina*. What did attract him was the world of smart journalism, the world of H. L. Mencken and Don Marquis and Christopher Morley and F.P. A., in whose *New York World* column, "The Conning Tower," White had published an occasional squib. These were the days, recall, of the wits of the Algonquin round table: Robert Benchley, Alexander Woollcott, Dorothy Parker, Heywood Broun, Frank Sullivan, and Ring Lardner. It was in the atmosphere of smart journalism, and through the efforts of such writers, that Harold Ross planned and brought to fruition his dream for the weekly magazine first published on February 19, 1925, and known as the *New Yorker*.

E. B. White's first piece in the *New Yorker* appeared in its tenth issue. It was one of those light comic compositions that at the *New Yorker* are called "casuals"; it was about how a copywriter might conduct an advertising campaign for spring. But White's real breakthrough at the *New Yorker* came with the publication, in the last issue of 1925, of a 650-word piece entitled "Child's Play," which was about the efforts of a man (the author) to retain his *savoir-faire* when in a New York restaurant—Child's, in fact—a glass of buttermilk is spilled on his blue serge suit. The delicate touch of humor in the piece, its precision and perfect tone of self-mockery, captivated the magazine's chief literary editor, Katharine Angell, who suggested to Harold Ross that he hire the author as a regular member of the *New Yorker* staff. Ross did. White and Katharine Angell eventually married, but the marriage of E. B. White with the *New Yorker* was perhaps the most crucial event in the magazine's history.

Although the *New Yorker* has accommodated in its pages writers as various in style and intellectual range as Hannah

Arendt and S. J. Perelman, A. J. Liebling and Kenneth Tynan, Harold Rosenberg and Garrison Keillor—its editorial capaciousness has been part of its genius—it is the magazine's tone that has been chiefly responsible for its success. That tone was early set by E. B. White, and even today, decades after White ceased regularly to supply the magazine with the editorials known as "Notes and Comment," the reigning tone of the *New Yorker* remains White's. The tone itself is an attempt at a compound of whimsy and common sense, modesty and decency, from which pretentiousness and heavy-handedness generally are excluded. The tone shimmers with an implied sensitivity, the chief implication being that we readers are ourselves highly sensitive characters—intelligent, good-humored, tasteful. It is a tone that encapsulates an attitude, and about this attitude no one has written better than Robert Warshow, in a 1947 review of E. B. White's *Wild Flag* in *Partisan Review:*

> The *New Yorker* has always dealt with experience not by trying to understand it but by prescribing the attitude to be adopted toward it. This makes it possible to feel intelligent without thinking, and it is a way of making everything tolerable, for the assumption of a suitable attitude toward experience can give one the illusion of having dealt with it adequately. The gracelessness of capitalism becomes an entirely external phenomenon, a spectacle that one can observe without being touched—above all, without feeling really threatened. Even one's own incompetence becomes pleasant: to be baffled by a machine or a domestic worker or an idea is the badge of membership in this civilized and humane minority.

Tone and attitude, the composition textbooks tell, commingle and in complex ways reinforce each other. But what can determine both is topic. Here, not E. B. White but Harold Ross had the whip hand. Ross was determined that his magazine, which provided serious criticism of the arts, would not

get serious about politics. What he termed "sectarian" opinions were *verboten;* taking political sides and espousing political causes were strictly outlawed. The *New Yorker* may have
been the only journal of its day not to touch on the subject of
Sacco and Vanzetti. E. B. White was the man who would change
all that.

Not that there is any compelling reason to believe that White
was burning to write about politics. He was not a very political
animal. As he had little interest in the main currents of avant-
garde art in his day, neither was he at all interested in radical
politics. He was a great deal less concerned with Trotsky's state
of permanent revolution than with his own state of permanent
nostalgia. He would write about the incursions of advertising
into modern life, or about the spread of commercialism into
places where he felt it had no place, or about the comic pretensions of science to make daily life better, or about the hopeless
complexity of urban living—about, in short, the little nui-
sances set in the path of mankind. The big "think piece," as the
boys in journalism used to call it, was not the specialty at his
house.

In the early years of the *New Yorker,* Harold Ross hired a
number of managing editors, who were charged with bringing
order to the natural chaos of a weekly magazine; these men,
would-be saviors, were known among the staff as Ross's new-
est Jesuses. But E. B. White, in Harold Ross's eyes, was the
Father and the Holy Ghost. White seemed to come through
for Ross as no other writer did; his were among the few contributions to the magazine that Ross did not devastate with
marginal queries. It was White who persuaded Ross to run
James Thurber's drawings; it was White who rewrote the large
sections of "Talk of the Town"; it was White who had the
perfect feel for "Notes and Comment." White was reliable on
deadlines, White had good taste, White's own prose was Ross's
ideal of good prose made flesh.

E. B. White and Harold Ross looked to have one of those

perfect editorial partnerships. White did not interfere with Ross's need for control, but when he felt the need to do so, he was able gently to guide him; Ross gave White the latitude and freedom he seemed to require. If White greatly aided Ross, Ross, in bringing the *New Yorker* into being, was the making of White. "I discovered a long time ago that writing of the small things of the day, the trivial matters of the heart, the inconsequential but near things of this living," White wrote to one of his brothers in 1929, "was the only kind of creative work which I could accomplish with any sincerity or grace. . . . Not till the *New Yorker* came along did I ever find any means of expressing those impertinences and irrelevancies." So there you have it: Ross needed White, White required Ross. "Symbiosis," as S. J. Perelman might have put it, "pleased to meetcha."

Harold Ross's devotion to the *New Yorker,* the child of his brain, was complete; E. B. White's was merely enormous. The artist in White could not quite obliterate himself for the larger purposes of the corporate effort. Perfect *New Yorker* editorialist though he may have been, White found himself struggling under the limitations of the form. "It is almost impossible to write anything decent using the editorial 'we,' unless you are the Dionne family," White wrote to his friend Gus Lobrano. Nor was he keen on the anonymity of the editorialist; at one point he asked Ross to allow him to sign his name to the "Notes and Comment" editorials, but Ross, who was against even printing a masthead in his magazine, refused.

The artist, with this artist's ample ambitions, began to stir in E. B. White. He preferred not to be called a humorist. He grew frustrated with his editorials; "my weekly sermon for the *New Yorker,*" he began to call them. To exacerbate matters, Ralph Ingersoll, one of Harold Ross's former Jesuses, who now worked for *Fortune,* published a long article about the *New Yorker* in *Fortune*'s August 1934 issue; in it he scored the *New Yorker,* which had flourished through the Depression, for ignoring the great economic and political issues of its time, and he cited in particular White's "gossamer writing" and editorials "so carefully swathed in whimsy" that they could not possibly affront anyone. This rankled. To the frustration of White's job was now added what he began to believe was the pointlessness of it.

By the middle 1930s E. B. White's fame, though more than intramural, was not yet anything like national in the way it was one day to become. He had published a collection of his *New Yorker* pieces, along with a few volumes of light verse and a collaboration with James Thurber entitled *Is Sex Necessary?* Around New York he was thought of as a pro—a man of modest but real talents who could get the job done. Such must have been the view behind Christopher Morley's offer to White, in 1936, of the editorship of the *Saturday Review of Literature,* which he turned down. Earlier, the publisher of the *New Yorker,* Raoul Fleischmann, badly on the outs with Harold Ross, had offered the co-editorship of the magazine to E. B. and Katharine White, but they were not interested in it. Editorial power was never really what interested White.

Art now began to be. In the summer of 1937, at the age of thirty-eight, E. B. White awarded himself a year's sabbatical. *Time* magazine, noting his departure from the *New Yorker,* remarked that he was giving "himself time to think about progress and politics, whether to get out of their jumpy way or to try to catch up with them." But *Time* was mistaken. White had taken leave to devote himself to a lengthy writing project. A bad idea whose time never came, this project was to be a long autobiographical poem, but White was able to make no headway with it, which redoubled his frustration. "I have made an unholy mess out of this 'year off' business," he wrote to Thurber. He spoke of envying those people who could write without being lashed to deadlines. Never quite comfortable in Manhattan, he now moved permanently to his farm near North Brooklin, Maine. He yearned to make something of his life; he yearned to be more than a mere journalist; he yearned—though he never used the word—for significance.

Although E. B. White continued to do various editorial chores for the *New Yorker* and would go on writing for it until the last few years of his life, in 1938 he made what appeared to be a break when he signed on to contribute a monthly essay of 2,500 words to *Harper's*. Appearing under the rubric "One Man's Meat," fifty-five such essays were published in *Harper's* from 1938 through 1943. Nearly the entire time White was writing for *Harper's*, Harold Ross kept a full-court press of attention on him, making him various counter-offers. (All the while, Katharine White continued to work as one of the principal editors of the *New Yorker* and White himself kept an office there.) Still, to make even this partial break with the magazine took a certain amount of courage. The *New Yorker* is one of those publishing institutions—the *New York Times* is another—that looms much larger than the people who work for it, and for people who cut loose from them the tendency is to lose stature and to lose it fast. A much smaller number of people gain in stature, and E. B. White was one of them.

The break, less than complete though it was, could not have been all that easy for White, even if he was eager to put an end, as he said, to "his long apprenticeship in the weekly gaiety field." Even before Heisenberg discovered it, uncertainty was a principle for E. B. White, who felt himself not only something of a lightweight but a sad failure as well. When, in 1938, he wrote a letter of general self-deflation to James Thurber, putting himself down for his own insignificance, Thurber responded that in the present tumultuous age, the need for humor was all the greater, and that White ought not to be ashamed of providing some of it. To Thurber, to give oneself over to a political age, as so many other writers had done, seemed a great mistake:

> It is the easiest thing in the world nowadays to become so socially conscious, so Spanish war stricken, that all sense of balance and

values goes out of a person. Not long ago in Paris Lillian Hellman told me that she would give up writing if she could ameliorate the condition of the world, or of only a few people in it. Hemingway is probably on the same path, and a drove of writers are following along, screaming and sweating and looking pretty strange and futile. This is one of the greatest menaces there is; people with intelligence deciding that the point is to become grimly gray and intense and unhappy and tiresome because the world and many of its people are in a bad way. It's a form of egotism, a supreme form. . . . How can these bastards hope to get hold of what's the matter with the world and do anything about it when they haven't the slightest idea that something just as bad and unnatural has happened to them?

Yet White could not quite take his friend Thurber's advice. To the gloominess of the times—the civil war in Spain, the ascendancy of Hitler in Germany and Mussolini in Italy, the entry of the United States into World War II—White joined his own gloominess of temperament. When he became a full-blown essayist, at least partially free from the "gaiety field," the "I" who emerged from the "we" of the editorialist was more melancholic, dark, and depressed than most of E. B. White's earlier readers would have been likely to suppose.

During his four-and-a-half-year stint at *Harper's,* E. B. White lived full-time on his farm in Maine. Life in the country in fact furnished a goodly portion of the subject matter of many of his *Harper's* essays. These essays, we know from White's correspondence, did not come easily. "A journalist," Karl Kraus once remarked, "is someone who, given time, writes worse." So it was for White, who found writing a monthly piece more painful than performing on his old weekly deadline at the *New Yorker.* After his first few *Harper's* essays, his "monthly encyclicals" as he called them, White wrote to Morris Bishop that "I sound like Thomas Mann on the Concord and Merrimack." That is very amusing, and not without a measure of accuracy. Perhaps, though, it would be more accurate to say that E. B.

White's essays sounded like Thoreau with hay fever and Norman Rockwell with a migraine.

"I trust," said a friend to White when he left Manhattan to live in Maine, "that you will spare the reading public your little adventures in contentment." He need not have worried. Anywhere you go, an old saying has it, there you are! While life in Maine for White was less anxious than life in New York—about which he had written a famous essay—he was still able to discover the cloud in every silver lining. Read cumulatively, the *Harper's* essays (brought together in a book entitled *One Man's Meat*) are dark indeed. There is the self-debasement—in one of the essays White describes himself as "a middle-aged hack"—that comes rather easily to a writer who elsewhere notes "the enormously important discovery that the world would pay a man for setting down a simple, legible account of his own misfortunes." There is the endless nostalgia, which causes White to be, rather predictably, against automobiles but, rather less predictably, also against the dismantling of the Sixth Avenue elevated. Then there are the bleak little touches: a school bus "as punctual as death"; a hen house taken over by "contagious hysteria and fear"; "faces desperate in the rain"; "the fierce bewildering night"; and more, much more, including, in June 1941, an imagination of doomsday, or, as White prefers to call it, "doomsmoment":

> I think when the end of the world comes the sky will be its old blue self, with white cumulus clouds drifting along. You will be looking out of a window, say, at a tree; and then after a bit the tree won't be there any more, and the looking won't be there any more, only the window will be there, in memory—the thing through which the looking has been done. I can see God, walking through the garden and noticing that the world is done for, reach down and pick it up and put it on His compost pile. It ought to make a fine ferment.

White seemed to have a positive taste for the apocalypse. In a story entitled "The Day They Did It," he took on the subject of the end of the world in a science-fiction fantasy. In "Notes and Comment" he wrote editorials about the fear of living in big cities during the atomic age. This fear of the end of the world, as we shall see, dovetails snugly with one of E. B. White's chief political ideas, that of world government, but it also is allied to his general gloom. As *One Man's Meat* makes evident, mankind made White edgy; men, through confusion, ambition, willfulness, were primarily great botchers, making the simple complex, the useful otiose, the beautiful ugly. White found the natural world not only more thrilling than the human one but less frightening as well. His essays form something like an extended commentary on Bishop Heber's quatrain about the isle of Ceylon, where "every prospect pleases / And only man is vile."

"Life," wrote White to Thurber, "is just about as alarming as it ever was, it seems to me." Life seemed to E. B. White almost perpetually alarming. He was very tightly strung. In 1943, his biographer informs us, without dwelling on the subject, he was under the care of a new doctor, "who had prescribed strychnine to treat his symptoms of depression." In his *Letters* White reported recovering from a "nervous crack-up" he had undergone in the summer of 1943. The following year he wrote to his brother that he had decided to go to a doctor "about my head, as there seems to be a kite caught in the branches somewhere." In another letter to his brother he spoke of having "mice in the subconscious" and announced that "the whole key to the neurotic life is simple," though he did not say what the key was.

Nor does Scott Elledge, White's biographer, specify what, precisely, was the matter with White, or what constituted his cure, if cured he was, for nervous breakdowns haunted him throughout his life. Elledge wrote his biography while White was still alive, and perhaps good manners stood in the way of probing his subject on this delicate point. I am more than a little hesitant to bring it up myself, lest it be thought that I am using E. B. White's mental problems against him; I do so only because it seems necessary in the effort to establish what kind of writer E. B. White was and why he was of this kind and no other.

White himself did not try to hide his mental fragility. Two pieces in his collection of 1954, *The Second Tree from the Corner,* deal directly with breakdown and madness. In a much reprinted sketch entitled "The Door," a narrator is comparing his own condition to that of rats who have been sent through mazes and put through other experiments. In a state of high agitation, the narrator remarks: ". . . I am confronted by a problem that is incapable of solution . . . and that is what madness is, and things seeming different from what they are." Later he will add: ". . . for although my heart has followed all my days something I cannot name, I am tired of the jumping and I do not know which way to go, Madam, and I am not even sure that I am tired beyond the endurance of man (rat, if you will) and have taken leave of sanity."

In a vignette entitled "The Second Tree from the Corner," one Mr. Trexler visits his psychiatrist late in the afternoons. He suffers from what he terms "the dullest set of neurotic symptoms in the world"; these include "the dizziness in the streets, the constricting pain in the back of the neck, the apprehensions, the tightness of the scalp, the inability to concentrate, the despondency and the melancholy times, the feeling of pressure and tension, the anger at not being able to work, the anxiety over work not done, the gas on the stomach." The visits to the psychiatrist avail him nought. The psychiatrist at one point asks Trexler what he wants from life. Trexler cannot say, but leaving the psychiatrist's office, he realizes that what he wants is

deep, formless, enduring, and impossible of fulfillment, and that it made men sick. . . . [that] what he wanted was at once great and microscopic, and that although it borrowed from the nature of large deeds and of youthful love and of old songs and early intimations, it was not any one of these things, and that it had not been isolated or pinned down, and that a man who attempted to define it in the privacy of a doctor's office would fall flat on his face.

At this, White continues,

> Trexler felt invigorated. Suddenly his sickness seemed health, his dizziness stability. A small tree, rising between him and the light, stood there saturated with the evening, each gilt-edged leaf perfectly drunk with excellence and delicacy. Trexler's spine registered an ever so slight tremor as it picked up this natural disturbance in the lovely scene. "I want the second tree from the corner, just as it stands," he said, answering an imaginary question from an imaginary physician. And he felt a slow pride in realizing what he wanted none could bestow, and that what he had none could take away. He felt content to be sick, unembarrassed at being afraid; and in the jungle of his fear he glimpsed (as he had so often glimpsed them before) the flashy tail feathers of the bird courage.

What E. B. White wanted, what I believe the second tree from the corner represented for him, was art—more specifically, he wanted, out of his vulnerability, to create something with the "excellence and delicacy" of true art.

In 1943 E. B. White returned to the *New Yorker,* whose ranks had been much thinned by World War II. In his letter of resignation to *Harper's,* he wrote to Frederick Lewis Allen, then that magazine's editor, that he "felt a peculiar disappointment, almost a defeat" in his work there; and he later added that "I want to write when and if I feel like it." Yet, however great White's personal sense of failure as an essayist at *Harper's,* there is no doubt that his stint there was the making of him.

Owing to a strong attack he had written for *Harper's* on Anne Morrow Lindbergh's *The Wave of the Future,* a book arguing the isolationist case against America's entry into World

War II, and other pieces he had written against Fascism and on behalf of democracy, White had become something of a spokesman for what in bygone days used to be called "the American way of life." (As an opponent of Fascism, White, it is worth noting, early condemned the Nazis' savage treatment of Jews in Germany.) Evidence of his new and greatly enhanced reputation is that in 1941 Archibald MacLeish, the director of the government Office of Facts and Figures, asked White to join Max Lerner, Reinhold Niebuhr, and Malcolm Cowley in collaborating on a propaganda pamphlet on the "Four Freedoms"; he, White, was to write on freedom of speech and then to serve as rewrite man for the entire project. He was offered— and refused—a judgeship at the Book-of the-Month Club. Around this time Irwin Edman asserted of White's *Harper's* essays that they contained "the poetry of observation and the philosophy of shrewd, usually gentle, sometimes biting moral insight." From such items are the altars of middlebrow gurus constructed.

How seriously did E. B. White take himself as a spokesman, guru, thinker? Elledge acknowledges that White "seldom commanded the patience and the intellectual staying-power needed for arguments involving a knowledge of history and the formulation of complex ideas." From his own letters one gets a sense that White was aware of his own intellectual indigence. On the dust jacket of *The Wild Flag,* his book of editorials on world government, White himself must have written: "Mr. White does not regard himself as a Thinker and says he feels ill-at-ease writing editorials on massive themes. He regards himself as a clown of average ability whose signals got crossed and who found himself out on the wire with the Wallendas." Yet, though he kept no bees on his farm, E. B. White would from time to time get a bee in his bonnet, and then his confidence in his powers of intellect could be very great. A case in point is, precisely, world government—a subject that he took up in the late 1930s and retained an interest in to the end of his days.

World government—or world federation, as it was sometimes called—was an aspiration, a belief, a panacea, for ending warfare among nations by introducing not international but supranational law into the affairs of nations. It made a broad appeal to humanity at large over and against narrow nationalism; it viewed sovereignty, as White once put it, as "a dead cat." It held out the hope for a world without enemies, which was an alluring hope indeed after World War II had introduced atomic weapons. In the late 1940s and early 1950s, world government had wide currency; among its adherents were Robert M. Hutchins and Mortimer Adler; many a political theorist lost many a weekend designing one or another world constitution. World government, in short, was an idea with everything to commend it and only reality and human nature to oppose it.

Although White wrote about world government in some of his *Harper's* essays, it was in the "Notes and Comment" section of the *New Yorker* that he really chopped away at this particular teakettle. Elledge maintains that after White's return to the *New Yorker,* "beginning with the issue of April 10, 1943, and continuing for the next four years, nearly one-third of White's weekly 'Notes and Comment' included at least one paragraph on the subject [of world government]." It is a tribute to Harold Ross's regard for White that he allowed him to editorialize so relentlessly on a subject that he, Ross, was not at all interested in. White's editorials did nothing, of course, to bring world government any closer to realization—neither, after all, has the United Nations—but they did have the effect of opening the *New Yorker's* pages to issues of social and political significance; they cleared the way for the magazine's political phase, which it has never left, so that today, in its "Notes and Comment" section, one can be almost certain of finding a weekly sermon on Nicaragua, or Star Wars, or fresh malfeasance on the part of the CIA.

Not that E. B. White was anywhere near so left-wing as the current tendency of the *New Yorker*. White's politics were a very great muddle, if that term does not give them credit for more coherence than they actually contained. White was, for example, against economic controls yet also against the profit system. He was, as we have seen, very much for world government yet against disarmament—on the grounds that until such time as we had world government, we would all need our weapons. (White never underestimated the ambition of the Soviet Union for world domination.) He was a civil libertarian, yet thought the country "babied" its labor unions. He worried (in print) endlessly about the future, yet seemed only to love the past. He claimed not to have understood the meaning of life, yet was full of advice for the living. E. B. White was a pessimistic utopian, a despairing optimist, a sour idealist, a man reputed to be a humanitarian who, when one got right down to it, was made edgy by most human beings.

These contradictions were not always apparent in E. B. White's writing, and for at least two reasons. The first is that, as an essayist, he was not a writer one was likely to read *en bloc,* and so one took him piece by piece and could not be expected to discover his inconsistencies. (It may well be that he himself never discovered them.) The second reason is his prose, which was clear, often shyly eloquent, and immensely seductive. All writers seek to seduce their readers, with reason or charm or brilliance, or a combination of the three. White did it mostly with charm, but charm of a special kind: self-derogating, homey, sensitive. He was the ostensibly bashful boy who sets out to win the hand of the beauty queen.

White wrote in what, technically, is known as the plain style. His specialty was the declarative sentence: subject, predicate, direct object, indirect object, in that order. His sentences contain few subordinate clauses, inversions, semicolons, or dashes.

His vocabulary is also plain: no foreign words, no arcane words, almost no abstract words, only occasionally a slang word like "dippy" or "loopy" that has its own charm. For the most part, an E. B. White essay is composed of plain words arrayed in plain syntax forming plain declarative sentences, one after another, back to back, on and on. In a prefatory note to his essay on William Strunk, the original author of *The Elements of Style,* White, after citing his uneasiness about "posing as an expert on rhetoric," said: "The truth is I write by ear, always with difficulty and seldom with any exact notion of what is taking place under the hood." That is the characteristic E. B. White tone.

White did have a fine ear for prose cadence. He also knew that the best-made sentences are those that have a small surprise waiting at their close. "In the still air," he wrote, describing a war-bond rally, "under the hard sun, gleamed the flags and the banners and the drum majorette's knees." Or, again, this time describing that moment in high summer when one realizes that autumn will soon follow: "The tides run in and out, clams blow tiny jets of seawater up through the mud, a white line of fog hangs around the outer islands, days tumble along in cool blue succession, and I hate the word September." This last sentence is perhaps, in Harold Ross's term, "writer conscious"—by which Ross meant artificial in the way that only an exhibitionist writer can be—but there is no denying White's descriptive powers. He was quite wonderful at describing buildings at dusk, snow in the bright sun, a lake in the rain.

Even with the plain style, variations exist. George Orwell used the plain style to convey that he, a man of plain words, could not be conned by fancy or false words. Behind E. B. White's plain style is the quiet but firm insistence that White is an unpretentious and sensitive man. One of the chief services performed by writers who project their own sensitivity—E. M. Forster and J. D. Salinger are two other such writers—is that they make their readers feel that they, too, are sensitive. Yet sensitivity can easily slide into sentimentality. Often it did in the work of White, who, in his editorial for the *New Yorker* on the death of Franklin Delano Roosevelt could invoke the guns fired at the dead president's grave and "Fala's sharp answering bark," or could write at the death of John F. Kennedy: "It can be said of him, as of few men in a like position, that he did not fear the weather, and did not trim his sails, but instead challenged the wind itself, to improve its direction and to cause it to blow more softly and more kindly over the world and its people." How sonorous, how beautiful, how not especially true!

Was E. B. White a great essayist? I, for one, think he was at his best when he was not preaching—when he set the teakettle aside and laid down his ax. But he was preaching a good deal of the time. Although he is now generally regarded as a cheery American writer—recall the *New Yorker* obituary's reference to "his inexplicably sunny inclinations"—White was by nature gloomy, and at his most moving when he gave way to his fear and sadness. To my mind easily his most beautiful essay is "Once More to the Lake," which is about his return in 1941, along with his eleven-year-old son, to the lake in Maine where White's own father used to take him and his family beginning in 1904. It is an essay that shimmers like a perfect poem; everything in it clicks.

In the essay White recalls the lake he once knew and now sees again through the eyes of his young son, who does everything at the lake that he did as a boy more than thirty years earlier:

> I began to sustain the illusion that he was I, and therefore, by simple transposition, that I was my father. This sensation persisted, kept cropping up all the time we were there. It was not an entirely new feeling, but in this setting it grew much stronger. I seemed to be living a dual existence. I would be in the middle of some simple act, I would be picking up a bait box or laying down a table fork, or I would be saying something, and sud-

denly it would not be I but my father who was saying the words or making the gesture. It gave me a creepy feeling.

"Once More to the Lake" is about generation, about birth and rebirth and death. White was fascinated by generation and haunted by death. Both obsessions come through brilliantly in this essay, where through his own son he relives his father's life and previews his own death. In the essay's closing paragraph, his son, after a rain shower, wrings out his bathing suit before going in for an afternoon swim. White writes: "Languidly, and with no thought of going in, I watched him, his hard little body, skinny and bare, saw him wince slightly as he pulled up around his vitals the small, soggy, icy garment. As he buckled the swollen belt, suddenly my groin felt the chill of death." This essay is dazzling and devastating, art of a heightened kind that an essayist is rarely privileged to achieve.

One does not usually think of E. B. White as a man writing out of his obsessions, yet obsessional he was, and perhaps nowhere more so than in his books for children: *Stuart Little, Charlotte's Web, The Trumpet of the Swan*. Children adore these books, and yet one wonders what they make of them. Children love living things and have their own fascination with the animal world—a love and fascination which White, clearly, shared. Yet children have this advantage over adults: they are permitted to love things they do not understand. But coming to these books as an adult, and loaded down with knowledge of their author's life, with its longings and fears, one cannot avoid reading them as fables about E. B. White's own life.

I hope I may be allowed to forgo a full-dress exegesis comparing E. B. White's life with that of the mouse Stuart, the pig Wilbur, and the swan Louis. But this much does require saying: all three are characters in need of rescue. Stuart is a mouse born to human parents who finds city life among human beings hazardous and indeed terrifying; Wilbur is a pig being fattened for slaughter; Louis is a trumpeter swan who is born mute and hence cut off from all communication. In these books, Stuart is impelled on a quest after a bird who is very much like a muse; Wilbur is saved by a spider named Charlotte who can write; and Louis learns to play the trumpet, a talent which allows him to find a mate and also earn enough money to redeem the reputation of his father, who broke into a music store to obtain the trumpet through which Louis learned to speak and eventually to live a fairly normal life.

I hope, again, that I do not betray the dreariness of my symbol-minded literary education when I suggest that Stuart's quest for the bird Margalo mirrors White's own quest in departing New York and journalism for art (at one point in the story Stuart is given charge of a class, and the lesson he teaches it is on the need for something suspiciously like world government); and that, at the close of *Charlotte's Web,* when Wilbur remarks of the spider who saved him that "it is not often that someone comes along who is a true friend and a good writer," White has in mind his wife, who was the mainstay of his always shaky life; and that Louis's attempt to make good his father's theft at the music store refers to the charges of fraud brought against White's own father at the Horace Waters musical-instrument firm.

In a letter, E. B. White reported that when Edmund Wilson, his colleague at the *New Yorker,* read *Stuart Little,* he announced to White: "I read that book of yours. I found the first page quite amusing, about the mouse, you know. But I was disappointed that you didn't develop the theme more in the manner of Kafka." But in fact White did develop his books for children in the manner of Kafka, if in a somewhat enfeebled and oddly American way; these books are Kafkaesque but with the American twist that they are Kafka with happy endings, and in their own manner they fulfill the prescription of William Dean Howells, who once remarked that what the American public wanted "was a tragedy with a happy ending."

A tragedy with a putatively happy ending might well stand

in as a description of E. B. White's own life and career. His was a life led in fear—"Everything scared me in those days," he wrote in an essay about his apprenticeship as a reporter in Seattle, "and still does"—and on the rim of nervous breakdown. His was a career that strained after significance; but despite all the honors he won, he himself was never quite convinced he had achieved it. The obituarists and eulogists (they were one and the same) who wrote about him at his death both praised and buried him, obscuring, in their exaltation of him as a "precious" literary resource and a man of "inexplicably sunny inclinations," both the man he was and the writer he wished to be. To be a writer vastly overrated and mostly misunderstood—this, for now, will have to pass for a happy ending.

Commentary 1986

George Santayana
and the Consolations
of Philosophy

PHILOSOPHERS, UNLIKE FISH, do best not to travel in schools. Josiah Royce once said that the philosopher does well to imitate the rhinoceros, who travels in a herd of one. George Santayana, a rhinoceros among philosophers, an all-ivory and very elegant one, went even further in stipulating that the philosopher ought not to share unreservedly the spirit of his age, or be subject to its dominant moods. One of Santayana's criticisms of Bertrand Russell was that "he could never shake himself free from his environment and from the miscellaneous currents of opinion in his day." Insofar as philosophy implies the long view and the high view—and insofar as it does not, philosophy is a great deal less interesting—this would seem to make good sense. If the world is among those phenomena that are not better understood close up, then philosophers should indeed cultivate detachment the way English pensioners do delphiniums: for motives above and beyond immediate profit. But is the world best understood from the distance, away from the fray and above the ruck? That, as a certain notable Danish prince was wont to say, is the question.

It was never much of a question for George Santayana, who in suggesting that the philosopher ought not to live too fully in the spirit of his age, might have been writing his own job description. Not that Santayana had to cultivate detachment; he seems to have been born with it, the way other people are born with, say, large feet. This quality of extreme detachment in Santayana has put many people off, in our own time and even more in his. He referred to his own "essential character as a traveller and a stranger, with the philosophical freedom that this implies." He felt that to be a stranger was his destiny and considered himself among those true travelers who, not "pining for a better cage," are content with their own condition of permanent transience. Nowhere in Santayana's writings will one find the least yearning to be amidst the fray or in and around the ruck. He was quite content to occupy his seat in the shade, a glass of good wine in his hand, watching the other people dance.

When Santayana remarked that being a stranger was his destiny, he could only have been alluding to the conditions of his birth and upbringing. He was the only child of his mother's second marriage, and was named after her first husband. His mother had earlier married the ninth child of the Boston merchant Nathaniel Russell Sturgis, with whom she had five children, three of whom survived. She had met her second husband, George's father, when he and her own father were officials in the Spanish civil service in the Philippine Islands, but did not marry him until many years later. In 1869, when George was six years old, his mother parted from him and his father to live in Boston among her deceased first husband's family, who were her main financial stay. Young George was left behind in the walled Spanish city of Avila with his father, who was then in his fifties. Three years later, along with his father, he joined his mother in Boston, to take his place as the youngest son in a shabby-genteel household with a remote connection to the wealthy and well-established Sturgises. When George's father found that he was too old to make the adjustment to life in the United States, he returned to Avila. His son would not see him again until he was at the end of his freshman year at Harvard.

Santayana did not have to worry about his mother's love; from nearly the outset, he knew he didn't have it. Such maternal love as she seemed to possess spent itself upon her first-born son, Victor, who died in the second year of his life. The death "made a radical revolution in her heart," Santayana would note years later in his autobiography, *Persons and Places*. "It established there a reign of silent despair, permanent, devastating, ruffled perhaps by fresh events on the surface, but always dark and heavy beneath, like the depths of the sea." He would claim that his half sister Susana, who was twelve years his senior, came closer to being his true mother. He frankly wondered what his parents saw in each other. As for him, he loved his father, whom he could not admire, and admired his mother, whom he could not love. Two interesting cards to be dealt so early in life.

Santayana's manner in writing about his mother in *Persons and Places* is characteristic of his detachment. It is evenhanded, but not cool; it is hot, but not red-hot. He ticks off her many and serious shortcomings: her coldness; her incuriosity, not to say philistinism; her pridefulness; her hostility to everything that interested her children; her mismanagement of the lives of those children who would permit her any control over their lives. Santayana, pretty clearly, was not among the latter. He wasn't because in many respects he and his mother were very much alike: in their independence of will; in their need to separate themselves from those around them; in their common inability to be much moved by the most tragic of events; and in their fundamental despair, which seemed to raise them both above great concern over ordinary matters. One may not like a man who tells you straightaway that he is a cold fish, but one tends to trust his word.

If few of the conventional comforts of family life were open to Santayana, those of patriotism were quite closed off to him. Born in Spain and raised in the United States, he was truly neither American nor Spanish, though legally he remained and died a Spanish citizen. When he first returned to Spain in 1883, in his twentieth year, he felt like a foreigner there "and could not do myself justice in the language." Language was no barrier to him in America—he spoke English with no marked accent—but he felt even more of a foreigner here. He would later say that in feeling he was Spanish and that in mastering English he might be said "to have been guilty, quite unintentionally, of a little strategem, as if I had set out to say plausibly in English as many un-English things as possible."

Almost by design, Santayana appears to have been a foreigner in every country in which he ever lived. In Spain, Santayana never sought out fellow Americans; in America he never sought the company of fellow Spaniards. Although he spent many a season living in Paris, the episodic and fashionable nature of French intellectual and artistic life put him off; so did the French mind, which he cited as "an exquisite medium for conveying such things as can be communicated in words. It is the unspoken things of which one feels the absence or mistrusts the quality [among the French]." He thought about settling in England after he had given up teaching philosophy at Harvard in 1912, which was as early as he could afford to do so. ("True serenity of mind comes, of course," as Murray Kempton once remarked, "to those who can dismiss Harvard.") But he decided, while living there during World War I, that he "was in danger of losing my philosophical *cruelty* and independence" (italics mine), and so departed once more, describing his farewell to England as akin to burying "a wife long divorced."

George Santayana was unassimilable by nature, a stranger by preference, a man without a country quite as much by choice as by circumstance. When in his sixties he finally settled in Rome, he did so not because he felt he had found an ideal society, but rather because he had found suitable lodgings in an ideal situation of solitude and independence, "after the fashion of ancient philosophers," as he put it, "often in exile, but always in sight of the market-place and the theatre." Of course, to be in exile one must first have a home country from which one has been ejected or has chosen to flee. As John McCormick writes in his excellent new biography of Santayana, "Wherever he was, he was at ease, playing his part on the stage, but he was not at home." Yet it would be a mistake, I believe, to imagine George Santayana as lonely, alienated, an *isolato*—a mistake, in general, to imagine that Santayana did not enjoy life, for he did, immensely.

How was Santayana able to do so without the consolations the rest of us require: love of family, of country, of friends? Consider only friendship. Santayana's friendships were sometimes intense but scarcely ever intimate. In regard to friends, he resembled a cousin of his father's, who "liked all that was likable, without being deceived by it." Such friendships as Santayana made as a young man were based not on social class, for his own was a bit blurry, or on membership in the same circle, for he belonged to no circle, but instead on his own two prerequisites to perfect friendship—"capacity to laugh and capacity to worship." Yet he felt, at least from the perspective of old age, that "modern life is not made for friendship," offering as it does too many distractions. The friend who seems to have meant the most to Santayana was Frank Russell, the second earl Russell and Bertrand Russell's older, equally scandal-prone brother; the long duration of their friendship, Santayana believed, was owing to the fact that "neither of us was ever a nuisance to the other." But this friendship, like almost all his others, would in time lapse. As he grew older, Santayana accustomed himself to lapsed friendships without bitterness. In a world where everything was transitory, friends could scarcely be otherwise, but for him this "involved no estrangement, no disillusion; on the contrary, the limits of each friendship perfected that friendship, insured it against disaster, enshrined it in the eternal." To live *sub specie aeternitatis*, under the aspect of eternity, is of course the way philosophers are supposed to live. Yet to come across a philosopher who actually does so live is startling and not a little spooky, and we tend to be chilled by it.

Marriage, the ultimate friendship, was for Santayana never a serious possibility. At twenty-two, studying in Germany on a Walker Fellowship from Harvard, he wrote in light verse to his friend Ward Thoron:

> I cannot part from what I prize
> For all I prize is in my head;
> My fancies are the fields and skies
> I will not change till I am dead,
> Unless indeed I lose my wits
> Or (what is much the same thing) wed.

Years later, now a professor at Harvard, when asked why he didn't marry, he replied that he wished to retain his freedom and, besides, he did not intend always to live in America. He also mentioned religious difficulties, for he styled himself a "free-thinking Catholic" (about which more presently), which left him in a socially impossible position in a Protestant country. He counted himself a *déraciné*, and, as he wrote in his auto-biography, "a *déraciné*, a man who has been torn up by the roots, cannot be replanted and should never propagate his kind."

Skeptical minds will want to know if all this isn't the sheerest twaddle and if Santayana was not in fact homosexual. It is a question worthy of Barbara Walters, but today, alas, all biog-raphers must ask it of their unmarried subjects, or even of those who have married too often. John McCormick, who does little poking about in sexual closets in his biography, nonetheless feels that he must flop one way or another on the question, and he flops, on a very thin mattress of epistolary evidence, too thin to air out here, on the side that says Santayana must have been homosexual. Although I much admire Professor McCormick's biography, and although his brief sexual inves-tigation does not in any serious way flaw his book, I wish he hadn't flopped at all.

I think a much stronger case can be made for the other side. In a letter to Morton Fullerton, who was later to be Edith Wharton's lover and a friend to Henry James, Santayana sets out the sexual choices, but eliminates "Paiderastia" because "our prejudices against it are so strong that it hardly comes under the possibilities for us." While he writes elsewhere in good Santayanan metaphor that "the chained dogs below keep barking in their kennels," he also avers that "love has never made me long unhappy, nor sexual impulse uncomfortable." But what seems to be clinching is his critical treatment of the dons at King's College, Cambridge—"my feeling when I was at King's was that the birds were not worthy of the cage"—during a time when the homosexual spirit was very much in the ascendant at that college. Santayana found E. M. Forster's friend and philosophical mentor, Goldsworthy Lowes Dickinson, hopeless in his utopianly sentimental moralizing. Oscar Browning "openly flaunted the banners of gluttony and paederasty, neither of them suitable for a teacher of youth. . . ." Of Lytton Strachey, another great Cambridge figure of this era, Santayana wrote: "*Obscene* was the character written all over him; and his expertness in secret history and satire expressed that character intellectually." To a correspondent who queried him many years later about Strachey, he replied: "No, I am *not* an admirer of Strachey. I knew him." Such sentiments scarcely seem those of a man, to adopt Professor McCormick's unfortunate phrase, of "homosexual temperament."

Very little else about Professor McCormick's biography is unfortunate. It is well written; it is comprehensive; it is devoid of nonsense. *George Santayana: A Biography* is a difficult biographical assignment brilliantly brought off. Of its difficulty, consider only the following: Santayana lived a long life (he died at eighty-eight) in which almost all the major events went on in his mind; *déraciné* by birth and as far from *engagé* as possible in his intellectual life, only his views, ideas, books matter. In *Persons and Places,* Santayana wrote one of the really splendid autobiographies of the twentieth century, and few things can be quite so discouraging to a biographer as his subject's having written well and truly about himself. One of those things may be to have this same subject also be among a small circle of extremely elegant English prose stylists, so that, next to his subject's, the biographer's own writing will often be made to seem rather dim, not to say a bit shoddy. (Careful readers will notice that thus far along in this essay I have myself refrained from quoting Santayana at length.)

In the nature of this case, a biographer does not figure to be as subtle, penetrating, or artful as his subject. But he ought not to be too much less so. A biographer who can write about a subject whose mind is as well-stocked and intellectually intricate as Santayana's is not easily found. To understand Santayana, one has to be interested in art and philosophy and to appreciate philosophy practiced as an art, which is the way he, Santayana, usually practiced it. John McCormick, who is not a professional philosopher but a teacher of comparative literature who has written on literary history and on the theoretical foundations of fiction, does understand all this. He is a worldly man, and a serious man, who writes lucidly, with power where it is called for, and with occasional enlivening flashes of wit, as when, in passing, he remarks that old age is a reliable cure for hypochondria, or when he says of Santayana and Ezra Pound, "Their difference in age was considerable; their difference in temperament was alarming." McCormick's treatment of Santayana is evenhanded; his general tone is one of appreciation not bereft of criticism. Unless one is wholly an aesthete, Santayana is not a writer one loves—Lionel Trilling, writing about Santayana's letters in the middle 1950s, noted that "indeed, it might be remarkably easy to dislike him"—but at the same time it is difficult not to feel fascinated admiration for him, so copious was his talent, so completely did he live his philosophy.

In his thirtieth year, in a letter to Norman Hapgood, Santayana wrote: "It becomes clearer to me every day that both in teaching and living our need is simplification, measure and docility to the facts." Of course his own needs were immensely simplified by his early understanding that he was among those with "no other purpose but that of living to observe life," which is to say, that he was a writer. Whatever his other deficiencies, he had, *in excelsis*, "the faculty of intellectual delight," which he never lost. On a traveling fellowship in Germany he wrote to his teacher William James that "philosophy seems to me to be its own reward, and its justification lies in the delight and dignity of the art itself"; and he later confessed to James that what initially drew him to philosophy was "curiosity and a natural taste for ingenious thinking." All this makes him sound very much the cool aesthete, for whom philosophy is above all a superior game. And so it might have been but for his talent for facing unpleasant facts, the least pleasant of which he knew by the time he was twenty-three, and perhaps much earlier— that "the world isn't run in our interest or with any reference to our needs." He calls this brute fact the "ultimate lesson of experience and philosophy," and by "our" he doesn't mean dreamy young men at Harvard but all human beings.

That the world is not organized in the interest of human beings, nor with any special reference to their needs, was the last thing Santayana was likely to have learned at Harvard, where a Protestant spirit of uplift prevailed. This spirit, it does not seem too strong to say, Santayana detested. It was akin to the spirit he found in the Unitarian churches of Boston, where people flocked "to hear a sermon like the leading article in some superior newspaper calculated to confirm the conviction already in them that their bourgeois virtues were quite sufficient and that perhaps in time poor backward races and nations might be led to acquire them." He considered the great New England god Emerson "a sort of Puritan Goethe," who had "slipped into transcendentalism and moralism and complacency in mediocrity, in order to flatter his countrymen and indirectly flatter himself." One of Santayana's many complaints against Harvard's president Charles W. Eliot (who brought the system of elective courses to the university) was that he, Eliot, thought that if a thing was moral it must also be true.

Santayana detected and ultimately condemned this spirit in the philosophy department at Harvard—a department that included William James, Josiah Royce, and, between 1889 and 1912, Santayana himself. "Protestant philosophy," as he called philosophy in America in *Character and Opinion in the United States* (1920), "was too conscientious to misrepresent what it found," but also too moral-minded not to undermine its findings. At Harvard, philosophers felt themselves bound "by two different responsibilities, that of describing things as they are, and that of finding them propitious to certain preconceived human desires." Josiah Royce, who loved logic, labored with a powerful contradiction at the heart of his work, adducing the existence of evil to prove the existence of good, and then feeling he ought to strive to eliminate evil. Not even William James, according to Santayana, could shake off the heavy hand of Protestant moralizing: "He was worried about what *ought* to be believed and the awful deprivation of disbelieving."

Santayana has the distinction of being one of the few people to speak ill of William James with a pretty fair consistency. The feeling was not reciprocated, even though James is famously known to have referred, in a letter to George H. Palmer, his colleague in the Harvard philosophy department, to Santayana's "perfection of rottenness in a philosophy" and to his "moribund Latinity." As Professor McCormick shows, these phrases were embedded in a letter of otherwise exuberant praise for Santayana's book *Interpretations of Poetry and Religion* (1900), about which James wrote: "Although I absolutely reject the platonism of it, I have literally squealed with delight at the imperturbable perfection with which the position is laid down on page after page; and grunted with delight at the thickening up of our Harvard atmosphere. . . ."

It is reasonably certain that Santayana never either squealed or grunted with delight at anything William James wrote. James was in no serious sense Santayana's mentor, but he was, within the Harvard philosophy department, his protector, helping to arrange a job for him, solidifying a permanent position, aiding in his promotion. Santayana may not have known this. Yet even had he known it, my guess is that he could not quite have let his disappointment in James be. In a letter to a Harvard colleague, after reporting that John Stuart Mill's psychologism repelled him, he went on to say: "Mill is a sort of ponderous and sober James." To the same man he earlier wrote: "I love W. James as a man. But what a singularly bad thinker he is!" Yet if he claimed to love him in a letter of 1904, when he came to write about him decades later in *Persons and Places* he noted:

> I was uncomfortable in his presence. He was so extremely natural that there was no knowing what his nature was, or what to expect next; so that one was driven to behave and talk conventionally, as in the most artificial society. I found no foothold, I was soon fatigued, and it was a relief to be out again in the open, and alone.

In *Character and Opinion in the United States,* Santayana really lowered the boom on James—a velvet-covered boom, to be sure, but one that could nonetheless knock off a man's head. There Santayana wrote that James was a spirited but not a spiritual man; that *The Varieties of Religious Experience* is a book that altogether overlooks the religious experience of the great mass of mankind, which "consists in simple faith in the truth and benefit of their religious traditions"; that James was chary of coming to philosophical conclusions, or, as Santayana put it, "liked to take things one by one, rather than to put two and two together"; and that, finally, "there is a sense in which James was not a philosopher at all."

Heavy praise was not part of the regular regimen of Santayana's intellectual exercise—the only thinkers who unwaveringly found favor with him are the Greeks, Lucretius, and, after a jump of seventeen centuries, Spinoza—but was there an air of spite in his treatment of William James? My own sense is that he was disappointed in James, whom he knew to be a superior man but unfortunately not superior enough to rise above what to Santayana was the stultifying atmosphere of *fin-de-siècle* Harvard. When James once accused Santayana of impertinence and of putting on airs, Santayana shot back: "I wonder if you realize the years of suppressed irritation which I have passed in the midst of an unintelligible sanctimonious and often disingenuous Protestantism, which is thoroughly alien to and repulsive to me, and the need I have of joining hands with something far away from it and far above it." In a later letter he charged James with not seeing "my philosophy, nor my temper from the inside." Part of this could be put down to sheer clash of temperament; yet perhaps a greater part was owing to William James's impatience with the type of the artist, which Santayana most assuredly was. Odd that a man such as William James, who had so much sympathy, should in this regard have had so little imagination. One remembers here his inevitably disappointing letters to his brother Henry about Henry's books, with his, William's, invocations to Henry to try harder to write for the multitude, to which Henry on one occasion responded: "I'm always sorry when I hear of your reading anything of mine, and always hope you won't—you seem to me so constitutionally unable to 'enjoy' it, and so condemned to look at it from a point of view remotely alien to mine in writing it. . . ." As for Santayana, when he met Henry James, for the first and only time, toward the end of James's life, he seems to have understood him immediately and completely:

> Those were his last years and I never saw him again. Nevertheless in that one interview he made me feel more at home, and better understood, than his brother William ever had done in

the long years of our acquaintance. Henry was calm, he liked to see things as they are, and be free afterwards to imagine how they might have been. We talked about different countries as places of residence. He was of course subtle and bland, appreciative of all points of view, and amused at their limitations.

Was it the artist in Santayana that discouraged the teacher in him? He never set out to become a teacher. Had he not been offered a half-time instructorship at Harvard, Professor McCormick informs us, he would have studied architecture at the Massachusetts Institute of Technology. Santayana preferred not to be thought a professor. A poet, yes; a philosopher, certainly; a continuing student, inevitably; but a professor: "I would rather beg than be one essentially." From the day he began teaching he started saving for the day he could cease teaching. He claimed that no close friend of his was ever a professor. Lee Simonson, the stage designer, who was a student of Santayana's, recalls him when lecturing "gazing over our heads as if looking for the sail that was to bear him home"— though where, exactly, home was could not have been all that clear even to Santayana, except away from Harvard.

"So you are trying to teach philosophy at Harvard," Henry Adams said to Santayana on the one occasion when they met. "I once tried to teach history there, but it can't be done. It isn't really possible to teach anything." Santayana, had he been older, would have disagreed; it could be done, all right; for him the question was always whether it was worth doing. In a beautiful but cool passage in *Character and Opinion in the United States*, Santayana neatly described teaching with an accuracy that only those who have *tried* to give their best to teaching will readily recognize:

Teaching is a delightful paternal art, and especially teaching intelligent and warm-hearted youngsters, as most American collegians are; but it is an art like acting, where the performance, often rehearsed, must be adapted to an audience hearing it only once. The speaker must make concessions to their impatience, their taste, their capacity, their prejudices, their ultimate good; he must neither bore nor perplex nor demoralise them. His thoughts must be such as can flow daily, and be set down in notes; they must come when the bell rings and stop appropriately when the bell rings a second time. The best that is in him, as Mephistopheles says in *Faust,* he dare not tell them; and as the substance of this possession is spiritual, to with-hold is often to lose it. For it is not merely a matter of fearing not to be understood, or giving offence; in the presence of a hundred upturned faces a man cannot, without diffidence, speak in his own person, of his own thoughts; he needs support, in order to exert influence with a good conscience; unless he feels that he is the vehicle of a massive tradition, he will become bitter, or flippant, or aggressive; if he is to teach with good grace and modesty and authority, it must not be he that speaks, but science or humanity that is speaking in him.

Complain about teaching though Santayana did, he had a most impressive roster of students attend his classes and lectures at Harvard. Among them, as Professor McCormick reminds us, were Conrad Aiken, Robert Frost, Gilbert Seldes, Max Eastman, Harry Austryn Wolfson, Samuel Eliot Morison, Felix Frankfurter, T. S. Eliot, and Van Wyck Brooks. Wallace Stevens never took a course from Santayana, but was very much aware of his presence, and later wrote a splendid poem about him, "To an Old Philosopher in Rome." Walter Lippmann while a graduate student was his assistant. Most of these figures came away greatly impressed by Santayana's teaching. Only T. S. Eliot would later describe his lectures as "soporific"; and Van Wyck Brooks, in his autobiography, claimed to find Santayana's "assumption of superiority" repellent and his "feline aestheticism" (Brooks was, avowedly, a canine man) no less so. Brooks was also put off by Santayana's distaste for things American, "though I could not deny that, wandering alone, a stranger and exile everywhere, Santayana lived the true life of the sage."

Did Santayana actually hate America? I think he came near to doing so, without quite hating Americans. Around the time of his preparing to depart the United States for good, he wrote to his sister that "I am far from wishing never to see my American friends again. It is only *their country* that I am longing to lose sight of." He felt America to be a country where people were interested in what might or should be, whereas his sympathies were all for preserving the already formed. In America, ideas and traditions were not refuted but simply forgotten. The serenity for which he longed was not available in America, not even in religion: "Be Christians," he claimed once to have heard a president of Yale tell his students, "be Christians and you will be successful." Returning from a trip to California and Canada, he wrote to his sister in Avila: "They are intellectually emptier than the Sahara, where I understand the Arabs have some idea of God or of Fate." In the same letter he remarked that at Harvard, "in the midst of the dull round, a sort of instinct of courtesy makes me take it [America] for granted, and I become almost unconscious of how much I hate it all; otherwise I couldn't have stood it for *forty years!*"

In 1911, Santayana worked out an arrangement whereby he would teach a single term at Harvard, leaving him otherwise free to live abroad, there to indulge his *"native* affinities to European things." But when his mother died, in 1912, he wrote, from Paris, a letter of resignation to President Abbott Lawrence Lowell of Harvard, saying that his mother's death marked "the moment when I should carry out the plan I have always had of giving up teaching, returning to live in Europe, and devoting myself to literary work. Each of these things is an object in itself sufficient to determine me, and the three conspire together." He was almost fifty, and free at last.

Henceforth Santayana would guard that freedom with the most scrupulous care. Financially independent—one of his

Sturgis relations had invested his money for him wisely— he
had no social ambitions, required no regular circle of friends,
no fixed abode, no round of engagements. He was not in any
way reclusive, and rather enjoyed such people as came his
way—the stray poet or philosopher, the handsome and agree-
able woman—but, as he put it in *Persons and Places*, "For con-
stant company I had enough, and too much, with myself."
Besides, he "liked solitude in crowds, meals in restaurants, walks
in public parks, architectural rambles in noble cities." Boundless and boundary-less, he roamed free, all of Europe his
demesne, like a Henry James character from the late period
with all the Jamesian sensibility, but without any interior conflict requiring resolution.

Santayana's cousin Howard Sturgis, who was a friend of
Henry James's and who lived in England, accused Santayana
of being abominably selfish. Santayana allowed that he was
merely "profoundly selfish," the distinction residing in the sense
that while he took pleasure in the life around him, he determined never to enter into relationships that would cause him
to surrender his independence. (In fact, as Professor McCormick
recounts, once his books began to sell well, Santayana was most
generous in providing financial help to family and friends.) He
then goes on to make the distinction that his selfishness is not
of a competitive kind. "I don't want to snatch money or position or pleasures from other people, nor do I attempt to dominate them, as an unselfish man would say, for their own good."
Master of irony that Santayana is, in owning up to his own
selfishness he makes us recognize that it is the unselfish man of
that subordinate clause who is the real menace.

The power of making distinctions, which can result in
parching dryness in a pedantic philosopher, is in Santayana
always a pleasure to behold. The smaller the distinction, often,
the more charm it has. Thus in *Persons and Places* one finds
people who are argumentative but not critical, others who are
cordial but not amiable, then others who have warmth but no

passion. One man—specifically, Spinoza—is "virtuous but not normal"; and another—specifically, Frank Russell—is "polygamous without being inconstant." A writer able to wield a linguistic probe with such skill makes one feel one's own prose has been cut, most coarsely, on a large buzz saw. Santayana also had the power, which Aristotle said cannot be taught, of constructing dazzling metaphors and similes. Thus (again) in *Persons and Places* one comes upon buildings whose surfaces are stark and unyielding, thin and sharp, "like impoverished old maids"; frail elms, "like tall young women in consumption"; an aunt said to be "living out the fifth act of the tragedy of her life"; the speech of William Lyon Phelps, "his every word . . . a cocktail, or at least a temperance drink." It was Santayana who once referred to those philosophers whose writing gave no aesthetic pleasure—among them Epicurus, Saint Thomas Aquinas, Immanuel Kant—as "leafless forests"; to retain that botanical metaphor a moment longer, his own prose is a field of orchids on a mountain slope.

But then, it occurs to me, Santayana might have been repelled by the metaphor. A field of orchids perhaps plays too strongly into the stereotype of Santayana's reputation as the most dandiacal among modern philosophers. Orchids are all very beautiful, but one cannot after all derive sustenance from them; and might not the same be said of Santayana's philosophy? Santayana is perhaps best known for his book on aesthetics, *The Sense of Beauty,* but in fact it is not a book he greatly esteemed (he also had strong reservations about his other well-known work, *The Life of Reason*); and Professor McCormick informs us that the book secured promotion for Santayana to an assistant professorship at Harvard. Yet, powerful literary critic though he could be, and thoroughly literary though his sensibility was—*The Complete Poems of George Santayana* (1979) runs to more than five hundred pages, and his single excursion into fiction, *The Last Puritan* (1935), had a popular success—Santayana thought of himself as a philosopher, and a philosopher primarily.

He was, however, a philosopher of a particular kind—and the kind can best be distinguished by his method and his temperament. He was not a logician and he did not come to philosophy through science, for he had no scientific training of any serious sort. He never claimed originality for himself, and once remarked that all he cared for was "to sift the *truth* from traditional *imagination,* without impoverishing the latter." As early as 1887, when he was twenty-four years old, he wrote to William James to say that he had no interest in the philosophy that sets out to solve problems, and that philosophy, for him, was "rather an attempt to express a half-discovered reality , just as art is, and that two different renderings, if they are expressive, far from cancelling each other add to each other's values. . . ." Nearly thirty years later he wrote to a younger man just beginning a career in philosophy that while he could not take the teaching of philosophy seriously, he did think philosophy "might be a life or a means of artistic expression."

For Santayana, of course, philosophy was both a life and an art: he lived his philosophy, and he lavished upon the production of it attention of the kind that the superior artist lavishes upon his art. As a philosopher, he was no system builder, and attempts at elaborate argument in his technical philosophy are often difficult to follow. He was himself well aware of this, and when Logan Pearsall Smith proposed the anthology of his work that eventually appeared under the title *Little Essays, Drawn from the Writings of George Santayana* (1920), Santayana, in remarking on Smith's initial selection, wrote: "My impression is that what I have to say is better conveyed in these occasional epigrams than in any of my attempts at argument or system." There was the additional difficulty that Santayana used certain key philosophical terms—"moral," "science," "genius," "substance," "intuition," and "spirit," among others—with special, sometimes quite slippery, meanings. This, too, he knew: "Philosophy seems to be richer in theories than in words to express them in; and much confusion results from the necessity of using old terms in new meanings." Owing to this, Santayana's philosophy, like certain poems, does not paraphrase easily, if at all.

Like many another artist, Santayana was a brilliant critic of practitioners of his art. Although he claimed to despise an atmosphere of contention and controversy, he could handle the stiletto with the best of them. Frequently he chose to do so in the privacy of letters, as when, in one such letter, he described G. E. Moore's *Principia Ethica* as a book that "seems to contain a grain of accuracy in a bushel of inexperience." Such is Bertrand Russell's intelligence and clarity, that "the more wrong he is the clearer he makes the wrongness of his position; and what more can you expect a philosopher to prove except that the views he has adopted are radically and eternally impossible? If every philosopher had done that in the past, we should now be almost out of the wood." To witness Santayana at work in his job as critic of philosophers one cannot do better than to read the brief book entitled *Egotism in German Philosophy* (1916), in which, with great economy, he works up—and over—the German philosophical system builders. When he is done the landscape of German philosophy resembles nothing so much as Berlin in early 1946: scarcely any buildings are left standing; only a few shabby figures shuffle past; the smell of smoke is in the air. Toward the close of his life, he wrote: "If I were not too old and could venture to write in French, I should compose a short history of *Les Faux Pas de la Philosophie.*"

At the heart of Santayana's philosophy is a desire to be unillusioned about the world and yet, unlike (say) Nietzsche, neither in despair nor in great anguish about it. "I was never afraid of disillusion," Santayana wrote in the opening essay of *The Philosophy of George Santayana*, the volume devoted to his work

in the Library of Living Philosophers series, "and I chose it."
Perhaps it is just as accurate to say that disillusion chose him,
given his upbringing in a house crowded with Spanish relatives, where, as a small boy, he witnessed women giving birth
and, not much older, he shared a room with a half brother of
adolescent years and normal appetites. His father was an atheist, finding the idea of the existence of God ridiculous; his
mother was a pantheist, believing God existed but was everywhere and hence was quite impersonal. Being born without
much of it, he early knew that money was not an illusion. He
never for a moment seems to have felt that the world was "a
myth, to be clarified by a little literary criticism." Yet everything in his background conduced against his overestimating
the importance of human beings in the universe. As he
announced in a lecture on Herbert Spencer entitled "The Unknowable," life is not "an entertainment, a feast of ordered
sensations . . . life is no such thing; it is a predicament. We are
caught in it; it is something compulsory, urgent, dangerous,
and tempting. We are surrounded by enormous, mysterious,
half-friendly forces." And yet this only makes it all the more
fascinating.

To feel the vanity of life—that everything changes and
everything simultaneously remains the same—was for Santayana "the beginning of seriousness." To trot out the "isms," he
claimed allegiance to materialism, the family of doctrines that
give a primary place to matter, and to naturalism, which in
Three Philosophical Poets (1910) he described as an "intellectual
philosophy" that "divines substance behind appearance, con-
tinuity behind change, law behind fortune." But more to the
point, Santayana believed that "man was not made to understand the world, but to live in it. Yet nature, in some of us, lets
out her secret; it spoils the game, but it associates us with her
own impartiality." That secret, as mentioned earlier, is that the
world is not organized for man, that "morally," as he put it in
Persons and Places, "all things are neutral in themselves. It is we

that bathe them in whatever emotion may be passing through us." A qualified pessimism, an almost happy pessimism, is at the center of Santayana's philosophy:

> I have never seen much evidence of happiness in human life; but personally I cannot complain of my lot. It has been tolerable enough to allow me to be disinterested in speculation and therefore happy in it, as musicians can be happy in music or mathematicians in mathematics. But as men we are all sad failures. The world is a blind power, is too much for us, even for a Napoleon or a Goethe. But the same world, as an object of thought, is a wonderful theme; to understand it, virtually and mythically, as a man may, is the supreme triumph of life over life, the complete catharsis. Nonetheless, from the point of view of the animal in man, the truth remains tragic. An animal can be confident and brave only if he does not know the truth.

This ought to be depressing in the extreme, and yet, somehow, it isn't—as it isn't in the company of two other American laughing pessimists, Justice Holmes and H. L. Mencken. There is something grand about someone who can think the worst— in this instance positing an existence in an uncaring universe whose end can only be oblivion—and yet play bravely on through. "Survival is something impossible," Santayana wrote, "but it is possible to have lived well and died well."

Santayana was in the odd category of being a nonbelieving (or free-thinking) Catholic—a believer, in effect, in the doctrine that there is no God and Mary is his mother. Although he grew up in the Church, he early lost his faith; yet he never quite lost his appreciation for the Church as an ancient institution of civilization, despite his belief that "the loss of illusions is an unmixed blessing." He tolerated what he once characterized as the "absurdity and fiction in religion" because he felt that men, having "no adequate knowledge and no trained courage in respect to their destiny," have "to believe something or other, and that is their necessary religion." He himself favored a belief in something beyond man, and, it is not going too far to say, detested those who believed in nothing greater than man. Yet he was gentler in his views of paganism than he was of other modern religions. "To be a Protestant is to be cross-eyed," he once wrote. And on the Jews he was much harder.

Professor McCormick's admiration for Santayana does not blind him to the fact that Santayana had what is euphemistically known as a "Jewish problem." It can scarcely be ignored. One will be reading along, swept away by Santayana's penetration or powers of formulation or elegant wit, and, bang!, up will pop the devil. Thus, lulled by the pleasant chat of a letter written from Madrid, one comes upon the complaint that Santayana found Florence in December beastly, because "the expatriated anaemic aesthetes and the Jews surprised to find that success is not happiness made a moral atmosphere not wholesome to breathe. . . ." Such remarks do not qualify as gratuitous; they are more in the nature of compulsive. How explain this? Some of it may have been owing to Brahmanic Boston, whose anti-Semitic spirit Santayana might have caught. But even more, one suspects, may be owing to Santayana's disgust at what, in a letter written when he was not yet thirty, he termed the Jews' "incredible conceit of believing that they had made a covenant with nature, by which the mastery of the earth and all the good things thereof were secured to them in return for fidelity to a certain social and religious organization." In Santayana's philosophy, nature (or, if one prefers, God) favors no one. Yet to allow such disgust to lead into such dismal slurs is a blot of prejudice, as Professor McCormick writes, "unworthy of a man of his fineness in other matters, and scarcely comprehensible in the man who wrote *The Life of Reason* and *Realms of Being*."

It is also a blot on Santayana's disinterestedness, for apart from his mania on the subject of the Jews, Santayana, when it came to disinterestedness, could make the calmer gods of Olympus seem as grubby as the asphalt-contractors lobby in the Texas legislature. Here was a man unassimilable by choice, who thought it an indignity "to have a soul controlled by geography" (that is, by patriotism), who wished to be associated with the impartiality of nature, and for whom it was axiomatic that "in the end every philosopher has to walk alone." When Santayana remarked that he was concerned about losing the "cruelty" of his philosophy if he remained in England, what he meant was that he was concerned about his thought losing its edge through his adopting the attachments and passions of ordinary men. However beautiful his manners or convivial his tone, there was a deep impersonality about Santayana. It was the impersonality of the classical artist devoted, in his case, to the art of philosophy.

> Time might transmute, without erasing, my first opinions and affections; I might wish to change my surroundings and way of living; I never undertook to change myself. I regard my occupations and interests somewhat as an actor regards his various parts or a painter his subjects. That a man has preferences and can understand and do one thing better than another, follows from his inevitable limitations and definite gifts; but that which marks progress in his life is the purity of his art; I mean the degree to which his art has become his life, so that the rest of his nature does not impede or corrupt his art, but only feeds it.

How did Santayana's impartiality square with his politics? Santayana was always interested in politics, but could he be said to have had politics? During World War I, he found himself siding with England, where he was living at the time. But he lived through World War II, now quite an old man, in Fascist Italy, without any qualms, above it all and, by then, choosing to be quite out of it. He was conservative by temper, and in his autobiography wrote that he loved Tory England

and honored conservative Spain, though not "with any dogmatic or democratic passion," adding: "If any community can become and wishes to become communistic or democratic or anarchical I wish it joy from the bottom of my heart. I have only two qualms in this case: whether such ideals are realisable, and whether those who pursue them fancy them to be exclusively and universally right: an illusion pregnant with injustice, oppression, and war." Yet in 1977 Sidney Hook, who when a young man much admired Santayana's *The Life of Reason,* published in the *American Scholar* a series of letters that Santayana had written to him, in one of which (dated June 8, 1934) Santayana wrote:

> But I love order in the sense of organized, harmonious, consecrated living; and for this reason I sympathize with the Soviets and the Fascists and the Catholics, but not at all with the liberals. I should sympathize with the Nazis too, if their system were, even in theory, founded on reality; but it is Nietzschean, founded on will; and therefore a sort of romanticism gone mad, rather than a serious organization of material forces—which would be the only way, I think, of securing moral coherence.

Others accused Santayana of being sympathetic to Fascism. Professor McCormick does not justify Santayana's late-life politics, but he does attempt to explain them, citing other factors that need to be taken into account: "He was never politically active; his attitudes were aristocratic, illiberal by any modern definition of the word, at base philosophical." I myself prefer to think it one of those embarrassing moments for a great philosopher, and an example of the danger of coming at the complexities of the contemporary world from too high, too lofty, yes, even too philosophical a position. The dogs may bark, yet sometimes the caravan is carrying parts for gas chambers and needs to be stopped.

When World War II began in 1939, Santayana was seventy-six years old and permanently settled in Rome. Two years later he moved into the Clinica della Piccola Compagna di Maria, or Hospital of the Blue Nuns, an Irish order so named because of the color of the habit. The fees for his stay were paid through another center the order maintained in Chicago, for his money, held in America, could not be sent to Italy during the war. There, isolated from the war, easily able to deflect all efforts by the nuns to convert him ("He has too much brains," he reported Mother Superior saying of him, in justification of their failure), he worked away at his final books. Unlike so many of his American contemporaries interested in artistic and intellectual life, unlike Oliver Alden, the hero of *The Last Puritan,* Santayana up to the very end showed no signs, in his own phrase, of "petering out."

When after the war Edmund Wilson, writing pieces for the *New Yorker* about Europe in the wake of World War II that would eventually be published as *Europe without Baedeker,* visited Santayana in his austere room at the Hospital of the Blue Nuns, he, Wilson, was immensely impressed. It seemed to Wilson that Santayana was "perhaps the most international— or, better, the most supra-national—personality I had ever met." The fire of intellect, Wilson found, still burned in the all but worn-out furnace that was Santayana's aged body. Wilson's meeting with Santayana appears to have been rather like Santayana's with Henry James. The least sentimental of men, Wilson on this occasion was greatly moved, and he closed his essay by writing that "the intelligence that has persisted in him has been that of the civilized human race—so how can he be lonely or old? He still loves to share in its thoughts, to try on its points of view. He has made it his business to extend himself into every kind of human consciousness with which he can establish contact, and he reposes on his shabby chaise longue like a monad in the universal mind." This is, of course, the way that every serious writer should like to end.

Wilson wrote that he did not imagine Santayana was troubled by the thought of his impending death, and he seems to have been right. It was cancer that reached his liver that finally brought about his death. When he knew he was going to die, he instructed his amanuensis Daniel Cory not to believe, should he not be present, any stories about his deathbed conversion to the one Church that had ever mattered to him. Two days before his death, when Cory asked if he was suffering, Santayana is said to have answered: "Yes, my friend. But my anguish is entirely physical; there are no moral difficulties whatsoever." Philosophy had been for him, as for Boethius, a consolation, but finally also life itself. In the end he died as a philosopher should, his thoughts in order, at peace.

The New Criterion 1987

Sid, You Made the Prose Too Thin

A MAN ARRIVES for his first appointment with a psychiatrist, and reports suffering from an unrelenting sadness and gloom. "It's not at all uncommon," the psychiatrist replies, after hearing him out. "I myself often feel depressed. I was feeling so earlier this week, and to fight it off took myself to see the great clown Joey Grimaldi, who's in town with the circus. In the briefest time, while I was watching Grimaldi's wonderful antics, the world suddenly came to seem a lighter and brighter place. My depression seemed to drop away and I left feeling like a new man. Take yourself to see Grimaldi while he's still in town. He'll cheer you up immensely, I promise you." At which point the man sitting opposite the psychiatrist rather sadly replies: "But, doctor, I am Joey Grimaldi."

It is an old story and a familiar one, and it also happens to be the story of the life of S. J. Perelman, who, behind a screen of habitual jokey phrasings, appears to have been dour most of his days and who, in middle age, so dark did his world become, required a regimen of anti-depressant drugs to continue, in the cold word of the clinicians, "functioning." From Pagliacci on, the notion of the clown laughing on the outside and crying within is old enough to constitute a cliché. So well-established is this notion that the modern clown Emmett Kelly actually worked in makeup that can only be described as sad-face. Although many a comedian has no doubt been undeceptively shallow, it is now nearly axiomatic that an intelligent man who makes his living from comedy will tend to view the world through sepia-colored glasses.

The question is, does the practice of comedy, with its concentration on the ridiculousness of humankind, turn the comedian dour? Or is it his natural dourness that turns him, in search of relief, to the practice of comedy? That may not exhaust all cases, as the philosophers say, but it can sure exhaust your damn patience, as Perelman might have retorted.

To a natural penchant for gloom Sidney Joseph Perelman added a relentless suspicion and a propensity for pessimism. This dolorous combination of qualities, natural and acquired, provided Perelman with a temperament that fitted him for becoming either a paranoid, a suicide, or a humorist. He took up the last as his life's work, and this, for a Jewish lad from Providence, Rhode Island, proved no easy dough to stow, at least to hear Perelman tell it, which he did over and over. Complaint and grievance and grudge were also part of the Perelman personality. So, apparently, were penny-pinching, skirt-chasing, and self-serving well beyond the call of duty. A funny guy, Perelman.

Both of S. J. Perelman's parents were East European Jewish immigrants. Although his father's family arrived in this country with more money than most, they soon lost it in bad real-estate deals in Colchester, Connecticut. "Most of the family's money evaporated," Perelman later wrote in a comic sketch, "in visionary schemes like a Yiddish musical-comedy production of *The Heart of Midlothian.*" Loss of family money forced Joseph Perelman, who was to be S. J. Perelman's father, to abandon a dream of one day becoming an engineer, and seems to have left him a permanently disappointed man. He married, found work as a machinist, lived in a Brooklyn tenement. In 1904, the year his son and only child was born, he moved his family to Providence, where opportunities for uneducated immigrants were said to be abundant.

Providence failed to provide, and there Joseph Perelman slowly failed in a dry-goods business and, later and more surely, as a poultry farmer. Like many a business failure, he turned to utopian socialism and strident attacks on capitalism (the world of *some* of our fathers). S. J. Perelman was raised without religious training. He knew enough Yiddish to fool the gentiles— if not really enough to speak to the Jews—and later used Yiddish phrases to salt his comic pieces. He was apparently a dreamy kid who whenever possible resorted to books, silent films, and any other form of fantastical hideout he could secure against the squalor and sadness of life at home.

The mature Perelman rarely spoke of his parents, according to Dorothy Herrmann, his biographer, and late in Miss Herrmann's biography one learns that Perelman installed his mother in a modest house in Los Angeles, where she complained, until her death at eighty-one, that he wrote checks but never visited. Allen Saalburg, a painter whom Miss Herrmann interviewed, told her: "I had the feeling that he wasn't quite pleased with his parents. Either he didn't like them or perhaps they weren't his style."

One also learns from Miss Herrmann that from his earliest years Perelman, who, one gathers from his mock-heroic self-descriptions, was not fond of his own looks, had "a divergent squint" in his left eye. Whether he lost it in later life, Miss Herrmann does not say. Symbolically, at any rate, he kept it; "a divergent squint" may in fact be the best way for a professional humorist to look upon the world. Certainly Perelman's experience at Brown University, where he enrolled as a freshman in 1921, did nothing to cause him to view the world more wide-eyedly.

Brown was a playboy school in those days, not yet the grimly permissive joint it is today. Fraternities were crucial to social success, and fraternities at Brown did not accept Jews. That Perelman was a commuting student, returning from class each evening to his parents' dying chicken farm outside Providence, merely compounded his isolation, for commuting students were felt to be rather *déclassé*. Poor and Jewish and a commuting student at a snobbish university, homely and dreamy and the son of a disappointed man, Perelman, it seems fair to say, had been dealt less than a perfect hand in life.

Among the friendships Perelman made at Brown, the most fateful was with a student from New York City named Nathan Weinstein, who was called by his friends "Pep," chiefly because he hadn't any. Nathan Weinstein later of course became Nathanael West, and Perelman, at twenty-five would marry his eighteen-year-old sister Laura West (née Lorraine Weinstein). West, whose family was well-to-do, introduced him to Brooks Brothers clothes; also to the writings of James Joyce, Ezra Pound, and other of the then still very much alive modernist writers. Perelman was himself something on the order of a corned-beef aesthete in those days, drawing cartoons with Beardsleyan touches and, when he became editor of a campus publication called the *Brown Jug,* writing fierce editorials in the vituperative style of H. L. Mencken.

At Brown it became clear that Sid Perelman, who now signed his cartoons and pieces S. J. Perelman, would find a career in journalism. He began as a cartoonist, publishing his early drawings in the old humor magazine *Judge,* of which Harold Ross, the founding editor of the *New Yorker,* was then a co-editor. He wrote for *College Humor,* and contributed to the *New Yorker* not long after it began publishing in 1925. Living in New York, he was a habitué of Jewish delicatessens, wore expensive duds, and sported a walking stick. He was in a small way part of the 1920s world of theater, show business, and smart journalism—a world that died in the Depression and never really revived. Unlike many another writer who came into maturity in the 1920s, Perelman was not a drinking man; apparently he could generate sufficient melancholy of his own without the aid of booze.

Writing comedy was then, as now, a hard dollar, but then, as opposed to now, there were more opportunities. There were the humor magazines, there were the radio comedy shows, there was the stage, there was Hollywood. Before he was through Perelman had worked them all. He wrote for the Fanny Brice–Royal Gelatine radio show; he wrote gags for, among others, Jimmy Durante and the harmonica player Larry Adler; he made many a foray onto the Broadway stage, once scoring heavily with a perfectly forgettable (and now justly forgotten) play he wrote in collaboration with Ogden Nash entitled *One Touch of Venus;* and he took several plunges into the schmaltz pools of Hollywood, about which he never ceased complaining (bitching all the way to the bank) and among which he is today best remembered for his work on the Marx Brothers' movies *Horse Feathers* and *Monkey Business* and on Mike Todd's *Around the World in Eighty Days.*

American cultural brows—high, middle, and low—were not yet quite so firmly set as they have since become; nowadays one could probably not expend one's talents on such a variety of (shall we call them) clients and still hope to be taken seriously as a writer. But for S. J. Perelman this proved no problem. Self-loathing at turning out such goods also proved no problem for Perelman. Instead of loathing himself Perelman loathed the people who paid him for the shoddy work they wanted. This is what is called cutting out the middleman, in some circles also known as artistic conscience. Nothing ever was permitted to get in the way of S. J. Perelman's high opinion of himself.

For the most part, it is fair to say, the world has shared Perelman's high opinion of himself. Robert Benchley once claimed that Perelman "does to our weak little efforts at 'crazy stuff' what Benny Goodman has done to middle-period jazz."

Dorothy Parker wrote: "Mr. Perelman stands alone in this day of humorists." (The day was 1957.) Perelman was chosen as an early subject for a *Paris Review* interview. The English critic V. S. Pritchett devoted an essay to him, giving him the best English minor-classic treatment. "Perelman commanded a vocabulary that is the despair (and joy) of every writing man," said E. B. White; "Sid is like a Roxy organ that has three pedals, fifty stops, and a pride of pedals under the bench. When he wants a word, it's there." Eudora Welty praised him regularly in prominent places, once in the *New York Times Book Review,* where she called him "a living national treasure." And Kurt Vonnegut, Jr., has now weighed in with: "Perelman handled the American language the way a virtuoso piccolo player plays 'The Stars and Stripes Forever.' " Were S. J. Perelman alive to read this paragraph, compact with kudos, he might, Perelman-esquely, reply: "Blurb me, daddy, eight to the bar."

And yet, in the subtle way in which the history of reputation works, one begins to sense an encroaching diminution of S. J. Perelman's high literary repute. This diminution owes less to what might be termed Perelman's retrospective ideological impurities—all homosexuals were for him screamers, on the interior-decorator model, and in his writing all women are either troublesome wives, wretched harridans, or luscious bimbos—than to revelations about his private life. One is of course entitled to be as unhappy as one wishes—it's a free country—but Perelman appears to have contributed to the unhappiness of others, and specifically to that of his own wife and children, and that is rather a different thing.

S. J. Perelman was not an altogether unpleasant man; he appears to have been unpleasant chiefly to those who needed him or relied upon him. He would switch publishers without provocation; he would drop an agent who considered him a friend, then use him in his writing under a name like Toby Swindler. When it came to money, he apparently believed, there are no friends, or rules, or ethics. Of course, in Hollywood and on Broadway he was often dealing with genuine financial thugs, and so one can forgive, or at least understand, his coldness.

But Perelman's dealings with his own family, if they are fairly reported in Miss Herrmann's biography, are less forgivable. For the Perelman marriage, the author leans rather heavily in her interpretation on a story by Josephine Herbst entitled "Hunter of Doves" *(Botteghe Oscure,* Spring 1954). A triangle of characters in the story is based on Nathanael West, Laura West, and S. J. Perelman. In the story Nathanael and Laura West are said to be devoted to each other with an intensity that is meant to suggest incestuous feeling. Miss Herbst writes: "For Bartram [the Nathanael West character] had been the beloved; would be so long as Nora [Laura West] had life. Baker [Perelman, who is Nora's husband] had been only his surrogate." Is this true? One has to remember that Josephine Herbst during these years was herself leading a quasi-secret lesbian love life, and may perhaps have been drawn to such sexy, under-the-table interpretations.

In her story, Miss Herbst writes: "Oh Baker was a devil with women. He did not have the appearance of a Romeo but he was successful with women. He was conspicuously untrue to his wife." About Perelman's philandering there is no serious dispute. Miss Herrmann reports that Perelman cheated on his wife the second day of their marriage. But then she had love affairs of her own, notably one with Dashiell Hammett. They had something resembling what we should now call an open marriage, which, as is usually the case, chiefly resulted in opening wounds.

Laura Perelman was a formidable woman. In Hollywood she often collaborated with her husband on movie projects, and as a paid screenwriter. She worked with him, too, on plays. The Perelmans' son, Adam, has said that he thinks his mother a better writer than his father. Doubtful though this seems, what is not doubtful is that Laura Perelman's was a hard life.

"She had that spiritually rattled look of a once beautiful, large woman who had gone through very difficult times," said Robert Gottlieb, who was one of Perelman's editors at Simon and Schuster. She became an alcoholic and was a member of Alcoholics Anonymous. Her brother's death in a car accident was devastating to her. She had more than the normal share of grief from her children. In her fifties she was discovered to have cancer of the breast. As her marriage worsened, her husband, after some forty years together, asked for a divorce, to which she reluctantly agreed. But before the divorce proceedings could be got under way, her breast cancer metastasized, causing blockage of blood to her heart, and she died in 1970, at the age of fifty-eight.

Other people have had equally sad, and even sadder, lives, but nobody else has had also to offer herself up for gags as Laura Perelman did in her husband's writing. In *The Swiss Family Perelman,* a book about a family trip around the world, one finds the following comic description of how Perelman came to be talked into such a trip in the first place:

> It was a story of betrayal, of a woman's perfidy beside which the recidivism of Guy Fawkes, Major Andre, and the infamous Murrel paled to child's play. That the woman should have been my own wife was harrowing enough. More bitter than aloes, however, was the knowledge that as I lay supine in my deck-chair, gasping out my life, the traitress herself sat complacently fifty feet below in the dining salon, bolting the table d'hôte luncheon and lampooning me to my own children. Her brazen effrontery, her heartless rejection of one who for twenty years had worshipped her this side of idolatry and consecrated himself to indulging her merest caprice, sent a shudder through my frame. Coarse peasant whom I had rescued from a Ukrainian wheatfield, equipped with shoes, and ennobled with my name, she had rewarded me with the Judas kiss. . . .

In reviewing how his wife had talked him into this trip, Perelman has her tease him about his philandering, as when he brings up the danger of snakes and scorpions in Southeast Asia, and she retorts: "You'll cope with them. You did all right with that viper on Martha's Vineyard last summer. The one in the electric-blue swim-suit and the pancake makeup." Two pages later, he warns her that there are no martinis to be had on such a trip. "For an instant, as she strove with the animal in her, my fate hung in the balance." It is a bad sign for a humorist when the reader winces after a joke.

Perelman's son and daughter were also used for comic copy. (He would refer to them as "the dwarfs.") The sad truth behind the jokes was that growing up with Sid and Laura Perelman could not have been easy: the fighting, the sulking, the boozing, the moving out to the Coast and back, all took their toll, especially on the Perelmans' son, who had eventually to be sent to reform school after a number of burglaries, muggings, and an attempted rape. After his son's second criminal offense, Miss Herrmann reports, Perelman began seeing a psychoanalyst. In a piece attacking contemporary advertising entitled "Tomorrow—Fairly Cloudy," he has a character say: "Yes, and thanks to Buckleboard the new triple-ply, satin-smooth dirt-resisting wall plastic we now have an ugly little playroom where we can sit and loathe each other in the evening." There, given a bit of biographical knowledge, goes that reader's wince again.

Biographical knowledge is often the apple in the literary Garden of Eden. Once one tastes it, one tends to cease trusting either teller or tale. In this respect S. J. Perelman has not been altogether fortunate in his biographer. Dorothy Herrmann is not an especially careful writer, yet she comes to her task without any apparent *parti pris;* she is not, for example, a strong feminist, nor does she ride any other of the dismal "isms" of our day. As she sets out the details of S. J. Perelman's life, however, they are overwhelmingly condemnatory—so much so that to reread Perelman today with any degree of pleasure one must frequently do what one can to block out what one knows about his life.

If Baudelaire was an unpleasant man, Emily Dickinson a bit mad, D. H. Lawrence hugely muddled in his politics, these flaws in their characters, the essential disequilibrium in their personalities, do not destroy their art but become, in a mysterious way, part of it. But from a humorist, alongside whom we are asked to laugh, a certain sanity, a certain decency, a certain balance is required. Even though the received wisdom in these matters instructs one to ignore the life and concentrate on the work, knowledge that such a man was fundamentally not nice does not lubricate one's laughter; quite the reverse, it can cause one to gag on the gags.

Paul Theroux, Chaim Raphael, I. J. Kapstein, Al Hirschfeld, and others who counted Perelman among their friends might disagree strongly with this judgment. Prudence Crowther, who knew Perelman after his wife died and who edited a collection of his letters entitled *Don't Tread on Me,* portrays Perelman in her introduction as a thoughtful and gentle man, full of polished anecdotes and rather comic crotchets, with a sweet tooth and an eye for the ladies. And the letters Miss Crowther has collected and selected for her volume do tend to make Perelman seem rather more charming than otherwise. Included are a number of inventive rambles, various bits done from within the personae of his standard comic pieces, some funny gossip about Dorothy Parker and Lillian Hellman, a few rather touching fatherly letters to his daughter (though none to his son), expressions of grief after the death of his wife, and sadness at his own eventual falling out of literary favor toward the end of his life.

It is almost as if there were two S. J. Perelmans to consider: the Perelman of Dorothy Herrmann's biography and the Perelman of Prudence Crowther's letters. As it happens, there is yet a third S. J. Perelman, the Perelman of the scores of comic pieces, the *feuilletoniste,* the high-*shticker,* the author of, as Jimmy Durante once put it, the "non-friction." This is the S. J. Perelman of whom Eudora Welty, in a review of a collection of

Perelman's entitled *Baby, It's Cold Inside,* noted: "Back of some of these pieces, and not very far, lies deep sadness, lies outrage."

There is outrage aplenty behind a good deal that S. J. Perelman wrote, but it is not always clear what he is so outraged about—or if his outrage and its putative target are even roughly commensurate. Ever since Buffon wrote on the subject in 1753, the style has been reputed to be the message, yet in Perelman it sometimes seems as if style has to make do in the absence of any message whatsoever. As for Perelman's style, when he was working well, it was no thing for a booby and a joy for the clever. "I can't write down to any special audience," he wrote to a friend. "Like any writer with self-respect, I've spent a good many years perfecting my tools and evolving a point of view and a manner that is characteristic." To read Perelman one has to have read a good deal else besides, for Perelman's style usually involves parody and pastiche, an attack on cliché, a raid on empty phrases, an exploding of unreality, leaving one who brings no bookish knowledge to his work in the literary equivalent of darkest nonsequiturial Africa.

At the heart of Perelman's style is his exotic vocabulary, which, in any given sentence, may play the slang off the arcane word, the Yiddishism off the Victorianism, the high-culture phrase off the low. A simple but characteristic S. J. Perelman sentence reads: "I fell back into my Barcalounger, utterly flummoxed." His frame of reference was wide, and a single page may include mention of Scipio Africanus, George Cable, and *Partisan Review.* He could strike off the comic simile with a double bite, as when, in one of his sketches, he describes himself as being as "glacial and reserved as Sumner Welles at a B'nai Brith picnic." Naturally enough, he had mastery over the standard comic moves, such as the poker-faced reversal: "They all laughed at Jean-Jacques Rousseau when he said man was perfectible, yet today we have people like Jody Powell."

There is also a Perelmanesque prose rhythm, a marching

cadence of false confidence, that is better conveyed in para-
graph-length quotation than in analysis:

> An old subscriber of the *New Republic* am I, prudent, medita-
> tive, rigidly impartial. I am the man who reads those six-part
> exposés of the Southern utilities empire, savoring each dark
> peculation. Weekly I stroll the *couloirs* of the House and Senate
> with T.R.B., aghast at legislative folly. Every now and again I
> take issue in the correspondence pages with Kenneth Burke or
> Malcolm Cowley over a knotty point of aesthetics; my barbed
> and graceful letters counsel them to reread their Benedetto Croce.
> Tanned by two delightful weeks at lovely Camp Narischkeit, I
> learn twenty-nine languages by Linguaphone, sublet charming
> three-room apartments with gardens from May to October, send
> my children to the Ethical Culture School. Of an evening you
> can find me in a secluded corner of the White Turkey House,
> chuckling at Stark Young's review of the *Medea*. I smoke a pipe
> more frequently than not, sucking the match flame into the bowl
> with thoughtful little puffs.

Out of such comic materials, Perelman created his comic
persona, or, more precisely, personae: the *faux-naïf* of the above
paragraph; and the Mittyesque fantast, who dramatizes everything and fools no one and whose characteristic tone is caught
in the following passage:

> Suddenly, without warning, the loungers by the pool were gal-
> vanized into attention. A man of imposing mien, who wore his
> white terry robe with the dignity of a toga and whose profile
> might have graced some early Roman post office, had approached
> the diving board. As he slipped from his robe, there stood revealed
> a body as flawless as a banana: the shoulders small and exquis-
> itely formed, a chest that would have shamed Tom Thumb's, a
> magnificent melon-shaped paunch that quivered like junket at
> its owner's slightest command. With the ease of a born gymnast,
> he dropped on all fours, crept out warily to the very end of the

diving board, crept back, and, sides heaving painfully, collapsed
on a beach mattress.

The cowardly hero, the elegant runt, the devil-may-care *schlep-
per*—these types would later be made to pay handsome profits
by Woody Allen, but S. J. Perelman was their progenitor.

Yet what did all of Perelman's comic gifts and skills come
to? I have recently read more than a thousand pages of Perelman—which may, I suppose, be likened to a man walking into
a room to announce that he has just eaten fifty pounds of choc-
olate—and I am not sure that I can say that they come to much.
Perelman's own ambitions were self-advertised as modest. When
friends encouraged him to write a full-blown comic novel, he
demurred, saying: "To me the muralist is no more valid than
the miniaturist. . . . I am content to stitch away at my embroidery hoop." In the concluding section of *The Most of S. J. Perelman,* he wrote: "If I were to apply for a library card in Paris,
I would subscribe myself as a *feuilletoniste,* that is to say, a writer
of little leaves. I may be in error, but the word seems to me to
carry a hint of endearment rather than patronage." These are
modest enough ambitions, but does Perelman truly live down
to them?

All too often, sad to report, he does. The received opinion
on S. J. Perelman is that he was a scream and then, suddenly,
late in his career, he lost his touch, and his humor became
forced and hopeless. Miss Herrmann, who leans toward this
view, sets the date for Perelman's decline in the early 1960s,
around the time that he himself was about to turn sixty. "His
comic persona," she writes, "was no longer the wistful, bespec-
tacled boy from Providence but an angry, cantankerous man,
condemning almost everyone and everything. He began to lose
the comic writer's most precious gift—a sense of humor." But
problems had set in earlier. In a letter of 1955 to a friend he
notes: ". . . I've been dithering about with a succession of snerd-
like little ideas, trying to convert them into pieces for the *New*

Yorker and achieving nothing more than daily frustration."

How much in Perelman's writing is snerd-like is depressing to consider. I do not refer to his writing for Hollywood, which he was wont to describe as "purest cat vomit," but to his *New Yorker* pieces and the pieces that went into his books. A great deal that Perelman wrote is an attempt to be funny not so much about wretched, as about merely silly excesses: the foolishness that regularly appeared in *Harper's Bazaar* and *Vogue,* idiotic advertising copy, show-biz vulgarity, dentistry, the melodramatic novels and movies he had read and seen in his adolescence. It is cruelly easy to summarize a piece of failed humor, but of the many that Perelman wrote perhaps the dreariest, reprinted in *The Most of S. J. Perelman,* is one that takes off from the copy on the back of a packet of frozen veal steaks, in which a veal steak addresses the purchaser. Taking a poor idea all the way out, Perelman has other foods in his refrigerator talk to him. Reading it you could die, but not from laughing.

Perelman's best work was that in which his anger was genuinely engaged. A good example is *Acres and Pains*, a collection of pieces about a city man (himself) lost in his fantasies of country living who is picked clean by rural merchants, artisans, and other local hustlers. He can be fine, too, at parody, as in his famous sendup of Hammett-like tough-guy detectives, "Farewell, My Lovely Appetizer," or of a John P. Marquand-like character recounting Waspy life on a summer estate in Newport called Chowderhead. He can be extremely funny on Los Angeles, which he loathed and once described as the "City of the Living Dead" and "the mighty citadel which had given the world the double feature, the duplex-burger, the motel, the hamfurter, and the shirt worn outside the pants."

One requires a word three-up in intensity from loathing to describe Perelman's feelings about Hollywood. There is, for instance, a passage in *Westward Ha!,* a comic account of his travels with the cartoonist Al Hirschfeld, and, as they used to say in radio days, "t'ain't funny, McGee":

A wave of nostalgia engulfed me as I remembered the decade I had spent writing motion pictures; a suspicious moisture glittered in my orb. What a splendid, devil-may-care band we had been in the 30's, brave lads and lasses all—ever ready to cut a competitor's throat or lick a producer's boot, ever eager to conform our opinions to those in authority, ever alert to sell out wife, child, and principle to attain the higher bracket, the fleecier polo coat, the more amorous concubine. Wave a paycheck at us and we could turn in our own wheelbase, strip ourselves inside out like a glove; the most agile, biddable, unblushing set of mercenaries since the Hessians.

Note the use of the first person plural, which strictly speaking precludes self-exculpation. Although Groucho Marx later complained that Perelman tended to take credit for the Marx Brothers movies, Perelman in fact took no pride in anything connected with his ventures in Hollywood, including the Oscar for best screenwriting adaptation that he later shared with the two other writers who worked on *Around the World in Eighty Days* for Mike Todd, whom he thought a standard Seventh Avenue huckster, not to mention a "psychopathic little bastard" and a "sinister dwarf." Perelman and Hollywood may have been an instance of a man eating his caviar and spitting in it, too.

Perelman did not make a vast sum writing for the movies though, in the Depression, he and Laura as a team were pulling in a thousand dollars a week. In later years he told Paul Theroux that he was among those writers who went out to Hollywood because, in the Depression years, they couldn't make a living elsewhere. That is no doubt partly true. Another part of the truth is that the Perelmans ran a complicated establishment, and always managed to live expensively but not well, with a place in Bucks County, an apartment in Manhattan, a separate office for him to work in, private-school fees, dogs, bills for psychotherapy—in sum, as we non-New Yorkers like to think of it, the full Manhattan catastrophe.

Perelman's view of himself as an artist was oddly riven. On the one hand, he had no complex feeling about being a sellout; he was unabashed in his yearning for a socko commercial hit. On the other hand, he was also perfectly unprepared to simplify his style to appeal to larger audiences. He was getting between $3,000 and $3,500 for his brief comic pieces in the *New Yorker*, yet, as he noted in a letter of 1957, he greatly resented the attempts of that magazine's editors to make "fussy little changes and pipsqueak variations on my copy." He complained regularly about how difficult writing was for him; according to his friend Heywood Hale Broun, after he had made a solid score with a television script entitled "Malice in Wonderland," he knocked off for a full six months. At one point he would insist on all the prerogatives, temperamental and otherwise, of the literary artist, claiming himself a writer, no mere humorist; at another point, he would avow only that "I try to write as well as I can on light subjects." On the wall of his office he kept a photograph of James Joyce, a writer he revered, yet he often conducted his own career as if he were Solly Violinski, Harry Ruby, Morrie Ryskind, or some other Broadway gagman.

If the humorist and the writer warred within Perelman, the humorist usually won. When the humorist won, not only the writer but the writing lost. A writer doesn't need subjects; a humorist scours newspapers, women's magazines, trade journals, for them. Perelman even claimed that in his search for subjects he had to travel so that he could find places "filled with things I can be hostile about." Dorothy Parker, who may have failed the test herself, once said: "There's a helluva distance between wisecracking and wit. Wit has truth in it. Wisecracking is simply calisthenics . . . with words." When the humorist in Perelman had the upper hand, wisecracks prevailed, and so did puns and funny names. A piece with too many funny names—Suppositorsky, Sir Hamish Sphincter, Marcel Riboflavin—is often a clue that Perelman is straining.

Part of Perelman's problem lay in being a full-time professional humorist. It is one thing to be humorous by the way, or on the side; it is quite another when *all* one is is humorous. "Humorous writing—humor meant to be read—is shrinking and passing out of existence," Perelman told an interviewer in 1962. And he was correct insofar as he was talking about the kind of humorous writing whose subject is little more than a pretext for joking. (Even the work in this vein of that appealing man Robert Benchley is now nearly unreadable.) Few things so improve one's chances of achieving wit as having a real subject to write about. One's chances are narrowed considerably, however, if one is writing about—to take three Perelman subjects that come to mind—trying to replace the favorite hat one lost at a party, establishing that all dry cleaners are crooks, or showing what dopes interior decorators are.

In a 1966 review of a new collection of Perelman pieces, Victor Navasky criticized him for writing about trivial things during a time of great political upheaval. Perelman resented the criticism, which reminded him of people who wanted him to line up on the side of the proletariat in the 1930s. "It isn't enough to make people laugh," he complained, "there must be messages." In the 1930s in a piece entitled "Waiting for Santy," he mocked the crude leftism of Clifford Odets (yet he himself also published in the *New Masses*). Politics, however, was not really his subject. He had fairly standard liberal politics, one suspects, but his general irritation with life went well beyond—or at least was outside—politics. He tended to find Richard Nixon and Jimmy Carter irritating in roughly the same way he would have found Des Moines or Fort Worth irritating. He could call Nixon "an everlasting *nudnick*," but also mock "the noble piety of the Hollywood folk," with their vast houses and large cars, immersing "themselves in the plight of the migratory workers and the like."

The larger subject awaiting S. J. Perelman was the culture at large during the years when it was becoming unhinged. Certainly he had the disdain required of the satirist, which comes through in neon in his letters. Hugh Hefner, he said, "nauseates me"; he referred to Johnny Carson as "that plastic character on the Coast"; and Barbara Walters was "the most insincere, brassy nitwit in the business." He also had a low opinion of John Updike and Donald Barthelme, who represented the new wave at the *New Yorker.* Taken to a stage production of Andy Warhol's *Pork,* he found it "unquestionably the most excremental, degraded, and degrading spectacle that has ever been vomited forth onto a public stage in modern times" and "the greatest corrective to sexual desire since the invention of saltpeter." As for the public falling-out between Lillian Hellman and Diana Trilling, he thought they ought to book themselves for a wrestling match at Chautauquas and county fairs, with the winner to be matched against Bella Abzug. Feeling out of it, he wrote to Frank Sullivan, his old friend on the *New Yorker,* to ask what Ring Lardner and Harold Ross would have thought of a professional foul-mouth like Germaine Greer.

None of this, unfortunately, got into his work, where, in transmogrified form, it really belonged. Perhaps he was too long used to playing for small laughs. "I don't believe in kindly humor," he once said, and apparently he didn't believe in courageous humor either. Instead he continued to work the old vein, "button-cute, rapier-keen . . . S. J. Perelman," as he once jokingly described himself in a parody of *Time*-style. But it no longer quite worked for him. Suddenly his pieces began to be rejected; the *New Yorker* began to hold back his work in that famous journalistic black hole known as its "inventory"; reviewers ceased to be kind; no one was any longer calling him a national treasure or treating him as a national monument, except, perhaps, in the way a pigeon treats a monument.

Doing a reversal on a boy named Finn, Huckleberry Perelman decided to light out for civilization, and in autumn of 1970 announced that he was departing the United States for permanent residence in England, where his reputation was strong and where among his appreciators he had counted no less than T. S. Eliot. He told a reporter for the *New York Times* that he thought it was "volcano time" in the United States, that he found New York "pestilential," and that in England there was a greater appreciation of eccentricity, not to speak of good manners and consideration. Besides, he said, quoting Swift, life is "nasty, brutish, and short."

But Swift didn't say that, Hobbes did. Perhaps it is a bad omen to leave a country on a misattributed quotation, for Perelman lasted about two years in England, where, after an initial full-court press put on him by the English as a minor celebrity, he soon fell into loneliness and homesickness, longing for a pastrami sandwich and the turn of idiom that had given him his living. As he told Israel Shenker of the *New York Times,* "My style is mélange—a mixture of all the sludge I read as a child, all the clichés, liberal doses of Yiddish, criminal slang, and some of what I was taught in a Providence, Rhode Island, school by impatient teachers. When I tried to think of an idiomatic expression in London, I had to reach for it. I felt out of touch with the idiom." He also told Shenker: "When I'm away [from New York], I miss the tension, the give and take. I feel it's a great mistake for any writer to cut himself off from his roots. One's work suffers by trying to transplant it to another milieu."

But in Perelman's case the roots had already pretty much dried up. His was a talent that showed no growth; and now he would continue to do the same old thing, only rather less well. He moved into the Gramercy Park Hotel. Needles-in-the-pants man that he was—the renowned world traveler Sir Sidney Shpilkes, as in imitation of his own style one might think of him—he continued his travels, but they didn't give him much pleasure. (He visited Israel and the Soviet Union for the first time and hated both.) He continued to write, but his writing no longer gave other people much pleasure. His

final book, published posthumously and entitled *The Last Laugh,*
included portraits of the Marx Brothers, Nathanael West, and
Dorothy Parker. Yet these pieces turn out to be chiefly anec-
dotal, played for color, and without much in the way of penetration into character. Whatever strong and complicated feelings
he had toward life and experience he could not finally reveal in
his writing, and these feelings died with him when he died at
seventy-five, alone in his hotel room, of a massive heart attack
brought on by arteriosclerosis.

In the front-page obituary of Perelman in the *New York Times,*
William Shawn, then editor of the *New Yorker,* was quoted as
saying that people were "so enormously entertained by him
that they sometimes overlooked his great originality and his
literary brilliance." Maybe so. Maybe, too, one can make a case
for Perelman's having been a fine critic of the unreality of
American life. Maybe one can, in the academic fashion of the
moment, sell him as an early and potent critic of the hopeless
instability and uncertainty of all language.

But more to the point is the remark made by the narrator of
V. S. Naipaul's autobiographical novel, *The Enigma of Arrival,*
who of himself as a young man writes: "I took refuge in
humor—comedy, funniness, the satiric reflex—which in writing, as in life, is often a covering up for confusion." Perelman
never surmounted the confusion in his life, at least not in his
writings. His comic response to life gave many people pleasure, which is no small blessing. Still, one cannot help thinking
that had things worked out differently, he might have been an
American Evelyn Waugh. Instead, wanting in ambition or soul
or the energy necessary for art, he had to settle for being a
humorist.

Commentary 1987

A Cottage
for Mr. Naipaul

WHEN I ARRIVED at the office of the Chicago-based encyclopedia where I was an editor on the morning after Martin Luther King, Jr., had been assassinated, I found, as on many another morning, my fellow editor Chandran Gajapathy already on the scene. Chan was often there early, to check his *Wall Street Journal* and his *Barron's,* so that he could get in his calls to his broker before the market opened in New York. Besides being a stock-market player of some intensity, Chan, a high-caste Indian, was also a chemist. Large and well-fed, with a round face whose features registered greater earnestness than penetration, he generally wore three-piece suits of rather expensive cut and was a determined if not very successful pursuer of women. Our relationship, Chan's and mine, was cordial with no serious prospect of becoming more than that. But on this morning in 1968, with the streets of Chicago still in flames after the riots following the murder of the civil-rights leader, he strode into my office. "Epstein," he said, an unfurled copy of the *Wall Street Journal* in his right hand, "after the death of Dr. King, I am so angry I could eat a white person." And out he strode, the financial newspaper flapping at his side.

None of this, I must tell you, did I find very convincing—not the anger, not the phrasing with its unfortunate suggestion of cannibalism and daintily correct use of "person," none of it. The *Wall Street Journal* detracted a good bit from the performance. (One had the feeling that assassination or no, had he seen a good thing in the morning's paper, Chan would have called it in to his broker.) So, too, did the fact that until this moment, I hadn't thought of Chandran Gajapathy—with his fine suits, his academic pretensions (he was a Ph.D. from the University of Chicago), his strong pursuit tactics with the white female subeditors and secretaries in the office—as at all concerned about, let alone sympathetic to, or indeed wholly identifying himself with, the American black civil-rights movement. Was Chan, so to speak, onto yet another good thing? Was he going to change himself into a black man, in other words, now that there were certain advantages to be gained by doing so? Or was he instead a lost soul, educated yet colored, quite rich yet emotionally broke, caught, like so many Indians away from home, in the cross fire of different cultures? I do not know. But what I do know now that I didn't know then, because in 1968 I hadn't yet read V. S. Naipaul, is that my colleague Chandran Gajapathy could have slipped out of the pages of a Naipaul novel.

V. S. Naipaul has made himself into a writer serious people cannot ignore. He has been able to fathom the crucial issues, questions, and problems of contemporary life well before they surface for even the most perceptive of us. Among living writers he has acquired, deservedly, the greatest reputation for facing unpleasant facts, for truth-telling, for grasping what is really happening in the world, and through his art demonstrating the personal consequences of public events. Everything Naipaul writes has the quality that used to be known as gravity, which derives in part from the subjects he writes about, his themes, and his inexorable manner of pursuing them. In part, too, it derives from his almost sovereign authority. *Sui generis,* he is a writer above nationality, above received opinions, above (apparently) normal attachments and loyalties. He is "a being organized for literature," as Henry James once described himself, but a being that not even Henry James, in all the richness of his imagination, could have anticipated.

Naipaul is a rare instance of a writer of world standing who comes from an island country in which, as he himself once put it, "the writer or the painter, unless he wins recognition overseas, preferably in England, is mercilessly ridiculed." Born in 1932, Indian by ancestry, British by education, and Trinidadian by origin, Naipaul is of a family that, though Brahmin by caste, arrived in the British West Indies toward the close of the last century as indentured laborers. Exotic though that vita sounds—and, in fact, is—the chief point is that V. S. Naipaul is a writer quite without precedent in the extent to which he has had, literally and literarily, to make himself. How a young man who left his home on an island at the mouth of the Orinoco at eighteen has been able to make such a strong impress on the world, so that one can speak confidently of people in real life as being "Naipaul characters," is itself an extraordinary story.

It is this story, precisely, that Naipaul has now begun to tell. Without the solid achievement that he has behind him—ten novels, eight books of history, criticism, political reportage—the story wouldn't quite exist; certainly, it would be nowhere near so compelling. V. S. Naipaul, whom people used fairly regularly to confuse with V. S. Pritchett, the English critic, and R. K. Narayan, the Indian novelist, V. S. Naipaul has become a writer of international stature, in a class with Milan Kundera and Alexander Solzhenitsyn. Even his face, visage, no, better, countenance, such is its formality and formidability, with its slightly disdaining mouth, has taken on a world-historical look. Gazing into photographs of that countenance, now in its middle fifties, pouched by discipline, shadowed by victories won doubtless at considerable psychic cost, one cannot find the face of the small, eighteen-year-old boy who, thirty-seven years ago, Indian relatives standing all about, boarded a plane at the crude airport at Port of Spain to fly to Puerto Rico, thence to New York, thence to London and eventually to Oxford to begin a career as a writer, about which, it is fair to say, he had only the dimmest notions.

In a contribution to a 1958 *Times Literary Supplement* symposium, Naipaul set out what seemed to him the apparently insurmountable problem of his career. This was that after producing in five years three books that earned him a total of three hundred pounds, he was a writer who wrote for an English audience about a country, Trinidad, which most people thought exotic at best. He was locked in as a regional author, his subject a region in which few people were interested. He could hype up his books with sex, or he could put race at the center of them, yet neither solution seemed to him very promising. (Of the former, he remarked that he would be embarrassed to make his novels sexier, for "my friends would laugh" and "my mother would be shocked, and with reason"; of the latter, he felt race much too complex to jam crudely into fiction, and he noted that it was unfortunate "that the *Manchester Guardian* should have carried a warm article by a Sinhalese about race discrimination in America at a time when his countrymen were killing Tamils in Ceylon.") He felt that he did not know English life well enough to write about it either. And he ended by stating that his continuing to live in England might "eventually lead to my own sterility; and I may have to look for another job."

Three years later V. S. Naipaul published a novel, *A House for Mr. Biswas* (1961), that is an authentic masterpiece, a great novel—as great a novel, in my view, as any written by a living novelist. *A House for Mr. Biswas* is long—590 pages in the Penguin edition—and splendidly intricate, with a vast cast of characters, an epilogue, and a sense for the roundedness of human personality that leaves the book's readers with the thoroughly satisfied feeling that nineteenth-century novels still produce. Although it is a long way from high-bourgeois Baltic Germany to chaotic Indian Trinidad, *A House for Mr. Biswas* is also Naipaul's *Buddenbrooks*. Like Thomas Mann's novel, it is an account in fictional form of the author's family history, of the kind that, apart from its intrinsic interest, provides crucial clues to his own spiritual inheritance.

Mohun Biswas, the novel's protagonist, is modeled on Naipaul's father, Seepersad Naipaul. A journalist, a short-story writer manqué, a late non-bloomer, Naipaul's father, in the account offered in *A House for Mr. Biswas* and in Naipaul's essay "Prologue to an Autobiography," was a man of delicate nervous organization, yet fierce pride, lacerating irony, and high ambition on which he could never quite make good. He had married into a family of wealthy Trinidadian Indian merchants and landowners, a family in which, owing to his irrepressible satirical streak and high opinion of himself, he could never find ease. Early marriage and many children weighed him down. It also forced him to live the better part of his married life among his despised in-laws in the maelstrom of an extended Indian family. The house that Mr. Biswas seeks in the novel represents his struggle to live in an independent way that comports with his imperishable sense of his own dignity.

A House for Mr. Biswas is, technically, a comedy. I say "technically" because, though the novel is filled with amusing things— many of them having to do with Indian domestic life, many with the madcap quality of provincial journalism in an island culture—its humor is finally bittersweet. Beneath its surface charm, *A House for Mr. Biswas* chronicles what life can do to pride, to ambition, to noble dreams; and what it can do is heartbreaking to behold. In an interview in *The Illustrated Weekly of India* (July 5–11, 1987), Naipaul himself remarked that when his novel was recently read on BBC radio, he could only bear to listen to a single episode. "I really can't do it too often. It's bad for me. I'm reduced to tears instantly." And elsewhere, recalling the anxiety of life in Trinidad, Naipaul has written about his novel: "It is that anxiety—the fear of destitution in all its forms, the vision of the abyss—that lies below the comedy of *A House for Mr. Biswas.*"

Running through the second half of the novel is the relationship between Mr. Biswas and his son Anand. Anand is a good student who wins a scholarship first to Queen's Royal College in Port of Spain and later to Oxford. He is pretty clearly V. S. Naipaul. In the novel, Anand has inherited his father's raw nerves, his propensity toward anxiety, and yet, as Naipaul writes, "Though no one recognized his strength, Anand was among the strong. His satirical sense kept him aloof. At first this was only a pose, an imitation of his father. But satire led to contempt, and . . . contempt, quick, deep, inclusive, became part of his nature. It led to inadequacies, to self-awareness and a lasting loneliness. But it made him unassailable."

As the novel draws to its close, the indomitable Mohun Biswas's ambition is transferred to his son, "and his visions of the future became only visions of Anand's future." But Anand will disappoint. When Mr. Biswas writes to him in England, Anand replies with self-absorbed, self-pitying letters. "But writing to Anand was like taking a blind man to see a view," Naipaul writes, and we recall that Naipaul is here essentially writing about himself and his feelings of remorse for not properly responding to his father during the last, sad years of his father's life. In the end, of course, Naipaul responded by writing *A House for Mr. Biswas,* memorializing his father, fittingly and for all time, through literature.

Contrary to that school of modern psychology which holds that owing to the unavailability of the real thing, every man wishes to marry a girl just like the girl that married dear old dad, the great figure in V. S. Naipaul's life was obviously his father. "My early work was very much an offering to him," Naipaul once told an interviewer, adding that from his mother he "got my other side—tenacity, toughness and self-reliance." Above all, Naipaul's is a life that reminds one how decisive the fate of a father can be for the character of a son. "When I get to your age," Anand tells Mr. Biswas, "I don't want to be like you." And Naipaul is not like his father, except that, like many another son of an unfulfilled artist (such hefty names as Beethoven, Yeats, Picasso, come to mind), he went on to fulfill his father's dreams. It was from his father that Naipaul acquired the notion that to write was to triumph over the darkness in the world, that writing implied a refusal to be extinguished, that the writer was a figure of nobility. Such is the subtext, the writing between the lines, in *A House for Mr. Biswas*. "The man who began that book," Naipaul has said, "is quite different from the man who ended it."

The man who ended it, the author of *A House for Mr. Biswas*, had paid off his debt to his region, and, though he would often look back, did not any longer need to think of himself as a regional writer. But, then, what kind of writer would he now be? V. S. Naipaul had left Trinidad hoping to become a writer on what one thinks of as the international metropolitan model. He early set out to invent a literary personality that would write about the world with great sophistication and exclude race and humiliation, both of which he knew a good bit about. His early novels about Trinidad—*The Mystic Masseur* (1957), *The Suffrage of Elvira* (1958), *Miguel Street* (1959)—expunged the childish notion that he might set up shop as a young Somerset Maugham. His quite magical achievement in his novel about his father had in large part put paid to his being a Trinidadian writer. He would have to await his subjects, find his form. Having no clear tradition out of which to write—"with Naipaul," Paul Theroux has written, "his tradition begins with him"—he would have to establish his own.

To say that V. S. Naipaul is a writer without a tradition is no small statement, given that Naipaul is himself highly tradition-minded. "The English language was mine," he has noted, recounting his education at Oxford, "the tradition was not." As a writer of immense literary ambition, he has carefully thought through the questions and problems surrounding his art. "Every serious writer has to be original," he has written; "he cannot be content to do or to offer what has been done before." Until this point in his career, Naipaul's originality has lain in his subject matter. I take this subject matter to be the modern world at the end of empire. To understand the true vastness of this enterprise, in Naipaul's hands, one must recognize that this has increasingly come to include *all* the modern world. Naipaul has written, in his novels and in his nonfiction, about Latin America, the Caribbean, Africa, India, and the world of Islam. He has written about Europeans in these places, and he has written about the inhabitants of these places in Europe. The collision of cultures has become, with him, *une spécialité de la maison*.

Naipaul's own move from Trinidad to England in 1950, as he would himself come to recognize, "was at the beginning of that great movement of peoples that was to take place in the second half of the twentieth century—a movement and a cultural mixing greater than the peopling of the United States, which was essentially a movement of Europeans to the New World." In Naipaul's own trope, the great cities of Europe were as Rome after the fall. "They were to be cities visited for learning and elegant goods and manners and freedom by all the barbarian peoples of the globe, people of forest and desert, Arabs, Africans, Malays." Perhaps that word "barbarian" has arrested your attention. It may well be that among living writers only Naipaul is able to speak of "barbarian peoples"; only he can say things that, though perfectly apparent, in the mouths of others would straightaway be declared racism.

He is permitted to do so in part because he is himself a dark-skinned colonial, one of these barbarian peoples, or, to use the old British derogatory term, a "wog." (For the British, the grisly joke had it, wogs began at Calais.) In even greater part, far from pressing this accidental (now) advantage of birth to align himself on the side of those who claim to speak for the new dawn of revolution, Naipaul has earned the right to plain speaking through his impartiality as a reporter and a novelist, his disdain for sentimentalizing and romanticizing, his almost angry analytical disinterest, his freedom from cliché.

Of course, it isn't only, or even chiefly, the dark-skinned who are barbarians in Naipaul's work. Many of the most despised characters in his pages are Europeans who, filled with the rant of political slogans, the cant of received wisdom, are quite incapable of that first act of civilization, independent thought. Of a young political adventuress in his novel *Guerrillas* (1975), he notes that she had a great many opinions but that, taken together, these failed to add up to a point of view. In *A Bend in the River* (1979), a French couple in a newly independent African country have parties at which they play the records of Joan Baez, about which the novel's narrator remarks: "You couldn't listen to sweet songs about injustice unless you expected justice and received it much of the time. You couldn't sing songs about the end of the world unless . . . you felt that the world was going on and you were safe in it."

Political content runs high in the novels of what I suppose it is by now appropriate to call Naipaul's middle period, from *The Mimic Men* (1967) through *A Bend in the River*. Aloof, dark, pessimistic, these novels force the question, Out of what kind of politics are they written? It is a simple question without a simple answer. In a novel such as *The Mimic Men*, whose narrator, Ralph Singh, is an exiled colonial politician now living in London, we get, in the voice of the narrator, a running criticism of the kind of men who have risen to the top in the countries of the third world:

The career of the colonial politician is short and ends brutally. We lack order. Above all, we lack power, and we do not understand that we lack power. We mistake words and the acclamation of words for power; as soon as our bluff is called we are lost. Politics for us are a do-or-die, once-for-all charge. Once we are committed we fight more than political battles; we often fight quite literally for our lives. Our transitional or makeshift societies do not cushion us.

Such men are elsewhere characterized as "totally ridiculous"; they are "men without talent or achievement save the reputed one of controlling certain sections of the population, unproductive, uncreative men who pushed themselves into prominence by an excess of that bitterness which every untalented clerk secretes. Their bitterness responded to our appeal. And in this response we saw the success of our appeal, and its truth!"

No one would ever describe V. S. Naipaul as coolly detached. Real anger, white-hot, runs through these novels, and it is anger above all at the corruption of spirit that allows men and women to use other human beings to stoke up their own greed, power lust, and fantasies. Revolution is not a game, Naipaul's novels make clear, and people are not to be treated as inferior without the most serious consequences ensuing. Perhaps the most terrifying single scene of violence in a serious contemporary novel I have ever read is that which Naipaul wrote toward the conclusion of *Guerrillas*. In this scene a white woman, a revolutionary camp follower, is gruesomely raped and murdered by a failed black revolutionary at the end of his spiritual tether. What makes it so terrifying is not altogether to be found in the writing, which is taut and vivid enough. What makes it so terrifying is that Naipaul quite makes you believe that this hideous fate—multiple stabbings following upon forced sodomy—was, if not warranted, understandable.

Having said all that, one has still not located Naipaul politically. Among those sentimentally aligned with the fate of the third-world countries—for whom one-party states are thought quite necessary at this point in history and every inefficiency, however epic in proportions, can be excused—Naipaul's name is sheer profanity. He is thought to be, anathema of anathemas, a conservative, which means unsympathetic to the travail of the world's newly independent people. His novels suggest no justification for revolution; his reportage puts forth no plans for reform. Offering no solutions, as they used to say in the bad old days of campus revolution, he is part of the problem.

Quite a different case could easily be made. It could, after all, be argued that everywhere Naipaul has looked—and as a world traveler, he has looked nearly everywhere—he has seen these same newly independent people conned, ill used, and generally diminished by their own would-be leaders and others with their own special agendas. It could be argued that by holding these leaders to a serious political standard of forthrightness and asking that they accept the consequences of their actions, Naipaul refuses to condescend to them. It could be argued that coming out of a colonial society himself, he understands how envenomed the history of these nations is, and how the poison circulating through these societies after years of servitude is not quickly discharged. But to grant all this would be to grant Naipaul's kind of conservatism a respectability that its enemies will not allow.

Not, one suspects, that Naipaul is himself eager to be thought conservative, or aligned with any other camp. An interviewer in a *New York Times Magazine* article of 1976 contended that "he [Naipaul] is beyond partisanship—neither a radical nor a conservative, but a disillusioned idealist who still believes in the possibility of man improving his world." A "disillusioned idealist" is another name for a man who can no longer believe, or even bear to hear, the same old lies. Except that Naipaul, owing perhaps to the skepticism learned from his father, never really believed all the old lies in the first place. The habit of truth-telling is ingrained in him. When asked how he feels about the recent immigrants from Asia and the Caribbean by an interviewer in *The Illustrated Weekly of India,* Naipaul replied:

> I feel there will be a lot of difficulty. I don't see how it can be avoided, especially with these immigrants who are not migrat-

ing to a new identity or a new kind of citizenship. They are migrating to allow their barbarism to flower, so they can be more Islamic or more Sikhish than they can be with the comparative economic stagnation of their home societies. I think it's very dangerous.

And this, please understand, is for consumption by an Indian audience.

Whatever his appropriate political label, Naipaul is certainly a conservative by temperament. He has a love for order of an intensity that can be held only by a man repelled by the disorder to which he was born. Naipaul's natural refinement comes through in all his writing—his hatred of crudity, his contempt for the blatant and the coarse. He has a keen, an almost excruciating sense of the perilousness of civilization. He cannot resist underscoring that near a golf course laid out in the administrative city of Yamoussoukro in the Ivory Coast, crocodiles are kept and fed live chickens. The power of day, in the places Naipaul visits, is perpetually battling the power of night. The bush is silently growing back, the sands shifting, the wild grass popping through the crevices in the cement, all inexorably mocking the notion that modernization is tantamount to civilization.

V. S. Naipaul is something of a psychological Hobbesian, for whom life is nasty and brutish, and he is short. He frequently mentions his own smallness. He notes his developing anxiety, his raw nerves, his fearful obsession with physical pain, his incipient hysteria, his panic. In Naipaul's books, human relations are frequently power relations, with status and security at risk, and humiliation always a distinct prospect. In his own life, Naipaul has remarked, the past for him "—as a colonial and writer—was full of shame and mortifications. Indeed, they became my subjects." A good part of Naipaul's art is about seeing through people's pretensions to their elemental desires and fears, their sadness, their fundamental vulnerability. Such skill puts high tension upon his page, persistent interest in his readers' minds.

Naipaul is a true writer, which is to say that, with a mind always engaged in brooding upon the problems of his art, he did not figure forever to confine himself to one subject, even so vast a subject as "the half-made societies that seemed doomed to remain half-made." That phrasing comes from an essay of 1974 that Naipaul wrote on Joseph Conrad. Reading him in his maturity, Naipaul found affinity with Conrad, another permanent exile who had lived in England and who, sixty or seventy years earlier, "had been everywhere before me." True, Conrad did not have firsthand experience of the racial politics on which Naipaul has become a connoisseur—the politics of evasion and overstatement practiced by those third-world leaders who blame everything on oppression caused by an ostensibly relentless racial enemy. But, more important, Naipaul and Conrad are alike in being writers without a society, who, in their wide experience, know many different societies from the outside but none securely from within.

This is part of the price one pays for being different. As a West Indian East Indian—or is it an East Indian West Indian?—Naipaul has always expected some recognition of his difference; and in an article written in 1962 he remarked that it "is only in India that I have recognized how necessary this stimulus is to me." (So much so that, while in India, tired of explaining that he was an Indian from Trinidad, he would sometimes find himself telling people that he was Mexican.) Along with his differentness, Naipaul has always had what has seemed a towering loneliness. He shares this quality with Conrad and with Henry James, who once averred that his loneliness was the deepest thing about him—"deeper than my 'genius,' deeper than my discipline, deeper, above all, than the deep counterminings of art." In fact, Naipaul is married, but his wife is never mentioned in any of his reportage or autobiographical

writings; and he seems, in his literary personality, to emphasize, if not cherish and cultivate, his solitude.

When I speak of Naipaul's literary personality, I have in mind
that personality, at once penetrating, unconnable, dour, that is
at the center of his nonfiction. Naipaul has come to the point
in his career where this personality is known to his readers.
The facts of his past have been revealed; his quirks and obsessions are fairly well established. I mention all this because in
his most recent work, *The Enigma of Arrival* (1987), Naipaul
has written a book that comes very near depending upon readers' having at least some prior knowledge of his life. Without
it, I believe, this new book would be extremely puzzling; it
might not even be quite comprehensible. *The Enigma of Arrival,*
which marks a turn in V. S. Naipaul's career, is built on
assumptions of a kind that only a writer of great ambition who
is confident of his quality could have made.

I have referred to *The Enigma of Arrival* as a "book," hiding
behind the safety of the general word, chiefly because, though
its publisher refers to it as "fiction," just what is fictional about
it is not evident. Perhaps English libel laws required that the
book be presented as a novel; perhaps the identity of living or
recently deceased persons has been disguised to avoid hurting
feelings. Doubtless characters drawn from life have been touched
up or transformed. But at the heart of the book is a narrator,
never mentioned by name, who shares the biography, idiosyncrasies, and style of V. S. Naipaul. (And style, for Naipaul, has
always meant not a way of arranging words in sentences but a
way of seeing the world around one.) When the narrator of
The Enigma of Arrival remarks, "Ever since I had begun to
identify my subjects I had hoped to arrive, in a book, at a
synthesis of the worlds and cultures that had made me," we
take him at his word that this is the book we are reading and
that it is an autobiographical account of the life of V. S. Naipaul. Naipaul is no John Barth or Donald Barthelme, playing
literary games, holding mirrors up to mirrors. I think one does

best to take this book as a nearly factual account of an important period in the life of V. S. Naipaul.

Of course the distinction between fiction and autobiography has in recent decades not so much blurred as caved in. Every novelist writes out of his own experience, some less directly than others, and the history of the novel has long known such variants as the young writer's autobiographical novel, the *roman à clef*, the novel whose author rambles on autobiographically about contemporary life under the thinnest disguise. Coming at things the other way round, in a classroom I not long ago heard Frank Conroy, whose book *Stop-Time* I had taken to be one of the better American autobiographies produced since World War II, refer to his own book as a novel. Which is it, I afterwards asked Conroy, novel or autobiography? He said that he thought it didn't make much difference. I replied that I thought the difference was crucial, and that if the book was an autobiography it was brilliant, but that if it was a novel it was mediocre. By this I meant that an autobiography is judged by among other things its candor, tact, and fidelity to fact, whereas a novel is judged by quite different criteria, among them the power of its plot and the elegance of its form.

Such questions, my guess is, are very much on V. S. Naipaul's mind. Every serious writer, he has said, "becomes aware of this question of form; because he knows that however much he might have been educated and stimulated by the writers he has read or reads, the forms matched the experience of those writers, and do not strictly suit his own." And in his essay on Conrad, he noted that "the novel as a form no longer carries conviction," and went on to say:

> Experimentation, not aimed at the real difficulties, has corrupted response; and there is a great confusion in the minds of readers and writers about the purpose of the novel. The novelist, like the painter, no longer recognizes his interpretive function; he seeks to go beyond it; and his audience diminishes. And

so the world we inhabit, which is always news, goes by unexamined, made ordinary by the camera, unmeditated on; and there is no one to awake the sense of true wonder. That is perhaps a fair definition of the novelist's purpose, in all ages.

The Enigma of Arrival appears to be Naipaul's answer, for now, to the questions about form that press upon him at this point in his career. In this book he has written autobiography within what he asks us to believe is a fictional frame. In doing so he has not only combined his already proven talents as a first-person reporter and as a novelist, but has managed to find a form that permits him to ask autobiography's chief questions—Who am I? How did I become the man I am?—while retaining the novel's interest in the larger world. The result is a book at once complex and serious and not quite like any other in contemporary literature.

The *mise en scène* for *The Enigma of Arrival* appears in a paragraph of a 1976 article by Mel Gussow about V. S. Naipaul in the *New York Times Magazine,* which reads:

> At present he has two residences—a small London flat, kept by his wife, where he stays when he is in the city, and a house in the country, where he is totally by himself. The house is an hour and 40 minutes by train from London, near Salisbury, on the chalky plains of Wiltshire. It is a simple, low, one-floor stone and stucco cottage, called "The Bungalow," set back from a winding road. There is no marker or mailbox, no near neighbors and only the telephone for contact with the world. Naipaul takes a bus to town to buy groceries. A housekeeper comes in regularly. Occasionally friends visit; they do not stop by. "I'm not in touch any longer," he says. "I used to know a few people, but relationships have all withered away, just withered away."

For ten years, Naipaul tells us in *The Enigma of Arrival,* while living in the cottage in Wiltshire, he was to find himself "in tune with a landscape in a way that I had never been in Trinidad or India," and was "to be cleansed in heart and mind" and able to turn this setting into a haven for concentrated work. But this period, punctuated by trips abroad on magazine assignments, also threw him back upon himself, leaving him much time during lengthy walks in the environs of his cottage to inquire into how he had become the kind of man and writer he is. Earlier, after a publisher gave him a hard time with his novelistic history of Trinidad, *The Loss of El Dorado* (1969), and while with trepidation he contemplated beginning his novel with an African setting that was to be *In a Free State* (1971), Naipaul, whom his readers generally take to be a detached observer, a man removed, began increasingly to think of himself as "a man played on, worked on, by many things."

A good part of *The Enigma of Arrival* is given over to the forces that made Naipaul: his education, his island culture, his fantasies, his anxieties, his ambitions. His education—which was more like a competition, for if one failed to win scholarships in Trinidad one was unlikely to be able to escape the island—was even more incomplete and abstract than most, if only because he read about things that existed nowhere in his environment. When he arrived in London, for example, he quite expected it to be the London of Dickens's novels which his father had read to him when he was a boy. He lived imaginatively in the cinema and in books, and his imagination, in Trinidad, never rubbed up against modern reality. Among the things he imagined was a writer's life for himself of a kind he was not in any remote way cut out to live. The education of Naipaul's adult years was in large part devoted to shedding all the half-baked and hopeless notions he had acquired when young. In this he is rather like the rest of us, only more so.

These autobiographical segments are woven among Naipaul's accounts of his Wiltshire walks, his descriptions of landscape, his meetings with his neighbors. Years before, in 1969, in an article about Jacques Soustelle, the French anthropologist and then politician in exile, Naipaul remarked that Soustelle's conversational method resembled that of neither the scholar nor the politician but came closer to that of the novelist, "making art of egotism, creating a private impenetrable whole out of fragments which from a distance might appear unrelated." Such, too, is the method of this book. The little dramas of plot are entirely absent from its pages. People die, there is even a murder; but we hear about all this from the author. Events matter less than what Naipaul makes of them. The interest of the book is not in its action but in the analytical intelligence that is controlling it.

In place of dramatic action, Naipaul supplies quiet revelation and superior observation, so that *The Enigma of Arrival*, which takes its title from Naipaul's immigrant's fascination with a painting by that name by Giorgio de Chirico, takes on something of the structure of an onion, layer after layer of which has to be peeled back until one gets to the nub of the thing. One learns that Naipaul's cottage, for example, is part of a large manor house built during the confident years of Edwardian England. Of a church in the neighborhood built at roughly the same time, Naipaul writes: "As much as a faith, it celebrated a culture, a national pride, a power, men very much in control of their destinies." Church and manor are emblematic of the spirit of the British empire; and it was this empire, as Naipaul acknowledges, that "explained my birth in the New World, the language I used, the vocation and ambition I had; this empire in the end explained my presence there in the valley, in the cottage, in the grounds of the manor."

Naipaul is of course writing at a time well beyond the end of empire. The man who owns and inhabits the manor house is a neurasthenic aristocrat with not very impressive artistic pretensions. The couple who look after him and his estate are rootless people. The gardener, who takes great pains with his clothes, lives with his handsome wife in colorless squalor. The cabman, whose father worked on the manor, becomes ensnared in sectarian mystical religion. All the people connected with the manor "were curiously unanchored, floating." No one any longer seems in charge of his fate; no one controls his own destiny. "Fifty years ago," Naipaul notes, "there would have been no room for me on the estate."

Bit by bit, Naipaul learns more about each of the people who works or lives on the estate. Slowly, he comes to understand that though technically all are "in service," as the English used to term the servant class, they "lived in a net of mutual resentment." Like the true novelist he is, Naipaul does not feel he knows a person until he knows how that person sees the world. Given the reticence of the English lower and lower-middle classes, this can take time. But in everyone Naipaul meets he eventually discovers a personal drama, an angle of vision, a different way of seeing that gives him insight into his or her character. The opinions of Bray, the cabman, for instance, are all borrowed from radio, television, and the popular press, but when filtered through his personality and personal history, they are original in combination, making him something like an anarcho-Tory.

It has always been the mystery of human character that most interests V. S. Naipaul, and in *The Enigma of Arrival* he makes an extended effort to understand his own. This is a book in which Naipaul recognizes that he has come to middle age, and therefore it is a book about change and death and the impermanence of life. The book closes with the death of his sister in Trinidad, an event that showed him "life and man as the mystery, the true religion of men, the grief and the glory." (Naipaul's brother Shiva, also a novelist, died not long afterwards.)

"It was strange," Naipaul writes, "but for myself, in my cottage, I never, never feared." The inner security that he found in Wiltshire was owing, in good part, to his relationship to the landscape, which he describes over and over in various seasons and from various angles. (Such descriptions constitute the only longueurs in the book.) The alternation of the seasons, the rhythm of gardening, the regular rounds of the staff at the manor and of the nearby farmers, gave a regularity and rhythm to Naipaul's own life that he had not known before. It was seductive, and productive—and not, finally, to last. As the years passed, death, disillusion, decay set in. Even in Wiltshire, the bush advances, creeping in on civilization, and ultimately bringing ruin. The following passage sums up Naipaul's feelings toward the end of his stay in his cottage and also illustrates what I have in mind when I speak of his conservative temperament:

> The very kind of people who, in the great days of the manor, would have given of their best as carpenters, masons, bricklayers might have had ideas of beauty and workmanship and looked for acknowledgment of their skill and craft and pains, people of this sort now, sensing an absence of authority, an organization in decay, seemed to be animated by an opposite instinct: to hasten decay, to loot, to reduce to junk. And it was possible to understand how an ancient Roman factory-villa in this province of Britain could suddenly, after two or three centuries, simply with a letting-go authority, and not with the disappearance of a working population, crumble into ruin, the secrets of the building and its modest technologies, for so long so ordinary, lost.

Civilization, for Naipaul, is a fragile thing, always in peril. Rural England, in his reading, is rather like Trinidad, or East Africa, or India; without the authority of tradition, it is, like every other place in the world, under siege by rot and at the mercy of rotters. In Naipaul's writing generally, there is a great, not ever fully expressed, longing for a society where he can cease the struggle, come to rest, feel at home. Although a British citizen, he remains, spiritually, a stateless soul, yearning for a society that the modern world just may not be able to provide. It is one of Naipaul's great themes, and perhaps the principal sadness of his life.

The Enigma of Arrival is a book about a journey, V. S. Naipaul's journey as writer and man, yet a journey still far from over. One feels this to be very much a transitional book, marking a turn in Naipaul's career. "As you get older," he once told an interviewer, "the work gets more difficult because the writing inevitably becomes more complex." But it only becomes more complex, one needs to insert, if you become a better writer, smarter and more impressed with the complexities of life. The enigma of Naipaul's own arrival has not been completely solved, and now, given the kind of restless writer he is, it will soon be time for fresh departures. Will he next write about life in the United States, in Europe, in the portion of the world that lives under Communism? Will his writing turn increasingly inward, in the manner of *The Enigma of Arrival*? Whatever he does next I take to be of the most serious consequence, for this man, the grandson of an indentured laborer, the son of an unsuccessful island journalist, is far and away the most talented, the most truthful, the most honorable writer of his generation.

The New Criterion 1987

Tom Wolfe's
Vanities

AMERICAN ENGLISH IS deficient in not having a word that, if not the antonym of "carpetbagger," at least suggests the idea of traffic going the other way. The carpetbaggers, it will be recalled, were those northerners who headed south after the Civil War to cash in on the Reconstruction. The word I seek would describe those southerners—southern writers, specifically—who, nearly a century later, headed north to cash in by describing the period of American history that may someday go by the name of the Deconstruction. I say "north," but I really mean Manhattan; I say "Deconstruction," but I really mean that scrambling of ideals and morals, that blurring of meaning about fundamental matters, which has been so notable a feature of contemporary life in recent decades. Truman, Bill, Willie, Tom, these southerners headed north as if toward home, to play off the title of an autobiography written by one among them. To Manhattan southern writers have brought their dreams, their subtle feeling for the filigree of status life (for outside a beehive, no place is more abuzz with status than a southern town), and their churning literary ambition.

Many of these southern writers scored early and heavily, and some among them ended sadly and boozily. Midge Decter, who worked as an editor at *Harper's* at a time when it was dominated by southern writers, once remarked that these southerners could be very impressive, but, funny thing, they always seemed to want to stop for a beer. That is no mere *mot,* for alcoholism, from Thomas Wolfe on, has long plagued southern writers. But between Thomas Wolfe and Tom Wolfe there is a vast difference, and the latter, a southerner from Richmond, Virginia, appears never to have stopped for a beer or anything else, except a Ph.D. in American Studies at Yale, on the way to a quite extraordinary career in contemporary American letters. And in Tom Wolfe's case, a career, in the root sense of a course of continued progress, it has distinctly been.

A careful caretaker of this career, Tom Wolfe may be the only writer since Mark Twain to dress for the job. Two white-suited southerners, Twain and Wolfe resemble nothing so much as characters who have somehow wandered off the stage of a production of Jerome Kern's *Show Boat*. In another sense, of course, a showboat is a show-off, and there is a strong element of calling attention to himself, of sheer showing off, in Tom Wolfe's work. Plainspoken and decorous in his personal utterances, Wolfe has written as he has dressed, which is gaudily. If exclamation marks were dollars, he would already have spent a million. If italics were neon, his prose would long ago have suffered a power outage. If punctuation could be patented, he could lay claim to the double-decker, triple-length ellipsis, which looks like this: : : : : : : : : : Along with flashy punctuation, Wolfe commands a vocabulary made up of up-to-the-moment street talk, academic locutions, and fairly arcane medical terms that, mixed together, often result in an amusing verbal salad. Abrupt shifts, wild transitions, loony interjections, and other prose pyrotechnics are frequently set off just to make certain that no one sleeps while reading Tom Wolfe's prose.

If Wolfe's manner can be raffish, his method has always emphasized realism. Realism in Tom Wolfe's journalism has meant a concentration on the grain and texture of everyday life as brought out in its concrete details. It was the concentration on detail, as Wolfe himself has argued, that gave power to the novels of Dostoevsky, Dreiser, Dos Passos, and other realists, for the element of reporting has always been crucial to story-telling of all kinds. As a newspaper reporter—once out of grad-uate school, with an appetite for the real world that only graduate study can give, Wolfe worked for the *Washington Post* and then for the *New York Herald Tribune*—Wolfe trained himself to pick up such details. I say "trained," but more likely he had a natural instinct for them, especially for those details that are important counters in what he once termed "the sta-tusphere." Wolfe can determine the status nuance of the frames around the photographs atop the piano in the apartment of Leonard Bernstein, of the sound a Bonneville car door makes when closing, of the length of a radical's sideburn. This may seem to some people pretty small game, utterly trivial, mere *kakapitze,* but I, who find it all fascinating, am not among them.

Tom Wolfe also early showed a powerful aptitude for insin-uating himself into the point of view of the people he wrote about. That takes work—legwork, the old-line journalists used to call it—and, if you do it with as ambitious a range of char-acters as Wolfe has dealt with over the years, it also takes imag-ination. Point of view had long been the almost exclusive province of the novelist; Wolfe was among those who first brought it into journalism. "The idea," he has written, "was to give the full objective description, plus something that readers had always had to go to novels and short stories for: namely, the subjective or emotional life of the characters." Wolfe used a straight point of view, shifting points of view, stream of con-sciousness, and every other literary device he could bring into play to enhance and enliven his journalism. The point was to lend journalism the density and intensity of literature while retaining the authenticity and excitement of dealing with real people and actual events.

This phenomenon of applying novelistic techniques to journalistic subjects came to be called the New Journalism. Tom Wolfe never claimed to have invented it, though he was its most energetic practitioner. A lot of it, you might say, was going around in the early 1960s. Some of the most prominent New Journalism was written by writers who were neither new nor trained as journalists. Truman Capote's *In Cold Blood* (1966), an account of the massacre of a prosperous Kansas farm family, was billed by Capote, who was a publicity genius, as a "nonfiction novel." Later, in 1967, Norman Mailer produced a book entitled *The Armies of the Night,* which he styled, in a subtitle, *History as a Novel, the Novel as History,* which is quite as nonsensical as it is inflated, apart from the obvious fact that Mailer, too, was using novelistic techniques—including writing about himself in the third person—in the production of autobiographical journalism. Gay Talese, Jimmy Breslin, and Hunter S. Thompson were also sometimes spoken of as New Journalists. But, as with all things that have the misfortune to be called new, the New Journalism, after a pretty good run of a decade or so, ran out of excitement.

Wolfe has argued that the New Journalism was able to generate the excitement that it did because the novel, after World War II, in effect vacated the premises by abandoning realism for sheer introspection or academic games-playing. True enough, there has, in American fiction, been a genuine *embarras de pauvreté*. True, too, many American novelists eschewed the great subject of American society—and at a time when that society was undergoing the social whiplash of the sixties and seventies—to contemplate rather exclusively their own navels and parts below. In a lengthy introduction to an anthology entitled *The New Journalism,* Wolfe wrote:

> . . . about the time I came to New York, the most serious, ambitious and, presumably, talented novelists had abandoned the richest terrain of the novel: namely, society, the social tableau, manners and morals, the whole business of "the way we live

now," in Trollope's phrase. . . . Balzac prided himself on being "the secretary of French society." Most serious American novelists would rather cut their wrists than be known as "the secretary of American society," and not merely because of ideological considerations. With fable, myth and the sacred office to think about—who wants such a menial role?

The novelist, in this reading, dropped the family jewels, leaving the (new) journalists to pick them up and pocket them for themselves.

After remarking that *"understatement* was the thing" among journalists and literati, Wolfe wrote that "by the early 1960s understatement had become an absolute pall." In his own journalism understatement was clearly out. It was out, too, in his discussion of the merits of the New Journalism, where Wolfe avoided it like Brooks Brothers. At one point, claiming that the New Journalism offered all the techniques of literature along with the simple but overpowering fact that what the New Journalists wrote about *"actually happened"* (italics certainly not mine), Wolfe went on to claim that the New Journalist "is one step closer to the absolute involvement of the reader that Henry James and James Joyce dreamed of and never achieved." Now that, no question about it, is really pushing it.

Wolfe, who can compare the tedium of graduate school with "reading *Mr. Sammler's Planet* at one sitting, or just reading it," is rather more kindly disposed to the creators of New Journalism and neglects to mention criticisms against it. Jimmy Cannon, an old journalist, once remarked that "my main objection to some of them [the New Journalists] is that they make up the quotes. They invent action. When I was a kid we used to call it faking and piping, smoking the pipe, opium smoking." That the New Journalists make things up may or may not be true—it is usually unprovable in any case; more interesting is the related problem of the reader's not being able to determine whether or not the author, the New Journalist, actually saw what he is reporting or is instead reporting what other people have reported to him that they saw. An example will perhaps make the point less abstract.

In *The Electric Kool-Aid Acid Test* (1968), Wolfe's New Journalistic account of the pharmacological adventures of the novelist Ken Kesey and those who gathered around him in the early and middle 1960s, there appears a lengthy paragraph that for sheer loathsomeness has been accorded a place in a mixed-media production that sometimes plays in my mind that I think of as Great Moments from the Sixties. It is a paragraph devoted to a gang-bang—not, technically, a gang rape, in which the victim is unwilling—of a married woman (she is described in the paragraph as "just one nice soft honey hormone squash") by a band of Hell's Angels. Further details are not required for anyone with the least scintilla of imagination, though Wolfe supplies details in sufficient abundance to make one feel that, next to what went on in the shack in which this took place, hell itself would seem no worse than Club Med. But since we are talking about what *actually happened,* it seems fair to insist upon knowing if the man reporting it to us was *actually there.* And if he was actually there—I could be wrong, but I suspect that Wolfe wasn't—then is the quality of his description, which is meant to be objectivity set out before us through the point of view of the Hell's Angels, appropriate to the occasion? I don't think this is a trivial question.

One could raise other questions and objections about the New Journalism: because of the large outlay of energy in legwork it requires, it seems to be chiefly a young man's game; because of the equally large outlay of time required to do what Wolfe has called "saturation reporting," large expense accounts or publishers' advances or independent wealth are necessary; because the amount of snooping required is great, not to speak of that special journalistic appetite for biting the hand that feeds you (the hand, specifically, of one's subject, whose permission one needs for interviews and for merely hanging around), not every literary talent has the temperament needed for New Journalism. But these objections have been rendered moot by time and nugatory by fashion. For the New Journalism the caravan passed years ago, and even the dogs have stopped barking.

If interest in the New Journalism has faded, interest in Tom Wolfe has not. He has been able to ride out the waves of fashion on the surfboard of his own remarkable talent. Fashion is after all Tom Wolfe's subject. By identifying and then (usually) attacking what is currently fashionable, he has himself become, not quite fashionable, but certainly famous. No other writer of our day has put more phrases into contemporary speech. "Radical chic," "mau-mauing," "the Me Decade" are all Wolfe's coinages; "the Right Stuff," which he took from the speech of test pilots, today has the currency of a full-blown cliché. "Wolfeian" has not thus far become a commonly recognized adjective, perhaps owing to the existence of Thomas and Nero Wolfe, but I myself have long begun to think of the phrase "to cry Wolfe" as shorthand for spotting a hot trend, shift in the current social scene, or new—my pen trembles in my hand as I prepare to set down the detested word—"lifestyle." Of the spread of the use of LSD in and around San Francisco in the early 1960s, and of the origin of the so-called Trip Festivals that initiated the psychedelic discotheques ("Civilization and its discotheques," Anthony Hecht once noted), Wolfe, in *The Electric Kool-Aid Acid Test,* wrote: "But mainly the idea of a new life style was making itself felt. Do you suppose this is the—*new wave* . . . ?"

Tom Wolfe is pre-eminently the chronicler of those people who do not so much live lives as they live lifestyles—which is to say, of people who do not live life very deep down or authentically. They are often very savvy, even self-reflecting, about the way they live, but finally the style dominates the life. To this day I can recall a brief piece about an advertising man alienated from his son that appeared in Tom Wolfe's first book,

The Kandy-Kolored Tangerine-Flake Streamline Baby (1965), in which Wolfe wrote that the man, whose name was Parker, called the short-brimmed, hard-crowned hat of the day a "Madison Avenue crash helmet." "He," Wolfe noted, "calls it a Madison Avenue crash helmet and then wears one." Of such people Tom Wolfe has made himself the leading connoisseur.

As a journalist, Wolfe has played the reporter who brings the news, some of it hot and new (as in the book on the California drug culture), some of it not so new but interesting nonetheless because it has been wrongly neglected by others (as in *The Right Stuff,* his 1979 book on the heroism of American test pilots and astronauts). Easily the most stir-causing single piece of journalism Tom Wolfe has written in this mode is "Radical Chic: That Party at Lenny's," which appeared in *New York* magazine early in the summer of 1970. That piece is, put simply, a devastation; it features that good old democratic joke, the rich making tremendous fools of themselves. In this case, it will be recalled, the fools in question were the guests of Leonard Bernstein and his wife Felicia—themselves greater fools still, for allowing Tom Wolfe past their front door—who organized a fund-raising party for the most militant of 1960s militant revolutionary groups, the Black Panthers, in their, the Bernsteins', Manhattan apartment. It was an event that can be likened to a French comte and comtesse's inviting Mme Defarge and a few of her friends over to dinner, then calling back and reminding her not to neglect to bring along the guillotine. Doing one of his point-of-view turns, Wolfe wrote:

> God, what a flood of taboo thoughts runs through one's head at these Radical Chic events. . . . But it's delicious. It is as if one's nerve endings were on red alert to the most intimate nuances of status. Deny it if you want to! Nevertheless, it runs through every soul here. It is the matter of the marvelous contradictions on all sides. It is the delicious shudder you get when you try to force the prongs of two horseshoe magnets together . . . *them* and *us.* . . .

The political consequence of "Radical Chic: That Party at Lenny's" was to take radical politics off the celebrity social calendar. By giving the disease a name, and by exhibiting its symptoms through the powerful microscope of literary ridicule, Wolfe demonstrated the egregious contradictions, the spiritual vulgarity, the sheer idiocy, inherent in reverse social climbing of the kind the Bernsteins and their guests thrilled to that night in Manhattan. After Wolfe's article had appeared in print, radicalism, at least as it was shown in the sexier news media, seemed to lose momentum and never again to have quite the same social luster.

Before the article about the party at the Bernsteins', it would not have been easy to say what Tom Wolfe's politics were. In writings about custom car designs, Pop Art collectors, stock-car drivers, rock'n'roll impresarios, the girl of the year, and other such subjects, Wolfe's political views did not seem a matter of pressing interest. Where they first became interesting was in *The Electric Kool-Aid Acid Test,* his book about Kesey and the drug culture. LSD, after all, is not a subject upon which it is possible to remain neutral, or so at least one would have thought.

Yet in reading that book, which exhibits prodigious reportorial skills, one couldn't resist asking where Tom Wolfe himself stood in relation to the patent destructiveness of the drug culture. One couldn't resist asking because, in truth, after more than four hundred pages, one still didn't quite know. Wolfe's admiration for Ken Kesey, which runs very high, came through in the book without equivocation. But did the worldly, then-young journalist also buy the mad talk about the higher consciousness that drugs were alleged to make possible? Was our author, to use a phrase much used in the book, himself on or off the bus—for or against what he was describing? Early in *The Electric Kool-Aid Acid Test,* Wolfe wrote: "I feel like I am in on something the outside world, the world I came from, could not possibly comprehend, and it *is* a metaphor, the whole scene, ancient and vast, vaster than . . ." By the end of the book, Wolfe had not filled in that ellipsis; and those may be the most unsatisfactory three dots in contemporary journalism.

After "Radical Chic: That Party at Lenny's" appeared in *New York,* Tom Wolfe's own point of view ceased to be problematical in his writing. He also seemed to become interested in politics. Perhaps writing that article helped him to understand that politics, for so many people, fell within the domain of "lifestyle"—proper political views being for them the ideational equivalent of proper clothes, food, and furniture—and could no longer be ignored by a writer with his literary ambitions. Perhaps he had something like a political conversion brought about by an awareness of the extreme contradictions inherent in contemporary left-wing views. Certainly publishing his article on the Bernsteins' party, which blew a very shrill whistle on left-wing absurdity, made him a permanent enemy of the Left. The article also gave him national fame of a kind that nothing he had hitherto written had brought. Before writing "Radical Chic: That Party at Lenny's," Tom Wolfe was a stylish journalist; after the article, he was something of a celebrity, whose point of view, far from needing to be suppressed for vague, possibly bogus, journalistic reasons, was now of considerable interest in its own right.

Wolfe's own status changed from journalist—"working pest," as a wag I know likes to put it—to something akin to social observer. He continued to do a certain amount of saturation reporting of the kind he had earlier vaunted as the literary wave of the future—certainly *The Right Stuff* is a work of this kind— but he now also did a turn or two at elaborate opinionation. In this realm, Wolfe was not about to fall into the journalistic trap of becoming a pundit; "paralyzing snoozemongers" is the way he had earlier described such pundits as Walter Lippmann and Joseph Alsop. Status and her sister Snobbery remained his key subjects, and comedy in describing their operation in the contemporary world his chief gift. As a social observer, he would charm through comic outrageousness.

Success, along with begetting success, begets confidence. It took confidence of high magnitude for Wolfe to take on his next subject, which was the contemporary art scene. *The Painted Word* (1975) is a comic sociology of that scene. In part, it delineates the relation of *le haut monde*—or *tout New York*—to visual art, just as "Radical Chic" delineated its relation to radical politics. In both instances an essential fraudulence lies at the heart of the relationship, with both radical politics and what passes for advanced taste in art allowing those rich and socially ambitious enough to dally with them to feel spiritual grace and gorgeousness of soul of a kind that sets them well above their class and even above the money that made it all possible to begin with. Wolfe plays all this for laughs, of which, as always when big money and social aspiration and culture get together, there is no paucity.

The Painted Word is an example—an extended essay on modern architecture, *From Bauhaus to Our House* (1981), is another—of Tom Wolfe operating in his emperor-has-no-clothes mode. He can be highly entertaining in this mode, except that he seems always to want to push things rather further than he ought. It is not sufficient to show that the emperor is undressed; it must also be pointed out that he has no kneecaps, clavicle, scrotum. Thus Wolfe, eager to show that the world he is depicting in *The Painted Word* is utterly fraudulent, must make everyone and everything in it a swindle. Thus, in his attempt to show the absurdity of much contemporary art criticism, he undermines entirely the relation of criticism to creation. Thus, in *From Bauhaus to Our House,* in his attempt to show that Walter Gropius and his European colleagues were utopian totalitarians, he all but asserts that all modern architecture is a hoax put over on Americans with a cultural inferiority complex. Throwing out the baby with the bathwater, along with being a cliché, is an old story; but when Tom Wolfe gets done, as in these two books, he has also removed the plumbing.

"Any work of art that can be understood," the line from the old Dada manifesto had it, "is the product of a journalist." It may well be that Wolfe's simplifications in *The Painted Word* and *From Bauhaus to Our House* are owing to his own training in journalism. Splendidly observant, intellectually alert, learned even (Dr. Wolfe, I presume), Tom Wolfe is an immensely entertaining writer, but he does seem to work almost exclusively in primary colors. Fine shading is not his specialty. His is not what one thinks of as a finely graded mind; the style he has developed is ill suited to fine gradations. On the bloody, three-dot, italic contrary.

Which is not to say that, as a writer, Tom Wolfe is without subtlety. He is extremely subtle, but on one topic chiefly: status. Wolfe has written on an impressive variety of subjects and on an astonishing range of characters—I consider the range between Leonard Bernstein and Chuck Yeager astonishing—but whatever the subject, whoever the character, the real story for Wolfe is status: who stands where on the rubber ladder. A foxy sort of hedgehog, Wolfe has written about everything and yet always about the same thing. In his pages, talent, money, audacity, all are measured by, and are rewarded with, status. Preoccupied with status though Wolfe is, he has not thus far in his career seemed himself snobbish. (Freud, after all, was not a sex fiend, nor Marx a miser.) Wolfe simply believes—or so, on the basis of his writing, I gather that he believes—that it is status that makes the world go round.

Certainly, Wolfe sees status as dominating literary life. Literary status, in his view, works through literary forms, or genres, and in his introduction on *The New Journalism* he mapped out a literary class structure with novelists at the top ("the occasional playwright or poet might be up there, too, but mainly it was the novelists"), the middle class occupied by the literary essayists and certain authoritative critics, and the journalists down in the low-rent district. "When we talk about the 'rise' or 'death' of literary genres," he went on to say, "we are talking about status, mainly." (I happen to think the subject is much more complicated than that, mainly, but this is no place for an essay-length footnote to prove it.) As Wolfe then (in 1973) saw it, "the novel no longer has the supreme status it enjoyed for ninety years (1875–1965), but neither has the New Journalism won it for itself. In some quarters the contempt for it is boundless . . . even breathtaking. . . ." Today the word "contempt" in that last sentence would have to be changed to "apathy."

Tom Wolfe has always liked to play being Jeane Dixon, shooting off predictions about forthcoming trends, and in his introduction to *The New Journalism* he predicted a new life for the novel, or, more precisely, a life for a new kind of novel:

> I think there is a tremendous future for a sort of novel that will be called the journalistic novel or perhaps documentary novel, novels of intense social realism based upon the same painstaking reporting that goes into the New Journalism. I see no reason why novelists who look down on Arthur Hailey's work couldn't do the same sort of reporting and research he does—and write it better, if they're able. There are certain areas of life that journalism still cannot move into easily, particularly for reasons of invasion of privacy, and it is in this margin that the novel will be able to grow in the future.

Fourteen years later Wolfe made this prediction come true by producing precisely such a novel himself. To put it Wolfe-ishly, *The Bonfire of the Vanities* (1987) is Tom Wolfe's bid to *make it—now!* . . . to break free from being a grubby journalist, however New and Glittering and Well Paid . . . and to become, are you ready for it, hey, give me a double (single-deck) ellipsis here . . . . . . *Literature!*

Not long after reading Tom Wolfe's novel, I came across a reference to an event of the kind from which it takes its title—

The Bonfire of the Vanities—in Thomas Mann's *Doctor Faustus*. In describing the town of Kaiseraschern, in which the narrator and Adrian Leverkühn came of age, the narrator remarks: "Rash it may be to say so, but here one could imagine strange things: as for instance a movement for a children's crusade might break out; a St. Vitus's dance; some wandering lunatic with communistic visions, preaching a bonfire of the vanities; miracles of the Cross, fantastic and mystical folk-movements—things like these, one felt, might easily come to pass." Savonarola, it will be recalled, beseeched the terrified citizenry of late-fifteenth-century Florence to toss their vain personal ornaments, including books and paintings, into a symbolic fire—a bonfire of the vanities—that would purge their sins. Early in Tom Wolfe's novel, when he first describes his main character's sumptuous Park Avenue apartment, he remarks that it is a place of the kind "the mere thought of which ignites flames of greed and covetousness under people all over New York and, for that matter, all over the world." Right out of the gate, then, we are under advisement that symbolic flames will follow.

The Bonfire of the Vanities is an audacious book. Its ambition is grand and so is its scope, for it covers life from the high tables of Manhattan down to the lockup at the Bronx County courthouse. It is a hefty tome of 659 pages, which would make fairly good bonfire of its own, and seems to have been written in defiance of the notion that if one wishes to make a major statement in our time, one had better make it short. It is audacious in yet another sense: it says things that no one else in our time has quite dared to say, at least not in print, not publicly. It posits that modern big-city life has become a jungle, full of danger and despair and disaster waiting to erupt. It further posits that there are men, some among them black men who are would-be leaders of their people, who profit handsomely from this arrangement. It has no regard for ethnic sensitivities, insofar as two of its most loathsome characters, both attorneys, are Jews, and makes the assumptions that ethnic groups generally live with one another in a perpetual state of not very deeply suppressed animosity. Roughly midway through the novel, reference is made to three V.I.F.s. " 'V.I.F.'s?' asked Sherman. 'Very Important Fags,' said Judy, 'that's what everybody calls them.' " This, then, is not a novel that has set its sights on winning the B'nai Brith Human Relations Award.

Much of the negative press—in the *Nation, New York,* the *New Republic* (whose review carried the title "The Right-Wing Stuff")—that *The Bonfire of the Vanities* has received has been owing to its politics. These are strongly anti-Left, at least insofar as Wolfe attributes much of the serious mischief in contemporary urban life to radical hustlers and soft-hearted (also -headed) liberal culture of a kind unwilling to admit unpleasant facts about contemporary life. One such fact is that the New York City public-school system is spiritually bankrupt, and its greatest victims are black and Hispanic kids. Of the students at the Colonel Jacob Ruppert High School in the Bronx, one Mr. Rifkind, a teacher with a minor role in the novel, remarks: "At Ruppert we use comparative terms, but *outstanding* isn't one of them. The range runs more from cooperative to life threatening." The same teacher says: "Written work? There hasn't been any written work at Ruppert High for fifteen years! Maybe twenty!" I would add that there hasn't been candor on such subjects, in our journalism or in our literature, for even longer.

Without an unblinkered view of reality, there can be no realism in literature. If one were to read the American fiction of the past few decades, one would be little likely to discover that large stretches of American cities are simply out of bounds to large segments of the population. Black or white, one can easily be killed in those streets. One can easily be killed, at least in spirit, in the media as well. One of the most terrifying moments in Wolfe's novel occurs as the members of the media are clos-

ing in on the main character, a successful bond broker named
Sherman McCoy, who has been indicted for running over a
black adolescent in the Bronx:

> They closed in for the kill. And then they killed him.
>
> He couldn't remember whether he had died while he was still
> standing in line outside, before the door to Central Booking
> opened, or while he was in the pens. But by the time he left the
> building and Killian [his lawyer] held his impromptu press con-
> ference on the steps, he had died and been reborn. In his new
> incarnation, the press was no longer an enemy and it was no
> longer *out there*. The press was now a condition, like lupus ery-
> thematosus or Wegener's granulomatosis. His entire central
> nervous system was now wired into the vast, incalculable circuit
> of radio and television and newspapers, and his body surged
> and burned and hummed with the energy of the press and the
> prurience of those it reached, which was everyone, from the
> closest neighbor to the most bored and distant outlander titil-
> lated for the moment by his disgrace.

Or, as Wolfe puts it in an earlier trope: "They were the mag-
gots and the flies, and he was the dead beast they had found
to crawl over and root into."

The Bonfire of the Vanities is about the wretched misadven-
tures of Sherman McCoy (Buckley, St. Paul's, Yale), a man in
his late thirties who lives in one of the best apartments in one
of the best buildings on one of the best streets in the most
important city in the world and who is earning only twenty
thousand shy of a million dollars a year and going broke. Sherman has a wife named Judy and a daughter named Campbell
and a dachshund named Marshall and a southern mistress named
Maria Ruskin, who is herself married to a rich, much older
man, a Jew whose fortune is built on chartering flights for
Arabs bound for Mecca. It is while driving Maria home from
Kennedy Airport, in his Mercedes roadster (engine size, oddly,
not noted), feeling masterful and atop the world ("There it

[Manhattan] was, the Rome, the Paris, the London of the twentieth century, the city of ambition, the dense magnetic rock, the irresistible destination of all those who insist on being *where things are happening*—and he was among the victors!"), that Sherman misses the off-ramp to Manhattan and finds himself, beautiful woman beside him in a $48,000 car, in the Apache territory of the Bronx.

Lost in a maze of dark streets, Sherman, on a lonely ramp, is about to be accosted by two young black men. Out of the car, he fends one off, while Marie, now at the wheel, backs up the Mercedes, which knocks over the other. They then drive off. Sherman wants to report hitting one of the two young men with the Mercedes, but Maria, reminding him of the complications this would cause—they are married, after all, and not to each other—persuades him, after a good bout of bonkering, otherwise. The boy who was hit by the Mercedes—he turns out to have been a high-school student—later goes into a coma and eventually dies. A Jesse Jackson-like figure named Reverend Bacon attempts to make great political hay over the incident, which, from the standpoint of the media, is a very sexy one: ghetto youth run over and killed by unidentified fleeing white couple in a Mercedes roadster. The main plot line of the novel is given over to the hunt, capture, and trial of Sherman McCoy for his part in the crime.

Tom Wolfe's handling of this material is altogether adroit. Cutting back and forth between five or six major characters, never lingering overlong with any one of them, or with the numerous subsidiary characters in this Russian-length novel, bouncing from social class to social class, subject to subject, *The Bonfire of the Vanities* is neatly paced, without a longueur in the book. Whether an upper-class homosexual lawyer or a black drug dealer is talking, an English journalist or a Jewish cop, a maître d' in a Manhattan Frog Pond restaurant or a lower-middle-class Greek bimbo, the dialogue in this novel always and everywhere feels right. The details are deft; a vast amount of information about the way some people (I won't say "we") live nowadays is dispensed. In sum, the book, as one thinks of them saying at editorial sales meetings, is a helluva read.

At this point, permit me to pose a question that I don't think will bore many people: How does a young man, not yet forty, without a drug or gambling problem and with no one blackmailing him, manage to be going broke on an annual salary of $980,000? It isn't that difficult to spend more than $980,000 a year in current-day Manhattan, as Tom Wolfe demonstrates in perfectly persuasive financial detail. I shall not rehearse all the details here, but it may give some inkling of Mr. Sherman McCoy's problem to say that for real-estate payments alone (loan repayments, mortgages, maintenance assessments, taxes) on a $2.6 million Park Avenue apartment and a house in Southampton, our boy is in for $368,000. Now toss in a few line items like $37,000 for restaurants and entertaining at home, $62,000 for servants (a nanny for the child, a cook and cleaning woman, a handyman for the place in Southampton), $65,000 for clothes and furniture, and a lousy $10,080 for parking two cars in Manhattan. You may think there is room for trimming things down here. Two and a half million dollars may seem a bit high for a pad, for example, but Wolfe, most amusingly, shows how little in the way of quality in an apartment one gets these days for $1 million ("8½-foot ceilings, a dining room but no library, an entry gallery the size of a closet, no fireplace, skimpy lumberyard moldings, if any, plasterboard walls that transmit whispers, and no private elevator stop"). It's a problem, no doubt about it.

But let us talk a bit further about clothes. The dandiacal Mr. Wolfe not only dresses his characters with care—that one would expect—but tells us the name brands of their clothes, the prices paid for them, and often the shops in which they were purchased. Thus we learn about a rubberized English riding mac "bought at Knoud on Madison Avenue"; a soft leather attaché

case of the kind that "come from Mädler or T. Anthony on
Park Avenue"; sport jackets that are bought at Huntsman, Savile
Row; Shep Miller suspenders; New and Lingwood shoes (lots
of these), at New and Lingwood, Jermyn Street, London. Ah,
me, in the 1890s dandies wrote for the *Yellow Book;* now they
use the *Yellow Pages.*

Clothes perhaps weigh too heavily in Tom Wolfe's reckoning of character. Some of his details about them, it must be
said, are very sharp. A down-on-his-uppers English journalist
named Peter Fallow appears in a once expensive blazer that is
beginning to show serious wear on its lapels; an assistant district attorney named Larry Kramer wears Nike sneakers and
carries his Johnston and Murphy brown dress shoes in an A&P
bag on the subway; the lawyer who defends Sherman McCoy,
a man named Thomas Killian, always dresses to the nines (make
that the thirty-sixes), and he is one of the few characters in the
book of whom Wolfe approves.

Is this sound novelistic practice? In having Larry Kramer
carry his not very elegant shoes to work in an A&P bag, Wolfe
is telling us that here is a dullish man, without flair or imagination, the reverse of a sport, essentially lower-middle-class, a
clod—all of which Kramer turns out to be, as well as being
cheap, lecherous, sycophantic, self-deluded, and dishonest.
Could he not, though, have been quite as dreary in, say, an
Alden tassled version of a full-strap slip-on in imported aniline
calfskin? How would Henry James have handled it? What did
Gilbert Osmond, that great snob, wear in *The Portrait of a
Lady?* All James says by way of description is: "He was dressed
as a man dresses who takes little other trouble about it than to
have no vulgar things." Henry James lets Osmond dress himself, or rather lets us dress him in our own minds, but then
James is fishing in deeper waters.

Henry James was interested in moral drama. Tom Wolfe is
here interested in the drama of social status, of which he ultimately morally disapproves. Yet his fascination with the drama

of social status is at least as great as his disapproval. In Henry James every decision has its moral price; in Tom Wolfe every piece of furniture has its retail price. In the drama of status, only one mode of thinking exists—that of comparison. Such a drama presents its players with a single problem—that of positioning themselves through their taste or wealth or political virtue or beauty or family standing. *The Bonfire of the Vanities* is a novel in which nearly every character searches for others down on whom he can look—and usually finds them. Take Larry Kramer, the assistant district attorney with the Johnston and Murphy shoes in the A&P bag. He and his wife, who has just had a baby, are living in an over priced, jerry-built Manhattan apartment and have hired for a few weeks, at the rate of $525 per week, an English baby nurse, about whom Kramer feels rather edgy, until the nurse speaks out against "the colored," who don't know "how good they've got it in this country." The edge, with that remark, is off. Wolfe has Kramer and his wife think:

> Thank God in heaven! What a relief! They could let their breaths out now. Miss Efficiency was a bigot. These days the thing about bigotry was, it was undignified. It was a sign of Low Rent origins, of inferior social status, of poor taste. So they were the superiors of their English baby nurse, after all. What a fucking relief.

"Everyone is striving for what is not worth the having," says Lord Steyne, in *Vanity Fair,* a novel to which *The Bonfire of the Vanities* has not infrequently been compared. *Vanity Fair* carries the subtitle *A Novel without a Hero* and this, by and large, is true, too, of *The Bonfire of the Vanities.* Among the crucial differences is that in Thackeray's novel not everyone is a swine, as nearly everyone is in Wolfe's, and in Thackeray there is still an aristocracy worth imitating whereas in Wolfe such aristocracy as America has known has by the time of the novel all but crumbled. (One of the sub-themes—and it is an important one in Wolfe's novel—is the decay and decline of the Wasp upper classes.) In *The Bonfire of the Vanities* just about everyone has his own agenda, his own fantasies of money, power, sex, mastery, all issuing in greater status—which is to say, everyone has his own towering vanity. I cannot recall a generous emotion or sentiment in this entire novel; everyone in it is in business absolutely for himself.

"Vanity only sins," wrote Lord Lytton, "where it hurts the vanity of others." Much of the artfulness of Tom Wolfe's plot is owing to his skill at setting vanities clashing against one another. The horror of Sherman McCoy's fall is that his own vanity is chewed up by the vanity of a great many others: an alcoholic English journalist who sustains his career in the gutter press by sensationalizing McCoy's accident and trial; a corrupt black leader for whom McCoy's manslaughter case is a godsend; a Jewish district attorney up for re-election in a black and Hispanic district for whom a case like McCoy's is equated to bringing in the Great White Whale (accent on "White"); and so forth and so on. After the assistant district attorney, Larry Kramer, expends money, time, and great emotional energy on seductive strategy, finally making his move on a young woman he has fantasized about for months, we learn that she is in fact a bit of a tart, bored by his self-dramatizing and principally interested in popping into bed. When an older man in the company of a journalist has a deadly heart attack at La Boue d'Argent restaurant, his face falling into a plate of *médaillons de selle d'agneau Mikado,* his companion, after the tumult and mess of removing the body from the restaurant, is presented with (you will pardon my French) *l'addition,* which, truth to tell, he hadn't counted on paying in the first place. Another night—afternoon, actually—in little ole New York.

"Who is ever missed in Vanity Fair?" asks Thackeray, and I fear something similar can be said about the characters in *The Bonfire of the Vanities.* However interestingly and accurately they are drawn—and they are drawn most interestingly and accurately—one does not long to hear more from them. Wolfe has been altogether too efficient at his job of demolition. (Look, the emperor has no fibula, navel, buttocks!) Wolfe puts Sherman McCoy through the full hell of the so-called criminal-justice system, exposes him to the complete torture of the media, fries him in betrayal, boils him in shame, and yet, so devastatingly has he earlier drawn him as a miserable mindless snob that the redemption Wolfe allows him at the novel's close seems unpersuasive, which is a milder way of saying aesthetically unsatisfying.

It is very hard to write a novel with no hero without, at the same time, revealing to one's readers exactly what it is you believe in. The author of *The Bonfire of the Vanities,* sad to report, is for the first time not always above the snobberies he depicts in his own work. He is not above mocking (in an unplayful way) New York accents, or belittling dreary apartments, or comically degrading a man who buys his clothes "from the Linebacker Shop, for the stocky man, in Fresh Meadows." When Wolfe lets his own point of view peep through, it isn't always pleasant to behold. His hatred for the high and vacuous celebrity culture is undisguised; his Olympian amusement at the nouveau riche has long been known. But what is surprising in his novel is to find him looking down his nose, as in the examples cited here, at the lower-middle class, or (as Marx neglected to call them) the *schleppoisie.*

The lower-middle class, my guess is, repels the dandy in Wolfe. Anyone who has ever seen Tom Wolfe's drawings knows that the quality of revulsion runs high in him. His drawings, with their ungracefully aging couples out jogging, their balding and ungainly intellectuals, their hopelessly overweight men on the disco dance floor attempting to hang in their with the young, their overdressed New York women who are all crotch and bust and bottom—all these drawings register pure disgust on Wolfe's part. As a penman, so as a draughtsman, he has always mocked other people's vanities, and the past few decades have kept him in full employment.

But does Wolfe believe in anything more than the need to skewer other people's vanities? "It is only to vain men that all is vanity," Joseph Conrad wrote in his story "Prince Roman," "and all is deception only to those who have never been sincere with themselves." In what does Tom Wolfe believe? Is there anything he admires? On the evidence of this novel, and of his earlier writings, I should say two things: command of craft and courage. Thomas Killian, the attorney in the novel, who is good at what he does, is one of the book's few characters who is not mocked. Neither, finally, is another character, a judge named Myron Kovitsky, who in the social jungle of the Bronx is absolutely fearless and takes crap from no one. When craft and courage combine, as they do in test pilots and astronauts, stock-car racers and navy fighter pilots, Wolfe drops his guard and writes in open, uncritical adulation. It was Ken Kesey's crazy courage that in large part attracted Wolfe in *The Electric Kool-Aid Acid Test*. In *The Bonfire of the Vanities,* Sherman McCoy is redeemed when he finds the courage—physical as well as spiritual—to face down his attackers. (Admiration for physical courage traditionally runs strong in southern men.) If one views the world as essentially a fraudulent place, a vanity fair, then perhaps all that one can trust are courage and craft. And yet this seems, for a novelist, oddly limiting.

To his journalism, Tom Wolfe brought the techniques of the novelist, and now to his novel he brings the temperament of the journalist. The latter arrangement turns out not to work quite so well as did the former. The journalist acquires his information in order to choose sides; the novelist acquires his information not for the purpose of choosing sides but for exploring human character. *The Bonfire of the Vanities,* impressive in so many ways, is nonetheless an almost paradigmatic case of the way that the journalistic mind works. The characters in the book are all fictitious, but none, so far as the author is concerned, is ever really innocent or capable of surprising or of teaching us anything about life.

The best qualities of *The Bonfire of the Vanities* are, at their core, journalistic ones: reams of fascinating information about the way people live, the way institutions work, and the way people can be ground down by both institutions and their own empty vanities. Novelists who refrain from making use of such material because they consider it merely journalistic are very great fools, but the serious novel, while including all this, goes beyond it. The difference, ultimately, between the novelist and the journalist is that the real subject of the novel is the truth of the human heart. Our greatest novelists have always known this, and now the greatest journalist of our time, who has missed this essential point, has proven it yet again.

The New Criterion 1988

A Boy's
Own Author

TASTE IN READING, like taste in food, tends to be formed early and changed seldom. Despite all the therapeutically salutary effects that Bruno Bettelheim claims fairy tales have on children, my own recollection is that, when read to me by my father, they bored the Doctor Dentons off me. I do not wish to exaggerate the sapience of my early childhood, but I do not think I lent much credence to stories about witches, spiders, and giants. I considered Hansel and Gretel dopes for letting themselves be so easily taken in; and as for Jack and the beanstalk, I felt that anyone dumb enough to trade a live cow for a mess of beans had whatever trouble he encountered coming to him. I preferred Robin Hood, with his heroism and battles against injustice. I was also nuts about Bible stories, read to me by my father in a children's version, which featured blood and thunder—like those of Abraham and Isaac, Samson and Delilah, David and Goliath—and in which something serious was at stake. Right out of the chute, then, my tastes in literature ran to realism, and to realism, now more than forty-five years later, they still chiefly run.

For someone given a rather nice literary start in life by a thoughtful father, I never read much on my own once I was in school, and hence I suppose it could be said that I dropped the ball. More precisely, once in school I picked up the ball, becoming a kid who played almost full time whatever ball game was in season. There were other fine distractions: radio programs, the movies, comic books. A company that produced comic-book versions of such classic adventure stories as *The Swiss Family Robinson, The Count of Monte Cristo,* and *Tom Brown's School Days* was then flourishing. For a minor racketeer such as yours truly, who already had too many strenuous demands on his time to allow for the reading of books, these were extremely useful as fodder for the classroom exercise known as book reports. Somewhere between the ages of nine and twelve I believe I read two books, *Hans Brinker; or, The Silver Skates* and *The Black Stallion.* I hugely enjoyed both, yet did nothing to search out others. My case was similar, I suppose, to that of Nancy Mitford's father, Lord Redesdale, who claimed to have read only one book in his life, Jack London's *White Fang.* "It's so frightfully good," he is reported to have announced, "I've never bothered to read another." For my part, I never bothered to find out if the authors of *Hans Brinker* and *The Black Stallion* had written other books; and to this day, in fact, I do not know their names.

Most children, I suspect, are inchoate New Critics, in that they are mainly interested in stories and poems, the work itself, and not in the man or woman who wrote it or the conditions of its composition. I must have heard the names of Dickens and Shakespeare, and possibly that of Mark Twain, but the first author who had a distinct existence for me when I was a boy was a man, still very much alive when I began to read his books in my thirteenth year (1950), named John R. Tunis. I don't believe anyone recommended a Tunis book to me; mine was not a crowd in which that sort of thing went on. (If there were any readers among the boys I ran with, they would have to have been closet cases.) But I do remember slipping a volume, bright-red and trimmed in black, off one of the lower shelves of the library of the Daniel Boone Public Elementary

School, my attention having been caught by its title, which was *All-American*. It was, as I had hoped, a story about football, high-school football; better still, among its characters, though not its protagonist, was a Jewish halfback named Meyer Goldman. It had lots of action, prejudice and snobbery, drawings by an illustrator named Hans Walleen, a fit moral—and the whole thing was brought in at under 250 pages. I lapped it up in a single sitting.

Over the next year or so I scrambled to locate every book by John R. Tunis that I could find. He had written a few nonfiction books, I discovered, but I took a pass on those and read only his novels and then only those novels in which sports played a central role. I read him on football, I read him on basketball, I read him on baseball (more on baseball than on any other sport), I read him on track, and I read him on tennis, a sport I had myself just begun to take up in a fairly serious way. I lived a good deal of the time between my thirteenth and fourteenth year in a world of John R. Tunis's imagining—that is, I imagined myself a character in one or another of Tunis's novels. " 'Pock' went the big serve, and Joe Epstein strode to the net."

John R. Tunis's novels were about a good deal besides sports—he was, as I have discovered on rereading a number of them, almost relentlessly preaching, a true and full-time message man—but it was the subject of sports that snared me. In his autobiography Sidney Hook reports that, during his early years as an elementary-school teacher, he was able to teach a class of mentally delinquent boys the rudiments of arithmetic and geography by demonstrating the use of arithmetic in compiling baseball batting averages and the use of geography in determining the location of big-league teams. My own mental delinquency was not quite so considerable, but the truth is that sports was all I cared to read about. The sports section was the only portion of the newspaper that interested me. Apart from thumbing through the pages of each week's *Life,* the only mag-

azine I read was a monthly called *Sport,* and this I read with
the intensity of a full-court press, cover to cover, the letters
from readers, up and down the masthead, the whole thing.
Among the editors were men with such names as Al Silverman
and Ed Fitzgerald (please note the locker-room familiarity of
Al and Ed, no Allans or Edwards permitted). The magazine
contained profiles of contemporary athletes. "Yogi likes plenty
of pizza in the off-season," a characteristic line from *Sport* might
run, "and can usually be found hanging out at his friend Phil
Rizzuto's bowling alley." The magazine also carried splendid
historical pieces, under the rubric of "The Sport Classic," about
such legendary figures as Jim Thorpe (the Carlisle Indian), Ty
Cobb (the Georgia Peach), Jack Dempsey (the Manassa Mauler),
and Bill Tilden (Big Bill, who, it was later to be revealed, liked
plenty of boys in the off-season). There was also a "Sport Quiz,"
which tested your knowledge of all sports, past and present. It
was the only test on which I ever cared passionately about doing
well.

In me John R. Tunis had an ideal reader—but not, I hasten
to add, in me alone, for thousands of boys similarly hooked on
sports read him with something like the same ardor. Tunis
published his first novel for boys in 1938, when he was forty-
nine years old, and from the outset generations have read him
and, apparently, still do. It is to Tunis I owe my first knowledge that reading can be as intense a pleasure as any that life
has to offer. This dawned on me when, to my own youthful
astonishment, I stayed home one sunny summer afternoon with
a Tunis novel, preferring, in this amazing instance, to read about
baseball when I could have actually been playing it.

An audience of youngsters is a tough audience to crack. Tunis
knew this very well. In his autobiography, *A Measure of Independence* (1964), written when he was seventy-five, he addressed
the question directly:

> A book written for my audience doesn't have to be merely as
> good as a book for adults; it must—or should be—better. Not

only does youth deserve the best, but also no youths read a book because it is on the best-seller list. There is no best-seller list. Nor do they read it because it has a huge advertising budget, or is well reviewed; they read it for one reason alone, they want to. They find it says something to them in an area they know and understand. These readers are important, perhaps the most important in the country today.

What, I wonder, did John R. Tunis's novels say to me when I first read them at thirteen? What did I think when, early in the novel *All-American,* I read the following sentence: "After all, it was something to have a father who had played football, who understood these things"? The man in question, Robert Perry, who is the father of the young hero of the novel, played, moreover, at Yale, has a high position in a bank, and sends his son to pick up his resoled golf shoes. My own father left school in Montreal to come to Chicago at seventeen, worked in the costume-jewelry business with men with such names as Sidney Gainsberg, Abe Levine, and Manny Dubinsky, and owned business shoes only. "Two different worlds," the old song runs, "we come from two different worlds."

The world John R. Tunis wrote about—small-town, Gentile, very American—was one about which I had the kind of intense curiosity available only to those who felt themselves ultimately excluded from it. What I did not know at the time, having no interest in authors apart from their ability to deliver an interesting story, was that so, in a way, was Tunis excluded from the kind of life he wrote about. Tunis was not a Jew, nor the son of immigrants, but he did grow up without a father and in highly unusual circumstances. His father's was a wealthy New York family, of Dutch descent, that had done extremely well in various kinds of speculation around the time of the Civil War. In the view of his family, Tunis's father made two crucial mistakes: the first was to leave the Episcopalian church to become a (Harvard-trained) Unitarian minister; the second was to marry a woman, three or so years older than he, whose father was a waiter. Tunis's father was disowned for this latter act; no Tunis appeared at his wedding in New York. Even though he later returned to Episcopalianism, when he died of Bright's disease—John was then seven, his brother five—no member of the Tunis family put in an appearance at the funeral.

In no John R. Tunis novel I have read—and, now, reread—does a mother figure as more than a sweet but mild pain in the neck. A mother in these books is generally someone who reminds a boy to take along his jacket or not to forget his galoshes. But in a case of art refusing to imitate life, John R. Tunis's own mother was a completely formidable woman, the chief influence in her two sons' lives, John's guide and critic and inspiration. After her young husband's death, she alone, quite without outside help, held her family together, kept up standards, and provided a model for her sons, both of whom loved her without qualification.

Caroline Roberts Tunis had gone to Normal College in New York (later Hunter College). When her husband died, she first took a job at the Brearley School for girls on the East Side of Manhattan. But before long she moved with her boys and her retired father—whom she never referred to as a waiter but always as a "steward"—to Cambridge, Massachusetts, principally, Tunis reports in his autobiography, because she wanted her sons to be near Harvard. "My mother had two articles of faith; first, that we should be brought up in the church of our father (Episcopalian), and second, attend Harvard, his college." Through her deceased husband's churchly connections, she arranged, with the help of Reverend Endicott Peabody, rector of Groton, to open an eating house for former students of Groton now at Harvard. This went quite well until 1904, when a student named Franklin Delano Roosevelt turned his fellow Grotonians against the idea of walking all the way to Mrs. Tunis's establishment in cold weather. Tunis's mother then turned to substitute teaching, along with teaching immigrants the English language at night, and she continued to teach until her retirement.

She was a Teddy Roosevelt Republican—her son John's one serious dissent from his mother was to become a liberal Democrat—a woman who believed in hard work, self-improvement, and the importance of culture. She read only serious books, usually with a critical eye; had reams of poetry stored in her memory; was often off to a concert or the opera; and read and argued with the editorials in the *Boston Evening Transcript*. In later life, she offered a running critical commentary on her son's books and articles—and later life lasted a good while, since she died at ninety-two. (Tunis himself died in 1975, at eighty-six.) "At ninety," she wrote to her son, "one does not get around as easily as at eighty-five. I find myself inclined to give in these days, instead of urging myself on as I once did." Perhaps the main reason John R. Tunis never included a mother figure like his own in any of his novels is that he did not have to, for his mother's spirit and idealism reign in everything he wrote.

Although Tunis grew up fatherless, without the security of money, written off by his father's wealthy family (which did later provide funds for him and his brother to attend college), he maintains in his autobiography that "never did we feel sorry for ourselves, for there was nothing to feel sorry about." One is ready to believe that, especially with so gallant a woman as his mother around, yet it must have been difficult watching her returning exhausted from cooking for other boys or from a double load of teaching. A boy growing up without a father, no matter how strong his mother, remains half an orphan; and this, too, could not have been easy. In many of Tunis's novels, the father is the moral center of the book, the figure whom a young man can turn to for balanced thought, perspective, good guidance. Where the father fails—as he does, notably, in *Yea! Wildcats!,* one of Tunis's Indiana high-school basketball novels—the coach steps in to play this role. Over many an adolescent crisis—involving physical courage, sportsmanship, masculine honor—a boy can turn only to a man for help.

It would be pushing things to say that Tunis grew up like

Stephen Crane's Maggie, a child of the streets, but it is true to say that, had his father not been disowned by his family, Tunis and his brother would have attended a school like Groton instead of seeing their mother cook for boys who had gone there. Still, there were much worse streets to grow up on than those in Cambridge around the turn of the century. Once when he and his brother were out playing, their ball hit a carriage containing the baby of Professor Irving Babbitt, who complained to the police. Babbitt lived across the street, and the Cambridge Public Library, which was important in Tunis's life, was not far away. A few blocks distant were the thirty clay tennis courts of Jarvis Field, used by Harvard students but also available to the Tunis boys, who hung around hoping to be asked to fill in for someone's missing doubles partner.

Sports was Tunis's passion as a boy, and he would later, of course, make a living out of writing about it. His grandfather taught him to read—to study is perhaps more precise—the sports pages in the daily newspaper. This same grandfather, his mother's father, took him and his brother to their first major-league baseball game, which happened to be played in a National League park and thus left him a National League fan for life. (American or National League is one of those choices a sports-minded boy makes early in life and rarely departs from.) His mother was puzzled by her son's passion for games, but did nothing to interfere with it. Tunis, ever the moralist, maintains that while as an adolescent he may never have learned the disciplines of working and saving, he did acquire the disciplines of sports, which meant, among other things, "how to accept defeat, a lesson most Americans hate to accept, although defeat comes to us all in the end and we had better be ready for it."

Tennis appears to have been Tunis's own best sport. Although he claims his brother was a more natural athlete than he— better coordinated, more stylish—he himself must have been a player of high competence. He played tennis for Harvard, and he mentions playing in what sounds like fairly serious second-line tournaments in Europe while working as a journalist abroad. Tennis was in any case the sport that lit him aflame with an excitement that went beyond the sport itself. In *A Measure of Independence* he tells how, in his fourteenth year, in 1903, he and his brother trekked out to the Longwood Cricket Club in Brookline to see the American national champion, William A. Larned, play a Davis Cup match against Laurie Doherty, who had won at Wimbledon, representing England. The Tunis boys had no money for admission tickets, so instead they watched the match sitting atop the huge barrels of a brewery wagon parked just outside the court. Tunis describes what he saw:

> I can still see Larned storming the net behind his powerful service, and Doherty passing him with an elegant backhand down the line, feet apart, his racket high in the air, poised in his follow-through like Mercury himself. Those fluid strokes, the crisp punched volleys of Larned, the classical purity of Doherty's shots off the ground, the attacks and ripostes of the two nervous men gave me, without my knowledge at the time, a feeling for art and beauty that was to be mine forever. This scene of grace and movement at Longwood that afternoon reached into me, touched my inner self, changed me for good. I was a boy no longer.

In this handsome paragraph, Tunis hints at a relationship between sports and art that I have never seen discussed. When he remarks that watching these two tennis players gave him "a feeling for art and beauty that was to be mine forever," he reminds me that sports provided my own first glimpses of mastery over materials, economy of execution, and elegance, which are among the qualities shared by the superior athlete and the artist. The superior artist is of course a figure of greater importance than the superior athlete, for what he creates has a chance to endure, but in the form, power of innovation, and authority of the athlete I, for one (and I suspect there have been thousands like me), had my first blessed inkling of what art can do.

That there is an artistic component to the athlete is a point never pushed but always subtly in the background of Tunis's sports novels for boys, though I cannot say that I myself picked up on it at thirteen.

Despite his mother's intellectual earnestness, Tunis was far from being a good student, and claims to have "possessed no intellectual disciplines, being ignorant, lazy, and uninterested." This did not prevent him from being admitted to Harvard in 1907, at a tuition fee—parents of today will be dismayed to learn—of ninety dollars, with the single condition that he take something called English A that sounds suspiciously like a remedial course. By his own reckoning, Tunis did not make very much of the intellectual opportunities at Harvard. He ran cross-country in the autumn, played tennis in the spring, and whenever possible sneaked off to the theater or a concert in Boston.

His closest friend when he entered Harvard was Conrad Aiken, the poet and critic, who, once at Harvard, began to move among such intellectually serious undergraduates as T. S. Eliot and Walter Lippmann. John Hall Wheelock, Van Wyck Brooks, Robert Benchley, and Norman Foerster were undergraduates at Harvard when Tunis was there, but he never saw them. He did become friends with a student—whom he describes as "a worse runner than myself"—named Frederick Lewis Allen, who later became editor of *Harper's*, for which Tunis wrote articles in the 1930s. (Joseph Kennedy, Sr., who was a year behind Tunis at Harvard, roomed across the hall from him.) The crucial—to hear him tell it, the only—intellectual experience of his Harvard days was hearing William Jennings Bryan speak at Sanders Theater; the Commoner's speech that afternoon turned him away from his Republican heritage and into a Democrat of strong populist-liberal strain.

In 1936, in the midst of the Depression, Tunis produced a book entitled *Was College Worth While?*, which was timed to mark the twenty-fifth anniversary of his own class of 1911 and which turned out to be a strong attack on the hidebound nature of most Harvard men. Surveying his own class, he noted that "we are practically barren of leaders of public life" and that only "a small minority . . . appear to have done any original thinking in their field"; and he ended by saying that the chief ambition of this same class of men, "if their record tells the truth, is to vote the Republican ticket, to keep out of the bread line, and to break 100 at golf." (In an interview given to Jerome Holtzman when Tunis was eighty-four, this was changed to "break 80 at golf.") He eased the stringency of his criticism of Harvard a few years later, when, in 1938, he published a novel entitled *Iron Duke,* about a boy from Waterloo, Iowa, who comes east to Harvard and feels left out, nearly flunks out, but finally wins out, though not on Harvard's rather snobbish terms but on his own: he becomes a track star, he makes the dean's list, he turns down membership in an exclusive undergraduate club.

This book, *Iron Duke,* written when he was forty-nine, changed John R. Tunis's career. He had written novels before, but this was the first work he produced that was sold, in the trade lingo, as a "juvenile." When he learned that this was how Alfred Harcourt, the founder of Harcourt, Brace, planned to sell his book, Tunis was astounded—"shocked, rocked, deflated," he reports in his autobiography—for he had not written it as a book for young readers. The book sold more than sixty thousand copies and twenty-five years after its publication was still bringing in respectable royalties. "I continued writing these so-called boys' books," Tunis told Jerome Holtzman, "but I've never considered them that." Perhaps herein lies the secret of the success of Tunis's books for young readers: an absolute absence of condescension in their composition.

Until *Iron Duke,* Tunis was a free-lancer, turning out as many as two books a year, picking up magazine pieces where he could, covering European tennis tournaments in the summers for American newspapers, knocking out roughly two thousand words a day six days a week—doing, in short, all the dog work of the sadly misnamed free lance. For a time he wrote sports pieces for Harold Ross at the *New Yorker,* usually for fifty dollars apiece and, as late as the early 1930s, two hundred dollars for a longish profile. Of Ross, Tunis wrote: "Curiously Ross knew less about sport than any male American I ever met." (This has a familiar ring; other writers have remarked that Harold Ross was equally ignorant about culture and politics; all he seemed to know, apparently, was what a *New Yorker* piece on any given subject ought to read like.) Tunis tells about the time that Ross, being strapped for cash, offered him sixty shares of *New Yorker* stock in lieu of payment he owed him for pieces. Tunis would have taken it, too, had he not met Frank Crowninshield, the editor of *Vanity Fair,* returning from lunch at the Algonquin, who told him that the magazine's future looked shaky and to go for the cash. He took Crowninshield's bad advice, later determining that, with stock splits and dividends, this little disaster on Forty-fourth Street cost him somewhere in the neighborhood of a million dollars.

Although Tunis had begun to sell fiction to *Collier's* and to write nonfiction pieces for the *Saturday Evening Post,* his (so-called) "so-called boys' books" were what eventually took him off the free-lancer's financial treadmill; they are also the chief reason for the endurance of such fame as Tunis still has. Of these books, Tunis, toward the end of his life, said: "They can be read by adults." Having just read—in most instances reread—nine of them, I would say that the remark requires some qualification. Tunis's books can be read by an adult, but then an adult can also eat a bag of gum drops. It is probably a good idea for an adult not to do either too often. Still, I found Tunis's books highly readable and, for personal reasons, very moving.

To return to the books one loved in one's youth is to risk disappointment—in both the books and in oneself when young. I should not care ever to return to Willard Motley's *Knock on*

Any Door, which at age sixteen I stayed awake through an entire night reading in the Brown Hotel in Des Moines, Iowa, while on the road working with my father. John Dos Passos's *U.S.A.,* which thrilled me the first time around at nineteen, many years later seemed, well, a bit hokey. As for John R. Tunis's books, there is nothing junky, or sickening, or second-rate about them. They do suffer from want of a very high level of complexity, but then I hardly expected Jamesian subtlety. In fact, upon rereading them I am rather proud of my thirteen-year-old self for thinking as well of them as I did. Although my memory of myself is of a fairly frivolous, genial goof-off, perhaps after all I was rather more serious than I remember.

I say this because, I now realize, the Tunis books are pretty serious, and I was utterly absorbed in them. All the novels I then read—and now have reread—are about sports, but they are only ostensibly about sports. Sports is the subject; other matters make up the theme. And even when sports is being discussed, things peripheral to the game itself loom interestingly large. Soon after *The Kid from Tomkinsville* (1940), which is probably Tunis's best baseball novel, gets going, Tunis invites his readers to consider the situation of the thirty-eight-year-old catcher Dave Leonard, on his way to spring training with the Brooklyn Dodgers. At thirty-eight, Leonard's mind is very much on staying with the club and even more on his future. He is making $12,500 (the year is 1940), which is a good salary. But he is a family man. "Twelve-five," he thinks. "They don't pay salaries like that to rookie catchers at any rate. Nor to veterans either, for long." Still, at his age, an age when most businessmen are just getting going, he is coming to the end of the line. "Twenty-five, yep, sounds like a lot of money. But he needed three years before some of his insurance came due and the load lightened."

What did I think of this when I first read it at thirteen? Why should a kid of thirteen give a rat's rump about the financial problems of an old guy of thirty-eight? I cannot recall exactly, but my guess is that I loved such passages in Tunis. For one thing, there was the realism of it (the son of parents who had come through the Depression, I had heard often enough how tough it could be to make a living); for another, it was fine to have such adult—such *real*—problems up for discussion. Material of this kind took you behind the scenes; it treated you, as a reader, like a grownup, which was a genuine compliment, especially since at thirteen you probably thought of yourself as a grownup anyway.

Tunis's books are studded with such stuff. In *Yea! Wildcats!* (1944) he tells you about the corrupt way that tickets are parceled out for the state high-school basketball tournaments in Indiana. The coach in that novel refuses to get tickets for anyone, an independent stand that, like all such stands in Tunis, comes to cost him dearly. Sometimes the presentation of inside material is conjoined with Tunis's own strong views. Although he had worked as a journalist himself, Tunis did not much care for the general run of the breed; he took them to be paid kibitzers whose self-appointed job was to spread dissension among athletes, increase pressure on everyone, and make trouble generally. In *Rookie of the Year* (1944), another of his baseball books, he sets out the various techniques that sports writers use to sniff out a story, and leaves them with the grandeur of, say, a third-class-hotel house dick. "An ounce of curiosity plus a pound of brass coupled with the sensitivity of a rhino and the pertinacity of a tiger," he writes in *Rookie of the Year*, "that's what makes a reporter." I am not certain what I made of that formulation at thirteen, but at fifty it seems to me quite on target.

Of course, how ballplayers feel about night games, the outside pressures on managers and coaches, the conditions of tournament tennis—none of this would have made much impression if John R. Tunis were not extremely good at telling a story. And telling a story, in a sports novel, largely means being able to describe action. This Tunis can do exceedingly

well. He has a commanding sense of pace; he knows when to
describe a game sketchily and when to go into intricate detail.
He has a nice sense of proportion, which prevents him from
ever allowing his heroes to become supermen, and hence
unbelievable, on the field. He is excellent at describing tennis,
good at football, a bit less sure of himself at basketball, and
perhaps best of all at baseball. He has the knack of instructing
while narrating without making a reader feel as if he were being
talked down to. Describing a double play in *Keystone Kids*
(1943), for example, Tunis writes:

> The two boys were off together. Both were near the ball, on top
> of it almost, so fast that either could have stabbed for it. But
> Bob suddenly realized his brother was the one to make the play,
> and as he neared the bag sheered away to clear the path for the
> throw. Spike picked up the ball a few feet from the base, and in
> one continuous motion touched the bag and hurled the ball to
> first in time to nab the fastest runner in baseball. Only an expert
> could have felt their understanding, their coordination as they
> made that decision in the fraction of a second when the ball
> roared toward them. The two men in the box behind the dug-
> out missed nothing. They looked at each other. Base hits, they
> knew, were a matter of feet. Doubleplays were a matter of inches.

John R. Tunis, as they say about superior infielders, could pick
it.

I suppose a boy of thirteen reading Tunis today might miss
an item or two of a factual kind. Such a boy, a habitual reader
of today's sports pages, might be mildly amused at the relatively small sums ballplayers then earned (there is talk in one
of the Tunis novels about a World Series winner's share of six
thousand dollars per player and endorsements earning only
$250). There is a real possibility that he might miss references
to such then-living figures as Grantland Rice, Al Schacht, and
Hank Greenberg. Will he know that the defensive shift used

against the character Cecil McDade in the novel *Highpockets* (1948) is based on the shift used on Ted Williams; or that an announcer named Snazzy Beane is based on Dizzy Dean; or that Jack McManus, the owner of the Brooklyn Dodgers in the baseball novels, is loosely based on Larry MacPhail? Then there are distinctly time-bound references to the Quiz Kids, the Aldrich family, Fred Allen (not the *Harper's* editor, the radio comic). Such a boy might be puzzled by the period slang—"Thunderation!" one character thinks, and the phrase "That was something like!" occurs repeatedly—or by the corny nicknames Tunis is in the habit of assigning his ballplayers: Spike and Bones and Razzle and Rats and Fat Stuff. A young boy today, rising from his personal computer, might be put off by any or all of this.

But it would be a pity if he were, for he would miss a great deal. Not least, he would miss Tunis's teaching, which is to say his moral instruction, which is to say his message(s). Recounting his own methods of composition in his books for boys, Tunis writes that the story must be told "simply, quickly, effectively," and that "when you allow a 'message' to take over, you are lost." He also remarks in his autobiography, apropos of the George Alfred Henty "Rollo" books he read in his own youth: "As boys have ever done—and thank God, ever will—we skipped the culture and the moralizing and gulped down the accounts of life in distant lands." Nothing of this applies to Tunis's own books, which taken together have more messages than Western Union. True, the messages in Tunis are generally artfully mixed with the action of the stories, but I know that I picked them up when young, and if I had not, so plain are they, I would have to have been declared a moral dyslexic.

Tunis's many messages divide into general and particular categories. In the general category, there are the lessons that sports teaches: the need for discipline, for the willingness to subsume one's own selfish interests in the greater good of the team, for the courage to come back from defeat. In *The Kid from Tomkinsville,* when the Dodgers come from well behind to make a stretch drive for the pennant, even the fans of the rival New York Giants at the Polo Grounds are impressed. "Because," Tunis writes, "sport offers no more inspiring spectacle than the man or the team who comes back, who takes the cracks of fate and pulls them together to rise once more." *Highpockets* is about a great natural athlete who turns from being a selfish loner, out only to compile impressive statistics that will earn him a larger salary, to become a team player. "That's the trouble with this country nowadays," an older player-coach tells him after he comes around, "everyone out for himself, aiming to hit the long ball over the fence."

The sense of a team is the great moment in Tunis novels; it is one of the overarching ideas in all his work. This applied to life as well as to sports. When a child is operated on in *Highpockets,* medicine, too, turns out to be "a sort of team, y'see." And what was this almost mystical entity, a team? "It was everything in sport and in life, yet nothing you touch or see or feel or even explain to someone else. A team was like an individual, a character, fashioned by work and suffering and disappointment and sympathy and understanding, perhaps not least of all by defeat." What Tunis is addressing here is character in its collective sense; in his novels the molding of character is always an individual matter, with a high-school athlete or professional ballplayer put through the test. Character, in Tunis, is won through discipline, through perseverance, through learning from defeat. This is a very old-fashioned notion. John R. Tunis taught me to believe in it when I was a boy. The odd thing is, I still do believe in it.

On the particular side, Tunis's messages tended to be those of the old-style liberal, the hater of snobbery and prejudice. *All-American,* a novel written in 1942, when the defeat of Hitler was far from certain, turns out to be a book about American democracy. In it a quarterback named Ronald Perry transfers from a prep school called the Academy to a public school called

Abraham Lincoln High. Many are this book's messages, a number of them delivered by the public-school principal: "In this school, Ronald, every pupil has to be responsible for himself. That's one of the principles of a democracy, isn't it?" Several are the book's conflicts, the concluding one occurring when Abraham Lincoln High's football team learns, after winning its conference, that Ned LeRoy, its fine Negro end, cannot travel with the team to an intersectional game in Miami because of southern segregation policy. The team, led by Ronald, decides not to play without Ned and so the trip is canceled, much to the consternation of the town's leading citizens. In Tunis's novels about high-school athletes, adults almost invariably are wrong when they take too keen an interest in high-school sports, interfering in a way that turns out to be detrimental to the boys and to the sport itself. A notable exception is Hooks Barnum, the coach of Ridgewood High, in *Go, Team, Go!* (1954), whose coaching and character have a salubrious effect on the team, "as the character of a good man always does in sport." But in the main the message is that, left to themselves, youngsters have fairly good instincts about fair play, and so they ought, in fact, to be left to themselves.

In *Keystone Kids,* Tunis takes on the subject of anti-Semitism in telling the story of Jocko Klein, the rookie catcher of the Dodgers, who is taunted by his own teammates as well as by opposing teams for being a Jew. Helping Jocko fight off the anti-Semitism of his own teammates is the young southern manager of the Dodgers, Spike Russell, who himself does not exactly possess an advanced degree in social work from the University of Chicago. Instead he has an instinctual sense of the unfairness of singling out a man in this way, a feeling that anti-Semitism is tearing apart not only the man but the team, and the strong belief that it cannot be allowed to go on. He offers some crude advice to Jocko—"You gotta think of yourself as a catcher, not as a Jew"—and some that turns out to be important to him: "Boy, you gotta take it in this game same as you gotta take it in life. Get me? Understand. . . . Don't quit."

And—need I say it?—Jocko does not quit; he eventually faces down his chief tormentor; the team finally unites and returns to the business at hand, which is winning the National League pennant.

Later in the same novel, Tunis runs through the ethnic origins, and offers potted histories, of the ancestors of the various members of the Dodgers, extending his concept of the team into a metaphor for America itself which not even so unliterary a kid as I could have missed. My guess is that when I first came across it, I was much moved. It reads strangely today, nearly thirty years after it was written and after the great efflorescence of ethnic pride that has swept this country in recent decades. Reading it now, I am still moved, even though the dream of America as a team made up of very different people—a dream that was also at the center of Tunis's vision as a writer—seems rather tattered and fading.

"Don't quit," Spike Russell tells Jocko Klein, in what may be John R. Tunis's essential message. It is the message that he apparently took from his own life. Of the difficulties of his own early free-lancing days, he writes in his autobiography: "Often I stumbled and fell; but usually got up, bruised and sore, and went on. It wasn't courage but stupidity that kept me going. . . . How many times in life when talent is lacking, sheer persistence pays off." I believe that, too. On rereading him now in my middle life, I find that there is not much at the heart of John R. Tunis's books for boys that I do not still believe. Whether I originally acquired these beliefs from him, or whether I had first to hack my way through jungles of intellectual obfuscation before returning to them, I do not know. But of the influences that helped form me, I now think of the books of John R. Tunis as a very real one.

"Highpockets had learned something," Tunis writes. "There's no easy way to a boy's heart. Like everything else, you have to work for it." John R. Tunis did, and he still has mine.

Commentary 1987